SO-AQH-197

THE CITY
in FLAMES

To John
Enjoy the story

Elizabeth von Berrinberg
November 26th, 2013

THE CITY
in FLAMES

A Child's Recollection
of World War II
in Würzburg, Germany

ELISABETH VON BERRINBERG

Copyright © 2013 Elisabeth von Berrinberg
All rights reserved. No part of this problication may be reproduced, stored in a
retrieval system, or transmitted, in any form or by any means, electronic, mechanical, photocopying, recording, or otherwise, without the prior written permission
of author.

ISBN: 978-0-9895915-1-5
Published by Berrinberg Publications, Minneapolis, MN
Cover design by Jeff Holmes
Interior design by Jim Arneson, Jaad Book Design,
www.jaadbookdesign.com
Illustrations by Paula K Yff
www.paulayff.com

Pictures from Wuerzburger Chronik, 1945. Copyright © 1947 by Schoeningh Verlag. Reprinted by permission of AdolfWolz.

Ebook available from most online ebook sellers.

For Information on obtaining interviews or permission for excerpts, contact the
author at lizvonb@q.com or Sybil Smith, publisher@SmithHousePress.com

Publisher's Cataloging-in-Publication

Berrinberg, Elisabeth von.
    The city in flames : a child's recollection of World
War II in Würzburg, Germany / Elisabeth von Berrinberg.
-- First edition.
    pages cm
    LCCN 2013950230
    ISBN 978-0-9895915-1-5
    ISBN 978-0-9895915-0-8 (ebook)

    1. Berrinberg, Elisabeth von--Childhood and youth.
2. World War, 1939-1945--Children--Biography. 3. World
War, 1939-1945--Personal narratives, German. 4. World
War, 1939-1945--Germany--Biography. I. Title.

D810.C4B47 2013   940.53'161
                      QBI13-600159

FIRST EDITION

Berrinberg Publications, Minneapolis, MN
Printed in the United States of America
10 9 8 7 6 5 4 3 2 1

*Dedicated to all the World War II soldiers
who liberated us from the Nazis.*

Table of Contents

ACKNOWLEDGMENTS

Many thanks to Sybil Smith of Smith House Press Publishing Consultants, a very patient mentor whose guidance helped me publish this book.

To editors Cass Erickson and Kellie Hultgren, who helped turn my draft into a piece of writing worthy of publication.

I am also grateful to intern Hannah Carpenter, who, fresh out of college, took on the task of putting the commas and hyphens where they belong.

To Carsten Gehring for his editing and computer skills and who is special because his family is also from my hometown in Germany.

Special thanks to Adolf Wolz, of the Schoeningh Verlag in Würzburg, Germany, for permission to use pictures from the book *Würzburger Chronik, 1945.*

To Paula K Yff for her delightful illustrations that captured the humorous side of our struggle to survive.

I also thank my twin sister, Rita Shannon, who reminded me of events that escaped my own memories.

And of course, my daughter, Lorraine, who chauffeured me to my meetings and presentations.

And last, but not least, a special thanks to a longtime friend, Janie Eilers, who was instrumental in helping me with my very first attempt to put my memoirs on paper.

INTRODUCTION

If I remember my first school day, it is only because that day also marked the beginning of World War II with the invasion of Poland. I was six years old.

Perhaps I was too young to fully understand the war's impact on the world, but the imprint it left on Germany and consequently on my own life is still reflected in many of my values. While World War II brought victory to the Allies, it brought defeat to those who conspired it. Nevertheless, the rewards of war, however meager they may have been, also touched the defeated. They showed us the value of ordinary life.

War taught us gratitude. We were thankful for every night that passed without interruptions from howling sirens. If they did disturb our sleep and send us to the cold and moldy cellar, we were grateful to leave the cellar alive.

I felt hunger many times and will always remember its ache. Now I feel guilty whenever I prepare a meal. The potato peels I flush down the disposal are thicker than the ones we once dug out of garbage cans. The heels from loaves of bread are still tastier at the time I discard them than the moldy bread we devoured at many meals. Even the tough outer leaves of the lettuce in my refrigerator taste better than dandelions. Would I feel guilt had I not experienced war's hardships?

War tore many bonds, but it strengthened the relationships that survived. Would I still be alive, had my mother not found the courage to distract a gunner pilot? She offered her life to save her children, a deed that only strengthened the bonds between us.

War also allowed us to experience compassion. A Russian prisoner of war, in spite of being our enemy, risked his life to save my family. And the Americans, whom we once called enemies, became the good guys to us. We even called some of them our friends.

One soldier stands out particularly in my mind. When first I saw him, I was performing my nightly chore of gathering dandelions for our rabbit. When he approached me, he handed me an orange, then turned around to return to camp. The next night he brought me a cream puff. I noticed a slight blush on his face as he handed it to me. I thanked him, but he just nodded, turned around, and walked away. I was certain he would come again the next night, and he did. It was a can of bread pudding he brought me then. I talked to him, hoping he could understand me. But he only smiled, and again I saw a blush on his young and gentle face. He bent over to help me fill my basket.

After that he never came back. Not once did he speak to me, and still, I remember him most of all. I remember his kind eyes and his warm smile. And wherever he is today, I want him to know that his gifts to me were the greatest reward of all. Did they not express his love? His love for all of mankind?

WARNINGS IN THE NIGHT

Chapter One

My *family lived in a four-story apartment house that was* owned by my maternal grandparents. At the beginning of the war, we had from four to five tenants who lived on the ground floor, second floor, and third floor. My parents, and my sister, Rita, and I lived on the fourth floor. My grandparents lived in a house next door. We were a close-knit family who loved each other very much.

One night, my mother's voice sounded far away. "Wake up! Quickly!" Was I dreaming? But again I heard her calling. I pretended not to hear, and with a sigh I rolled over. Suddenly I was being shaken by two arms, and my feather bed was lifted and pulled away from me.

"Gee, Mama, why do I have to get up? I just went to bed an hour ago!" I complained as I glanced at the wall clock. The light was dim, but I could see that the clock's hands had not yet reached midnight.

"The sirens!" my mother exclaimed. "Didn't you hear them?"

"Hurry up in there!" yelled my father from the kitchen.

I searched for my socks. "Where are my shoes? I can't find my shoes," I growled to myself. Sleep was still in my eyes, and I could barely open them.

"Are you ready?" my father asked impatiently.

"In a minute!" I hollered back.

"Now!" came the voice from the kitchen. It was then that I heard the planes. With one shoe on my foot and the other in my hand, I stumbled down the three flights of stairs of our apartment building toward the cold and moldy cellar.

The year was 1945. The place was Würzburg, Germany. I was born there as the second of twin girls. I was twelve years old—well, almost thirteen—and half of those years I had been living in fear. It was on my first school day, September 1, 1939, that it all began. The invasion of Poland meant the beginning of World War II.

But now the war was nearing its end—at least so we hoped—for D-Day had passed and the Allied front was penetrating Germany.

Air raids had become a daily event. *Will they bomb us?* we all wondered many times as we sat, sometimes for hours at a time, in the cave-like shelter beneath the house. It was a safe place to hide while the bombers crossed over. *Which city will it be tonight? Nuremberg? Schweinfurt? Well, as long as it isn't Würzburg!* we hoped selfishly.

I was proud of our beautiful city. Its numerous church spires reached into the sky, and its narrow streets still reflected the splendor of bygone eras. It looked so charming huddled into the wide valley of the Main River. On the hills surrounding the city grapes grew, which were used to make the unique and earthy-tasting Frankenwein, a favorite of wine lovers the world over.

Centuries had shaped this festive city, where kings and emperors had sojourned. In Würzburg, Tilman Riemenschneider carved his incomparable Madonnas, and Balthasar Neumann designed a palace for the prince-bishop.

Many students from the University of Würzburg rose to international fame. Sir Winston Churchill was one of them. Was this the reason Würzburg had been spared? There were rumors that no one would dare bomb the city where the great Churchill was once a student. Whatever reason the Allies had not to bomb Würzburg during all these years of war, it was fortunate for us. The city was spared until a month before the war ended.

But we still suffered. We felt fear and anxiety every time the sirens howled and every time the sound of airplanes reached our ears.

Maybe this time? Will they dive this time, to drop their cargo of death among our houses? Or will they continue on their course toward Nuremberg? Then all we would feel was a gentle tremor in the ground, whereas only a hundred kilometers east of us, death was on its way.

What would happen, should they decide to attack us? The thought was frightening. Would we survive? Or would we burn to death, or suffocate on poisonous gases escaping from fractured pipes? How would it feel to be crushed to death by tons of steel and stones? *Dear God! Don't let it happen! No! I am too young to die!*

"Get up!" My mother tapped me gently on my shoulder.

"Is it over?" I asked, startled, as I jumped up from the corner in which I had curled up, my blanket tightly wrapped around me.

"Yes, of course it's over," my sister assured me, looking at me in surprise. "Didn't you hear the all-clear sound off?"

"I was dreaming," I said with a yawn.

My legs were numb from the long wait in the corner. Wearily I staggered back up three flights of stairs, stumbling over the blanket that slipped from my shoulders and now dangled between my feet, part of it dragging behind me.

The wall clock chimed twice. Two o'clock. Good! I thought. This meant school would start at ten tomorrow. Had the alarm ended before midnight, school would have started at eight as usual.

Sleepily I slipped out of my shoes and coat. Still wearing the rest of my clothes, I dropped into my soft bed.

"Thanks, Lord, for sparing us again," I prayed, and minutes later sleep came to me.

Ration Stamps

Chapter Two

*L*ife *became much the same for everybody, rich or poor, since* money didn't matter anymore. Ration stamps were essential. Those small sheets of colored paper printed with numbered squares became a treasure. They could not be replaced, should they be lost. If a person found a ration stamp and returned it to the address printed on it, it was a noble gesture, for many of us had become selfish and rude.

Each type of food had a different color of ration stamp. Meat stamps were blue, those for bread or other baked goods were red, milk stamps were pink, stamps for staple goods were orange, and vegetable stamps were, of course, green. Each member of a family received one set of ration stamps monthly.

Every year the ration amounts became smaller. In 1940, the amount of meat per person was four pounds per month. By 1945, the amount diminished to one pound per person. Bread had been cut to less than half the amount issued five years before. Some commodities, such as bananas, oranges, and other tropical fruits, had long vanished from the markets, and only on holidays like Christmas or Easter was a special distribution arranged.

Getting these rations involved long hours of waiting in line. Not only the special issues, but also even the smallest item sometimes demanded hours in line. You would often wait only to be told that the person in front of you got the last one. It was a strain to stand in line, and on hot days it was not unusual to see someone in the crowd suffer heatstroke or faint from exhaustion.

Electric refrigerators were unknown in those days. Perishable items had to be bought on a day-to-day basis. But even staple goods were rationed in such a way that daily shopping was necessary because some ration stamps were only valid on certain days.

We preserved food only by the means provided by nature. In cold weather we would set the pot of milk, after it had been boiled, outside the window. By the time it was needed, it usually had to be defrosted, and sometimes we just sucked on pieces of frozen milk that we had chipped off with an ice pick.

In the summertime we used the coal cellar to keep our food cool. It was a chore for my sister and me to bring food down to it and back up from it. Nobody ever volunteered, so we had to take turns, and sometimes, when both of us were too stubborn to go, we flipped a coin.

Equipped with a pot and a metal spoon, I would make my way to the dusty hole beneath the house. I would bang the spoon against the pot to produce a deafening noise. This was to scare the rats away.

Not everybody was lucky enough to have such a cellar, so they had to find other means of preservation. Many used wooden boxes lined with tin and then filled with ice—another item to stand in line for.

One of our tenants thought up a scheme to save hours of standing in line, not only for ice, but also for bread and meat. Supermarkets were unheard of then, so every shop specialized in different products. It was at the store that sold ice, though, where her scheme was uncovered.

After this lady learned that expectant mothers did not have to stand in line, she showed sudden signs of pregnancy. But her condition lasted only a few days. On the day she bought ice for her cooler, which she usually did once a week, she must have worn a loosely fitting dress. As she bent over to load a block of ice onto her cart, she suddenly "delivered" a pillow.

"There was a scene!" she recalled as she related the incident to my mother. "I was lucky they didn't beat me up!" Curious inquirers who noticed her quick change to a shapelier waistline were casually informed that she suffered a miscarriage.

So the struggle dragged on day after day. If it wasn't over a block of ice, then perhaps it was over a space in line at the butcher shop or the vegetable market.

There were three types of butcher shops. One was the regular butcher shop, which sold roasts of beef or pork. But one such roast cost most of the month's meat ration stamps. If one wanted to stretch one's meat rations, then one shopped at the second type of butcher shop. There, the meat was available for only half the stamp value: two pounds for one stamp.

A terrific buy, if you happened to like horsemeat—and in those days, everybody liked it. The third type of butcher shop offered even better bargains. There, only one-fourth of the stamp value was needed. This shop sold meat from cattle that had to be done away with. A blackboard in the shop's window noted the reason for which the animal was killed. Perhaps it had broken its leg or swallowed a nail. When an animal had tuberculosis or a rupture in its intestines, however, the meat was entirely exempt from rationing.

Occasionally such half-stamp sales were also conducted at bakeries, although only rarely. There simply was no such thing as day-old bread or yesterday's rolls.

It is a European custom for a bakeshop to operate a cafe on its premises, sometimes with no more than two or three tables, though the shops are usually quite roomy and always busy. Wartime did not change this custom much, except that ration stamps were needed even to buy a cup of coffee. This could easily spoil an afternoon of kaffeeklatsch with a friend or neighbor you happened to meet. First of all, it wasn't coffee from beans, but Ersatz, a substitute concocted from roasted barley and a dash of chicory. It tasted like nothing more than brown water. If you hoped sugar would improve its taste, the waitress could supply you with it, but not without clipping a 10-gram stamp of sugar off your ration card. If you didn't have a 10-gram stamp, you would have to use a 500-gram stamp, and with a smile the waitress would return your change: forty-nine 10-gram stamps.

For some products other than food, a special *Bezugsschein* had to be obtained. This purchase permit entitled the lucky recipient to shop for a new shirt, pair of shoes, or dress, or, if they were especially fortunate, even a coat. Standing in line at the office that issued such permits by no means guaranteed that the applicant would receive one, though. The office kept close records on everyone, and if a person received a permit within a certain period, chances were he or she would be turned down.

Most children are rough on shoes, and my sister and I were no exception. Keeping them in shape was a task for my grandfather, because his talents for making old things new again extended into many fields, including shoemaking. One of his contributions was "tapping" our worn-out shoes. Since no leather was available, he simply nailed the rubber from an old bicycle tire over the holes. Of course, the nails could only be bought with a special iron-purchase permit.

We were growing fast, and our shoes did not contain our feet for long. But the solution was simple. With a pair of scissors, we cut off the tips of our shoes to make space for our toes. In the summer we walked barefoot, but on rainy days we had our *Holzklapper*—wooden sandals that grandfather carved for us. They were a bit noisy on cobblestones, but they kept our feet dry.

Cigarettes were as scarce as everything else. Nicotine lovers would await their turn at the tobacco shop with anticipation. The lines there often stretched longer than those at the butcher shop.

My favorite pastime was to walk the streets, my eyes fixed on the ground in search of cigarette butts or the chewed-up remains of a fat cigar. I would gather them into my container, which usually was an old tin can, but sometimes it was my apron pockets—all kids wore aprons in those days. Then I would rush home to proudly present my finds to my grandfather. After spreading a newspaper on the dining-room table, we would carefully unwrap the tiny butts and shake the tobacco onto small pieces of paper, which my grandfather then artfully rolled into new cigarettes. The cigars he cut into shreds of tobacco, with which he stuffed his pipe. This operation would usually stink up the whole house. My grandmother, upon discovering he had used her best scissors for this smelly project, would throw open every window and door in the house in protest, regardless of the temperature outside.

Then it would be my turn to be scolded for supporting such a nuisance. After listening to a lecture on smoking, how it smelled up the house, ruined the drapery, and most of all, how it occasionally burned holes in the tablecloth (of which my grandfather usually knew nothing), I would promise to use my spare time for more creative projects. But soon grandfather's tobacco ration would go up in smoke, and again, but ever so secretly, I would be on my way to collect a supplement for his pipe. He paid me with candies or other rare sweets, which my grandmother had acquired by way of her connections in hope that she could divert my grandfather's cravings toward something less habit-forming. Every time my grandfather lit up a cigarette, she would shove a candy into his mouth. Soon it became obvious that he didn't mind this extra treat, and to my grandmother's horror, she discovered he had now become hooked on both.

"THANK HITLER FOR IT!"

Chapter Three

As the years passed, the morale among the Germans had fallen, and many who believed in Hitler's lunatic ideas now joined the skeptics. Though they wouldn't dare admit it, they no longer praised him or believed in his insane ideas. My grandfather was one of them. Though a passive member of the party, he defended Hitler's actions even when the average citizen did not approve of them. Nobody would dare to publicly reveal their disapproval, though, because this would mark them a traitor, for which the penalty was life—or was it death?—behind the barbed wire of Dachau. No one could be trusted, so discussions took place in whispers, or best at home, where no one could eavesdrop on us.

At our house, it became a routine. On cold Sunday afternoons in winter we gathered together, usually at my grandparents' house, across the courtyard from our house. There we would sit around the lace-covered table and enjoy home-baked apple strudel. My grandmother poured Ersatz into delicate, hand-painted cups, which had in better days emitted the inviting aroma of real coffee. Sugar, too, was a rare commodity and used sparingly, so we used saccharin to sweeten our coffee. When my grandfather, the lover of sweets, complained about artificially sweetened food, my grandmother would usually reply with her favorite answer: "Thank Hitler for it!"

This would start an argument that lasted way beyond the kaffeeklatsch hour, sometimes extending into the evening. Occasionally it would be interrupted by an air-raid warning, which would leave my grandmother triumphantly repeating "Thank Hitler for it!"

My father disagreed with my grandfather when it came to Hitler, and my grandfather would try to change his mind. When he failed to convince my father, my grandfather would usually call him a Communist who didn't know any better.

My father was not a Communist and did indeed know better. He was a man of logic. And though not politically educated, he relied on his power of reasoning. Many men, like my grandfather, were blinded by the power wielded over them and misguided by ruthless leaders who became murderers of their own kin.

I loved my grandparents as much as I loved my mother and father, and though I was too young to understand the arguments about Hitler, I knew my grandfather was a kind man. And when he became angry at my father, I sensed he argued in compassion, to convince my father that he was wrong.

How could he know that it was he himself who had been misled?

February 19, 1945

Chapter Four

*I*t *was practically impossible to keep up with the air-raid* warnings, so the German authorities provided a system by which one could determine how acute or immediate the danger was. The newspaper printed a map to be clipped and kept for orientation. The map showed Würzburg and an area of about a 100-kilometer radius. When enemy airplanes approached that area, there was acute danger. Radio stations broadcast bulletins with information on the course and the estimated number of airplanes involved. They also named cities in danger of being attacked. If Nuremberg was among them, it meant immediate alarm for us, because their course would bring them directly over our city.

It was the evening of February 19, 1945, when a voice announced over the radio, "Single enemy airplane in the vicinity of Frankfurt. Course: east. No immediate danger is expected." This was good enough for us. No sirens had sounded yet, and we were hoping they never would, since we were ready to retire.

My father, however, had different ideas. "Let's wait a little while yet," he suggested. "If there should be an alarm, we at least won't have to leave our warm beds." He was right. It had happened so many times before, and it was an awful feeling. Just when you were all cuddled up in your cozy bed, ready to go to sleep—or worse yet, if you were already asleep—there they were again, those howling, monstrous sirens sending their fearful warnings across the sleeping city.

Well, still no sirens that night. No further warnings on the radio, either.

"I'm sleepy, Papa. Please can I go to bed?" I said.

"Psst," he interrupted me. He lifted his head from the newspaper and listened intently. My heart pounded, and I held my breath.

"What is it, Papa?" I whispered, frightened.

"Turn the lights off, quickly!" he ordered me.

Hastily I reached for the switch. I still couldn't hear anything except my pounding heart. My mother was napping in her chair. A book slipped off her lap and fell noisily to the floor.

"Quiet!" my father urged in a hushed voice.

My mother, awakened by all this, said, "How come it's dark in here? Brr, I feel a draft; have you got the window open?"

My father would not answer. His head was between the blackout window shade and the open window. Now we all heard it: the sound of a single airplane coming closer. Suddenly the steady hum of the plane's engine changed its pitch. The aircraft was diving. My father had survived four heavy bomb attacks in other cities, making him the veteran in our family. When he heard that sound, he knew what was going to happen.

"Run!" he yelled at us, almost screaming. "Run for your lives!"

The room was still in darkness, but now more than ever I wouldn't dare turn the lights back on. I fell over a stool.

"Where is my coat? I can't find my coat," I cried. I fumbled around in the dark, feeling my way to the door. I touched a briefcase, which I grabbed, but still no coat. I started slowly for the cellar. I had walked these stairs countless times, so I should have found my way in the dark easily. But fear and panic disoriented me, and I ran head-on into a wall.

I was approaching the second floor when suddenly there was a deafening noise. The entire staircase shook, and glass flew from the windows. Part of a window casing fell on top of me, but I was too terrified to feel any pain. The impact of a bomb that hit three houses away made our own house shake in its foundation. Huge chunks of plaster broke away from the ceiling and crashed all around me. The force of the bomb's impact pushed the right side of my body against the banister. I grabbed hold of the steps after the banister gave way, and the briefcase slipped out of my hands.

"Oh, dear God," I whimpered, "don't let me lose that briefcase. It contains all our valuable papers and money." I sat in total darkness, feeling around for the briefcase. Now cold winter air rushed through the hole in the wall where a window had been shortly before. Broken glass covered the stairs. I found a shred of stiff paper, the remains of a window shade, and with it I swept away some of the debris so I wouldn't trip and fall.

Until that moment, I hadn't thought about my family. I knew that Rita, my sister, had run out the door before I did; she must be in the cellar by now. But what about my mother? My father? On my hands and knees, I started back up the stairs, calling for them: "Mama! Papa! Hurry!"

My father was in the hallway on the third floor, and my mother was still in the kitchen, desperately searching for the briefcase.

"Forget about the money and papers!" my father shouted.

"I got it!" I yelled upstairs, even though I didn't have it anymore. Again I started for the cellar, though not without warning my parents about the loose banister on the second floor.

It was on the ground floor that I found the briefcase. A small beam of light coming through the open door of the cellar lit up the spot where the precious case had landed. It was leaning against the wall, just like it had been neatly put there.

"Thank God!" I said aloud and picked it up just in time to hand it to my oncoming mother.

We had just reached the last step of the cellar stairs when a second bomb hit. This one landed half a block away on the other side of our house. It must have been twice as big as the first bomb. The impact was so tremendous we thought the bomb had hit our house. The canned goods on the cellar shelves came tumbling down, hitting some of our tenants before crashing to the ground. Instinctively we braced ourselves against the rough, moist walls of the cellar to await another hit. My grandmother, her rosary between her folded hands, had already been engrossed in silent prayer, but now she fell to her knees, and the other women joined her and prayed aloud. The men, too, joined in, their hands folded as they stood against the wall, ready to drop to the ground should another bomb fall from the sky.

After we had been in the shelter for about an hour, my father and a few other men felt it was safe enough to emerge and see what was happening outside. Just then we heard the all-clear sound in the distance. Our own neighborhood alarm system must have been damaged in the attack, for we never did hear it.

Then everybody felt brave enough to go upstairs. Both entrances to our street were blocked by flames bursting from the roofs and windows of the houses that had been hit. People filled the street, and everyone was in a panic. There were people trapped in the houses, but the heat was so intense that no one dared go near. A fire truck was on its way, someone said. But would it come in time?

Sparks and burning debris flew through the air, carried by a breeze that swept through the cold February night. This created a new danger. The fire could spread. People started evacuating rapidly. Featherbeds flew out of windows. Suitcases tied to ropes were lowered to the ground, and baskets filled with fragile objects were carefully carried to the center of the street.

Nobody dared to sleep that night. When we finally returned to our apartment, morning had begun to dawn. What awaited us made us forget our sleepiness. Every window was broken, and a cold draft filled with the smell of smoke had settled in the house. We tried to look over the rooms for damage, but the electricity was out, so we had to wait for the morning sun.

When I entered my bedroom, a chill came over me. There in my bed, right on the pillow, rested a stone too big for me to lift. It had broken out of the wall. Our house had been in the family for many generations; it was built from natural stones of various sizes. The one in my bed was about two feet square.

Despite the terror and sadness of that night, my sister and I couldn't help but laugh when we saw our naked Christmas tree.

"What's so funny?" my father asked in a somber voice, sticking his head through the living-room door.

"Look at it!" My sister laughed as she pointed to the tree.

The tree leaned against one of the walls, its branches stripped of needles, which now covered the floor, table, and chairs. Some even made it to the kitchen, where they had settled on top of the potato soup in the pot on the stove.

The tree's decorations had vanished too. Only pieces of string dangled from this skeleton, the sad remains of the symbol of Christmas, the season of peace. It was late February, and we still had our tree. Why we kept it that long, we didn't really know ourselves. It was as though we had known that this would be the last Christmas we celebrated in this house.

After looking over the rest of the damage, we realized it was impossible to live there without windows. So we prepared to move to our summer cabin for what we hoped would be a short stay.

The naked Christmas tree

Our new home on Nikolaus Hill

The Cabin on Nikolaus Hill

Chapter Five

Our cabin was located on a hill southwest of the city. The Nikolausberg is one of the highest hills in the Franconia region.

My father's hobby was growing things. By "things" I mean anything that would grow in the ground. Our land was planted with apple, pear, peach, cherry, and plum trees. A large strawberry patch was bordered with bushes of gooseberries, boysenberries, and raspberries and beds of beets, carrots, cabbage, lettuce, tomatoes, and numerous types of flowers. There were also pumpkins, cucumbers, beans, and lots of weeds.

The cabin, covering a 10-foot square, was built with overlapping lumber and topped with a wooden gable. Black tar paper waterproofed the roof and the weather side, on which evergreens had spread their creeping leaves.

The interior was simple. Four bunk beds lined one wall; the first one was level with the floor, and the fourth was surrounded by ceiling beams. The two windows faced opposite directions: one to the south, the other to the north. Below the latter was a wooden board fastened on hinges. It served as a table at mealtimes but folded down to make space when not in use. The east wall held the door and a row of nails that served as a clothes-rack. A small wood-burning stove and a faded, blue-painted cupboard with a couple of drawers beneath it completed the furnishings.

As a whole, the cabin resembled a toolshed more than a cottage. But it was only meant to be an overnight shelter, a place to spend weekends in the summer. It was not ideal for sub-zero weather, snowdrifts, or long, cold nights. But this was February, and spring was on its way, so we didn't worry about winter, which was almost over anyway.

Fyodor: A Russian POW

Chapter Six

Twice a day, we loaded our four-wheeled cart with our household goods and took them up to the hill. After three days we had not made much progress. The cart was small, and many more trips were necessary. My father, a craftsman, worked during the day and could help us only with the second load, which we timed to be ready at the end of his work day. This load was always heavier, because one more adult on the team made a difference.

Our muscles were sore from the strain of the last few days, so we were relieved when Andreas, a family friend who owned a farm, offered us one of his wagons, complete with horses and driver.

Throughout the war, a substantial number of prisoners of war worked for the Germans. Farmhands, for example, were mostly POWs. One such prisoner, a Russian, drove Andreas's wagon. His name was Fyodor, and I shall never forget how he risked his life to save ours.

It was during our second trip with the horse wagon that we became the targets of an air attack. Just as we reached the peak of the hill, we left the wooded area to cross a field. Out of nowhere they came: planes! One? Two? Three? I don't know how many—I was afraid to look up—but it sounded like twenty.

They came down fast. Then, almost in unison, they fired their machine guns. The bullets hit the dirt road, leaving a cloud of dust that stopped abruptly as their trail crossed into the muddy field and toward us. Then two strong arms pulled me from the wagon. I heard words shouted in a language I did not understand. Then a spray of bullets hit the wagon.

"Oh God, why?" my mother pleaded. "Why do we have to suffer like this?"

I, too, pleaded with the Almighty, although in silence because fear left me mute.

The planes vanished from the sky; only a distant hum remained in the air. When it, too, faded away, I opened my eyes and found myself lying under the wagon, my face and clothes covered in mud. I looked around and found my mother and sister in the same position. Now Fyodor bent over to look at us; his face was beaded with sweat, and his eyes expressed concern. One by one he pulled us out from under the wagon. With his handkerchief he wiped the mud from my face. His gestures were accompanied by a swarm of words, which I could not understand, but I am certain they expressed his concern for our well-being. My mother in turn spoke a few words of gratitude, which he probably didn't understand either. He must have known their meaning, though, for my mother kept shaking his hand.

During the attack, after he helped us into the shelter of the wagon, he stood there, an open target, as he tried to calm the horses, which were bucking frantically. Miraculously, no one was hurt, and not until a long time after the incident did we learn why this might have happened. Like all prisoners, Fyodor was wearing a coat marked with the letters *POW*. Could those three letters have saved our lives? The planes were low enough to enable the pilots to read them, and of course, they wouldn't shoot an ally.

The city of Wurzburg in ruins but a steeple remains untouched

March 16, 1945: A Night in Hell

Chapter Seven

The days went by fast. We had most of our clothing and some dishes in the cabin. Now we were ready for the bigger items, like furniture. We asked Andreas to lend us his horse team once more. A last-minute change, however, made it impossible for him to spare the horses that day. So we used the hand-cart again and loaded it with my mother's sewing machine. Just then, an air-raid warning interrupted us, and we had to find shelter.

It was early in the afternoon when the warning sounded, but by the time we left the shelter the sun began to sink behind the roofs of the city. We did not speak much on our way up the hill. Everyone was busy with his or her own thoughts. I was looking forward to the halfway point of our trip because then we would stop to rest for a few minutes. This we had done many times before. We stopped there not only since we started evacuating, but also on weekends when we went to relax at the secluded summer cabin. But today we did not stop. My father was tense and nervous.

"Please, Papa! Let's rest for a while!" my sister and I pleaded.

"Not today, girls!" my father said resolutely, wiping his forehead with a handkerchief.

We tried to bargain: "Five minutes, maybe?"

But my father remained firm. He rushed us, as if he had an intuition that something was going to happen. So we kept on pushing the cart, sadly looking back to the spot where many times before we spent a few minutes stretching and taking in the spring air.

It was almost seven in the evening when the sound of sirens rang in our ears. Another alarm! The 335th since the beginning of the war. We were already going at a fast pace, but now we hurried and pushed the cart with all our strength. We all had the feeling that something was going to happen that night. There had been rumors that there would be another air attack.

At 5:30 p.m., 660 air wings took off from a base near London. Intercepted radio messages revealed at least one of their destinations: Würzburg! The fate of our city had already been sealed.

Hastily we pushed the cart over the last few meters, and the air began to swell with the sound of approaching airplanes. Hundreds of them. Slowly the sound drew closer and closer. Two-engine planes, probably Mosquitoes or Marauders. There was no time for us to waste. Drenched in sweat and breathless from exhaustion, we arrived at our gate. It was not safe to stay in the cabin, yet it was just as dangerous to lie on the ground, so we hid in what we called our dungeon, a four-foot-square manhole located in the northeast corner of our garden, put there to hold our water meter. We had to squeeze ourselves into it. We used it before when we were surprised by an alarm on a quiet Sunday afternoon, so we stocked it with some logs for seating. We left the cast-iron lid off, because the air supply in such a small chamber would not last long.

Now we heard planes directly over us! For four minutes they dropped thousands of orange-red flares. How beautiful and yet so cruel was the sight. It was just as if a giant Christmas tree, lit up with candles, was slowly descending from heaven. My father pulled the lid over the opening of our dungeon. Seconds later, it all turned into hell, four engine bombers filled the sky. For nineteen minutes, hundreds of airplanes dropped a total of four hundred thousand bombs.

The roar of diving planes, combined with the shrill whistle of falling bombs, brought upon us an unconquerable fear for which we knew only one cure: pray to the Almighty that He might spare us!

The impacts felt like an earthquake. Our shelter began to rock, and we had to hold on to each other to keep from being slammed against the walls. Our ears began to hurt.

"Leave your mouths open so your lungs don't burst," my father warned. Gradually the sound of planes faded into the distance. Then there was dead silence. My father opened the lid. And it was high time because we began to run out of air. He stuck his head out, and then quickly withdrew it. His face showed agony, and his voice trembled when he said, "Oh my God!"

My mother rose to look outside. Seconds later she cried out, and it took minutes to calm her. My sister and I started to cry, even though we had not yet seen what awaited us. Finally, we crawled out. If there is anything to which I could compare the sight, I do not know about it, for I have never seen such an inferno as what lay before us. The sky was lit by the flames that consumed what once had been a city. In 17 minutes, British Lancaster bombers destroyed about 88 percent of Würzburg—what centuries had built and generations had inherited. Standing there, helpless and still crying, we suddenly remembered that my grandparents were still in the house when we left the city. For them to have survived would have required a miracle, for the valley before us was burning in every corner. Every few minutes a blue flash extended from the flames into the sky, warning us that seconds later another time bomb would explode.

Smoke started to fill the air. The sound of collapsing buildings carried throughout the night on the wind that developed in the vacuum caused by the tremendous fire.

The narrow and otherwise quiet country road by our property suddenly came to life. Men, women, and children passed by in an endless stream, seeking refuge in a village a few kilometers west of our land. Most people were quiet because many were in shock, but the children cried. Some people limped, some trembled, and some carried others. Many wore no more than their sleepwear or blankets and bedsheets wrapped around them.

We sat by our gate, for we hoped we might find my grandparents among the passing survivors. Never ending was the stream of refugees, and the sight became more and more pathetic. Blinded by the smoke, scorched by the fire, they fumbled aimlessly forward.

A young girl pushed her grandfather in a wheelbarrow. The old man whimpered in pain, and the girl desperately tried to calm him. He wanted to scream, but his voice was hoarse from the dense smoke in the air and only moans came from his lips.

My father offered him some water. When he held out the canteen flask, he noticed pieces of clothing wrapped around the man's arms. Blood was dripping from them. My father held the flask to the man's mouth. Just then the old man started to slouch forward, and slowly he fell off the wheelbarrow onto the ground. The cloth around his arms came loose and fell open. He had no hands. He had bled to death.

My mother broke into tears again. "I can't look anymore," she cried. "I can't stand the sight of it anymore!"

Some people stopped to rest, to sit beside us by our fence. They gratefully accepted the water we offered. The people on the road became fewer as the hours elapsed. But still no sign of my grandparents.

"Please, Lord! Please don't let them die!" we prayed to heaven and cried. "Please spare them!"

When the last weary survivor passed by our gate, the sun had already risen.

Divine Intervention left Madonna and child unscathed

SEARCH FOR GRANDPARENTS

Chapter Eight

We left for the city, determined to find my grandparents. Soon we reached the asphalt road we traveled on the night before with our cart. The fear we felt then was replaced with desperation as daylight revealed the results of the previous night's holocaust.

A new wave of refugees trekked up the hill, passing us on our way to the burning city.

"You're crazy! You can't go down there!" a man shouted at us in disbelief. "It's hell down there," he said, more to himself than to us, as he resumed his walk uphill. It was a great risk to enter the city, we all knew that, but we hoped that God was once again on our side and would let us find my grandparents—alive!

The smoke became more intense as we neared the foot of the hill. We crossed a small park near one of the bridges connecting the suburbs to the inner city. The bridges were still intact. A small calculation by the bombers, perhaps, as they might be useful for invaders someday.

We began to cough as smoke filled our lungs, and we had to don our gas masks. Everybody in sight wore one now; it would have been hazardous to go without one.

A truckload of German soldiers, also wearing masks, passed us on the bridge. A row of houses that collapsed into the street was still in flames. The truck could go no further. The soldiers dismounted and equipped themselves with shovels, picks, and other tools for use in rescue. Their leader saw us, and with a wave of his hand he motioned for us to follow them.

"Where are you going?" he asked my father with a frown.

"My Oma and Opa!" I exclaimed before my father could answer. "We've got to find them! Please can you help us?" The soldier turned toward me and said, "I am sorry, little girl, but we have orders, and they are to lay free the exit of the public shelter in the Adolf-Hitlerstrasse."

"We are going toward Oberthür-Gasse," my father interrupted. The soldiers were not familiar with the streets of the city, as they had come from a garrison in a nearby town. The two streets ran parallel to one another. My father led the soldiers toward their rescue mission.

"What a waste!" my father lamented as he scanned the fiery surroundings. The soldiers remained quiet; they were not allowed to voice their opinions, but their faces reflected their thoughts.

"This way!" my father said and pointed to the next corner, leading us into a narrow street. Mounds of stones and debris blocked passage, and the hollow structure of a burned-out house leaned dangerously to one side.

"Let's try the next one," my father suggested, gesturing to a side street ahead. But it, too, was filled with fallen debris, and burning lumber blocked off any remaining openings. A cry came from a cellar beneath one of the still-burning houses. There it was again! In minutes the soldiers cleared a window leading to the cellar below the street level. One of them lowered himself on a rope held by the rest of the soldiers. When he emerged, a child clung to his body. Nobody spoke—we were too moved.

"The rest are dead," the soldier reported as he untied himself. The child was a girl, about seven years old. How she survived while the others with her had died was beyond our knowing.

With every step we took through this giant pile of stones and ashes, our hopes of finding my grandparents alive shrank more and more.

We reached the public shelter, which was the soldiers' destination. Another group of military personnel already arrived carrying the bodies they found in the shelter to the street. An entire block was already lined with victims.

Our family occasionally used this shelter. It was only a block away from our house. We went there especially in the winter, when our own cellar became too cold.

Is it possible Oma and Opa decided to use this shelter last night? Dear Lord, I hope they didn't! I thought.

My mother must have had the same thought. "We are looking for my parents," she said to one of the soldiers who emerged from the shelter, carrying a dead child.

"There are only a few bodies left down there, but they all look like children," he said, breathing heavily as he lowered the lifeless bundle to the ground.

"This child," I said as I stared at the little girl on the ground, "looks familiar."

"It's Ingrid!" my sister exclaimed. "Oh, Ingrid! Ingrid!" she cried to the little body, as if she could awaken it.

I looked over the rest of the bodies as I walked past them. "Oh God!" I cried. "Don't let me find them here. No! Not here." I reached the end of the lineup and turned around. Again, I looked over the lifeless remains before me. "Anneliese," I said, recognizing another of my playmates. She, too, had died, like her little sister, Ingrid.

My father walked toward me. "The rest of her family lies over there," he said, pointing to the other side of the street.

"Why?" I sobbed. "Why did they have to die? They didn't hurt anybody."

"Come!" my father said, his voice choked-up as he led me away, his arm around my shoulders. "We'll go to our house now," he added, turning to see if my mother and sister were following us. We were all in tears, even my father, although he tried not to show it.

More people looking for their family members came toward us, heading in the opposite direction.

"How does it look over there?" my father asked one of them, pointing to our street.

"It's all gone!" the man said wearily. "I doubt anyone got out of there alive."

"Oh no!" my mother said tearfully. "I won't believe they're dead. We must find them!"

Rubble cluttered the street, leaving only a narrow path. Soon there was no street at all—just piles of stones and smoking lumber between rows of ruins. Single file, we paced our way over mounds and climbed carefully around twisted beams of steel.

"Don't touch them," my father cautioned us. "They might still be hot from the fire."

There it was! Our house—our family's home for generations. Or was it a house? No! Only the four walls remained intact, though burned. The graceful furniture, delicate china, and polished silver were destroyed. A lonely chair leg peeked out from crushed stovepipes, broken tiles, and chunks of smoldering mattress.

"The cellar did not collapse," said my father.

"Maybe they are still down there!" we all exclaimed. Feverishly we began to remove stones and dirt from the entrance to the cellar, but every time we pushed the rubble away, more came rolling down.

"It's no use," my father said as he brushed the dirt from his hands, which began to bleed. "We've got to get a pick and shovel."

"*Ja!* And perhaps some soldiers," my mother said with hope in her voice.

We did not take the route by which we came. Instead we walked to the other end of our street, but soon reached a point where passage was almost impossible. Heavy, yellow-colored smoke rose from a cavity in the ground. It looked like something exploded there. The strange odor made us cough. Hastily my father buckled his gas mask back on his face and, still coughing, he motioned for us to do the same. We removed them earlier, because the hot air made the rubber stick to our skin, causing us to perspire.

Soon we reached the end of our street. We took a side street, which, if passable, would shorten our trip back to the shelter. We hoped to find some soldiers to help us, but they left. Only the dead remained, and a few more were added since we'd left. There was a woman with a dog on a leather leash still tied to her wrist and two men, one of whom lay facedown. Their clothes were half burned off their bodies.

"They must have found them in another shelter," my father commented. "There was no fire in this one. They all suffocated from the smoke that entered from outside."

"Let's go!" my mother urged. "We've got to find help! Maybe on the Residenzplatz."

The Residenzplatz consisted of a wide-open area that was used as a parade ground in bygone days. The plaza stretched out in front of a majestic baroque castle that also suffered. Black smoke still rose from one of its wings. Since the castle was a sturdy structure, it remained standing.

A mass of people occupied the plaza. Some were still there from the night before when they fled their homes, realizing escape from a caved-in house or a collapsed cellar was impossible. The plaza was free of danger from falling beams and whirling stones. Could Oma and Opa have had the same thought and left the house or cellar before the exit was sealed off? We quickened our steps, jumped over one last pile of debris, and ran toward the crowded plaza.

"Oma! Opa!" my sister and I called out, searching the crowd. Faces blackened by smoke still reflected horror and shock. Some people lay on the ground, too weak and exhausted to stand any longer.

"Mutter! Vater!" my mother called. A woman approached us. "They are here," she called out to my mother. "I saw them." She pointed in the direction of where she had last seen them. Only then did we recognize the woman as one of our neighbors. Her appearance had changed.

"They're alive! They're alive!" my mother shouted in excitement as she turned toward us to reassure us of what the woman said.

My sister, staring in the opposite direction, suddenly ran, her arms waving in the air, as she yelled as loud as she could, "Oma! Oma! Over here!"

I had not spotted my grandmother yet, but I ran across the cobblestoned ground as fast as my feet could carry me. I stumbled but quickly recovered my balance and continued my pursuit. But now I lost sight of my sister. My parents followed behind, out of breath from running after us. Then I saw my sister walking toward us with two weary figures beside her. It was them! My grandparents! We barely recognized them at first. Their eyeglasses were gone, their hair and eyebrows had burned off, and their clothes smelled of a sickening odor. My sister recognized my grandmother from a distance only by the color of her sweater. My grandfather stood right beside her. He was clad only in his pajamas and house slippers, without his mustache—it, too, had been singed away. He looked eerie.

But they were alive! We embraced them and stood in silence. No words could express our feelings at that moment.

Our eyes filled with tears once more, but this time they were tears of joy. Our search ended and our prayers had been heard.

I raised my eyes to the smoke-filled sky and whispered, "Thank you, God!"

Opa and Oma's Survival

Chapter Nine

"*It was just like any other night,*" *my grandfather began after* he settled into the broad sofa at my aunt Katrina's house in one of Würzburg's suburbs. He held a cup of hot peppermint tea between his still-trembling hands. He took a sip and out of habit wiped the spot where his mustache had been. With a grimace he withdrew his hand because the spot was still sore.

"It will grow back," my aunt Katrina assured him, and she dabbed the area with a soothing salve. My grandmother sat beside him. A bath refreshed them somewhat, but fatigue still marked their faces. Cuddled in my aunt and uncle's bathrobes, they were ready to tell us about their ordeal.

"I guess you'll have to put up with us for a while," my grandfather concluded with a look at his oldest daughter Katrina.

"Of course you can stay with us," my aunt assured him. "Where else would you go?" My aunt was right. The cabin was no place for my grandparents. It was a little safer in the suburbs than on Nikolaus Hill, and their house was spacious enough for two more people.

"Are you sure you feel like talking?" my mother asked, concerned.

"I don't think I can sleep yet," my grandfather argued mildly and held out his cup for a refill. "It was just like any other night," he began again. "Just another alarm, we figured."

"Father was in bed already," my grandmother joined in. "He didn't feel well, so I told him to lie down and I would make him some tea."

"Never had a chance to drink it," Opa recalled.

"Did you go to the cellar?" my father asked.

"Yes, we did," my grandfather continued. "No sooner were we down there than the bombs began to fall. First in the distance, then closer. A direct hit made the walls sway. When the lights went off, we panicked. The heavy cellar door broke from its hinges and slid down the stairs, leaving a mound of rubble. Then there was darkness."

A shiver raced down my spine. I often envisioned a scene like the one my grandfather described. "How did you get out?" I asked.

Grandfather continued, "We heard a crackle above us and smelled fire. Smoke drifted down. We knew remaining there would mean certain death."

"We broke through the thin wall that separated us from the shelter of the house next door," Oma explained. "But debris blocked the exit. We entered the shelter beyond that one by breaking through one of the emergency exits, but there was no escape from there either."

There was a short pause. Then my grandfather said, "I was almost at the end of my strength, but there was one more wall we had to break through to get to the public shelter beyond. But it looked empty. The people using it must have left in a hurry because there were suitcases and bags of clothing left behind. A baby carriage was tipped over on its side, and infants' toys were strewn beside it."

Oma joined in again. "We even found a baby bottle half filled with milk."

"What happened next?" my mother asked.

After another sip of tea, my grandfather continued, "The shelter looked safe, so we decided to stay and wait for the fire outside to die. But then an explosion in the opposite corner of the shelter tore away a huge steel door. The impact knocked us to the ground, and for a moment we lost our breath. Smoke came billowing in. We had to leave fast.

"We quickly unbolted the steel door on the other side of the shelter. Then we found ourselves in a little garden surrounded by stone walls with a wooden gate. Flames devoured a pavilion and a wooden table and chairs. On the other end of the garden, there was a stone cherub glowing in the light of the flames, and a small cistern containing animal waste for fertilizer. Off to the side, a door led to the house, or what was left of it—as well as the stairs that led to the shelter from which we emerged. There was no escape in that direction."

My mother, apparently familiar with the garden, asked, "Did you leave through the gate then?"

"Yes, but not for a while," my grandmother said. "The gate was just barely burning, but it was locked. So then we sat on the ground and awaited our fate." Her voice trembled, and her eyes filled with tears. Without words, my aunt handed her a handkerchief. After a short pause she continued, "By then, daylight had begun to break."

"There was no ladder, and the table and chairs were too burned to be of use," Opa now recalled. "We searched for some kind of tool that would help us break open the gate, but all we could find was a pair of rusty pruning shears.

"But then we had another idea. Why not speed up the fire on the wooden gate? It was already burning slowly on the upper corners, but the metal trimmings retarded the flames. The best way to burn an opening would be from the bottom up.

"With the pruning shears, we picked up some of the burning lumber from the pavilion and set it under the gate. Time was running out. The smoke became more intense, and the house adjoining the garden was ready to cave in. It did not take long to set the gate on fire. It was already hot from the heat around it, so in seconds the entire gate was engulfed in flames. This was more than we counted on, and now there was no time to waste. But if we went through it at this point, it would mean our deaths. We had to wait until the opening became large enough for us to pass through without getting touched by fire.

"The firestorm became stronger, sucking up loose debris and whirling it into the air. Then our glasses were sucked up by the vacuum.

"We were about to give up again when another idea came to mind: the blankets. We found them in the last shelter and decided to take them with us. On our hands and knees, we crawled toward the cistern. Our eyes hurt from the smoke, and even breathing became hazardous. But only a few more inches and we reached the cistern in the ground. We dropped the blankets into the basin to let them soak up the manure. A swarm of flies burst aimlessly around us, hitting our faces. The blankets quickly soaked up the heavy liquid, and the weight of it had us struggling to retrieve them from their bath. The smell was sickening when we wrapped them around us.

"Now we were ready to exit through the furiously burning gate. We could only open our eyes for seconds at a time, though even then we saw an endless blur. Without our glasses, we were blind. We crawled toward the gate. We could only hope that whatever was on the other side was more bearable. 'Lord, be with us,' we prayed before we rose from our hands and knees and blindly ran through the fire. Not a minute too soon did we reach the other side. The house caved in, sending huge stones and burning pieces of lumber into the garden. Our hair had burned away, and pain overcame us. With what little strength remained in us, we made our way to the plaza . . . ," slowly my grandfather's voice trailed off, "and that's where you found us." His tired voice now turned into a soft whisper. Seconds later he entered a deep and restful sleep.

Friedhof

Chapter Ten

The cemetery near the eastern edge of the city became the center of activity.

We never noticed the sunny sky. Less pleasurable thoughts occupied our minds when we returned to the still-smoldering ruins of the city to pay one last tribute to those who had lost their lives a few nights before.

The resting place of the dead had not been spared from destruction. Tombstones lay overturned, some broken into pieces, and grave markers were strewn about. Flowers and greenery that had formerly decked the graves were now wilted and forlorn, covering the aisles and paths.

"Look!" my sister said, pointing at a piece of bone that stuck out from a pile of dirt. The bomb damage was heavy in this section. Deep craters caused by demolition bombs exposed the aged remains of skeletons. Entire graves had vanished.

"Even the dead cannot rest in peace!" my mother lamented.

"I hope ours is still there," my father said doubtfully, referring to our family plot. The section where it was located was sealed off by ropes tied to the trees. A piece of cardboard with a hastily written message, *GEFAHR!* was nailed to a nearby tree.

"What kind of danger?" I asked my father. He was spared an answer. A man with a shovel mounted over his shoulder like a rifle approached.

"There are duds in there," he informed us. "One of them went off this morning," he added to convince us it was not safe beyond the ropes.

"Let's get out of here," my mother said. The day before she had seen a wagon, drawn by a team of horses, set off such a bomb. A farmer helped some citizens salvage belongings that had not been completely destroyed. Just as he was leaving the city, the entire load, the wagon and horses, was thrown into the air.

"It just tore them into shreds," my mother recalled with a shiver.

We continued walking aimlessly. Was this the same Friedhof, or court of peace, I had so often visited? Although I was too young when my brother died to remember his funeral, I made weekly visits to his grave for years. He died at the age of nine from a leak in his intestines. Led by my mother's hand, I carried flowers from the fields and meadows we passed on the way to trim his resting place. I remembered the many funeral processions I witnessed, the mourners all dressed in black, and the women's faces enveloped in veils to hide their tears. At a calculated pace they followed the coffin carried by somber-looking men clad in dark suits and hats. A small group of brass musicians led them toward the burial site.

But what I witnessed now bore no resemblance to my memories. The graveyard was swarming with people. Many of them were digging holes. Not big holes, just something deep enough to hold whatever was used in place of a casket. A water bucket, deformed and rusty, stood near the edge of a freshly dug hole. A wrinkled newspaper was tightly wrapped around its contents. A man bent over to collect some of the wilted flowers strewn about, and with loving care he arranged them on top of the bucket. Then he slowly lowered the bucket into the ground. He whispered words of prayer as he returned the earth to the hole. He picked up the grave marker beside him; with his pocketknife he made one last adjustment on its newly inscribed words before he sunk it into the ground.

"Hier ruht in Frieden—unser Sohn Thomas," it read in white, painted letters. Underneath were the freshly carved words, "und seine Mutter, Maria."

A woman passed us. The cart she pulled held an oval-shaped laundry tub. A lifeless limb protruded from beneath shreds of scorched burlap.

"Can we help you?" my father asked in sympathy. She did not answer. Apathetically she raised her hands to decline his offer and quietly continued her journey.

A young soldier pushed his bicycle up the road. A cardboard box balanced on the frame of his bike. Carefully, so as not to drop his load, he steadied the box with one hand while he steered the bike with his other hand. As if he could read our thoughts, he stopped to say, "It's my baby!" He nodded toward the box.

"I am sorry," my mother said.

"I haven't found my wife yet," he said.

Not knowing what else to say, we stood and stared at the box. Slowly, the soldier continued up the road. "My baby! My baby!" he wept. I fought back tears, but like acid they burned my eyes and face. Won't they ever stop? I remembered my grandmother saying, "If you run out of tears, you have run out of faith!"

A steady line of trucks rumbled toward the cemetery. Just outside the gate was a narrow, wooded park. Men with shovels clustered around a huge hole in the ground.

Piled up in the hole were hundreds of bodies. A truck backed up to the edge. The hydraulic lift was set into motion, and another load plunged into the hole. The truck moved away, and the workers mechanically swung shovels filled with a white compound, a disinfectant, until a layer formed over the bodies. A layer of dirt followed.

The next truck in line rolled up. With jerky movements the bin rose to empty itself. When the truck finished dropping bodies into the hole, one body remained. Caught on a metal hinge, it hung in midair. A worker poked at it with his shovel, but it would not come loose. Another man walked up to it. He dropped his shovel, and together the two men pulled on the corpse. The driver shifted gears to pull away from the hole. One of the men shouted for more gas. The driver stepped on the accelerator. The body fell at their feet. Lifting it by its arms and legs, they swung it back and forth. "Hoooh-roock!" someone yelled. Like a sack of flour, the body fell through the air, with arms spread as it plunged into the pit.

My eyes had become immune to the sight of death, but my stomach revolted against the odor of decomposing flesh. I had to fight back the nausea. I quickly ran to some nearby bushes.

"I want to go home," I pleaded with my father.

"Weitermachen! Weitermachen!" the overseer yelled at the workers. Another truck approached the pit. The whining hum of its hydraulic lift was carried off by a mild breeze, and in the distance we could still hear the truck ridding itself of its cargo.

Nearly five thousand citizens lost their lives. When the pit was full, it held three thousand and nine of the bodies. Sixty-two of them were our friends and neighbors.

Water barrel artillery

Water: A Precious Commodity

Chapter Eleven

*O*ur hopes of living in the cabin only temporarily vanished. Now that we lost most of our belongings, we had to face the fact that the cabin would be our home indefinitely. Perhaps for months, maybe even for years to come. What did the future hold for us? Was it death? Perhaps from another air attack? As it turned out, we lived there for more than two years—from February 19, 1945, to just before Christmas in 1947.

"How many potatoes do we have left?" my mother asked as she prepared to fill a pot from the nearly empty sack.

"I'm afraid this is it," my father said, pointing at the sack.

"Remember? We never got the rest," I joined in. "The horse wagon was supposed to bring them up here!"

"That's right," my mother recalled, "the fire probably made baked potatoes out of them."

At most there was a week's supply, and potatoes made up most of our diet. It was too early in the season to harvest any fruits or vegetables from our own garden, which had been neglected lately anyway. The city's traffic, commerce, industry, and economy were at a complete standstill. We never had electricity in the cabin, so we didn't miss it. But the candles—how many were left? Would they last? But even candles were dispensable. Water, however, was essential.

Höchberg, the village about three kilometers west of our land, was our only hope. A wooden barrel in the garden that caught rainwater now became our means to haul water from the village up to the hill.

The village square was crowded. It looked as if the entire population of Höchberg was gathered in front of the fountain. The village's utility centers suffered, and the spring fountain had to provide water for everybody. The fountain pumps occasionally lost pressure, and then only a trickle of water ran from the spout.

Every other day we left for the village to fill our barrel. While my sister and I waited in line at the fountain, my mother waited her turn at the grocery store. Whoever was first to accomplish their chore waited by a bench near the edge of the village.

Climbing the hill from the west was not easy. Bumps and stones in the dirt road made the cart tilt and spill the precious liquid, so that sometimes only half the water remained by the time we reached the cabin.

"No bath tonight!" my mother would conclude. But this was all right with us. A cold bath gave us no joy. Sometimes, when we made the trip alone, we did not always notice the big stones in the road.

One time we returned with no water at all. But that time it wasn't bumps and stones that rid us of our load, but bullets from a machine gun.

"He wore a red scarf!" my mother exclaimed, running across a field to come to our assistance, a pair of field glasses still dangling around her neck.

"Who wore a red scarf?" my sister and I asked. Still shaken from the sudden attack, we sat on the edge of the road. Though more amazed than scared by what happened, we waited for our mother to reach us.

We had been only a short distance from the cabin when a single plane, as usual out of nowhere, attacked us. Our ears, trained to be alert to any noise like the engine of an airplane, picked up its approach. The short ravine lined with blackthorn bushes ahead was a good hideout. Leaving the cart behind, we ran toward the dense scrub to conceal ourselves from the plane. A flock of birds took noisily to the air.

"They could give us away!" I said as we crawled deeper into the bushes.

"Don't be silly!" my sister answered. "They know where we are. Where else is there to go in the middle of a country road?"

With our cart abandoned on the road, we awaited the attack. But none of the bullets came near us. The plane targeted the water barrel instead. Full of holes, the barrel leaked its water onto the ground.

"Fink!" my sister shouted, waving her fist at the plane, which had long disappeared into the clouds.

My mother, who had also spotted the airplane, quickly scanned the road through her binoculars. The rolling hills partly obscured her view, so she could not see us from her vantage point. But when she saw the plane dive toward the ravine, she knew that was where we had to be.

"The pilot," she answered our question now, "he wore a red scarf."

It didn't matter to us what color scarf the pilot wore. We were too tired to care at that point, but my mother was trying to tell us how low the plane was flying.

"I yelled at him and waved at him," she continued, still excited.

"What did you tell him?" my sister asked, trying to keep a straight face.

My mother was not short of an answer: "I told him that he couldn't shoot at you, that you were only a couple of innocent kids. 'Here!' I told him. 'Shoot at me if you have to shoot somebody, but leave my children alone!'"

My mother meant what she said. She stood out there in the open, waving at the pilot in desperation, hoping to save us from death. Only God knows what the pilot thought when he saw my mother standing there in the middle of an open field, waving at him.

A thought occurred to us as to why only our water barrel was attacked, while we got away with only a few tears in our skin from the thorny bushes. After several mishaps at the fountain, we brought along a piece of unused stovepipe, complete with a curved knee. We used this to guide the water into the barrel without having to lift it from the cart. Lifting a hundred-liter barrel full of water was too strenuous for undernourished girls.

A barrel mounted on a cart was quite innocent-looking by itself. But with a stovepipe attached to it, it may have resembled a piece of artillery from the air.

So now that our water barrel had suffered from a case of mistaken identity, it was no longer of any use to us. We had lost not only our water supply for the day, but also our means to carry it in the future. One more hardship was added to our lives.

Village Life

Chapter Twelve

S*tanding in line in Würzburg was a tiring experience, but here* it was even more exhausting. The village was not prepared for the sudden rise in population, and more and more refugees arrived seeking shelter. This situation affected everyone. The bakers could not keep up with the demand for bread, and many times a long wait, often in a line the entire length of the main street, was in vain.

Rules made by the shopkeepers were grudgingly obeyed by the villagers. One such rule allowed only one loaf of bread per family. Everyone knew each other, and no one was able to break this rule. But we were strangers, and we hoped that might be an advantage for us. We arrived at the bakery at different times. We stood at reasonable distances from each other and by no means let it be known we were related. With this plan we hoped to buy three loaves in one day. But the woman behind the counter noticed a certain resemblance between my sister and me. Identical twins. Of course! We should have known better. Well, we got two loaves among the three of us, and in only two hours of waiting, which was more than we hoped for.

The next trip, however, was again in vain. After four and a half hours of waiting, my mother, together with the rest of the people in line, was told to come back the next day. Choked with tears, she walked back to her bicycle. But as she rounded the corner of the building, the unmistakable smell of freshly baked bread wafted toward her. Tracing the aroma, she found herself in the storage room of the bakery, surrounded by shelves, all of them filled with still-steaming loaves of bread.

"Hallo, ist jemand da?" she called out.

My mother was determined not to return home empty-handed. If she could persuade the baker to make an exception and sell her a loaf of bread, she would at least not have to fear being turned away again the next day.

She called again, "Hello, anybody here?" Still no answer. She was about to give up when an idea struck her. *I'll just take a loaf and leave the money for it on the shelf,* she thought. Quickly she grabbed a loaf. As she searched for her billfold, she heard footsteps coming from the basement stairs. Now that she had the bread in her possession, it could be a nasty situation if she got caught. She left the room in haste. It was not until she was pedaling her bike along the country road that she realized what she had done.

"May God forgive me for what I have done," my mother muttered when she set the bread before us.

"What happened?" my sister asked.

"Not a word to Papa!" she said and made us promise; she told us what happened.

Having become a thief bothered her so much that she confessed her misdeed to the baker—though not until a long time after the incident. He just laughed and, instead of taking the money she offered him as a belated payment, rewarded her for her honesty by presenting her with another loaf of bread, which was just as fresh and aromatic as the one she stole.

One time the rain set in and lasted for four days. We gave up our daily trip to the village while it rained and instead set up every available pot and pail, which left us with plenty of water. But bread, unfortunately, did not fall from the sky.

In hopes of a shorter wait in line because of the unpleasant weather, my mother left for the village. Wrapped in my father's raincoat and holding an umbrella, she swung herself onto her bicycle. We watched her pass the ravine. Only the black dome of her umbrella was visible now, but we knew she would soon come into sight again after she reached the other side of the hill. But the road remained empty. There was no way we could have missed her. Fearing that something happened to her, we prepared to leave for the ravine. Without any proper clothing to shield ourselves from the rain, we wrapped bedsheets around ourselves. By now we were certain something happened to our mother because her figure never appeared on the ascending road.

To shorten the walk to the spot where we suspected her to be, we crossed through the fields rather than following the road. The ground was soaked, and we sank ankle-deep into the mud. It slowed us down, but it was too late to take the road.

When we spotted my mother we knew she was hurt. Her bicycle lay on the side of the road. Her umbrella drifted into a field, blown further away each time a gust of wind caught its frame.

"Mutti!" my sister and I called to let her know we were near. We could hear her sobs as she lay in the mud, unable to raise herself. Mud and tears covered her face. She looked at us with a strange expression.

"Are you all right?" we asked.

"My children?" asked my mother, wiping her face with the back of her hand.

"Ja," I answered, wondering at her strange question.

"Who did you think we were?" my sister asked. "A couple of ghosts?"

In a weary gesture my mother motioned toward us as we stood there, enveloped in white bedsheets—well, they were white when we started out—but her movement brought back the pain in her hip. She cried out when she tried to shift her position.

I unwrapped myself from the sheet, and together we tried to slip it underneath our mother. It was a painful procedure for her, and watching her suffer, we, too, were about to cry.

"All right now," I said comfortingly and covered her with my sister's sheet.

"You just lie still, and we will carry you back," I told my mother.

"You can't," she cried, trying to discourage us. "I'm too heavy for you!"

"We can't leave you lying here," my sister said, determined, and we lifted up the ends of the sheet beneath her.

With the hundred and fifty pounds we now held between us, our footsteps sank even deeper into the muddy ground. After a few meters we stumbled and lost our balance and with it, our grip on the load we carried. My mother fell to the ground, and a glimpse at her face assured me she was in great pain.

"I'll get Herr Hefner," I decided.

"No, get the cart," my sister suggested. "And some blankets," she called after me as I pounded toward the cabin.

Before I left for the ravine with the cart and the blankets, I quickly exchanged my drenched clothes for some dry ones. As an afterthought I left a note for my father to let him know where to find us. The time passed quickly, and it was nearly evening. If I waited long enough I might see my father come home.

"The note will do," I decided and speedily returned to the ravine. This time I took the road.

After unsuccessfully attempting to lift my mother onto the cart, my sister and I lost most of our strength. My clothes were again soaked by the rain, and my pigtails opened, letting my hair to fall loose onto my neck and shoulders, clutching against my cheeks as the wind blew past me.

Then we finally saw my father. He looked worried when he saw my mother's condition. "You will be lucky if you don't catch pneumonia on top of it," he said, concerned, "all of you."

The experience stayed with us for a while. All of us, including my father, came down with a cold. My mother's dislocated hip kept her from doing even the smallest chores. The task of cooking and other household chores were completely in the hands of my sister and me. But with guidance and comments coming from the bunk bed in which my mother was laid up, we had nothing to worry about. Or did we?

"You've got to do the cooking," my father said.

Cook with what? Dandelions tasted all right if properly prepared. But without vinegar to season them, they tasted bitter and were hard to digest. There was another edible weed, stinging nettle, but harvesting it was an itchy chore. Whenever we spotted a spread of stinging nettle, we stood clear from it by walking a big circle around it. The slightest touch caused uncomfortable itching and it even left a rash on people with more sensitive skin. It was not nearly as bad as poison ivy, but it was annoying enough. But it was edible, and that was all that mattered at the moment.

With an anticipation stimulated only by the pain of my empty stomach, I left in search for our supper.

"Only the tips," my mother advised me. "And grab them firmly. That way they won't sting."

When I returned to the cabin to prepare my harvest, I felt short on hands to scratch myself.

"This stuff better be good," I grumbled as I filled my plate.

"Hunger can bring out the genius in man," my father said as he tasted the green mass on his plate.

"And some less admirable traits, too," my mother finished.

An Odorous Adventure at Midnight

Chapter Thirteen

Stealing a loaf of bread might have been my mother's first dishonest act. As it turned out, however, it was not her last. Our never ending search for edibles became less successful from one day to the next. We needed milk, but there was none available.

"Run over to the Hefners' cottage," my mother urged me, "see if they can spare some goat milk today."

"We just got some yesterday," I reminded her, hoping she would change her mind. But she insisted I try anyway, so with a tin cup tucked into my apron pocket, I set out for our neighbors' cottage. I loathed going near their place because every time I approached it, my childish imagination took hold. I could see myself as one of the victims in the fairy tale of Hänsel and Gretel, which still gave me shivering memories.

Wild rosebushes and tall grass surrounded the Hefners' cottage. The stucco that once covered the bricks crumbled away, and only random patches remained. The green shutters were hinged to small, mullioned windows that were so densely coated in dirt and grime that even the curtains were no longer visible from the outside.

No one in our family—and, for all we knew, nobody else— had ever set foot inside of their cottage. Occasionally, we were invited in, but we could not accept because of the odor that greeted us every time we tried to enter. From the front door, we saw chicken droppings covering the hallway, trailing toward the kitchen, where the smell of spoiled garbage mixed with the scent of cat droppings. A menagerie of animals gathered about the cottage, which we eventually dubbed the "gas chamber." There was a goose – her gander was no longer around, since somebody stole him – and, of course, the chickens roamed the house. A forever-pregnant cat lazily stretched out on top of a buffet, and an aging tomcat usually lay wrapped around Mrs. Hefner's neck.

Herr Hefner, though long retired, still wore his traditional butcher's garb, including a black-and-white-striped denim shirt with a mandarin collar. All but one of its buttons was replaced with safety pins. His once tall stature shrank from age and hard work, which gave him the appearance of a hunchback. His hands with only seven fingers remaining – the rest of them got lost in a meat grinder, as he once told us – were habitually hiding behind the bib of his ankle-length apron, which was long overdue for a laundering. There was no way of telling whether he had any hair because his head was never without the protection of a shielded cap he wore backwards whenever he milked the goat.

Frau Hefner covered her stringy gray hair with a moth-eaten wool scarf, even on hot days. The scarf matched the dingy gray skirt that reached her boots. Their laces had long ago been replaced with pieces of rope that were never tied.

"My arthritis," she would explain. "Couldn't get into my own shoes today, so I'm wearing my husband's boots."

Her gout-crippled hands were as ever tucked into her seemingly bottomless skirt pouches from which she simultaneously extracted bits of bread crumbs from one and kernels of grain from the other, to sprinkle them amongst her squawking and cackling menagerie by which she was constantly pursued.

■ ◆ ◆ ■

Regardless of how formidable the neighbors were, we needed milk. So I ventured over there one day. The ring of a chime became audible as I pulled on a thin wire attached to the frame of the wooden gate. Soon I could hear a voice from the inners of the cottage, then footsteps.

The first thing I saw when the door opened was Frau Hefner's nose as she stuck her head through the door. It must have been one of those days when her arthritis troubled her, for a cane – a homemade one carved from a branch of a pear tree – now supported her frail body.

Again I noted the uncanny resemblance between her and the witch in "Hänsel and Gretel." Instinctively I peered at the rosebushes, as if I might find an oven behind them.

When she saw the tin cup in my hands, her toothless face grimaced, and before I had a chance to air my request, she waved me off.

"Can't spare any milk today!" she huffed and shut the door. The next day was no more successful.

"This old witch would rather feed it to her cats than let us have any!" my mother said when I returned with an empty cup.

But all was not lost, my mother decided. By now she had sufficiently recuperated from her bicycle fall and was back on her feet again. So this was a good time for what she was planning.

The night was black. Not even the stars were visible. The ground was dry, so our footsteps would leave no trace. A perfect night for our venture.

"I hope it works," I whispered as I followed my mother, who strode along the narrow path to our neighbors' garden.

"Look," my mother said reassuringly. "I milked a cow once, so a goat should be easier yet."

"Once?" I asked. "Once you milked . . ."

"Psst," my mother interrupted. We had reached the hedge surrounding the mesh fence. We knew from prior investigation that there was an opening in it that led directly to the goat's shed.

Having tucked the kettle under my sweater, I used both hands to separate the branches of the dense bushes. My mother slipped past me to the other side, and then my sister and I followed. My sister's task was to stand by the opening so that if a hasty escape was necessary, we would not have to search for the exit in the dark.

A sudden fear struck me. What if Herr Hefner decided to stand watch over his domain? Recent attempts to rob him might have provoked him to sacrifice his sleep and stand guard.

"Got the kettle?" my mother whispered. I handed it to her.

The goat's stable was about the size of a doghouse. The door was narrow, and a person could hardly stand up inside it without touching the roof. Waste saturated the straw on the floor. The wind sometimes carried the odor as far as our cabin.

Carefully, so as not to make a sound, my mother opened the slide bolt. She entered the shed. There was a thud and a splash, then a howling moan. Mother had not counted on the narrow board above the ground, part of the frame that held the door. Her fall aroused the goat, and judging from the noises, I clearly pictured what was happening.

Between my mother's special selection of German curses and the goat's cries of "M-a-a-ah! M-a-a-ah!" I heard my sister's subdued giggle, which drowned out my own warning for silence.

"Shut up, you beast!" my mother shouted at the goat.

A light appeared in the distance, coming toward us from the Hefners' cottage. My heart sank with fear.

"Hurry up!" I urged my mother, who was still fumbling around in the shack.

Her broad gluteus region came out the door first. On her hands and knees, she backed out of the byre. We slipped through the opening to the other side of the fence. With my mother leading, we ran straight ahead into a field. There was no need to cause any suspicion about who those night prowlers were. If our neighbor saw us leaving in the opposite direction, he would think we were strangers.

I could still smell manure, even after we put a considerable distance between the goat shed and ourselves. I learned the reason for this when I grabbed my mother's dress sleeve to slow her down.

"How much farther do you want to run in this direction?" I asked. I felt a slippery substance on my fingers. One sniff confirmed my fears. In the dim light of the moon, my mother stripped off her dress.

"Where are we going?" I asked again.

"To the village!" my mother exclaimed.

I could think of no reason for us to go the village in the middle of the night, and curiously inquired, "Why?"

"There is not enough water at the cabin," she explained impatiently, now clad in nothing more than her underwear.

I had a fairly good idea of what she was planning to do once we reached the village. The fountain stood forlorn. An unusual sight, as it was ordinarily surrounded by people at most hours of the day.

With a deep breath, my mother submerged herself in the trough by the fountain.

"Horch!" I cautioned. A sound came from the village's main street. Dawn lit the sky, and a glance in that direction confirmed what I thought I heard. A herd of cows was approaching, and the farmer guiding them took notice of us. My mother, busily washing out the rest of her clothes, was unaware of the approaching herd until she found herself eye-to-eye with a cow.

What followed was a sight the farmer may well have talked about many times thereafter. Whether he was believed is another matter. Who wouldn't have doubts when told of a woman bathing in the village fountain in the middle of the night who, after being interrupted by a herd of thirsty cows, ran the length of the main street in dripping-wet underwear, letting out a swarm of unintelligible sounds accompanied by the hearty laughter of two girls desperately trying to catch up with her?

Our mother bathing with the cows

Bartering with the Farm Wives

Chapter Fourteen

M*y mother soon found a solution to replenish our provisions:* making weekly trips on her bicycle to nearby villages, where she bartered for flour, eggs, and sometimes a big slab of bacon.

On one of our salvage trips into the ruins of the city we discovered a cellar beneath a bombed-out house. The cellar contained a huge pile of paper sacks containing a white powder. We decided to load our four-wheeled cart with several of the bags.

We were still not sure what exactly we had found. Tasting it was not an option. Once my mother decided that we had found laundry detergent, we returned to the cellar to load up whatever our cart could hold.

My sister soon regretted our find. As we pushed the cart up the hill to the cabin, one of the bags slipped off the cart and landed on her big toe. It took weeks for the nail to heal.

With an abundance of the white powder, my mother decided to do some bartering, especially after she was certain—after several loads of laundry—that she was dealing with laundry detergent.

This worked well. The farm wives were happy with their exchange until one day when one of the farmers realized his wife was washing laundry with fertilizer!

It was an honest mistake by my mother. She really did think it was laundry detergent and swore to its getting the laundry clean. Unfortunately, her bartering with "laundry detergent" had come to an abrupt end.

To the best of my memory, it took months to use up the remaining bags. Finally, after only a small amount was left and curiosity had gotten the better of us, my sister and I decided to find out if it really was fertilizer. So what better way than to sprinkle some of it on our own vegetable garden?

I don't remember the exact results, but our father could never figure out why a certain patch of cabbage was covered with a white substance that burned little holes into the leaves.

EASTER 1945:
WHERE IS THE EASTER BUNNY?

Chapter Fifteen

At night, the front came closer with every hour.

It was difficult to keep track of the days without a calendar. Let's see . . . the wind came from the west this morning, so we could hear the bells of the village church—it must be Sunday.

"Happy Easter, everybody!" my father jokingly commented as he spooned a piece of bread from his bowl of coffee. Our Easter dinner: imitation coffee or Ersatz with hard bread soaking in it.

"Remember how we used to hunt Easter eggs on this day?" my sister reminisced.

How could I forget that annual event! It was the same every year for as long as I could remember. Saturday afternoon we would leave the city, loaded down with knapsacks that held our provisions for the weekend. On holiday weekends, we always had something special to eat. Our family's favorite meal consisted of wiener schnitzel and potato dumplings. Next morning at sunrise, my father snuck out to the garden to hide the eggs. By the time we awoke, he was back in bed. Sometimes he snored in his sleep, but other times he just pretended. That way he could overhear our whispered conversation:

"Hey, Rita, are you awake?"

"Hmm."

"Think the Osterhase has been here?"

"I don't know. Why don't you look and see?"

By that time, the rhythm of the snoring coming from the bed above us was cut off with a loud "Chrrrauh!" My mother had punched my father's mattress above her to end the snoring.

When my father pretended to snore, it usually ended with a long, loud yawn, which let us know we no longer had to whisper. Then we heard movement. An arm reached down to pull back the window curtain.

"There it is—the Easter Bunny! Look, quickly!" my father would exclaim.

This was our cue to begin the egg hunt. The Osterhase long disappeared by the time we crawled out from our bunks, and we never got to see it, except once. The timing of my father's Osterhase sighting coincided with the visit of a wild hare, which somehow made it into the garden despite the fence. Unaware of us, it sat there in a vegetable bed, munching away on our carrots. Although I expected the Easter Bunny to be pink, the sight of this long-legged, rather homely looking creature strengthened my sometimes-wavering belief in the existence of the Osterhase.

Now I almost longingly watched the fields and meadows, hoping to see a wild rabbit that would give this day at least some sign of Easter. But the wild animals we used to watch had gone. Some had been scared away by our dog, Flora, who constantly chased them without ever catching any. Others had been trapped by farmers for food.

"I wonder what next Easter will be like?" my mother pondered.

My father was about to answer when his eyes caught a figure nearing our fence. It was a German soldier. His helmet was tied to his belt, and his coat was loosely draped over his shoulders. The rifle he carried was tied to his back, with the strap crossing over his chest. This was no soldier out to fight a war. He smiled wearily when he saw us.

"I was hoping to find someone here," he said.

My father walked up to the fence. "Where is the front?" he asked the soldier. It was odd for a single soldier to be in our vicinity. An entire company had passed through the day before, heading toward the southeast corner of the valley. He came from that direction.

"It's down there someplace," he said, motioning behind himself without looking back. Then, his voice subdued, he asked, "Do you have any civilian clothes I could borrow?" We told him we lost our belongings and were about to decline his request when we remembered our scarecrow.

"Help yourself," my father said and motioned to where a weathered wooden stake, clad in a weatherworn assortment of rags, towered amidst rows of blooming strawberry bushes. Still there from the previous summer, it barely survived the winter's icy snowstorms and tearing winds.

The soldier accepted our offer. Curiously, Rita and I watched from behind the curtain as he stripped his clothes to exchange them for the rags. After shaking off some of the hardened bird droppings, he slid into the baggy pants.

"What kept you out?" he asked my father.

"A kidney," my father replied. "Had only one since I was fourteen."

"You were lucky," the soldier said.

He rid himself of his rifle and other war accoutrements while passing some bushes along the road. Soon he had disappeared into the distance.

"Look!" my sister said with a laugh. "Our scarecrow got drafted!"

The scarecrow in its new attire, the uniform of the Deutsche Wehrmacht, looked very real. Not real enough to scare the birds away—one had already landed on its extended arm— but real enough to cause trouble should the Allies see it.

"Get me some matches," my father ordered me.

Hours passed. The bright afternoon sun now transformed into a glowing ball of fire that slowly lowered itself beneath the horizon. The shadows from the branches of the bulky cherry tree began to dance in the sand as the breeze grew stronger. The small pile of ashes amidst the strawberry bushes was picked up by a mild gust of wind, which carried it, along with fallen leaves and small debris, off on an unknown journey.

Moments later, artillery fire penetrated the peaceful quiet of the evening.

The scarecrow got drafted

LIBERATION

Chapter Sixteen

The time had come! American tanks surrounded Würzburg. Only hours from now we would know our fate. Would it change for the better or for worse?

Even though it was clear that every effort to hold off the Allies was a lost cause and a waste of human lives, there were still some stubborn Nazis who thought they could save Würzburg, or Germany, or whatever was left.

Boom, boom! The cannons echoed through the dusky sky. We ran for the dungeon, our shelter in the ground.

"Will they find us, Papa?" I asked.

"We are not hiding from them," my father explained. "Only from their bullets."

It was dark outside now. The wind shifted directions, and the thunder of guns grew fainter. Between short intervals of silence we could hear the rebellious growl of our empty stomachs. We wondered if it was safe to go back to the cabin.

The moon, high in the midnight sky, hid behind clouds chased by the chilling April wind. Occasionally its light reached the earth around us, but another cloud soon drifted over its path and left us in darkness again.

"Now," my father whispered when another cloud enveloped the moon.

Hastily we crawled out of the narrow shelter opening.

"Keep down," my father cautioned. We crawled back to the cabin on our hands and knees.

The guns subsided. The sudden quiet was eerie. What was happening in the city? Had the Allies left? Advanced toward the east? Fatigue and hunger won over our fears, and after a meager meal of stale bread and uncooked oatmeal stirred into water, we fell asleep.

The thunder of heavy artillery woke us at dawn. The windows shuddered, and the cabin rattled suspiciously with shockwaves in the air. Our cabin was in the midst of the battlefield.

It was impossible to go back to the shelter in the opposite corner of the garden.

Boom, boom! Boom, boom! The cannons shouted. Our dishes fell from the cupboard and crashed into pieces around us. My father opened the door to grab an ax. Black smoke rose to the sky from behind the forest. Speedily my father chopped out some floorboards, enough to make an opening for us to climb beneath them.

The earth was cold and moist. As we descended to the floor below, a strong smell of mold greeted us. The space between the floor and the ground was, at most, an arm's length. Barely enough to be comfortable. We covered the ground with our blankets, and then it was almost cozy. Then my father thought it would be safer for us to lie on our stomachs. And we couldn't forget our helmets. By "helmets" I mean our entire stock of pots and pans, three in total. One short, we improvised even more. So what did my father wear? A colander that already had about three hundred holes. It was a funny sight, and in spite of our dangerous situation we had to laugh at ourselves. But at heart, we were scared to death. The field mice were scared, too, and they joined us under the floor – much to our dismay.

"I am thirsty, Mama!" I said.

"I am hungry!" my sister joined in.

We knew there was nothing left to eat in the cabin. But talking, we thought, made the time go by faster. The time passed, but ever so slowly. Then all became quiet.

My father lifted a floorboard. "It must be dark outside by now," he said as he looked into the cabin. The moon had spread its beam over the ghostly land, but the cabin was dark. "Where are they?" my father wondered as he scanned the fields through the space between the curtains. Stiff and cold, the rest of us emerged from our confinement.

"I am hungry!" I cried. The hunger pains became stronger, making me dizzy when I tried to stand. An entire day passed. We hadn't eaten anything in nearly twenty-four hours.

"I wish I was Flora," my sister grumbled. "At least then I could stuff myself on mice!"

"I have an idea," my father interrupted. Willingly we listened to his suggestion. "Remember now," he warned us, "keep down at all times."

Like snakes we slithered through the damp grass to cross a muddy bed along the fence. There was a space between the ground and the lower edge of the mesh wire. Flora dug it out one day when she spotted a rabbit in the field. No one dared to speak. Not even a whisper. Carefully, not making any noise, we crawled through the tight opening. The field on the other side of the fence had not been cultivated. Most of the land lay fallow. The farmers feared the enemy planes and guns and abandoned their ploughs. Straw stubble still stuck in the ground, and strewn among it were whole stems, still bearing wheat kernels from the previous harvest. Swiftly we gathered a bundle and retreated to our cabin.

"You've got to chew them real good," my father explained. In the dark of the cabin we cowered around the pile of straw, searching for the kernels. The field mice must have gotten to them before us, for nearly half the straw held only empty husks.

"I could make some salad," my mother suggested.

"With what?" my father asked.

"From dandelions," said my mother.

"We can wait until morning," my father decided. It was not wise to let anybody know that the cabin was inhabited. Our presence could easily be mistaken for that of German soldiers. If there were any Allied scouts in the area, they might throw a hand grenade and blow us all up.

Our worries and precautions were uncalled for, because the scouts didn't arrive until the following morning. I was the first to be awakened by a strange noise. It came from the highway in the valley below us like an endless thunder: the sound of hundreds of tanks rolling toward the city. Würzburg was liberated!

Soon daylight came, and only moments later we had our first face-to-face encounter with our enemy. Across the valley, a hill caught our attention. We saw people coming out of the woods, heading for the clearing on the edge of the hill. No roads or trails crossed this particular part of the landscape, so we found it strange to see people around. Were they citizens from the village beyond the forest, running from the Allies? But they would have passed through their community by now.

The guessing came to an end when we noticed an American jeep slowly proceeding down our road. Soon another jeep followed; both carried mounted machine guns. Then came a tank with its guns fixed on our cabin.

"Take cover!" my father shouted excitedly. Instinctively we reached for our helmets. With our hearts pounding at twice their normal speed, we waited. And waited. We knew they would come soon. Our eyes were fixed on the window. Many thoughts raced through my mind. *What if they are hostile? Maybe they will kill us? Or rape us? Maybe take us prisoner?*

Minutes seemed like hours. Then, there they were! None of us had seen them coming. We heard voices outside. Voices speaking in English.

"Hello! Anybody home?" Fear-stricken, my father opened the door. His knees were shaking, and he could hardly stand.

"Raise your hands," my mother whispered from behind. Slowly he stepped outside. A soldier motioned for him to open the door entirely. Now they could see us, and we could see them. Three soldiers aimed their bayonet rifles at us.

Moments of silence passed. Then one of them, presumably the one in charge, stepped forward to ask, "Do you speak English?" In unison we shook our heads. So then he spoke in German, asking us whether we had any weapons. No, we didn't – at least, not any more. There was a .45 around for a while, but my father thought it wiser to put it out of sight. So he buried it under the elderberry tree.

"Are there any German soldiers hidden here?" the soldier asked.

"Nein," my father replied.

Then, with a smile on his face, the American asked, "Do you have any whiskey?"

At this point, we didn't even have any water, so my father burst into laughter. We all joined in, including the three Americans. The tension passed. With friendly but firm words, the soldier advised us to raise a flag of surrender and at all times wear a white handkerchief. Before the Americans left, the soldier in charge pointed to the colander on my father's head. "You can take that off now," he said with a grin.

Immediately we began to construct a flag of surrender. Minutes later, a white bedsheet mounted on a broomstick and attached to the chimney, blew proudly in the wind.

A new phase in our lives had begun.

"You can take it off now"

THE METAL BATTLE: THE CATFIGHT OVER AN AIRPLANE WING

Chapter Seventeen

Flowers of various sorts were blooming in the fields, the fruit trees were beginning to show their harvest, the vegetables were sprouting, and even the weeds were growing in abundance. Summer had arrived.

The front had passed us. It was east of us now, making its way to Berlin.

What a beautiful feeling! To walk about without fear of bombs, or the machine guns of low-flying planes. Now we could watch planes pass over us and perhaps even wave at them. I recalled the time when my mother waved at a pilot out of desperation, pleading with him not to shoot us.

The black tar paper on our roof had long been in need of repair. The crows picked holes in it, and whenever my father sealed up the holes, the birds picked new ones.

My father grew weary of sleeping with an umbrella every time it rained through the night. Sometimes he would place a pan on his stomach—mostly during thunderstorms, when the rain was especially heavy. But the steady drip, drip, drip kept all of us awake. That is, all of us except my father; one rainy night, after he had fallen asleep, he turned over. My mother's resulting protests convinced him to resort to the umbrella.

The holes in the roof eventually outnumbered the available pots and pans we had to set under the leaks. Since there was nothing else for us to do on rainy days, my sister and I invented a game, "Catch the Rain." With a coffee cup in each hand, we leaped from one end of the cabin to the other, calculating the timing of each drip so it would land in the cup. For every drop we caught, we gave ourselves a point. To make the game more interesting, we decided to do it to music. The old hand-cranked gramophone, a bit outdated, but still in working condition, supplied us with a variety of tunes. Amongst them were songs sung by the much-celebrated voice of Enrico Caruso and "Schmaltz Hits" and "Who Rolled the Cheese to the Railroad Station?"

It was a challenging game, and we were almost sad when the tar paper was replaced with metal from a plane that was hit in a dogfight with a German aircraft. It happened during our hibernation beneath the floorboards. A neighbor witnessed the scene. He claimed to have seen one of them go down, but he couldn't tell which one.

Afterward, the sun brought it to our attention. It caused a bright glare, a reflection we could see whenever the sun struck the bright object in the distant field at a certain angle.

"It must be that plane that crashed," we figured, and soon we set out to investigate. Getting close, we had our doubts about whether it was a plane and not another dud. The bulky mass rested in a vertical position, part of it penetrating the earth. We had seen our share of bombs, not only as they fell from the sky, but also at close range in Nazi exhibits, where they were set on pedestals as if they were art. We soon realized this was not a bomb.

Black letters and numbers were stenciled on the olive-green paint that coated the metal, a heavy aluminum. None of the writing made any sense; it was foreign to us.

"Just what we need for our roof!" my mother exclaimed.

"Where is the rest of it?" I wondered, scanning the area. There was no trace of any other debris. It was only part of a plane that we found, probably a wing tip, from what we could tell by the shape of the metal.

"We need tools to pry it loose," my mother said.

Equipped with a spade, to dig out the embedded part, and our clothesline, with which we planned to tow the wing away, we returned to the site. A figure moved about the pile of metal. It was a woman, a stranger to us. We knew everyone who lived on the hill. Judging by her movements, we knew her intentions were the same as ours. The moment she saw us, she took on a defensive position.

"That's mine!" she shouted from a distance.

"Nein," my mother replied calmly. "This belongs to us. We were here first. We just had to leave to get some tools."

The woman shouted back, "I was here before, too, and now I am back!" Had she been there before, she, too, would have brought back some tools. Instead, all she came with was a small wicker basket partly filled with some wild herbs.

"Look," my mother said in a subdued voice. "There is plenty for all of us. We could divide it somehow."

"It's mine!" the woman insisted, and with that she walked toward my mother and slapped her in the face. My mother, not prepared for such an attack, lost her balance. But just as the woman swung out to strike a second blow, my mother regained her balance. And so it began: both women pulling each other's hair and shouting obscenities at one another until they were both out of breath.

"Hooh!" came a voice from behind. It was a farmer pulling his team of horses alongside the scene of the battle. A big grin spread over his face. "Who won?" he asked, laughing thunderously as the two women readjusted their hair and wiped the dirt from their clothes.

My sister and I explained the situation.

"This is my land," he said. "Anything on it belongs to me—"

"It's mine! It's mine!" the woman interrupted, yelling in rage.

"Get off my land!" the farmer ordered her. His fist tightened around his horsewhip. "Get off my land!" he repeated, his face grim. A swarm of curses and other foul language rang in the air as the woman stomped away, shaking her fist as she turned around to throw another curse at the farmer.

"Madwoman," the farmer said to himself, dismounting from the wagon.

"Let's go," my mother said. And, to the farmer, "I guess it does belong to you."

"What would you use it for?" he asked.

"It's our roof," my mother began, and soon she had the farmer listening to a story that was probably the saddest he had heard in a long time. "It's almost like sleeping under open sky," she said.

"As I was saying," the farmer said, "anything on this land belongs to me, however," he paused to light his pipe, "I don't have any use for an airplane wing at this time." He laughed.

So there it was. A new roof, constructed from the wing tip of an airplane. How fortunate for my father. No longer did he have to sleep with an umbrella, nor did he have to balance a cooking pan on his stomach anymore (see picture on page 20).

As for us kids, it was less fortunate, for how were we to kill the time on rainy days now?

LAUNDRY

Chapter Eighteen

Fraternizing with Germans was not encouraged amongst the Allied troops, and sometimes it was even forbidden. But as time passed, the regulations were less strictly enforced until finally they were lifted entirely.

It didn't take us long to make friends with the soldiers, especially after we offered to do their laundry. A cousin of ours spoke English. With a note he wrote for us, we approached the soldiers of the camp on the hill. "Have you any laundry to be washed?" it read. Word got around quickly among the troops, and soon we had so many customers that the entire family was involved in our laundry operation.

First, we had to have soap and brushes, so the soldiers supplied us with them. Our swimming pool—well, our pool anyway, it was big enough to swim one stroke—became our oversized laundry tub. Water was available again via pipelines from the city. The long board from our teeter-totter, a plaything we had long outgrown, was placed across the pool and used as a scrubbing board.

Since the washing was done in cold water, a thorough overnight soaking of the laundry was necessary. Each morning at sunrise we assembled in the pool. Submerged to the waist, we waded amongst floating uniform pieces: T-shirts, shorts, and socks. Everything had an olive-green color, even the towels and handkerchiefs.

Ironing was a time-consuming project, which took three of us to perform. Without electricity, the only way to heat up an iron was to put it on the stove. With the temperatures of thirty degrees Celsius outside, it was forty degrees inside the cabin. After we lit the stove, the temperature increased to about fifty degrees Celsius.

There were two irons. One of them was a vintage tool from a time closer to the year of my grandmother's birth than my own. We heated it on the stove, though the traditional means was filling it with smoldering charcoal.

Once our project started, it became necessary to work as a team, and a typical day of ironing proceeded in the following manner.

"Ready?" my mother asked, placing herself in front of the garden table, padded with a couple of blankets and a white bedsheet—formerly our flag of surrender. The clean clothes lay beside her, ready for pressing.

"Ready!" my sister confirmed, and she ran from the cabin with an iron. After placing it before my mother, she returned to the cabin to pick up the other iron. If it was the antique one, she had to use potholders to hold onto it, for the wooden grip had long since burned away from its handle. By the time she reached my mother again, the iron she used was ready for reheating. We repeated this procedure continuously, and only seldom was it interrupted.

Meanwhile, I busied myself with breaking wood, small twigs, and branches from pine trees, to fuel the stove. We also used pinecones for fuel. However, we saved our logs for the cold season to come.

While sitting in front of the stove and stuffing it like a hungry mouth, I stripped off my clothing. By the time I heard the much-awaited words "switch jobs," I wore nothing more than my underwear. With a sigh of relief, I took a plunge into the sudsy but refreshing pool water before I took on the job of iron carrier.

By the time the last piece of uniform passed under my mother's tired hands, she, too, was no longer dressed. Even the bathing suit for which she had exchanged her earlier attire had become unbearable.

"Wasser! Wasser!" she moaned. This was a cue for me to perform another one of my tasks: keeping my mother cool. Placing myself on a stool in front of her, I gave her a shower by squirting her with the laundry sprinkler.

"More! More!" she said and quivered in anticipation while I refilled the bottle with the garden hose. The refilling progressed slowly, so I resorted to the quickest method available and aimed the entire water hose at her. One time this method created a disaster of which I have still painful memories!

I placed the hose on the ground, and while I went to turn it off, the hose suddenly snapped up, spraying the pile of pressed and folded uniforms. Panic-stricken, I raced for the knob, but in confusion I turned it to full blast.

Until then, I thought I was familiar with the entire vocabulary of German curse words and other profanity. But the words I heard that day taught me otherwise.

As I fled from my pursuing mother, my foot hit a sharp stone. She decided that was punishment enough because it took days before my swollen big toe fit into my shoe again.

When the time came to deliver the laundry, it was a day full of anticipation. Our rewards made it worth all the hard work and sweat (and pain) we suffered. Cartons of cigarettes—a hot item on the black market—fruit, chocolate candy, corned beef, and many more goodies filled our baskets upon our return.

Soon we recuperated from the previous wash day, and we would again leave to collect a new load. When one company moved on, another one would take its place, and we made new friends and customers.

After practicing the pronunciation of the words on our note, we soon approached the newly arrived troops. After exchanging a few greetings, ever-so-proudly showing off our English we asked, "Have you any laundry to be washed?"

Our Communion Dresses that Fell from the Sky

Chapter Nineteen

A religious holiday was only a week away—what better time to wear our white communion dresses? They were among the few items of clothing we brought to the cabin before the bombing on March 16, 1945.

We celebrated our first Holy Communion in April of 1942. Our grandmother prepared a Festessen for which our Aunt Katrina offered one of the geese she bred. Gänsebraten became a rare commodity for city folks, but Aunt Katrina lived on the outskirts of the city, where it was permissible to keep farm animals. She had chickens, ducks, geese, rabbits, and even at one time, a pig. I still remember the day when my mother and grandmother were summoned to help grind the meat, which was then stuffed into the cleansed intestines to make sausages.

Grandpa, a retired civil servant with connections, managed to secure some wine to go with the meal. And from another one of his connections he hired a carriage, complete with a white horse, to bring us to the church.

But now it was 1945, and my sister and I were almost teenagers. Our communion dresses turned into dresses with miniskirts, we had grown so much. This was not an issue. Short skirts, long skirts—most people were wearing hand-me-downs because new clothing was not yet available. What did become an issue was the fabric from which our dresses were made.

The day arrived, and we donned our outgrown dresses. The chapel was on the opposite end of Nikolaus Hill, and to reach it, we had to pass the nearby army camp.

We had long before befriended some of the soldiers. We passed them every day on our way to the forest to gather firewood. When we stopped to say hello, we were usually rewarded with a candy bar or whatever they were willing to share.

As usual, today we stopped to talk with the soldiers. While we spoke with one of them, another soldier approached us from behind. He touched the sleeve of my dress, and with a frown on his face he asked, *"Woher hast du das?"*

Why would he want to know from where my dress had come? A little startled, I shrugged my shoulders. *"Ich weiss nicht!"* I answered.

He spoke a few words in English with the other soldier, and then walked away without another word to us.

Back at the cabin, we told our parents what took place at the camp. My mother showed concern. "I don't want you to pass by the camp anymore!" was all she said. But we wanted to know why.

I remembered the day a seamstress came to our house to sew the communion dresses. She usually came about

Communion dresses from the sky

once or twice a year to help with alterations or sewing new garments. My mother unrolled a white linen tablecloth to reveal the fabric for our dresses. Suddenly the conversation turned into whispers. What exactly was said, I do not know. But the shock on the seamstress's face told us something strange was going on.

Now our mother decided we were old enough to learn of the enigma surrounding our dresses. She told us that Grandma bought the fabric from a farmer on the black market. He casually mentioned that it came from a parachute. After the transaction was completed, he said, "There was a dead soldier attached to it!"

We never knew what happened to the soldier. And it is just as well. Whenever I look at the photograph of our first Holy Communion, I am reminded of the horrors war brought upon us. It will forever stay in my memory.

KÄFERLES SUPPE: PEAS AND BUG SOUP

Chapter Twenty

Life at the cabin became routine. My father worked for the Americans now, repairing broken windows in the formerly Nazi-occupied buildings that served as headquarters for the Allies.

In the cellar beneath those buildings, the Nazis hoarded commodities no longer available to citizens without ration stamps. Sacks of sugar were piled up on shelves there. A fire must have melted the sugar, because the sacks contained only hardened brown globs. After gaining permission from the Allies to salvage whatever was still edible, my father chopped off chunks of caramelized sugar.

There were also sacks of dried peas. They had been spared from fire damage, but tiny bugs floated to the top of the pea soup my mother made. After scooping them off, then stirring up the soup to make the peas release more of their inhabitants, we were able – albeit reluctantly – to fill up on what we called "Käferles Suppe." Bug soup tastes okay if you are hungry enough.

Then there was the bread. Round loaves of *Kommissbrot,* so called because it keeps longer than regular bread. Unfortunately the *Kommissbrot* could not withstand the cellar's moisture and grew moldy. But we removed the moldy parts and ate the rest.

One item my father brought home is still in my possession. One of the soldiers at headquarters was to be shipped out. Faced with limits imposed on what the soldiers could carry with them, he offered my father a small China teapot he "found" in an Italian villa before he was transferred to Germany. My father gave it to me as a keepsake on the day I left for America with my husband.

I am sure its value could be enormous because a self-proclaimed expert told me it came from a dynasty of a bygone era. But it sits on the mantel above my fireplace, where it shall remain while I am still alive.

Yellow Round Things: What Are They?

Chapter Twenty-One

One day, a truck loaded with crates of fruit and vegetables for the nearby army camp passed us on our way up the hill. The driver gave us a friendly wave and a sample of his German, asking, *"Wie geht's?"* to which we replied, "Fine, zank you!" He quickly turned his attention back to the road and the nearing summit. When he shifted gears, the truck jerked, causing one of the crates to fall off. Even if he had noticed the crate's fall, the driver could not have stopped or his truck would have rolled backward. With a crash, the crate landed at our feet. The fruit rolled and bounced downhill with us in hot pursuit.

"What are they?" we wondered, after we gathered whatever didn't get away from us. They weren't lemons—that much we could tell. And though we hadn't seen oranges for some time, we knew these were not oranges. We peeled them, licked them, and bit into them, only to spit them out again.

"Mama will know," we decided. But where to put them? We had no purse or bag. When we finally arrived at the cabin, we looked like a pair of overgrown packrats. We stripped off our knee-high socks and filled them with the yellow round things. But the socks couldn't hold all of them, so we stuffed the rest into our clothes. Our skirt pockets were too small to hold even one, but our sweaters had plenty of space to be filled, especially since nature had not yet provided us with certain endowments.

Now our mother performed a thorough examination of the fruit. But she, too, had no name for them. In the end, we squeezed them, diluted the juice with water, sweetened it with saccharin, and drank it. Eventually, a neighbor told us it was grapefruit!

Then there was peanut butter, that brown sticky stuff that stuck to our gums. At first we thought it was some kind of shoe polish, but with our ever-present appetites we eagerly tasted anything we could find.

Our biggest supply of food came from the garbage cans of the army camp near our cabin. There we discovered such delicacies as the necks, gizzards, and wings of chickens and, on one occasion, a turkey carcass with lots of meat left on it.

Our stomachs, used to less culinary varieties of foods, such as potatoes and bread, with the occasional vegetable stolen from some farmer's field, could not handle the richness of the chicken soup we had one day. We spent the following day trying to beat each other to the little outhouse behind the cabin.

During one of our garbage collections, a soldier noticed us.

"Is this for your dog?" he asked me, after I withdrew a half-filled can of beans from a barrel. I didn't understand what he said, so I shrugged my shoulders and said, "Nix versteh. Nix versteh English."

"Hmm." The soldier pondered for a moment. But then he had an idea. "Is this for your . . . your woof-woof?" he said and smiled after getting on his hands and knees to imitate the four-legged animal.

"Oh! *Wau-wau!*" I exclaimed, finally understanding. "Nein," I said and shook my head. "Our dog eats mice. We eat this." I gestured at the can.

"Come!" the soldier commanded.

With mixed feelings, we followed him toward the entrance of the mess hall, a barrack set up near the roadside.

"Wait here," he said as he motioned to us that we should go no farther. For a moment he disappeared into a side chamber. Upon his return he presented us with a loaf-shaped can. "Corned Beef" read the label. The words didn't have any meaning for us, but we knew it had to be something good.

"*Danke schön!*" we called back as we ran toward the cabin, and again, "Vielen Dank . . . eh, zank you very much!"

We barely believed our eyes when we saw the can's contents. Meat! Good, clean meat! Fresh from a can instead of a barrel in which flies and other insects dropped their eggs.

Not always did we encounter soldiers as good-hearted as the mess-hall cook. We actually expected to be treated with hostility and a certain amount of contempt by the Allies and were, therefore, pleasantly surprised when we experienced kindness. But when we were treated rudely, it made us somewhat sad, as on the day we dug for food in a huge hole in the ground near the woods.

A soldier walked up, threw a whole chicken into the hole, and walked away. This was odd behavior. Why did he throw it in there? Why couldn't he just hand it to us? Slowly we walked toward the spot where the chicken had landed. This was what he was waiting for! Quickly he turned around to walk back to the hole. With a big grin on his face, he unbuttoned his pants and exposed himself to urinate into the hole, aiming right for the chicken. We couldn't believe our eyes.

My sister and I looked at each other. Our faces turned white, then red. We didn't speak, we just ran. How he must have hated the Germans, to show it with such an awful gesture!

Satan's Servants

Chapter Twenty-Two

If some of the troops showed hostility toward the Germans, no one blamed them. Many of us deserved it. Being German felt like being of a savage race—the child of a nation without a soul. Our minds had been poisoned by a man who exploited a people still hungry from the Great Depression.

The life he promised was supposed to be different. "In time, the faces of your cities will change, and you will not recognize them," he proclaimed. Well, that's one promise he kept. The bombs did change our cities beyond recognition. But still, Germans continued to listen. Mesmerized by his speeches, they would cling to their radios to absorb the words of their leader.

"Silence! Our Führer is speaking!" one would hear, should one dare to speak above the transmitted voice. What fools we were! How naive and gullible! How could it happen that an entire nation was lured into his trap?

"We didn't know they killed them," was the answer of my elders whenever they were asked about the Jews whose lives ended behind the walls of Dachau. Perhaps they spoke the truth. The vast majority did not know what transpired behind those walls.

We had a tenant who was a confirmed Communist. Buchenwald was the camp where he spent many years of his life. Then, one day, he was sent home on furlough. During his stay at home, he worked his trade as a baker. He spent many hours in the cellar beneath the house with the rest of us. He was a trustee, he told us, when asked about his leave from the concentration camp. I also overheard the word Spitzel. Upon inquiring, I learned it meant "informer!" He was to spy amongst us and identify those who might find the courage to voice their suspicions. Then he was to report them. Never once did he speak of torture and killing!

Could it have changed the fate of his fellow prisoners? Could it have changed the course of the world, had he spoken out? Not likely. It would have meant the end for him and nothing more. When the masses finally awakened, it was too late. They had kept their minds closed for too long.

The Allies came, and suddenly there weren't any Nazis. No one freely admitted that they belonged to the party. Those who did had nothing to lose anyway. My grandfather, a passive member of the party, paid his dues once a month. The swastika pin that proved it had long since vanished from his lapel. The last I heard, it fell into the river as he leaned over the railing on a bridge one day.

"So you didn't know what was going on in Dachau?" the Americans asked the Germans. "Well, we will show you then!"

They transformed a school building into a movie theater, and they forced us, including the children, to watch film footage of the concentration camps. We saw the bodies piled high and the gas chambers on the screen. This was proof of what the rest of the world already knew. Perhaps many suspected what happened in the concentration camps, but they either didn't care or were powerless to stop it. Newspaper headlines everywhere shouted in many languages: "Murderers!"

How we must have looked to them! Guilt and shame assailed us. What were we guilty of? It was the Nazi leaders, the SS or SchutzStaffel, who were the executors. They were the murderers! All we were guilty of was ignorance. But will the world ever forgive us? Even centuries from now, history will talk about us. And generations yet to be born will learn about the Nazis, the SS, and the millions who died at their hands.

The SS! It might be forgotten what these letters stood for. But it will never be forgotten that the men who wore them on their uniforms stood for something against all the principles of humanity. Against all the laws of God!

The SS. Could it have stood for Satan's Servants?

Return to the City

Chapter Twenty-Three

We had become used to life at the cabin. Winter came and went twice before the house in the city was rebuilt.

The ruins of my grandparents' two-story house were my mother's inheritance, and the proceeds from the sale of our ruined four-story apartment house were divided among her siblings.

By Christmas of 1947 our father decided that we could move to our house in the city. It still needed a staircase to the second floor, so we used a ladder instead. There was no furniture either, so we slept on the mattresses from the cabin on the half-finished floor. But at least my father kept his promise that we would celebrate Christmas in our new home.

The term *celebration* was a slight exaggeration. A pine branch hung on the wall, decorated with some store-bought pretzels. A tin filled with chocolate candies, another find for 300 Reichsmarks on the black market, was a treat for all. I don't remember the meal we had, but after my parents both dozed off, my sister and I were curious about the candies at the bottom of the tin. Were they the same as the ones in the top layers?

Carefully, one by one, we lifted the tiny paper cups and spread them on the floor. They were all the same. No variety. Just candies filled with a sticky liquid. When my mother, who was still napping, decided to roll over, she landed on the precious sweets. It must have been the fact that it was Christmas that made her refrain from her usual selection of swear words.

Shortly after the holidays we were informed that our school was ready to conduct classes. Our parents tried some homeschooling, but without books it was mostly hands-on learning. Hiking in the forest, we learned to tell a pine tree from a spruce, and an oak from a beech. It was a fun way of learning about nature. We even learned to grow green beans by sticking beans into the ground beneath our mesh-wire fence at the cabin. Canning them, stuffing them into beer bottles with rubber and porcelain caps secured with metal clasps, was boring, though.

Little by little, life in the city returned to a makeshift existence. Stores were rebuilt, the streets cleared of debris, and the streetcars were back in operation.

Sadly, some of the ruins had been untouched for many years, as their owners perished in the bombing. If there were no next of kin, then by law the authorities could not touch the property for thirty years. Only then could they raze the ruins and take possession of the lot.

COMING TO AMERICA

Epilogue

War *changed our lives, putting us through hunger and fear.* But some good came out of it.

We were freed from the grasp of a madman whose delusions convinced him he could change the world. And by the grace of God we became friends with the Allies, whom we called enemies shortly before.

But were those drafted soldiers really convinced their mission would bring a solution? Did bombing cities full of innocent women and children achieve anything? Unfortunately, it still happens.

My life changed when I fell in love with one of those soldiers. It was in 1954, when a veteran of the Korean War ended up in a division stationed in my hometown. With my limited knowledge of the English language and his equally limited German, our courtship was enriched by the help of a German/English dictionary and by a friend of the family who offered to serve as a translator and chaperone. When the time came for my beau to ask my parents for my hand in marriage, it was again with the help of a dictionary.

I still remember clearly. My mother had already retired when my father summoned her to the kitchen. In her nightgown and cap, she and my father sat across from us at the kitchen table. Then, with trembling hands, my friend began to leaf through the pages.

"*Darf ich Ihre Tochter heiraten?*" he asked.

My parents had trouble understanding him, so I repeated his request: "He wants to know if you permit him to marry me!" After a long silence, my mother began to cry.

He felt bad, so he asked if that meant yes or no. "Ja?" he asked again, and my parents gave their blessing. He quickly became part of our family.

This marriage business involved a lot of paperwork, but finally in November of 1955, I was on my way to board a military transport ship that brought me, after nine seasick days, to the land that was to be my new home.

I could see the Statue of Liberty in the distance, and in my mind I envisioned her waving at me to say, "Welcome to America!"

About the Author

Elisabeth von Berrinberg was born in Würzburg, Germany, and migrated to the United States in 1955 after marrying an American soldier. In addition to raising her daughter, Lorraine, she had a long career as a darkroom technician both in Germany and the United States. She also held various volunteer positions; she worked for the Red Cross during the Vietnam era and as a captain in the Civil Air Patrol. Ms. von Berrinberg has given numerous presentations on her World War II experience, which prompted her to write her story.

She is also the author of *The Cozy Connection*, a cozy mystery series featuring *The Adventures of Countess von Schleppmeister, The Jewel Heist, The Cruise, The Missing Madonna, A Culinary Experience, Mystery at the Pearly Gates, and The Doppelgänger.* She is presently working on a series of children's books.

595

S0-AQG-224

THE ART AND PRACTICE
OF HAWKING

THE
ART AND PRACTICE
OF HAWKING

BY

E. B. MICHELL

CHARLES T. BRANFORD COMPANY
Newton, Massachusetts 02159

First published 1900
Holland Press Edition 1959
Second impression 1962
Third impression 1964
Fourth impression 1967
Fifth impression 1969
Sixth impression 1971
SBN 8231 2009 0

© *All rights reserved*

Printed in Great Britain by
A. Wheaton & Co., Exeter.

TO THE

EARL AND COUNTESS OF WARWICK

AND ALL OTHER LOVERS OF HAWKING

THIS BOOK IS DEDICATED

BY THE AUTHOR

PREFACE

NOTWITHSTANDING the large number of books, both ancient and modern, which have been written on the art of Hawking, it cannot be said that the English-speaking people generally have more than a very vague idea of the character of the sport, or the mode in which it was, and still is, conducted.

Yet, in an experience of Hawking which extends over more than thirty years, the author has found that a great and increasing curiosity, and even a real interest in the subject, prevails, especially amongst sporting men, who are in many notable instances beginning to believe that hawks and their owners have been unduly disparaged, and that there is more to be said in their favour than has for the last two centuries been imagined.

There has not been space in this volume to discuss the much-vexed question how far the use of hawks is compatible with the preservation of game. But it may be said here, without any reservation, that wherever experiments have been actually tried, Hawking has been found not to spoil but to improve the shooting.

The object of the author has been to describe as briefly as was consistent with clearness the birds now chiefly used in the chase, and the manner of training and flying them. His hope is that some of the sportsmen who read these pages may, in spite of the difficulties which they will have to encounter, resolve to give this old and honourable sport a trial.

The use of technical terms has been avoided as far as possible ; and those which could not be excluded have been explained in the text. When the reader is puzzled by any word, a reference to the Index will direct him to the page where the meaning of it is given.

CONTENTS

CHAPTER I

HISTORY AND LITERATURE

CHAPTER II

THE BIRDS USED IN HAWKING

CHAPTER III

FURNITURE AND FITTINGS

CHAPTER IV

EYESSES AND HACK HAWKS

CHAPTER V

PASSAGE HAWKS

CONTENTS

CONTENTS

LIST OF ILLUSTRATIONS

THE ART AND PRACTICE OF HAWKING

CHAPTER I

HISTORY AND LITERATURE

I T would be easy to fill a large volume with dissertations on
the antiquity of the art which is now called Falconry, and
with records of its history in different countries during the
many centuries that have elapsed since it was first practised.
In a treatise on practical hawking, such as the present, there is
no room for such matter ; and the omission will be the more
readily excused when it is explained that only a short time
ago the antiquities of the art, and the literature in which its
records are embodied, were most carefully and ably explored
by Mr. J. E. Harting, the erudite Secretary of the Linnean
Society, whose catalogue of books on hawking contains a reference to every known publication on the subject (*Bibliotheca
Accipitraria*, London, 1891). The actual origin of hawking, as
of other old sports, is naturally hidden in the obscurity of the
far-away past. No one would suppose that it was practised as
early in the world's history as the sister sports of hunting and
fishing. But Mr. Harting's researches have resulted in con-
vincing him that it was known at least as early as 400 B.C.,
although its introduction into Europe must clearly be placed at
a much later date. It is remarkable enough that the Greeks,
whose country abounds in wild hawks, should have known
nothing of their use in the service of man. Homer, indeed,
speaks of the mountain falcon as "the most nimble of birds,"
(ἠΰτε κίρκος ὄρεσφιν, ἐλαφρότατος πετεηνῶν, *Il.* xxii. 139) ; but Sophocles,
in alluding to the triumphs of man in taming and using wild
creatures, omits all mention of the training of hawks, which is
certainly more worthy of notice than mere bird-catching or
the breaking-in of oxen (Soph. *Antig.* 343). Even the later

Roman authors refer to the use of trained hawks as an un-familiar practice, in vogue only amongst some of the barbarian tribes.

Until at least some centuries after the Christian era, China and other countries in the Far East seem to have been the chief if not the only homes of falconry. But the Lombards, when they settled in North Italy, in the latter half of the sixth century, were acquainted with the art; and before the end of the ninth century it was familiar to the Saxons in England and throughout the West of Europe. Henry the Fowler, who became Emperor in 919, seems to have been so nicknamed on account of his devotion to this form of sport, which was already a favourite with princes and magnates. The Saxon King Ethelbert wrote to the Archbishop of Mayence for hawks able to take cranes. King Harold habitually carried a trained hawk on his fist; and from the time of the Norman Conquest hawking was a sport as highly honoured in the civilised world as hunting. The greatest impulse that was ever given to the sport in Western Europe was derived from the returning Crusaders, many of whom, in the course of their travels to the East, had become acquainted with the Oriental falconers and the Asiatic modes of training and flying hawks. Conspicuous amongst such Crusaders was the Emperor Frederick II., who brought back with him some Asiatic hawks and their trainers, and who not only was himself an enthusiastic and accomplished falconer, but even declared that falconry was the noblest of all arts. From that time—early in the thirteenth century—for' more than four hundred years falconry flourished in Europe, as well as in the East, as a fashionable sport amongst almost all classes. As in the case of hunting and fishing, its attractions as a sport were supplemented by the very material merits it possessed as a means of procuring food. While the prince and the baron valued their falcon-gentle for its high pitch and lordly stoop, the yeoman and the burgher set almost equal store on the less aristocratic goshawk and the plebeian sparrow-hawk as purveyors of wholesome delicacies for the table. Even the serf or villein was not forgotten in the field, and was expected, or at least allowed, to train and carry on his fist the humble but well-bred and graceful kestrel.

During this long period the example of Henry the Fowler was followed freely by many of the most celebrated and powerful rulers in European countries. Hardly a prominent personage amongst the great conquerors and lawgivers in mediæval times was unacquainted with the art. Most of them were as enthusiastic in their devotion to it as they were to the more serious objects of their ambition. It would be wearisome to recount the long list of royal falconers ; and it will suffice to merely mention a few of the most notable examples. Thus Edward III. was accompanied on his warlike expedition with a whole train of falconers. His father had been indulged in his imprisonment with liberty to go hawking. Shakespeare has familiarised his readers with the hawking parties of Henry VI. and his Queen (2 *Hen. VI.* ii. 1) ; and few people have failed to read the story of the broken leaping-pole which precipitated Henry VIII. into a ditch as he was following a hawk. Louis XI. and a host of French kings, including Francis I., were ardent falconers, as were many of the kings of Castile and Arragon, Sardinia, and Hungary. Henry of Navarre was excelled by few men in his passion for this sport. James IV. of Scotland gave a jewelled hood to one of the Flemings, because the latter had won a match in which his hawk flew against the King's. And James I. of England enjoyed nothing more keenly than a day's hawking, declaring that if a man had only patience and good-temper enough to contend with the disappointments inseparable from it, the sport would be preferable to hunting. Catherine II. of Russia was as great at falconry as at most other things, and specially delighted in the flight with merlins. Ecclesiastics, both great and small, were not a whit behind the laity in their devotion to the sport of the air. It was thought no scorn for a holy-water clerk to carry a "musket" or male sparrow-hawk, Not only did Cardinal Beaufort fly his falcons with those of the great Duke of Gloucester, but no less a potentate than Pope Leo X. was constantly in the field at Ravenna, and even incurs the blame of the great D'Arcussia for being in the habit of too soundly rating his comrades during a flight. The hawking establishments of all the earlier Bourbons were kept up in more than royal style, and were supplied annually with rare falcons from many parts of the world.

It was the invention of shot-guns that struck the first and most deadly blow at the popularity of hawking. It was soon discovered that wild-fowl, rabbits, and most kinds of game could be captured much more easily and cheaply by the aid of "vile saltpetre" than by the laborious and costly processes involved in the reclaiming and moulting and conditioning of hawks. Economy, as well as novelty, pleaded in favour of the new sport of shooting. At the same time, the common use of fowling-pieces added a fresh and formidable danger for the owners of hawks, already exposed to a thousand unfair risks of losing their favourites.   In the unsettled state to which Europe was reduced by the innumerable wars consequent on the Reformation, it was impossible for falconers to identify or punish those who recklessly or deliberately slaughtered a neighbour's lost hawks ; and although the offenders were still liable to serve penalties, they could snap their fingers at the protective laws.   Finally, the more rapid subdivision of the land, and its enclosure with fences for agricultural purposes, spoilt, for the falconer's purposes, large tracts of country which had formerly been the most suitable, and was especially hurtful to the flying of the long-winged hawks, for which an expanse of open ground is indispensable.   On the Continent these various causes operated surely but slowly to displace falconry in the public estimation.   But in England a special circumstance almost ruined it at one blow.   The outbreak of the Great Civil War interrupted rudely all peaceful sports, and its disasters destroyed a vast number of those who were the best patrons of hawking.   From the blow then struck English falconry never rallied in any general sense.   Certainly it did revive, or rather survive, to a certain extent.   It would be wrong to suppose that the sport has ever been extinct in the British Isles, as so many writers are fond of reiterating.   But its devotees have kept it up without any of the pomp and show which once distinguished it, carrying on in comparative privacy, and in the retirement of rather remote spots, an amusement in which the difficulties always besetting the sport were aggravated by a thousand new dangers and annoyances.

The annals of falconry, since it was deposed from its fashionable place—in England by the Great Rebellion, and afterwards in France by the Revolution—are obscure, and for the most part buried in oblivion.   Here and there the name of a notable falconer, professional or amateur, emerges from the mist, showing us that the sport was still carried on with vigour by a few.   In the middle of the eighteenth century Lord Orford flew kites in the eastern counties, and this sport, as well as rook-hawking and heron-hawking, was successively carried on by the Falconers' Society, the Falconers' Club, and the High Ash Club, which latter existed from about 1792 to later than 1830, and included amongst its members Lord Berners, Colonel Thornton, and other sporting celebrities.   In Scotland falconry has always been kept up.   The life of John Anderson covers the whole of the last half of the eighteenth century, as well as more than a quarter of the nineteenth.   This accomplished trainer of hawks was for the first twenty years or so of the present century in

charge of the Renfrewshire establishment kept by Fleming of
Barochan, and flown chiefly at partridges and woodcocks.
During the early years of the same century, until 1814, Colonel
Thornton did a great deal of hawking on his own account, at
first in Yorkshire, and afterwards at Spy Park, in Wiltshire.
From 1823 to 1833 Mr. John Sinclair flew woodcocks with
success in Ireland. In 1840 Lord O'Neill and Colonel Bonham
took a moor in Ross-shire for hawking; and in the following
year the Loo Club was started for heron-hawking in Holland,
under the auspices of Mr. E. Clough Newcome. This influential
club continued to flourish till 1853. Its place was taken, not
many years after, by the Old Hawking Club, which, although it
has never undertaken the flight at herons, continues to carry on
an annual campaign against rooks and game with great credit
and success. In France a hawking club was started in 1865,
under the title of the Champagne Club, but was not long-lived;
and several minor attempts at organising new clubs have been
made in England during the last thirty years. There are at the
present moment at least thirty private establishments in England
alone where trained hawks are kept and flown, besides several
in Scotland and Ireland. The names of several of the leading
amateurs now living will be mentioned in this and following
chapters.

Of professional falconers, the supply has sadly dwindled
away since the time when the office of Grand Falconer was
something more than the hereditary title of the Dukes of
St. Albans. It was not, however, until quite recent years
that the supply became quite unequal to the demand. At
the death of John Anderson in 1832 there were able suc-
cessors to keep alive the best traditions of the old Scotch
school. Foremost among them was Peter Ballantine, of
whom, as well as of Mr. Newcome, excellent likenesses are
published in Mr. Harting's fine work, *Bibliotheca Accipitraria*.
This accomplished trainer survived until 1884. Nearly con-
temporary with him were the brothers Barr, whose names
are frequently mentioned in these pages. While these and
others upheld the sport in Scotland, England, Ireland, and
France—for John Barr acted as the falconer of the Champagne
Club—John Pells in Norfolk, once falconer to the Duke of
Leeds, attained to great efficiency and repute; and the names
of Bots and Möllen became celebrated in Holland as the
successful hawk-catchers and servants of the Loo Club. Later
still, John Frost acted for eighteen years as the energetic and
skilful falconer of the Old Hawking Club. He was succeeded

by George Oxer, who, with the Retfords (James and William) and the sons of John Frost, is still living.   There are at the present moment several very young falconers who bid fair to attain distinction, though their training is derived mostly from lessons imparted to them by the amateurs who have brought them out.   It is to be hoped that, now the facilities for travelling are so immensely increased, some modern imitator of Frederick II. will bring back from India a native falconer or two, whose experience in the tropics would be invaluable, and thus infuse new life into the professional world of Europe.

Of amateurs there has been for some years past no lack in England ; and want of space alone prevents the enumeration of the distinguished falconers who still keep up in the British islands and dependencies the best traditions of their art. Amongst these it would be unfair to pass over the most conspicuous names, such as those of the late Lord Lilford and Captain Salvin and Mr. William Brodrick, the first named as justly famous for his acquaintance with hawks as for his knowledge of ornithology.   Captain Salvin first familiarised the modern English people with the training of cormorants, and with the flight with peregrines at rooks.   Mr. Brodrick illustrated with his own admirable coloured figures the handsome and useful book on falconry which he published jointly with Captain Salvin.   Another joint-author with the latter was the Rev. Gage Earle Freeman, who for many years most successfully flew, in a far from perfect country, peregrines at grouse, merlins at larks, goshawks and sparrow-hawks at various quarry. The small book which owes its authorship to these two masters of the art has long been out of print.   It is impossible to praise it too highly as a handbook for beginners.   Of living falconers, no one can be compared in experience and general knowledge with Major Hawkins Fisher, of the Castle, Stroud, whose game-hawks have for more than fourteen years annually killed good bags of grouse at Riddlehamhope, in Northumberland, and whose favourite peregrines, such as " Lady Jane," " Lundy," and " Band of Hope," have been a terror to partridges in Wilts and Gloucestershire.   Mr. St. Quintin, of Scampston Hall, Yorkshire, probably the most successful game-hawker of whom we have any record, has recently brought to a high degree of perfection the flight with peregrines at gulls.   The fine sport shown at rooks every year in Wiltshire by the Old Hawking Club, is due chiefly to the ability and energy of their secretary, the Hon. Gerald Lascelles.   In flights with short-winged hawk of both descriptions, Mr. John Riley, of Putley Court, Herefordshire, is *facile princeps*. The late Rev. W. Willemot did some good work with falcons at gulls before this branch of the sport was taken up by Mr. St. Quintin; and the late Mr. T. J. Mann, of Hyde Hall, Sawbridgeworth, was successful with rooks and partridges in Cambridgeshire. Probably the most splendid establishment of hawks in England during the last forty years was that of the late Maharajah Dhuleep Singh at Elvedon. Falconry in India has been extensively practised by many English officers quartered in that part of the world, and notably by General Griffiths, and more lately by Captain S. Biddulph, who has probably killed a greater variety of wild quarry than any European now living, and whose portraits of trained hawks are above all praise. Colonel Delmé Radcliffe, Colonel Brooks-bank, Colonel Watson, Captain Crabbe, the late Sir Henry Boynton, Mr. A. W. Reed, Major Anne, and Mr. Arthur Newall, are all enthusiastic and successful falconers. Colonel Ayshford Sanford, Major C. W. Thompson, of the 7th Dragoon Guards, and the writer of these pages, have had considerable success with merlins.

In France, the names of MM. Barachin, Sourbets, Arbel, and Belvallette for the short-winged hawks, and MM. Pichot and Paul Gervais for other kinds, require honourable notice ; and in Russia that of the late M. Constantine Haller will always be remembered. It is not many years since the latter originated and carried into effect the scheme of an International Hawking Congress, to be held near St. Petersburg. This was attended by many Asiatic falconers, and one from England. But the impossibility of finding suitable wild quarry in accessible places sadly interfered with the success of the meeting ; and the result was not proportionate to the great trouble of organising it.

It will naturally be supposed that a sport so fashionable, so prevalent, and so difficult as falconry, has been discussed at length in many writings and in many languages. For the very extensive literature treating of its art and practice in different parts of the world, the reader is referred to Mr. Harting's *Bibliotheca Accipitraria*, already mentioned, in which a full account is given of no less than three hundred and seventy-eight works on the subject. Of these, eighty-two are in English, and eighty-four in French. The German publications number forty-six, the Italian thirty-eight, the Japanese fourteen, and there are several in Spanish, Russian, Latin, Greek, and Chinese.

The most notable works, besides those already mentioned, are the Latin treatise written by the Emperor Frederick II.; *The Boke of St. Albans*, by Dame Juliana Berners, 1486; the volumes published by Turbervile in 1575, by Latham in 1615, and by Bert on the short-winged hawks in 1635. Still more interesting are the books written in French by Charles d'Arcussia, which date from 1598 to 1627. The nineteenth century has produced several important works, including the small treatise by Sir John Sebright, 1826, and the splendid illustrated volume by Schlegel and Wulverhorst, 1853. The Badminton Library contains half a volume on Falconry from the very able pen of Mr. Gerald Lascelles ; and the *Encyclopædia Britannica* has an article on the subject by Colonel Delmé Radcliffe.

To look for any real revival of falconry in Europe would be altogether quixotic. Lucky indeed may the falconer of the future consider himself if the art even survives. Already the goshawk, the ger, and the golden eagle are almost extinct in England ; sparrow-hawks have become so rare that constant advertisements offering to buy one remain without response ; the harmless hobby and innocuous merlin are ferociously persecuted, and have been exterminated in most of their favourite haunts. A lost hawk has become almost a synonym for a murdered hawk. Owners are beset with enemies on every hand, besides being plagued and pestered by ignorant and impertinent intruders, if ever they venture with their hawks into a public place. The country becomes more and more unsuitable for hawking purposes. Upon many of the most open spaces bricks and mortar intrude ; upon other parts the vexatious small plantations designed as shelters for game. Even when a suitable grouse-moor or partridge-ground is found in want of a tenant, obstacles may be raised. A baseless but deep-rooted prejudice deters many lessors from allowing trained hawks to be flown over their land, on the absurd plea that it will spoil it for subsequent tenants. In short, the impediments with which the modern falconer has to contend are too many and too great for any but a few very determined sportsmen. These, when they have once mastered the initial difficulties, usually persist in preferring the sport to any other. "Once a falconer, always a falconer," is a maxim of universal truth. And the fraternal spirit which animates most English falconers—and, for that matter, most falconers throughout the world—is not the least agreeable feature presented by this ancient and honourable field sport.

CHAPTER II

The Birds used in Hawking

OF the numerous birds of prey which are found in various parts of the globe, a good many have been employed in the service of man as agents in the pursuit of other birds and of four-footed animals, partly for purposes of supplying him with food, and partly for sport. It is more than probable that others might be similarly trained and flown, especially some of the American and Australian hawks, which seem suitable for the purpose, but which have never yet, as far as we know, been thus taken in hand. It is not, however, proposed to describe at length any members of the large family of Raptores, except such as are known to have been used in hawking; and with regard to those which have been flown only in remote parts of the world, considerations of space necessitate a very brief reference.

It has usually been said that the list of birds used in hawking includes only two main divisions—the long-winged hawks, as falconers call them, known to naturalists under the name of "falcons"; and the short-winged hawks, to which the men of science apply specially the name of hawks. This ornithological classification of falcons on the one hand and hawks on the other, is not a very happy one; for in the general public estimation, as well as in falconers' phraseology, every falcon is a hawk, although every hawk may not be properly called a falcon. The one term is of classic, and the other of Teutonic origin; and it was too late, when books about birds first began to be written scientifically, to attempt to establish a hard-and-fast difference between words which had already passed current for centuries as meaning pretty much the same thing. Moreover, hawking, which, if the naturalists' view of the matter were accepted, ought to be concerned, like the French *autourserie*, with the short-winged hawks only, has long been considered in England a mere

9

synonym for falconry, which also, if interpreted strictly according to the ornithological theory, ought to be regarded as dealing with the long-winged species.

The two-fold division, however, no matter whether it is into falcons and hawks, or into short-winged and long-winged hawks, seems to be insufficient and unsatisfactory. For eagles, which have been, and still are, extensively used in a sport for which the only English names are hawking and falconry, remain unincluded in the two usually accepted classes. No eagle can properly be called either a hawk or a falcon; and in order to find a place for them amongst the birds trained and flown at quarry, it seems necessary to institute a third class. What order of precedence should be taken by such new class is a matter of small consequence. In symmetry of shape, in its mode of flying, its character, and its tastes, the eagle is as inferior to the true hawk as the latter has always been deemed to be to the true falcon; and in this work, as in others on falconry, the first place has been retained for the long-winged hawks, and the second for the short-winged, leaving a third place for what little it seems necessary to say about such eagles as we know to have been flown at game.

The long-winged hawk is known by the following characteristics:—The second primary feather in the wing, reckoning from the outside, is the longest, or at least equal in length to any other, as in the merlin, which has the second and third feathers very nearly or quite of the same length. The upper mandible has on each of its sides, about a third part of the distance from the point to the cere, a projection somewhat resembling a very blunt tooth. The eye is dark brown. The wing is long enough in the outer joint to come down, when closed, considerably more than half-way between the end of the tail coverts and the end of the tail itself, and in some cases, as in the hobby, as far as the tail, or even farther.

In the short-winged hawks the wing is comparatively short in the outer joint, and, when expanded, presents a rounded appearance at the end, the fourth primary being the longest, and the first very short. That emargination, or narrowing in, of the feather near its end, which is observable in the first two primaries of the long-winged hawk, is still more pronounced in the short-winged, and is conspicuous in the third and fourth primaries also. The tail is long, and large when expanded. The iris is of some shade of yellow, light or dark. The upper mandible curves in a smooth line, without any projecting tooth.

In the eagles the tail is shorter and stouter. The outer

WING of LONG·WINGED
HAWK

WING·of SHORT-
WINGED·HAWK·

WING·of EAGLE

SHAPE OF WINGS

joint of the wing is shorter than in the falcons, the wing deriving its power from the feathers near the body rather than from the outer ones. The beak is longer in shape than that of the other two sorts, and the legs are proportionately stouter. The size of the smallest eagle is very much greater than that of the largest falcon or hawk.

The differences which exist in the shape of the wing between the three classes will perhaps be best appreciated by a glance at the accompanying illustration, in which a characteristic wing of each kind is figured.

The French have convenient terms (see Belvallette, *Traité d'Autourserie*, Paris, 1887) which express in themselves, with great perspicuity, though perhaps a little exaggeration, the different methods of flying employed by the short- and the long-winged hawks. The latter they describe as *ramiers*, or rowers, because their mode of progression through the air resembles that of an oarsman, or rather sculler, striking with repeated beats of his sculls ; whilst they describe the short-winged hawks (with eagles and all birds that have rounded wings) as *voiliers*, or sailers, maintaining that their impulse is gained by the pressure of the air against the wing, upon which it acts as upon a sail. Many people may be inclined to call such a distinction rather fanciful, and even question its truth ; but the mere fact that the two words have been accepted as correctly denoting the two separate styles of flying, shows what a marked difference between them has been generally admitted to exist. It will be seen that the mode of flying the " rowers " and the " sailers " at quarry is also very distinct.

In accordance with the three-fold classification above suggested, I now proceed to mention the various birds used in hawking under the successive headings of—(1) Long - winged hawks ; (2) Short-winged hawks ; and (3) Eagles.

I. THE LONG-WINGED HAWKS (Falcons) [1]

Perhaps the leading characteristic in the flying of this kind of hawk is that it habitually captures its prey, or, as falconers

---

[1] It should be observed that although the term falcon has an established meaning among ornithologists as a name for the long-winged hawks, it is used by falconers in quite a different acceptation. In hawking phraseology it is applied, in contradistinction to the term tiercel, to the female of the larger sorts of long-winged hawks, and especially to the female peregrine. Thus when a falconer is described as being possessed of "two falcons," or a hare is mentioned as having been taken by a "falcon," the reader is expected to know that the female peregrine is referred to, and not a male peregrine, or a saker, lanner, or any other kind of hawk.

term it, "quarry," by making a dash or shot at it, technically called a stoop, from some position where it can command an advantage in speed and force.   In many cases the bird is itself so conscious of this natural aptitude for stooping in preference to mere following, that it habitually places itself, when on the look-out for food, at a considerable height, from which it can descend with great ease and velocity upon any victim which may happen to be passing beneath, using the principle of gravity to increase the force of its downward flight ; and in several departments of the falconer's art the trainer endeavours to encourage the tendency of his hawk to mount and make the most of the advantage so gained.   The long-winged hawks are as a rule trained to come to the lure, and not to the fist, although for the sake of convenience it is sometimes found advisable to make them to both practices.

GREENLAND FALCON (*Falco candicans*)

Female—Length, about 23 inches; wing, 16.5 ; tail, 9.   Male —Length, about 20 inches ; wing, 14.5 ; tail, 8.

The general colour in the adult of both sexes is white, with more or less faint bars of light brownish grey on the upper plumage, and spots of the same colour underneath.   The young birds of both sexes are considerably darker than their elders, with a much larger allowance of darker grey brown on the plumage both above and below.   These dark patches and markings become fainter and less abundant at each moult, until in very old birds they almost vanish, leaving the hawk to appear at a distance merely white.   The bars on the back, shoulders, and wings are often shaped like the two arms of an anchor ; and the spots on the breast are mostly tear-shaped, especially after the first moult.   The legs, feet, cere, and eyelids are bluish grey in the young birds, but after the first moult become yellow, strengthening in colour at each moult.

It will be seen by reference to the remarks on comparative merits of falcons (Chap. XVIII.), that in proportions this species excels all the other gers.   It is also the most majestic in its appearance and attitudes, and the most noble in the expression of its eyes and, if the term may be permitted, of its countenance.   It was not so much used in the Middle Ages as the other gers, by reason of the difficulty of obtaining it, but was probably the most highly valued of all.   The late Lord Lilford, who in quite modern times had a good deal of experience with this species, opined that it was an excellent flier and stooper, but a poor " footer," that it was the reverse of hardy, and difficult to keep in condition. When observèd in the wild state in Scotland it was found to kill a great many rooks, and to be dreaded by the wild-fowl, but not to be partial to game, though it was seen to make an ineffectual stoop at a blackcock.

ICELAND FALCON (*Falco islandus*)

Female—Length, about 24 inches ; wing, about 17 ; tail, 9¼. Male—Length, about 21 inches ; wing, 15 ; tail, 8¼.

In young birds the upper parts are dark greyish brown or brownish grey, each feather barred and tipped with a much lighter grey. The under plumage is dusky white, splashed more or less profusely, especially on the breast and flanks, with streaky spots and splashes of greyish brown. At the first moult the brown tinge begins to disappear, and the spots on the breast and flanks become more heart-shaped than longitudinal, and less profuse. In subsequent moults the spots become smaller and smaller, and the whole plumage fades to a lighter grey, the bars on the upper plumage often softening gradually to a greyish white. The sides of the head and lower nape are white, with brownish lead-coloured shaft marks in the immature plumage, fading and diminishing as the hawk moults. The moustachial streak is wanting in this variety.

This species of ger was very highly esteemed in antiquity; and individual falcons were occasionally presented by the kings of Denmark to foreign potentates as a high compliment. In modern times it has been found delicate, and difficult to keep in health. Mr. Newcome had some which flew well at herons, but did not find them so generally effective as peregrines. The late Maharajah Dhuleep Singh flew them with success at hares. Lord Lilford, however, was unable to get them to fly rabbits or hares, and found them liable to a troublesome affection of the feet.

NORWAY FALCON (*Falco gyrfalco*)

Female—Length, about 22 inches ; wing, 16 ; tail, 9. Male—Length, 19½ inches ; wing, 14 ; tail, 8¼.

In the young the general colour of the upper plumage is a lead-coloured brown, each feather tipped and margined with a somewhat lighter brown or buff. The flight feathers are also similarly margined. The lower back is sometimes tinged with grey. The tail is tipped with white, and barred rather closely with a speckly buff. The breast is profusely streaked with longitudinal blotches on a white ground, as in the peregrine ; but these markings are of a rather duller brown.   At the moult the markings on the under plumage diminish greatly in size and number, especially on and near the chin, and become more or less tear-shaped—this tendency to decrease continuing in subsequent moults.   In the upper plumage the brown is replaced by slatey grey, barred with a lighter blue-grey, which in patches, especially upon parts of the feathers which are habitually hidden, are nearly white.   The tail becomes slatey brown, with narrow bars of brownish grey.   This species has a broad well-marked moustachial streak, which is dark brown in the immature and dark grey in the adult.   The cere and eyelids are blue-grey, and the legs and feet bluish lead colour ; but all become yellow in the adult.

This species is found not only in Norway, but also along the whole expanse of Northern Europe and Asia.   It is the nearest in colouring and disposition to the peregrine, and the most remote from the Greenlander.   Lord Lilford considered that it was not so fast as the Greenlander, and its shape is certainly not so indicative either of speed or of strength.   John Barr was sent over by Captain Dugmore some few years ago to Norway, and brought back sixteen of these hawks.   They flew beautifully to the lure, turning more quickly than a peregrine, and stooping with greater dash, but were of little use in the field, and mostly fell speedy victims to the croaks or other maladies.

LABRADOR FALCON (*Falco labradorus*)

This is another species of the ger family, found, as its name imports, in Labrador.   It is of a much darker coloration than even the Norway falcon, but not very different in measurements. It has not, as far as I can learn, been trained for sporting purposes, though no doubt it very well might be.[1]

---

[1] Although the name gyrfalco—the gyrating or circling falcon—is now appropriated by most ornithologists to the Norway birds, all the foregoing were included by the old falconers under the name ger, gyr, or jer.   They are all so styled, and very properly, by modern usage.   They are indeed little, if anything, more than climatic varieties of the same bird, and although it has not been ascertained beyond a doubt that they interbreed, this is highly probable.   The lightest variety of each one species is almost, if not quite, undistinguishable from the darkest of the next ; and the character of all is similar enough to admit of their being trained and treated in the same way.   From the falconer's point of view, there will certainly be less difference between one Iceland falcon and one of either of the two nearest allied species than there may be between two individual specimens of *F. islandus*.   They will all therefore be dealt with in the remaining chapters under the same general name of gers, unless when any special consideration involves a more specific indication.

The difference of size between the two sexes in the case of these splendid birds is, as it will be seen, considerable. But both are so superior in speed and strength to any creatures at which they are at all likely to be flown in England, that the list of quarry suitable for the gerfalcon will, with a very few exceptions, serve for the ger tiercel also. This list includes gulls of all kinds, herons, rooks and crows, wood-pigeon, black-game, grouse, partridges, hares and rabbits, wild-duck of all descriptions, Norfolk plover, and all the sea-fowls found on the coasts of Great Britain and Ireland, except swans, and perhaps wild geese. The gerfalcon will also take these latter, as well as kites and cranes, peacocks, ptarmigan, and bustards, at which the best of them may be flown in countries where such birds are to be found in sufficiently open places. It is recorded of Henry, king of Navarre, that he had a gerfalcon which Scaliger declares to have struck down in his sight a buzzard, two wild geese, divers kites, a crane, and a swan (Sir Thomas Browne, cited by Harting, *Bibliotheca Accipitraria*, xxvii.). The flight of the ger is marked by an appearance of power suitable to its size and shape, and combines in an extraordinary degree swiftness and the power of turning readily. When taught to wait on, it does so in majestic style, often at a stupendous height ; and its stoop from that direction is so " hard," as the old falconers termed it, or in other words so swift and impetuous, that the quarry is less often clutched and held than struck down with a blow as the hawk passes, and is often found either killed or altogether disabled by the violence of the shock. So great, indeed, is the vehemence with which the ger flies and stoops, that the old masters warned their pupils not to work them long on any occasion, for fear of tiring them, and thus lowering their " pitch," or impairing their powers of mounting.

Gers have not had a very fair trial in the hands of modern falconers. They have seldom come into their possession under favourable conditions. Greenlanders, especially, have for the most part been brought to European shores by ships, upon which they were caught at sea by men quite unacquainted with the proper mode of treating a wild-caught hawk. Almost always their plumage has suffered badly ; and they themselves, having been kept alive on unsuitable or scanty food, have been reduced so low as to permanently lose some of their natural strength and vitality. The same thing may be said of several Icelanders and Norwegians which have reached the hands of the falconer in pitiable plight. Gers are very seldom taken on the passage in Holland, although one tiercel, captured by

Adrian Möllen in 1878, was acquired and trained by the Old Hawking Club, and proved a fine performer at rooks. Reference has already been made to the gers brought by John Barr from Norway. Mr. Newcome, who in the treatment of peregrines was excelled by no falconer of modern times, was dissatisfied with the gers which he trained, and found them difficult to keep in condition.

D'Arcussia, who, of course, had many gers under his charge, declares that their principal excellence was in mounting, whereas in the downward stoop the peregrine might be awarded the palm. This opinion, however, can hardly be reconciled with the more forcible and striking words which he uses in another passage, where he tells us that having trained some gers for partridges he took them out before a company of experts, who, after seeing these hawks fly, were "disgusted with all other hawks."

PEREGRINE (*Falco peregrinus*)

Female—Length, about 18 inches ; wing, 14 ; tail, 7 ; tarsus, 2¼.   Male—Length, about 16 inches ; wing, 12 ; tail, 6 ; tarsus, 2.

In young birds of both sexes the upper plumage is a more or less dark brown, inclining in some individuals to chocolate colour, and in others to black, each feather of the back, wing, and tail coverts tipped with a lighter and more rufous brown. The chin, neck, breast, thighs, and whole under plumage is more or less dull creamy white, streaked plentifully with longitudinal blotches of dark brown, which are thin and small at the neck, but become broader and bigger as they approach the lower part of the breast, dying away again towards the vent. The tail is greyish brown on the upper surface, tipped with more or less rufous white, and barred with five or six rather irregular and rather faint bands of darker brown. The under part of the tail is very faint brownish grey, barred with a somewhat darker hue of the same colour. The sides of the head and neck are dull creamy white, streaked with very small dashes and markings of dark brown. On the under side of the eyebrow, passing round the eyelids, is a patch or streak of very dark brown, and a broad streak of the same colour or of black reaches like a moustache from near the back of the upper mandible backwards for an inch.

The legs, feet, cere, and eyelids vary from light blue-grey to greenish yellow and pale ochre ; beak, light bluish grey, darkening to black at the tip; claws—called always by falconers "talons"—black, as in other hawks of all kinds. In the first moult the brown of the whole upper plumage is replaced by a slatey blue, each feather from the shoulders to the end of the tail barred transversely and tipped more or less distinctly with a lighter shade of blue-grey. The slate colour on the crown and side of the head, including the moustache, is of a dark hue. The under plumage, instead of being streaked longitudinally with brown, becomes at the first moult spotted and splashed with markings of dark grey, which are partly transverse and partly shaped like an arrow-head or tear-drop, especially on the throat and gorge. At each successive moult these spots and markings become more transverse and bar-like, and also narrower and more sparse on the parts nearest the chin, until in very old birds they disappear on the chin and throat, leaving a blank surface of pure creamy white. Even before the first moult the feet and legs begin to assume a yellow colour ; and by the time the first moult is over, they and the cere and eyelids have changed to a more or less decided yellow, which as the bird grows old develops into a rich gold.

Both sexes undergo the same changes in plumage, but it should be said that these hawks at all ages vary considerably in size and shape, and still more in their colouring. It is not unusual to see an eyess which has the head and parts of the upper plumage nearly black, while the brown of others at the same age is as light as cocoa, with buff edgings. Some detailed remarks as to the size and shape of peregrines and other hawks will be found in Chapter XVIII., where it will be seen that some are of much more prepossessing appearance than others.

Speaking generally, the peregrine may be regarded as the most perfect type of combined strength, speed, and destructive power in birds. The proportions are such as could not be altered with any advantage, and adapt the hawk to a greater variety of flight than any other. This reason, and the fact that it is to be found in almost all parts of the habitable world, have always made it a favourite with falconers ; and at the present day it is more highly esteemed in Europe than any other, even including the nobler gers.

The female—to which sex alone falconers allow the application of the name of falcon—may be flown with success in this country at herons, gulls of all kinds, ducks of all kinds, crows, rooks, grouse, black-game, partridge, pheasant, woodcock, landrail, Norfolk plover, curlew, and other sea birds of about the same size, magpies, wood-pigeons, and doves. She may also generally, if desired, be taught to fly at hares, and no doubt at rabbits. Occasionally she may take plovers and snipe, jackdaws, kestrels, and smaller birds. In India her list includes wild geese, cranes, bitterns, ibis, and bustard.

The male peregrine—always called a tiercel (tassel, or tiercelet), because he is about a third smaller in size than his sister—may be flown at gulls, teal, widgeon, partridges, woodcock, landrail, starling, and the smaller sea birds, magpies, and doves ; and when exceptionally strong and courageous, will succeed to a greater or less extent with rooks, crows, jackdaws, grouse, wood-pigeons, and kestrels. In India and Eastern countries the francolin and the florican, and several sorts of duck and plovers, may be added to the list.

The peregrine at different ages was described in old times by a great variety of names, some of which are now little used, or even understood. Thus, in the eyrie or nest, from the time when she was "disclosed," or hatched, for a fortnight or three weeks she was called an eyess (or nyas, from the French *niais*). When able to move about on her legs she became a ramage hawk ; and when she could jump or flit from branch to branch, a brancher. After leaving the nest and becoming fledged, as the term is for other birds, she was described as a soar-hawk or sore-hawk (French, *sor*, from the Latin *saurus*, reddish brown) ; and when her feathers were all fully grown down she was said to be summed, whereas before this time she remained unsummed. The period during which she could properly be called a soar-hawk lasted, according to some eminent writers, from June 15 to September 15, when the migrating time begins, and she came to be more properly spoken of as a passage-hawk (or true *pélérin*). This designation carried her down to the end of the year, when she assumed, according to the French falconers, the title of *antennaire* ; that is to say, a hawk whose feathers, or whose whole self, belong to last year (*antan*). Many of the English falconers, however, gave her no new title until at or near the arrival of Lent, when they called her a Lantiner, Lentener, or Lent-hawk, for as long as Lent lasted, that is to say, till near moulting-time. The great similarity of the two names Lantiner and Antennaire, given as they were to the same hawk at the same time of her life in the two countries, suggests a strong doubt whether the former was not a mere corruption of the latter. During the whole of this time the unmoulted peregrine was known, from the colour of her plumage, as a red hawk ; and this term is still constantly employed. Many writers also called her during the same period merely a soar-hawk, neglecting the finer distinctions. It seems also that for a hawk which had been taken in August or thereabouts, and kept in captivity, it was quite correct to continue the name soar until her first moult was over.   Passage-hawks and lantiners were those only which had been caught in late autumn or late winter; and these words could never be used for such as had been caught before.   As for the terms " gentle " and " slight," they seem most properly to belong to peregrines which had been caught after they left the nest, but before they began to migrate.

In spring or early summer the young peregrine naturally begins to moult; and as soon as this tedious operation is concluded she becomes, if wild, a " haggard," and if tame, an " intermewed " hawk.   In any case she is described as " blue," and not " red." There is some doubt as to the meaning of the term haggard, many authorities, including the lexicographers, deriving it from the Saxon *hag*, meaning hedge.   A more rational explanation seems to be that which traces it to the Hebrew word *agar* or *hagar*, meaning wild, as it is used in the Old Testament. Wildness, indeed, is always regarded by Shakespeare and other writers as the characteristic of the adult wild hawk, and not any liking for hedges, to which no peregrine is very partial.

The language, or jargon, of falconry appropriated to the falcon, and, by analogy, to other hawks, especially of the long-winged species, special terms for various parts of her body and various movements and conditions; much in the same way as several of the Oriental languages describe the actions of royalty by special names.   Thus her wings are sails: the long feathers of them are flight feathers; and of these the outer are principals; and next to them are the flags.   Her tail is her train; and the two central feathers of it are deck feathers.   Her lower leg is an arm, and her foot a hand, with petty singles instead of toes, and talons instead of vulgar claws.   Her nostrils are nares; her breast feathers are mails; her lower intestine is her pannel; and her crop her gorge.

A host of the commonest actions are dignified by more or less quaint appellations.   When a hawk sleeps she " jowks "; when she sips water she " bowses."   When she seizes her quarry in the air she " binds " to it; and when her companion in the flight comes up and also takes hold, she or he is said to " join." When she strips the feathers of the " pelt," or dead body, of the quarry, she " deplumes "; and as she passes the food from her crop downwards she " puts over."   To " endue " is to digest; to " feak " is to wipe her beak after eating; to " rouse " is to shake herself; to " mantle " is to stretch out the leg in a sideways and backward direction, and afterwards stretch the wing

B

over it; to "mute" is to evacuate; and to "cast" is to throw up the refuse feathers, bones, and other indigestible matter which remains in her crop after a meal has been digested. When a hawk is pushed or forcibly held down by the hands she is said to be "cast" (French, *abattue*); and when she is bound up in a wrapping, so as not to be able to move, she is "mailed." When a silk thread is passed by means of a needle through the upper eyelids and made fast under the chin she is said to be "seeled," and the process of undoing these fastenings is called "unseeling." When she stretches her wings upwards over her head she "warbles." When quarry is put up for her, she is "served" with it. When she drives a quarry to take refuge in covert she is said to "put in"; and when she rises in the air over the place where the quarry has gone into hiding she "makes her point." If instead of doing this she goes and takes perch on a tree or other place of vantage, she "blocks." When her digestive organs are brought into good condition she is said to be "enseamed."

Most of these words can be used indifferently for both long-winged and short-winged hawks; but others are inappropriate for the latter. Thus it is wrong to call the claws of a short-winged hawk talons; and a goshawk or sparraw-hawk does not "mute," but "slice."

BLACK SHAHEEN (*Falco peregrinator*, or *Falco atriceps*)

This hawk is decidedly smaller than the true peregrine, the female hardly exceeding a big tiercel in length or weight. It is distinguished by the darker colour of its head, and especially of the sides and moustachial streak, which may be called black. The under parts of the body have a more or less pronounced rufous tinge; and the ends of the wings, when closed, approach more nearly to the end of the tail.

The black shaheen is docile, and more easily reclaimed than the peregrine; and is a great favourite with some of the Indian falconers, although the many distinguished Europeans who have flown hawks in that country express themselves less satisfied, and rather doubt the courage of peregrinator in the field. The quarry is the same as that of the peregrine, but it is only the strongest individuals which can be expected to cope with such heavy birds as the latter can tackle. Of the rapidity of its flight there can be no doubt; but Colonel Delmé Radcliffe says that it is inferior to the peregrine in "ringing" flights.

RED-NAPED SHAHEEN (*Falco babylonicus*)

Female—Length, about $17\frac{1}{4}$ inches; wing, 13; tail, $7\frac{1}{4}$.
Male—Length, $15\frac{1}{2}$ inches; wing, about $11\frac{3}{4}$; tail, $6\frac{1}{4}$.

This is another very near relation of the peregrine, also a favourite with the Indian falconers, both native and European. It is slightly smaller than the black shaheen, from which, as well as from *F. peregrinus*, it is readily distinguished by the reddish chestnut colour of the back of the head. The foot is smaller proportionately than that of the peregrine, and shaped rather more like that of the desert falcons. It is easily caught and reclaimed, and is said to develop a sort of affection for its trainer. When trained it is a most useful servant, and will fly with readiness and success at almost any of the innumerable Indian birds which are anywhere nearly of its own size. It excels particularly in the flight at wild ducks ; and a specimen which was brought to England not many years ago proved a first-rate game-hawk. Latham asserts that it can be flown successfully at wild geese, but should be followed closely by well-mounted men, who should dismount quickly and secure the quarry, which may otherwise severely damage the hawk with its long and strong wings. He appears to have known a tiercel which flew rooks, and seldom missed as much as one in ten flights. It is a better moulter than the peregrine, and can sometimes be fully moulted by August.

BARBARY FALCON (*Falco barbarus*)

Female—Length, about $13\frac{1}{4}$ inches; wing, $11\frac{1}{2}$; tail, $5\frac{1}{2}$.
Male—Length, about $12\frac{3}{4}$ inches ; wing, $10\frac{3}{4}$; tail, 5.3.

This beautifully-shaped hawk is the smallest of those which have been commonly called miniature peregrines ; and the resemblance is hardly so marked in either of the last-mentioned varieties. For the barbary is even more powerfully armed and feathered than her bigger cousins, having not only the wings conspicuously longer and more pointed than *F. peregrinus*, but also distinctly larger feet and talons, and a larger beak proportionately to her size. The colouring is the same as that of the peregrine, except that the young birds are generally lighter, especially about the head, which has a slightly ruddy tint ; and the feet are more usually yellow than grey-blue. In adults the thighs are strongly marked with arrow-headed streaks. This hawk is sometimes called the Tartaret. It is found in the southern portion of the temperate zone, especially on the African and other shores of the Mediterranean.

The falcons and strong tiercels will fly well at partridges, pigeons, and doves. Quails, of course, are easily taken by them, as they are exceedingly fast on the wing. If a cast of haggards could be trained for peewit or snipe, and well entered, they would probably have as good a chance as any hawk which could be selected for these difficult flights.

LESSER FALCON (*Falco minor*)

This hawk very much resembles the last, but has longer legs, and a slight rufous tinge on the plumage. It is found chiefly in South Africa.

The PUNIC FALCON (*F. punicus*), the JAVANESE FALCON (*F. melanogenys*), and the CHILIAN FALCON (*F. cassini*), all more or less resemble the peregrine, but with variations in the colour of the plumage, and of smaller dimensions.

SAKER (*Falco sacer*)

The measurements of this hawk, as of a great many others, are given in the so-called scientific books, even of highest repute, with hopeless inaccuracy. One of the authorities which is most often referred to gives the length of the female saker as 18½ inches, or the same as the peregrine, whereas every naturalist ought to know that the saker is a very much larger bird. On the other hand, the *Royal Natural History* (1895), coming much nearer the truth, says that "the female falls but little short of 25 inches, and the male measures more than 18½." The proportions of this hawk, excepting the feet, do not differ greatly from those of the ger, although the colourings and general appearance are completely dissimilar. The weak point, from the falconer's point of view, is the smallness of the feet and shortness of the middle toe, as well as the poor quality of the feathers, which have about them none of the glossy smartness so noticeable in the ger and the peregrine.

Young birds have the crown and nape buffy white, lighter on the forehead and over the eyebrows, and in other parts profusely streaked with dark brown. The upper plumage is a rather dull dark brown, with fulvous and rufous buff edgings. The tail, excepting the deck feathers, is marked with irregular oval spots, which range themselves into a sort of band. There is a distinct moustachial stripe. The under parts are buff-coloured, liberally streaked with splashes of dark brown, especially on the flanks; but the buff colour grows lighter on the upper parts, and at the chin becomes nearly white. The cere, legs, and feet are pale bluish or greenish grey.

In adults the head becomes much lighter, and sometimes dull white, but with a more or less rufous brown tint and streaks of darker colour. The upper parts are dull and rather pale brown, the feathers margined, and in some parts barred, with light fulvous buff. The flight feathers are faintly barred with a lighter brown, and all the tail feathers barred with light buff. The sides of the face, chin, throat, and breast are nearly white, the latter being spotted rather than streaked with brown, but not transversely barred. The moustachial streak fades away. The cere, feet, and legs assume a more or less pronounced yellow colour.

The saker is a tolerably common bird throughout almost the whole of Central and Southern Asia, and is there very highly valued for practical purposes. It was also largely imported into Western Europe in the Middle Ages, and later it was used even in France and England for the flight at kites. It is for this fine sport that it is now chiefly prized in India. The list of quarry taken by this very serviceable hawk is extremely large, and includes, besides the various kinds of tropical kites, hubara, or bustard, herons, black ibis, ducks, and a whole host of smaller birds. The flight at the short-eared owl is especially fine, and the quarry often rings, and attains to a very great height before the saker can get up. The female saker will take hares well, and also ravine deer.

The tiercel of the saker is more properly called a sakret, sakeret, or sackeret. This hawk is the largest of those called desert-hawks or desert-falcons.

LANNER (*Falco lanarius*)

Female—Length, 18 inches; wing, 13.3; tail, 7.2. Male or "Lanneret"—Length, 16½ inches; wing, 12; tail, 6½.

The dimensions of this desert-hawk do not differ widely from those of the peregrine, but the feet are much smaller, and the tail longer. The feathers are of an inferior quality, and the light colour of the head prevents all risk of confusion. The wings are slightly longer and heavier. Young birds have the whole back up to the nape of the neck and down to the tail coverts dark brown, each feather tipped with a lighter and more rufous brown. Wing and tail feathers darker brown, narrowly tipped with rufous buff. The deck feathers are plain, but the others are barred with lighter brown on the upper surface, and with dull brownish grey bands of two shades underneath. The crown of the head is light greyish buff, with narrow streaks of light brown. The lower plumage is more or less dull white, very variously marked in different individuals, but generally with longitudinal splashes of more or less dark brown. The change to the adult plumage is not very marked. The breast markings do not change to transverse bars ; but some old birds have the brown markings so arranged as to appear like irregular bars. These markings, however, generally become very sparse, and often disappear entirely on the throat and upper breast. The upper plumage alters to a slatey brownish grey, most of the feathers being barred with a darker brown, and still tipped with a rufous line. The cere and feet change from a bluish to a yellowish grey.

The lanner is common in North Africa, as well as in Central and Southern Asia, and is very frequently trained and flown in all these parts of the world. It was also formerly very largely imported into England, and used chiefly for game-hawking. It enjoys, nevertheless, anything but a good character. The old English writers describe it as " slothful and hard mettled," and of an " ungrateful disposition," while the French characterise it as *vilain* and *rebelle*. The Indian and Afghan falconers get it, as well as the saker, into condition by frequent physicking ; and the list of drugs formerly used for it in England is of portentous length. In modern times the dosing of this as well as other hawks is imperfectly under-stood by European falconers ; and the lanner is consequently in most cases a disappointing bird. When thrown off, she flies in a heavy style, and only after considerable delay will begin to mount. Very often, too, she will not mount at all, but go to perch on a tree, or even on the ground. She is apt to rake away and check at pigeons, plovers, and what not, and to be dull and obstinately slow at coming to the lure. To ensure obedience she must be fed a good deal upon washed meat, and that in moderate quantities, her appetite, like that of all the desert-falcons, being apt to grow slack on the least over-feeding. The lanner is very partial to mice, and in the wild state appears to devour lizards and other reptiles. She is not, therefore, at all particular as to diet, and may be regaled with coarser food than the nobler falcons.

Once properly conditioned, however, and " on her day," the

lanner—or for that matter the lanneret, as the male is called—is a useful and deadly hawk. Both sexes will kill partridges freely, not waiting on so often when the quarry has put in as taking perch on a neighbouring tree, and waiting, like a sparrow-hawk, to start from there. The female has also been known to take wild-duck well, and will wait on, when she likes, at a stupendous height. For magpies the lanner would hardly be quick enough. Pheasants can usually be taken by the females at the first stoop. It is said that the Arabs fly the lanner at small gazelles and a kind of bustard, which it stoops at when-ever it takes wing, and without actually striking it, frightens it on to its legs, so that it can be run down with hounds. This bird has the faculty of ejecting a slimy matter from its mouth and vent, which, if it reached the hawk, would incapacitate her from flying. Ringing flights are flown at a bird called the chakhah, resembling a golden plover ; and the lanners which excel at this fetch a price equivalent to £50 or £60. The Arabs also fly the lanner at sand-grouse and francolin.

D'Arcussia declares that the sakers and lanners do better in stormy weather and high winds than the peregrine. Neither of them bear the heat well in temperate climates.

The SOUTH AFRICAN LANNER (*F. biarmicus*) and the TUNISIAN LANNER, or ALPHANET, are local species, having a more strongly rufous coloration than *F. lanarius.*

LUGGER (*Falco jugger*)

Female—Length, 17 inches ; wing, 13.6 ; tail, 8. Male—Length, 15 inches ; wing, 12 ; tail, 7.

An Indian hawk, rarely found out of the peninsula. It is much used by the natives for a variety of quarry, and does a lot of useful work.

ELEONORA FALCON (*Falco eleonoræ*)

Female—Length, about 15½ inches ; wing, 13.3 ; tail, 7.5. Male—Length, about 13½ inches ; wing, 11.8 ; tail, 6.5.

This is a hawk of the hobby type, much darker on the under parts, and with a good deal of black and rufous on the under surface of the wings. The feet are at first pale yellow, develop-ing later into orange. The wings are long, but do not project, like the hobby's, beyond the tail.

This hawk is common on the eastern shores of the Mediterranean.   It was observed and reported upon by Brooke in Sardinia, and Kruper in Greece, which latter observes that it is "a noble falcon, and was in early ages used for falconry."   I have not discovered the chapter or verse in which this use is mentioned; but the hawk is obviously quite big enough to be flown at partridges, if willing to go.   Both the above-named naturalists maintain that its food consists principally of birds, and Dr. Kruper declares that he found in its nests the remains of six different kinds of bird, including quail and hoopoe.   A specimen was trained by Lord Lilford in 1868, who found it very obedient to the lure, but of no use in the field.

HOBBY (*Falco sabbuteo*)

Female—Length, 13 to 13½ inches; wing, 11¼; tail, 6¼. Male—Length, 11 to 12 inches; wing, about 10½; tail, 5½.

This very beautiful and graceful little hawk may at once be identified by the exceeding length of its wings, which, when closed, extend a full half-inch beyond the end of the tail. It is conspicuous also by its very marked colouring, which is in young birds almost black on the upper parts, each feather, however, being tipped with fulvous brown.   The lower plumage is creamy white, streaked profusely with dark brown splashes, and tinted on the throat and sides of the head with a warm buff. There is a broad black patch below the eye, and a black eyebrow, with a small streak of buff above it.   The moustache is broad and strongly marked.   The cere is greenish grey; and the feet, originally of the same hue, develop gradually into light yellow, and later into gamboge and bright orange.   The deck feathers are plain, but all the others are barred both above and below by about ten cross-bands of lighter brown.

In adults the upper plumage changes to a uniform dark slate colour, nearly black towards the head.   The flanks and thighs, especially in the male, assume a more and more distinct rufous colour.   The feet are proportionately small, and the legs decidedly weak.

There are strong evidences that the hobby, when commonly bred in Western Europe, was used with success for taking larks, not only by the process of "daring" referred to later on in the chapter on lark-hawking, but in actual flight, and that the female was used for taking partridges in the same way. The failure of modern falconers to make any practical use of this elegant and prepossessing hawk, is noticed in detail in the same chapter.   Owing to its natural tameness, the hobby is especially liable to fall a victim to persecution by gamekeepers and naturalists, and has as a result been nearly exterminated in England.

A wild hobby has been seen by credible witnesses to take a swift on the wing in Bulgaria. A trained female has been known in England to take house-pigeons.

MERLIN (*Falco æsalon*)

Female—Length, 11½ to 12 inches; wing, 8½ to 9; tail, 5¼ to 5¾; weight, about 8 oz. Male—Length, 10½ to 11 inches; wing, 8 to 8¼; tail, 4¾ to 5; weight, 6¼ to 6¾ oz.

Females and young males have the whole upper plumage a rich chocolate brown, with reflections of purplish grey, each feather on the back and upper wing coverts tipped with a somewhat lighter brown, and crossed by a buff bar, which is usually not to be seen except when the plumage is disarranged or ruffled. Each feather also has a black shaft, which is conspicuous in strong lights on a close view. The primaries and all the principal feathers of the wing are very dark brown on the upper surface, barred with several patches of light brown or buff. The under surface of the wing is very light silvery grey, with numerous bars and spots of brownish grey, each feather having a dark grey shaft, which is white underneath. The tail feathers on the upper surface are of a slightly lighter brown than the back, and light grey underneath, barred with more or less oblique bands, which are buff-coloured above, and light grey-brown underneath, and are all tipped with white. The under plumage of the body is creamy white, more or less tinged with light buff, especially on the sides of the head and throat. It is liberally streaked with longitudinal splashes of dark brown, which on the upper throat are very small, but on the lower flanks are broad and large. There is a facial patch and a moustache of dark brown, but these are not so strongly marked as in the peregrine and hobby. The beak is light blue, darkening to indigo, and at the tip to black. The cere and eyelids, light bluish grey. The legs and feet vary from light greenish or blueish grey to light yellow. The toes are long, thin, and flexible.

Adult females do not change, except that they lose much or all of the purplish sheen of nestlings, and that the edging of the feathers is less marked. Adult males undergo a very striking transformation. The whole upper plumage changes from brown to a rich bluish slate colour, deepening in the long wing feathers to greyish black. Instead of the light bars on the tail, there is a single broad grey-black band nearly at the extreme end.

The breast at the same time assumes a warmer tint, deepening from cream colour at the chin to a rich buff lower down, and deep russet at the flanks. The cere, eyelids, legs, and feet assume a deep golden or light orange colour. The wing and tail feathers have a stronger and stiffer appearance than before the moult, and those of the tail are generally somewhat shorter as well as stouter than they were. Very old females occasionally, but not often, put on the livery of the adult male; and this is the case sometimes also with old female kestrels. In merlins of both sexes the third feather of the wing is usually exactly equal in length to the second, and it is only exceptionally that it is even fractionally shorter.

The name merlin is in orthodox phraseology reserved to the female merlin only, the male being more properly spoken of as a jack. The former, when exceptionally strong and courageous, may be flown with some success at partridges, and will also take house-pigeons and probably doves. They have been known to capture and kill wood-pigeons. Both sexes may be flown at quails, and are more deadly at this business than sparrow-hawks. In the wild state they kill blackbirds, thrushes, starlings, and almost all kinds of small birds, and the trained birds may be kept with more or less success to any one of these birds of quarry. It has been thought that a good cast of merlins might take snipe, and it is said that such a feat has been in former times achieved. With tropical snipe in an overfed or moulting condition, it is possible that this might still be done; but it is to be greatly doubted whether any trained merlin or merlins could take fully-moulted English snipe. The flight, however, for which merlins are usually reserved, and for which they are renowned, is that at moulting skylarks, and in this sport the jacks are very nearly as successful as their sisters, as will be seen in the chapter on lark-hawking. The merlin will follow her quarry when she can into covert; and when her victim is larger than herself, kills it by strangulation, gripping it tightly round the neck.

INDIAN MERLIN (*Falco chicquera*)

This hawk, a little larger than the European merlin, is flown at much the same quarry, but also at rollers and hoopoes, which latter afford a fine ringing flight.

The AFRICAN MERLIN (*F. ruficollis*) has the markings on the breast closer together.

KESTREL (*Falco tinnunculus*)

Female—Length, about 13 inches ; wing, 9 ; tail, 7. Male —Length, about 12 inches; wing, 8¼ ; tail, 6½.

Females and young males have the upper plumage reddish brown, transversely barred on the shoulders, wing coverts, and tail with black ; the flight feathers, blackish brown ; the under plumage, very pale fawn colour, streaked on the breast, and splashed on the lower part with brown. Adult males have the head, lower part of the back, and upper surface of tail, light slatey grey. The tail with a broad black band near the end, and tipped with white ; and the head with dark shaft-streaks ; the shoulders, upper back, and upper wing coverts, pale chestnut, with small black spots of a triangular shape. The wings, dark horn colour, with lighter edging. The under plumage, pale fawn colour, becoming more rufous at the lower part and on the thighs ; streaked with dark brown splashes on the breast, and spots on the abdomen. The cere, feet, and legs are pale greyish yellow in the young, and brighter in the adult.

This little hawk has, structurally, all the characteristics of what the naturalists call a true falcon—more so, in fact, than the more highly reputed merlin. Its shape, indeed, but for a want of size in the feet and a somewhat exaggerated length of tail, is very symmetrical, and indicative of fine flying powers. It is the least shy and most familiar of all European hawks, and survives in tolerably large numbers throughout England, where, together with the owls, it is a chief agent in keeping down the inordinate increase of mice. Its powers of flight are very considerable ; and it remains on the wing generally for a considerable part of the day, not soaring so much as beating the ground at a height of two or three score feet, and hovering from time to time with its eye on any small creature that may be moving about or hiding in the grass below. But notwithstanding its fine proportions, its muscular power is not great, and its extreme pace is not to be compared with that of the merlin. If pursued by a fairly good peregrine in a pretty open place, it frequently succumbs.

In the field a kestrel is of no practical use. It will indeed generally take sparrows and other small birds thrown up from the hand when it is waiting on. And instances have been known where it has flown and taken a few wild birds. There is even a story extant of an eyess kestrel which was flown at a young partridge and took it. But these facts, if true, must have been entirely exceptional. As a rule the trained kestrel refuses all wild quarry, and it has never been known to persevere in killing any.   I am not sure whether a fair attempt has been made to fly her at rats, which would probably afford the best chance.   But kestrels can be reclaimed and taught to fly to the lure in exactly the same way as the proudest peregrine or the most majestic ger.   They will wait on beautifully, and stoop very prettily at the lure.   And while at hack their movements are exceedingly lively and graceful.   Thus for a beginner the kestrel is, in my opinion, undoubtedly the most suitable hawk upon which he can try his hand.   In the breeding season eyesses may be procured pretty easily, and at an insignificant cost ; and throughout the year many of both sexes are captured in the nets of bird-catchers, who would part with them readily for a few shillings if they were notified beforehand that any amateur would give a fair price for the captives.   In reclaiming and manning a kestrel, in learning how to keep her feathers un-broken and clean, how to hood her, bathe her, house her, and weather her, and how to diet her, the tyro can very easily and cheaply acquire all that elementary knowledge of the difficult art of falconry which it is advisable that he should possess before he attempts to succeed in training and flying a valuable hawk.   Whereas if, without any preliminary experience, he begins, as so many writers advise him, with an eyess merlin, he is almost certain to meet with a more or less discouraging failure.   Far better to observe the old maxim, "*Fiat experi-mentum in corpore vili.*"   Let the young falconer not attempt to run before he can walk fairly well.   When he has taught his kestrel to wait on and stoop to the lure, and has either by preventive care or by successful imping got her in perfect plumage, let him feed her up and "whistle her down the wind" to shift for herself, and then consider himself qualified to make a more serious attempt with a sparrow-hawk, merlin, or peregrine.

II. THE SHORT-WINGED HAWKS

Regarded from the falconer's point of view, the short-winged hawk differs essentially from her more honourable cousin of the long wings in the following particulars.   She cannot be taught to "wait on" in the air.   Although she will on occasions stoop from above at her quarry, she does not habitually capture it by a downward stroke or blow, but by following it from behind and "trussing" or "binding" to it.   She manifests her readiness to fly by a condition of body which is called by the quaint, and apparently Oriental, name of "yarak," in which she shows evident signs of eagerness and excitement, and is obviously on the *qui vive*—attentive to every sight and sound which she may suppose to indicate the presence of quarry or the hope of a flight. She kills her quarry, when taken, by crushing it in her strong foot and piercing it with her long and sharp claws, or pounces. She follows her quarry, when it is possible, into covert; and when this is not possible she takes stand readily on some convenient resting-place, such as the branch of a tree, the top of a wall, or on her trainer's fist. As a general rule she does not need to be kept to any one particular quarry, or flown at any particular time of day, but may be thrown off at anything, whether fur or feather, which she thinks she can take, and will do almost any amount of work at almost any hour.

It will thus be seen that though, from the purely artistic and sporting standpoint, the long-winged hawk deserves the more honourable place which has always been accorded to her in the most civilised countries, yet, taking the more material and matter-of-fact view of the matter, and regarded as a "pot-hunter," the short-winged is at least equal to her in merit. There is, it is true, in the flight of the latter little of the grandeur and dramatic excitement which so often attend the efforts of the former. No silent pause while the pointer stands and the hawk mounts steadily to her lofty pride of place above him. No spiral climbing of quarry and hawk into the distant blue sky. No lightning descent, which in a second or two brings down the hawk from hundreds of yards high to within a few feet of her trainer's head. But there is plenty of excitement of a different and not less healthy kind. The wary stalking of a shy quarry while the well-trained hawk on the fist trembles with eagerness for the chase. The rush and bustle of the start; the quick burst of riding or running to keep the chase in view; the hurry and scurry when the quarry has to be routed out from his place of refuge; the tussle for mastery when he has once been seized; and, last but not least, the abundance and variety of the bag which on a successful day is carried home.

One very great advantage attached to the short-winged hawk is that she can be flown in an enclosed country, or at least in places which are only very moderately open. Woods and forests are of course tabooed; and any land which is very undulating or very steep should be avoided. But the grass land and arable land which is commonly found in some four-fifths of the area of England, and especially that part of it which is not cut up into too small fields, is available, as well as the downs and commons, even though an occasional spinny or small plantation intrudes itself into the campaigning ground. Another merit of the short-winged hawk is that she is less likely to be lost. Trained as she is, or should be, upon missing her quarry, to come back to the falconer himself, and remain with him until her quarry is again actually on the wing, or, in the case of ground-game, on its legs, there is little temptation either to "rake away" or to "check." Again, the length of the flights, counting each separate bout in the pursuit as a flight, is very much less; so that the falconer—or ostringer, to give him his correct name—has a far better chance of keeping in sight when the quarry is either taken or put in. Finally, neither of the species of short-winged hawks usually trained and flown is much addicted to the vice of "carrying"; and thus the risk of losing a hawk or wasting valuable time by reason of this vexatious habit is much less to be feared. It should perhaps be added that constant exercise is less necessary for a short-winged than for a longed-winged hawk, as the former may be left idle for considerable periods, and when brought into yarak again seems to have lost little if any of her speed or her merits.

At the same time, the temper and disposition of the short-winged hawks are undeniably worse at the first than those of the long-winged. Both goshawks and sparrow-hawks, whether eyesses or wild caught, are naturally suspicious and mistrustful of mankind. They are easily alarmed, and very ready to take offence, and, once alienated or frightened, can with difficulty be conciliated. Savage and vindictive by nature and habit, they are subject to almost ungovernable fits of rage and sulkiness, which can only be subdued and guarded against by the exercise of much patience and good temper on the part of the trainer. They are jealous and cruel, and cannot, as a rule, be flown in company with other hawks, even of their own species and sex. Once lost for any considerable time they resort to their wild habits, and are difficult to re-capture. Unless carefully dieted they are very subject to apoplectic fits. Their long tails, although flexible and elastic under moderate pressure, will not always stand a very severe strain, and are likely, in a serious struggle either with any big quarry or with an awkward trainer, to be broken. The short-winged hawks should generally be belled on the tail. They are apt sometimes to crouch down on their quarry when taken, in which case a bell on the leg is hardly sounded.   Besides this, if flown when snow is on the ground, the snow will choke the bell and make it useless.

Taking the whole world over, the families of the goshawks and sparrow-hawks, which practically merge into one another, are very extensive, comprising more than thirty species, many of which could without doubt be pressed into the service of man. Only three of these have, however, commonly been trained.

GOSHAWK (*Astur palumbarius*)

Female—Length, 22 to 24 inches; wing, 12½ to 13½; tail, 10 to 12; tarsus, about 3.5.   Male—Length, 19½ to 21½ inches; wing, 10¼ to 12½; tail, 9 to 10; tarsus, about 3.

Females and young males have the upper plumage a dull liver brown, broadly margined and barred with much lighter brown; the tail, barred with five broad bands, dark brown. The under surface of the tail is pale whitish grey, with five bands of dark brownish grey.   The rest of the under plumage is pale or rusty cream colour, tinted more or less faintly with salmon pink, and streaked irregularly on the breast and flanks with longitudinal patches or splashes of dark brown.   The cere and legs are greenish yellow.   The eyes are very light, and clear yellowish grey, and so bright that the Greeks gave to this hawk the name of ἀστερίας ἱεράξ, the star-eyed hawk.   Adult males have a decided grey tint on the upper and under plumage. At the first moult both sexes change the longitudinal streaks on the breast, thighs, and flanks into more or less irregular bars of dark greyish brown; and as they grow older the bars usually become narrower and more regular.   The tail is now barred on both surfaces with four broad bands of dark brown or grey. The cere, legs, and feet become yellow; and the eyes change to a deeper yellow, and ultimately to deeper and darker orange.

Goshawks vary greatly in size and strength.   Those which are imported from Norway are often exceptionally big and strong, while the specimens from Germany and Central Europe have a reputation for weakness.   Although this hawk formerly bred commonly in England, it is now practically extinct; but some nests are still annually found in France.

The list of quarry at which the goshawk may be flown is very large, including, for the British islands, hares, rabbits, stoats, weasels, squirrels, and rats; herons and wild ducks—flown as they rise—pheasants, partridges, landrails, water-hens, jays, and an occasional magpie or wood-pigeon.   In fact, any moderate-sized bird which gets up close in front of a goshawk must bustle himself if he intends to escape the first quick dash of this impetuous and greedy pursuer.

In India and other tropical countries the female "goss" will fly, with a good start, at crows, neophrons, minas, florikin, francolin, jungle-fowl, and even such big birds as kites, geese, cranes, and pea-fowl.   Even in England she was formerly flown with success at cranes, wild geese, and other large water-fowl ; and the old books contain elaborate directions as to stalking these birds "with grey goshawk on hand."   In some parts of Asia goshawks are said to have been flown at ravine deer and bustard ; but this would probably be with some assistance from dogs.

The male goshawk, much smaller in size than his sisters, is less valuable to the sportsman, but is usually accounted rather swifter on the wing.   The best specimens will catch a partridge in fair flight ; and most of them, with a tolerably good start, will overtake a pheasant.   A very strong male will sometimes catch and hold a full-grown rabbit, and the others may be expected to kill half-grown rabbits and leverets, if kept to such quarry.   Landrails and water-hens make a more or less easy flight.   Jays and magpies may sometimes be taken, as well as blackbirds.   Rats, weasels, squirrels, and "such small deer" are, of course, available.   Occasional specimens of the male goshawk are extraordinarily fast and strong.   Colonel Delmé Radcliffe had one which actually killed grouse in Scotland, and another which took storks and geese in India, as well as partridges.

SPARROW-HAWK (*Accipiter nisus*)

Female—Length, 14 to 16 inches ; wing, $8\frac{1}{2}$ to $9\frac{1}{2}$; tail, $7\frac{1}{2}$ to $7\frac{3}{4}$; tarsus, 2.4.   Male—Length, $11\frac{1}{2}$ to $12\frac{1}{2}$ inches ; wing, $7\frac{1}{2}$ to $8\frac{1}{4}$; tail, 6 to $6\frac{1}{2}$; tarsus, 2.1.

The sparrow-hawk is remarkable for its very long and slender legs and middle toe, and its small head.   Young females have the beak and upper plumage sepia brown, each feather edged with rufous brown ; the nape varied with white or rufous white.   The wing feathers are dark brown, with five bars of still darker brown on the outer primaries.   The tail rather lighter brown, with five dark brown bars.   The under plumage is dull white, more or less tinged with rufous, spotted with irregular patches, streaks, or bars of greyish brown.   In the adult the brown of the upper plumage assumes a slatey grey hue, and the edgings of lighter colour vanish.   The breast and under parts are barred with transverse markings of mixed fulvous and brown, and develop a rusty red colouring on the abdomen and inner thighs. The legs and feet become more distinctly yellow or gold colour, and the eye deepens in colour to light and ultimately to dark orange. Males in the immature plumage differ from females only in having a somewhat more rufous hue on the lighter part. But after the moult this rufous colouring becomes still more conspicuous, and spreads to the flanks and under surface of the wings, as well as to the upper throat. In both sexes the bars on the breast and thighs become narrower and of a fainter grey as the birds grow older ; and the eyes deepen in colour.

Female sparrow-hawks—very much bigger and stronger than their brothers—may be flown at any bird of the size of a partridge, or smaller, which is not very swift or quick in shifting. In the wild state they undoubtedly kill a certain number of wood-pigeons, taking them at some disadvantage, as, for instance, when they pass under a tree in which the hawk is at perch. Probably the wild sparrow-hawk also picks up an occasional peewit, snipe, or woodcock. She is fond of young pheasants, which she will pick up from the ground when insufficiently guarded by the mother or foster-mother. Young chickens sometimes undergo the same fate under similar circumstances. The uses of the trained sparrow-hawk, both male and female, are described in the chapter devoted to this hawk.

BESRA SPARROW-HAWK (*Accipiter virgatus*)

This species, considerably smaller than *A. nisus*, is very common in the tropics, both in the wild and in the trained state, and is thought by many to be quite equal, if not superior, to it in courage and ability.

Other sparrow-hawks which may be trained include the large species called the Levant sparrow-hawk (*A. brevipes*), *A. minullus* and *A. tinus*, from South America, *A . cirrocephalus*, from Australia, *A. badius*, and the miniature *A. polyzonoides*.

III. THE EAGLES

In Western Europe no great use seems to have been made by the old falconers of any kind of eagle. D'Arcussia in the early editions of his book makes no reference to them as objects of the trainer's care, and some of the early English authors expressly speak of them as useless to the falconer by reason of their great weight, making it impossible, as they believed, to carry them on the fist, and also their powers of fasting, which, they supposed, precluded all chance of reducing them to proper obedience. In the East, however, they have from time immemorial been trained with success, and flown at a great variety of quarry suitable to their size and strength. For the far greater part of the knowledge which we now have about flights with eagles, we are indebted to Mr. J. E. Harting, who obtained much valuable information on this subject from the late Mr. Constantine Haller, an enthusiastic falconer, and president of a Russian falconry club which had its headquarters at St. Petersburg in 1884–85. Notwithstanding the efforts of these two very competent authorities, it is still exceedingly difficult to say with any certainty what sorts of eagles are now employed by the Kirghis and Turcomans and other Asiatic peoples, and what other sorts are regarded as unserviceable. As to the golden eagle and Bonelli's eagle there is no doubt; but the evidence as to the others below-mentioned cannot be said to be at all conclusive.

The speed of the eagles in ordinary flying is inferior to that of the hawks, though superior to that of any quadruped at his best pace. Their usual mode of capturing their prey when in the wild state, is by soaring and scanning the ground below, and, when they see a good chance, dropping with a powerful stoop on to the back or head of the victim. In training they cannot be made to wait on, and must therefore be flown from the fist, so that winged game of all kinds is usually able to show them, if not "a clean pair of heels," at least a clean set of tail feathers. Consequently their quarry consists almost entirely of four-legged creatures. Large birds of various descriptions might be flown at when they are on the ground, and might be taken before they had time to get fairly on the wing; but such masquerades of real hawking can hardly be called flights.

The golden eagle, and most other eagles, are naturally more or less ill-tempered, and require the exercise of considerable patience on the part of the man who undertakes to reclaim them; but the method employed differs in no material respect from that applied to the short-winged hawk. Only, when a goshawk or sparrow-hawk is once properly reclaimed and manned, she generally says good-bye to her bad temper. The eagle is said to be sometimes apt, even when fully trained, to become so enraged, either at missing her quarry or by some other *contretemps*, that she will attack the men of the party, and perhaps have a flight at a native just by way of a relief to her outraged feelings.

Eagles are carried to and in the field on a crutch, which is formed of an upright pole with a cross-bar at the top, the lower end of the apparatus being fitted into the saddle, and the staff of it attached by a strap to the rider's girdle. The lure, to which they are called when they do not come back to the crutch, consists of the stuffed skin of an animal made to resemble the quarry at which they are meant to fly.

The following are the eagles best fitted for training:—

GOLDEN EAGLE (*Aquila chrysaetus*)

Female—Length, about 35 inches; wing, about $27\frac{1}{2}$; tail, about 14; tarsus, 3.8. Male—Length, about 32 inches; wing, $24\frac{1}{2}$; tail, 13; tarsus, 3.7.

The plumage is generally of a ruddy brown or fawn, inclining in parts to dark brown, and in others to dull brownish gold. Adult females become very dark, and males also assume a more dusky hue as they grow older.

Of the fact that the golden eagle is now and has been for centuries commonly trained and flown in Central Asia there is no manner of doubt. Many excellent authorities maintain that it is the species used by the Kirghis and other tribes subject or tributary to Russia under the name of Kholsan. This was also the opinion of M. Paul Gervais, who became the owner of a veritable Kholsan, imported into France by M. Maichin, who purchased it from the Kirghis for £40 and a gun. This trained eagle, which was a female, would take foxes well, and after binding to them was accustomed to grip them by the fore part of the mask, thus obviating the chance of a dangerous bite. In Central Asia the Kholsan is flown at bustard, hare, fox, and antelope; and the females will tackle such heavy quarry as wild goat, wolf, and even wild boar.

BERKUTE (*Aquila nobilis*)

About the identity of this species there is even more doubt than about the Kholsan. Mr. Harting inclines to the view that it is no more than a golden eagle in a different phase of its plumage. Others suppose that it is the imperial eagle, and others again regard it as Bonelli's eagle.   It appears that in the Russian provinces of Asia it is still more commonly used than the Kholsan, and at much the same quarry, which would suggest the conclusion that it is not at any rate a larger bird than *A. Bonellii*.

WHITE-CROWNED EAGLE (*Haliætus leucoryphus*)

A specimen was owned by a Russian falconer, who found it worth while to keep it over two moults, and must have taken a favourable view of its merits.

SPOTTED EAGLE (*Aquila clanga* or *nœvia*)

This large eagle is trained by the Kirghis, under the name of Kara Gush, *i.e.* black eagle.

IMPERIAL EAGLE (*Aquila imperialis*)

This is a smaller eagle than *A. chrysaetus*, the female measuring about 32 inches and the male about 31.   It appears to be susceptible of training, and is thought by many to be included in the list of eagles commonly used in Turkestan.   It is found throughout the greater part of Asia, and occasionally in South-Eastern Europe.

STEPPE EAGLE (*Aquila nipalensis*)

This bird is described by some naturalists as a hawk-eagle. It is of a taking and sportsmanlike appearance, the eyes of old specimens being of a fiery yellow, though in young birds they are dull grey.   Colonel D. Radcliffe obtained several specimens in India, both eyess and wild caught.   He says that in the wild state it takes pine martens and also the musk deer.

BONELLI'S EAGLE (*Aquila Bonellii*)

Female—Length, 26½ inches ; wing, 18¼ ; tail, 11½ ; tarsus, 4. Male—Length, 24½ inches ; wing, 17½ ; tail, 11¼ ; tarsus, 3.9.
This small and rather long-legged eagle is probably the easiest to train, and the best for purposes of falconry in Europe, as it is of a more handy size than the bigger species, and strong

enough for all practical purposes. A trained specimen was kept and flown by M. Barachin in France at hares and rabbits. It is described by Canon Tristram as a more dainty feeder than most of the eagles; and Mr. Hume says that in the wild state it kills many water-fowl. The tail is barred. The weight of the male hardly exceeds 4 lbs.

In concluding the list it must be observed that several birds which might have been comprised in it are omitted. The Chinese and Japanese falconers of bygone times undoubtedly trained hawks which are figured in their books, but cannot now be identified. Falconry is extinct in Japan, and nearly so in China. The hawks themselves, which were once highly honoured in their country, will probably before long be exterminated by the ever-increasing horde of skin-collectors.

Some readers may be surprised at the exclusion from this list of some such birds as vultures, buzzards, and even some owls. These I have designedly omitted. I find in a work called the *Natural History Picture-Book* a statement by Mr. Wood, that the kite (*Milvus regalis*) "has even been trained for purposes of falconry, and found to perform its task to the satisfaction of its owner." Either the owner must have been very easily pleased, or the kite must have changed very greatly in disposition and habits within the last few centuries! With shrikes the case is different, for it appears that they were actually trained to fly at small birds. D'Arcussia tells us plainly that amongst the numerous hawking establishments kept up by Louis XIII. was one of shrikes, and relates a very quaint story of one of these little birds owned by the king, which would fly up to a heron on the wing and whisper in his ear!

Several of the falconets might certainly be utilised in the field, and amongst them especially Feilden's falcon, which is very common, very bold, and very tame. Indeed, some of the Malays are said to train these little hawks. Davison says that he has seen the black-legged falconet (*Hierax fringillarius*) stoop at a rock-thrush, and killed one on a partly-plucked swallow. Other likely varieties are the white-legged and red-legged falconets (*H. melanoleucus* and *H. cærulescens*).

There can be little doubt that such birds as fly-catchers could be trained and flown at butterflies; and possibly, when the naturalists and Cockney sportsmen and egg-collectors have succeeded by their united efforts in exterminating all hawks, our descendants may resort to this form of sport as their best substitute for falconry as we now know it.

CHAPTER III

FURNITURE AND FITTINGS

BEFORE the intending falconer takes any preliminary steps even towards becoming the owner of a hawk, he must make himself thoroughly familiar with the necessary appliances which he will have to use, and first of all with the hawk's furniture, or articles of attire and daily use.

The "jess" (or jesse) by which the hawk's feet are secured is a strip of leather fastened round the leg, just above the foot. It is, of course, of a different length, width, and stoutness, according to the size of the wearer. For a peregrine or ger the same stuff may be used as for strong riding or driving gloves ; and the softer and more pliable it can be, consistently with strength, the better. For a gerfalcon 8 in. is not too long. For a peregrine tiercel 6½ in. is long enough, and for hawks of intermediate size the length may vary according to their proportions. In the case of the smaller hawks, from the female sparrow-hawk to the tiny jack-merlin, the length for ordinary purposes should be from 4½ in. to 6½ in. But when a jack-merlin is flying ringing larks late in the season, or indeed at any time, and it is important that he should carry the very smallest possible amount of extra luggage, his jesses may be made out of a thin kid glove, well stretched and greased, and need not be more than 3½ in. long, by ¼ in. wide, bulging out to ⅓ in. at the place where they encircle the leg, and at the other end, where they are hooked to the swivel. In all cases the jess is attached in the same way. After it has been well stretched and greased, a short slit is made near the broader end of the leather (see Fig. 1), and another a little farther down. The distance between the two slits should be about the same as the circumference of the hawk's leg—not greater, nor much less. This part of the leather between the two slits is applied to the hawk's leg, and the shorter end, being brought round the

40

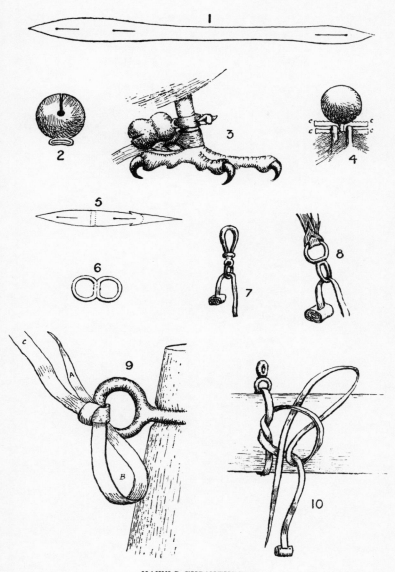

HAWKS FURNITURE, I.

1 JESS 2. BELL 3. HAWK'S FOOT WITH BELL AND JESS ATTACHED 4. BELL FOR TAIL
OF SHORT-WINGED HAWK 5. BEWIT 6. RING SWIVEL 7. SPRING SWIVEL
8. LEASH, SWIVEL AND JESSES 9. FALCONER'S KNOT 10. ATTACHMENT
OF LEASH TO POLE, PERCH OR CADGE

leg, is pushed through the second slit as far as it will go. Then the longer end is in its turn passed through the first slit and pulled tight. Some falconers pass the long end of the jess through both slits before pulling it tight; but the reason for this extra precaution has never been made plain. After the long end has been pulled through—or before, if preferred—a hole is punched in the leather at a short distance from the tip, and another and larger slit is made for the purpose of attaching the jess to the swivel. But if the hawk is destined, immediately after the jesses have been put on, to be turned out to hack, this end slit is not required, and should never be made, as it is possible that it might loop itself round some thorn or other peg-like object, and hang up the hawk, causing her death or some irreparable injury. Whenever a jess is released from the swivel, it is a good plan, when there is time, to twirl up the end, rolling it between the finger and thumb, so that the slit does not form a loop. It is then less likely, in case of the hawk being lost, to lead to a misfortune of the kind referred to.

Trained hawks always wear jesses. As soon as one pair is worn, and shows signs of weakness, another pair should be put on ; and after they are attached, the old ones may be cut off with a sharp knife or scissors and thrown away. Valuable hawks have been lost by the owner's neglect to renew the jesses. Of course it usually happens that one of a pair wears out before the other, and the breaking of the weakest gives warning before the other has given way. But when one jess has become so dilapidated as to be on the point of breaking, his fellow will not be in a much better case, and a jerk caused by suddenly bating at the block, especially when sitting there after a bath, may liberate the hawk when you feel least prepared for such a mishap. The old falconers seem to have almost always attached the ends of the jesses to "varvels," which were small rings of silver, or other metal, upon which often the name and address of the owner were engraved. Possibly the jesses so used were very short, so that the risk of "hooking up" did not arise. But the practice has long been abandoned by European falconers.

Bells for trained hawks are of the greatest possible use. They betray the whereabouts of the wearer, and save an infinity of time and trouble when she has killed out of sight; and besides this, they proclaim to every stranger who sees a lost hawk on the wing that she is private property, and not wild. They are, practically, no impediment to the hawk's flight, except in the case of the very smallest species ; and their sound probably augments the terror inspired in the quarry by a stoop that has only just missed its mark.   Bells have been used in all countries from time immemorial.   The best are now made in India; but for the larger hawks, those supplied by Mr. Möllen, at Valkenswaard, in Holland, are good enough, and very cheap. The European bells are spherical, with a plain flat shank (Fig. 2), and those of Indian manufacture are of the shape shown in the illustration (Fig. 3).   Anciently, silver was much used for bells for the more valuable hawks, but the metal now used is chiefly brass.   A good bell should be capable of being heard distinctly on a still day more than a quarter of a mile, even if lightly moved.   The bell is attached to the hawk's leg by a " bewit," which is fastened on in the same way as the jess.   The bewit is a small strip of leather shaped as in Fig. 5.   It is pulled through the shank of the bell until the latter is at the place indicated by the dotted line near the middle.   The shank is applied to the hawk's leg above the jess, and the end (A) is passed round the leg and pushed through the slit (B).   Then the thicker end is pushed through the slit at the thin end, and pulled till the ears or jags at the side have come through the opening.   These then act as barbs to prevent the end slipping back, and the thin part of it can be cut off.   Hack bells are used not only to give notice where the hawk is, but also to serve as a weight to handicap her when, at the end of her time of liberty, she begins to chase chance quarry. They are therefore much bigger, in proportion to the size of the wearer, than the bells used in the field.   A falcon's or tiercel's bell will not be too big for a merlin or jack.   Sometimes hawks' bells are even loaded with lead.   A merlin which is flying ringing larks does not wear bells, for it is impossible to get any which are sufficiently light, and at the same time loud enough to be of any use.

Short-winged hawks should generally be belled on the tail, and for this purpose the bewits should be of a different shape, as in Fig. 4.   The aperture on each side of the bewit should be made to encircle the shaft of one of the " deck " feathers, that is, the central feathers of the tail, near to its base; and the double ends (C, C) should be lapped or tied together with waxed thread, so that the fastening cannot slip from its place.

Of course when it is intended to put on new jesses or bewits, the hawk must be " cast," or held.   And some considerable attention is required to cast a hawk properly.   To seize an unhooded hawk, especially short-winged, and forcibly thrust her down on her breast would constitute, in her eyes, a deadly and perhaps unpardonable offence. To meddle with her when she has a full crop would be a great mistake. A time should be chosen when she has little or nothing in her crop. She should be hooded and held on the fist, while on the "operating table" is placed a cushion and the apparatus required, including tweezers and a sharp penknife. Then a silk handkerchief, once folded, can be thrown over the hawk's shoulders, and the falconer's assistant, standing behind the hawk with his hands over her back, the thumbs close to her back-bone, will, with a quick steady lowering of the palms, grasp her firmly round the body, with the fingers enclosing the sides of her wings and thighs. Lifting her off the fist, he must deposit her on the cushion, holding her down steadily on her breast. A man should be employed for this purpose who is not likely to be nervous or flurried.

The jesses are made fast to the swivel when the hawk is not intended to fly; and swivels are of two kinds. The safest (and the most troublesome to put on and take off) is the ring-swivel (Fig. 6), consisting of a double ring in the shape of a figure 8, each end working freely on a pivot which keeps the two rings close together. It is made of brass or iron, and very good and cheap ones are to be had from Mr. Mollen, of Valkenswaard, in North Brabant. To attach the ring-swivel to the jesses, pass the end of one jess from right to left through one of the rings, and, after it is through, pass both rings through the slit in the jess, and pull tight. When the first jess is fast, pass the end of the other jess through the same ring upon which the first jess is fastened, but in the opposite direction, from left to right, and then pass the two rings through the slit as before. The second jess will pull up tight over the first, and both will be fixed firmly at the outer end of the same ring.

To get the ring-swivel off, the extreme end of the jess which was last put on must be pulled until that jess becomes slack enough for the two rings to be passed through it, or, in other words, for the opening in the leather to be pulled over the rings, and, this being done, it will come away at once. After releasing one jess, take care to hold it tight between the fingers of the left hand while freeing the other jess. Otherwise, if the hawk is fidgety and jumps off, she may jerk the other jess out of your hand, and go off bodily, leash and all, into the next parish.

Spring-swivels (Fig. 7) are very handy contrivances for use in the field, but not so safe for a hawk when sitting unhooded on the perch or at the block. They are shaped like the swivel by which watches are usually attached to a watch-chain, and must be so made as to turn quite freely on the pivot. To attach them to the jesses, nothing more is required than to press the side with the thumb-nail, making the spring yield, and then hook the curved end through the slit in both jesses, after which the spring is released, and the jesses remain encircled by the metal. Only, if the spring is stiff or does not work properly, there will be disasters. The unhooking process is of course even more easily and quickly effected.

The leash can now be attached to the swivel. And leashes, again, may be of two kinds. The orthodox leash for peregrines and big hawks is a strip of tough leather, about half an inch wide, and a yard long, provided with a stout button at one end, which is made in the following way :—In cutting the leash, three inches or so at one end are cut rather broader than the rest of the strip. This broad end is then rolled up tightly by doubling it over and over upon itself. After the broad part has been rolled up, a hole is punched right through the roll, and the other end of the leash, which is tapered to a point, is pushed through and pulled tight. A sort of square button will thus be formed at the thick end of the leash (Fig. 8) ; and if the thin end of it is passed through the outer ring of the swivel—that ring to which the jesses are not attached—it will run right through until the ring encounters the button, which is too big to get past. The whole length of the leash is then available for the purpose of tying up the hawk to her block, or to a peg in the ground.

There is a right and a wrong way about even so simple a matter as tying up a hawk. Blocks and pegs ought always to be provided with a ring or staple, round which to tie the leash ; and it should be tied in what is called a falconer's knot, which can easily be negotiated with one hand. To begin with, pass the thin end of the leash through the ring. Then make a loop in the part which has gone through the ring, and pass the loop round that part of the leash which has not gone through the ring. Pull tight, and the leash will assume an appearance resembling that shown in Fig. 9. Next pass the end (A) through the loop (B), and again pull tight. It will be impossible for any strain upon the leash at C to undo the knot. And when it is desired to undo it, the end (A) can easily be picked out with the fingers through the tightened loop (B), and a simple pull upon A will then undo the whole fastening.

For attaching hawks to the screen-perch, a sort of double falconer's knot is required for fastening the two ends of the leash round the pole. But it is learnt with the greatest ease. Nothing more is necessary than to take the two ends of the leash—the thick and the thin—and pass one over and one under the pole. Then tie them together, just as if you were tying a black necktie, except that you make only one bow instead of two. Let this one bow, when the knot is pulled tight, be about four inches long; and through the loop formed by it pass the two ends of the leash, which will naturally be found on the reverse side of the knot (Fig. 10). When the hawk is carried on the fist, the ends of the jesses, the swivel, and button of the leash will often lie in the palm of the left hand. The leash will hang down for some inches, perhaps a foot, and then, forming a loop, be gathered up to the little finger, round which the lower part, a few inches from the thin end, is wound for the sake of extra security.

Smaller leashes in the same style, but made of less stout leather, can very well be used for the smaller hawks, and usually are so. But when these hawks are doing a great deal of flying, as they should, and doing it twice a day, the trouble of constantly unfastening the ring-swivel from the jesses and fastening it on again becomes very tiresome, and even vexatious; and it is a common practice to use spring-swivels permanently. The outer ring of these (unless they are made specially) is too small to admit the passage of a flat leash; and it will be found more convenient to use thongs shaped like a porpoise-hide boot-lace. In fact a long leather boot-lace makes about as good a leash as can be wished for. The function of the button is fulfilled by a simple knot tied in the end of the lace. Or in order to save still more time, the lace may be permanently attached to the spring-swivel in the manner shown in the diagram (Fig. 25). By making the knot an inch or two away from the ring of the swivel, instead of close up to it, enough length of tether is left, when the leash is tied round the pole, to enable a merlin or sparrow-hawk in short "racing jesses" to shift about a bit on the perch.

The proper place for a hawk, when not out of doors, is the screen-perch (Fig. 23). The bar on which the hawk stands may run from wall to wall of the hawk-house, or, if this is not convenient, it may be supported on arms or brackets reaching out from the wall to a distance of not less than 30 in. for a big hawk, or 2 ft. for a little one. Where this arrangement is also impossible the bar may be supported at each end on a post or tressels so securely fastened or weighted that they cannot be upset or moved out of place. Round the bar, which should be of wood, is wrapped a padding of baize or other soft stuff, and over it a covering of canvas stretched very tight. The canvas may be nailed to the pole, or stitched together, on the under side. A screen, or curtain, of canvas must be attached to the under side of the perch, and hang down from it for more than two feet, to form a sort of ladder, by which any hawk may climb up again as often as she bates off and hangs by her leash and swivel. The ends of this screen may be kept down with weights attached to it, or stretched by a sort of guy ropes from the lower corners, so as to keep the whole flat and taut. In perches for small hawks, the same canvas which is rolled round the pole is often allowed to hang down and form the screen. In this case slits or holes are made in the canvas just below the pole, through which the leashes may be passed when fastening the hawks to the perch. A space of at least 2 ft. should be left between each big hawk and that which stands next her on the perch; and 18 in. between each of the small ones; and there should be rather more space between the end hawk and the wall or the bracket of the perch, whichever it is.

Underneath the perch must be spread a good thick layer of sand or sawdust, extending in the case of peregrines and gers for a good yard on each side of the perch, and about 18 in. in the case of the smaller long-winged hawks, to catch the mutes. As for short-winged hawks, the layer must be very much farther extended, and in the case of goshawks should reach at least three yards from the perch. And if the perch is near a wall, the wall itself must be protected by a shield of paper, or other cheap material which can be changed every other day, for these hawks "slice" to a very great distance almost horizontally. The sand or sawdust must either be removed daily, or at least freed from the mutes which have fallen into it. In or near it will also be found the "castings," or pellets of refuse feathers and other indigestible matter thrown up by the hawks. These castings should be looked for every morning by the falconer, and each one should be examined before it is thrown away, as it is by the appearance of them, as will be seen later on, that the state of health of each hawk is to a large extent ascertained. Both castings and mutes, with the sand or sawdust adhering to them, should, when collected, be immediately removed from the hawk-house. A dirty or ill-smelling room is not only a disgrace to the falconer, but injurious to the inmates, which, though possessed of no sense of smell, require the purest possible air to breathe.

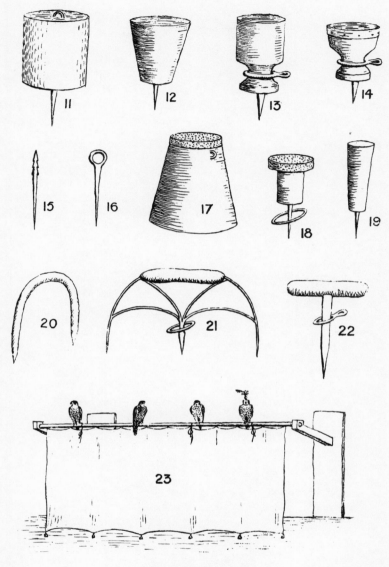

HAWK'S FURNITURE, II.

BLOCKS AND PERCHES

11. PLAIN BLOCK FOR LONG-WINGED HAWK   12. BLOCK FOR SAKER, MERLIN, ETC.
13, 14. IMPROVED BLOCK FOR LARGE AND SMALL HAWK   15. SPIKE FOR BLOCK
16. RING PEG   17, 18. BLOCKS WITH CORK TOP   19. FIELD BLOCK
20, 21. BOW-PERCHES   22. CRUTCH-PERCH   23. SCREEN-PERCH

For out-door service, blocks are used for the long-winged hawks, and bow-perches for the short-winged. Blocks are of various shapes, as shown in the illustration. The simplest are made of mere chunks of tree or sapling sawn off level (Fig. 11), and having a staple of iron or brass driven into the top or at the side, to which to attach the leash. They should be from 8 inches to a foot in height for a peregrine or ger, and for all other hawks of such a height that when the hawk is standing on them her tail may just clear the tops of the blades of grass. A high block is not good; for then the leash, if it is not to catch in the shoulder, must be a long one, and when the hawk bates she will be brought up with a too sudden jerk as the leash tightens. For the smaller falcons—hobbies, merlins, and kestrels—as well as for sakers and lanners, the block should always be larger at the top than at the bottom, so that it may not be fouled on the sides with the mutes (see Figs. 12, 14). It is a very good plan to have a groove made round the body of the block, and to have a metal ring fitted round it, so that it will run freely in the groove. This hoop of metal may be looped out into a smaller ring on one side, to which the leash may be tied (see Figs. 13, 14). As the hawk jumps off to one side or the other the ring will run round; and thus all risk is avoided of the leash getting hitched up or wound round the block. A spike (Fig. 15) is firmly fixed into the middle of the base of the block to hold it fast in the ground. Of course a block which is larger at the base than on the top may be used without a spike, and without any ring or staple in it, if the leash is fastened to a ring-peg (Fig. 16) in the ground. But even if this peg is driven in on the windward side of the block, that is, on the side towards which the hawk is pretty sure to bate off, the risk of entanglement is not wholly avoided; and a hawk so attached should not be left alone for long. The top of the block should be covered with cork (Fig. 17), or it may be padded and covered with leather. But in the latter case it must not be left out in the rain. Wood is too hard for hawks to stand on for any length of time, and is apt to give them corns or sore feet. No hawk should be allowed to stand on a wet block. A simple and not a bad plan for making merlins' blocks, is to saw off a chunk from a pole or tree branch, about $2\frac{1}{2}$ in. in diameter and 5 or 6 in. long. Into one end insert a spike, and on to the other nail a 4-in. or 5-in. bung (Fig. 18). A 4-in. metal curtain-ring, measured from outside to outside, can be placed on the ground and the spike driven into the earth in the middle

C

of the ring, which will run freely round the block when the leash is attached to it.   Care must always be taken to drive the block well home to the ground, or the leash may get jammed under its lower edge, and cause a dire mishap. Fig. 19 is a little field block which I use for merlins.   It can be carried in a side-pocket when out on the open downs. After one of these little hawks has done her day's flying, or before her turn comes, instead of putting her, hooded, on the pole cadge, her leash is made fast to the looped creance, which comes from a ring in the top of the block.   The spike is driven into the ground in a sheltered spot, and the hawk is deposited on the top of the pigmy post, where she will sit, if not exactly " like patience on a monument," at least more comfortably than if merely pegged out on the prickly grass or still more uninviting stubble.

Bow-perches for goshawks and sparrow-hawks may be made by simply bending a length of yew or other tough wood into the shape of an arch, and sticking the two sharpened ends into the. ground (Fig. 20).   A more elaborate apparatus made of iron, with three spikes and a padded top, is shown in Fig. 21. In any case it is proper to pad the uppermost part of the arch. The ring for the leash runs loosely on the outer frame of the perch.   The crutch-like perch shown in Fig. 22 is simple, and has its merits.   Probably for an eagle it is the best resting-place that could be provided.   When fixing up bow-perches or crutch-perches care should be taken that they are placed broadside on to the wind, so that the hawk as she takes perch on them may directly face the wind.   It is perhaps needless to say that for an eagle the spike should be very long, and hammered deep into the ground.

The hood, or to speak more exactly, the hood proper, is an article of attire with which every educated person is vaguely familiar.   The exact shape is shown in Fig. 24.   It is made of stiffish leather, fashioned on a wooden block made of the size and shape of the hawk for which it is intended, and stitched together.   Some amateurs have arrived at a certain proficiency in making their own hoods.   Captain Salvin, for instance, could manufacture very good ones.   But such excellent hoods can be obtained from Mr. Möllen, for all sorts of hawks, at so small a price, that it is scarcely worth while to be at the trouble of making them.   The hooding of hawks is an art in itself, and will be referred to in a later chapter.   When the hood is well on the hawk's head and the beak well through the opening in front, the longer and thinner of the braces at

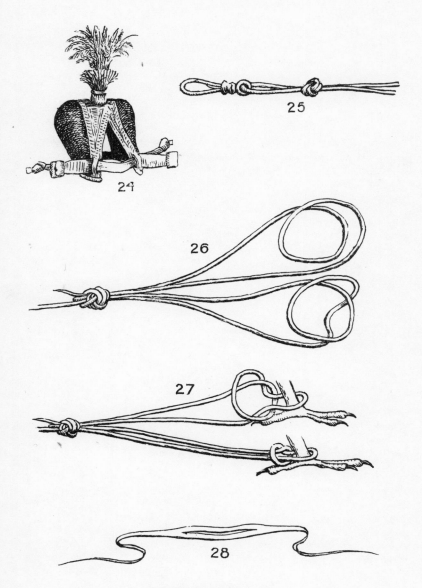

HAWK'S FURNITURE, III.

24. HOOD-PROPER 25. SPRING SWIVEL AND LEASH FOR SMALL HAWK
26, 27. DOUBLE RING LEASH 28. BRAIL

the back (A, A) are pulled apart, and the back of the hood is thus drawn tight, so that it is impossible to remove it. The shorter and stouter ends are pulled when it is desired to slacken the fastening, so that the hood can be taken off by lifting the plume forwards. Usually each of these operations is performed with the aid of the right hand and the teeth. As the hawk stands on the falconer's left fist with her tail outwards over his knuckles, he takes hold with his right finger and thumb of the brace which is on the hawk's left side, and then catches hold with his front teeth of the brace which is on the hawk's right side. A sharp pull brings the ends apart, and the hood is braced up or slackened, as the case may be. Before any hood is ever put on, the falconer should remember to look inside it to see that no dust or dirt or stray feathers or anything else has found its way in, and it is as well to blow a puff of air into it to clear it of any particle of dust.

The rufter-hood is made of much softer leather, with no plume, and a simpler fastening. It is used for newly-caught hawks, and hardly need be described in detail, as before the beginner has occasion for it he will have learnt more about hoods than can be taught in any book. Indian hoods are also made of softer leather, with a different and smaller plume. They are fastened by braces which run round the lower side, passing in and out of the leather and working by friction.

This completes the list of ordinary hawk's furniture. But there are a few other appliances with which the beginner must become familiar before he can undertake to train, or even to keep, a hawk.

A brail (Fig. 28) is a sort of manacle for an unmanageable hawk, which keeps on bating and fidgeting with her wings. It consists of a narrow strip of fine soft leather, having a slit two or three inches long down the middle. Into this slit is inserted the pinion joint of the hawk's closed wing. The upper end of the brail will then of course extend upwards over her back, and the lower will hang downwards by her side. Now take the upper end and pass it down under the under part of her wing between it and her ribs. Pass the lower end in the contrary direction upwards under the under side of the same wing. The two ends will now be pointing in the opposite direction to that first described. Next bring them together on the outside of the wing, and tie in a plain bow-knot, making the bows very short and passing the single ends through them.

The hawk will be unable to open the wing, which will be to all intents and purposes as useless to her, as long as the brail is on, as if all the flight feathers in it had been cut.

A bath must always be offered to a trained hawk at least twice a week, and oftener in fine and warm weather. And it is not a thing which can always be improvised very easily. The best baths are sunk in the ground, so that there are no upstanding sides round or under which a leash can get entangled. But of course, unless great care is taken, the ground round the edges of such a bath is apt to become slushy and dirty, if much used. Whenever it is impossible to sink the bath in the earth it is necessary that some person should be at hand when the hawks are bathing, so that if the leash gets entangled he may come to the rescue.

Many hawks have a tiresome way of jumping on and off the sides of the bath, and running round it — in fact, as Winchester boys say, "funking on the bank"—in complete oblivion of the fact that they are thereby hitching up their leashes. For such hawks it is best to take off the leash and substitute a creance three or four yards long, attaching the end of this to the block on which they are deposited at the side of the bath. All baths should be of a sufficient size. For gers they should be nearly a foot deep at least, and well over a yard in diameter. For the smallest jack-merlin they should be not less than four inches deep. A hawk will not fully enjoy her bath unless she can wade into it, if she chooses, up to her shoulders and over. In shallow water she is more or less uncomfortable. Like Alexander the Great, in the small world of antiquity, *æstuat infelix angusto in limite*; and her back and the nape of her neck are never properly wetted, however much she may splash about in the endeavour to throw the water over them. The bath should be tilted up, so that it is shallower at one end than the other, and the bather may get in, if she chooses, at the shallow end, and wade out as far as she likes towards the other. According to immemorial custom a few pebbles should be thrown in to lie on the floor of the bath. When the weather is very cold, a cup or two of hot water may be added, to take off the chill; and if the water used is taken from a deep and cool well it should be allowed to stand for some time in the sun before being put out for the hawks. Cemented basins in the ground make, of course, capital bathing-places. But they are troublesome to keep clean, and even to empty; and the surrounding edges are

likely to become small quagmires. Perhaps the most serviceable bath is a common flat bedroom bath, sunk into a cavity
in the ground, and removable at will. A pretty tall block
or for short-winged hawks a bow-perch, should be placed
near the bath, so that the bather, having finished her ablutions
may at once jump on to it.

In some places it is possible to indulge the hawks with a
natural bath. When there is in the neighbourhood a stream
of clean water with a sandy or gravelly bottom and shelving
banks, the hawk may be carried down to a suitable part of
the bank, the block set up, and the creance attached. She
may be left on the block while the falconer retires to a short
distance, and will come back, when bathed, to her post. After
the bath, every hawk should remain out, bareheaded, for about
an hour, in the sun, if possible. She will busy herself first in
spreading her feathers to the sun and wind, and then in
pluming and arranging them—a work exceedingly agreeable
to those hawks which are particular about their own appearance.

The lure will be more particularly referred to later on. It
may suffice to say here that it is a rough imitation of some bird
—or, if the hawk is to be trained to ground-game, of some
beast—used as a bait to which the hawk is taught to come for
food. It is attached to a strong cord or thong a yard or more
long, and sometimes to a swivel. It is the invariable companion of the falconer in the field, though never allowed to be
seen by the hawk, except when she is required to come to it.
The lure should be a sort of magnet, operating to draw the
hawk towards it as surely as iron will attract a magnetised
needle.

A cadge is a most necessary apparatus when a man is the
possessor of more than one hawk. The orthodox and historic
cadge—such as one sees in representations of *As You Like
It* on the stage, or, as once I remember, at a Lord Mayor's
Show—is a circular or square or oblong frame of wood, three
or four feet across, having straps by which it can be suspended
from the shoulders of a man, who in classic phrase is termed a
"cadger," and who stands or walks in the middle, with the
frame surrounding him. At each corner of the frame is a small
jointed leg, which can be hooked up when the cadge is being
carried, and let down when it is to be deposited on the ground.
The bars which form the body of the frame are padded on the
top, and on these stand the hawks, hooded of course, and

fastened by their leashes to the frame. The man with the cadge (whom in these days you will not address by his right title, unless you wish him to give you a month's notice) will, if he is a sharp fellow, so carry the cadge that all or most of the hawks upon it face the wind. On windy days—and at rook-hawking time it is mostly pretty windy — the cadge should be rested as much as possible under the lee of some shelter, generally a rick. All hawks very much detest a wind ; and should not be unnecessarily exposed to it. In fact, trained hawks must be, in this and in all other things, whether at home or in the field, subjected to as little vexation and annoyance as can be. Like other creatures, they have tempers of their own—sometimes very queer ones ; and they have enough to put up with, as it is, when trained, without any extra trials that can fairly be spared them. A cadge is shown in the illustration.

A still greater luxury for the field, especially in rook-hawking, is the hawk-van, which is a sort of omnibus, fitted with screen-perches, and hung on very easy springs. In it are conveyed the hawks which are not for the time being in use, and also spare lures and other furniture and properties, not forgetting the luncheon-basket. Such a vehicle will be too pretentious, as well as too costly, for most private individuals, but it is used successfully by the Old Hawking Club, whose excellent arrangements and methods of training and managing hawks will be repeatedly noticed in these pages.

The box-cadge is a very simple apparatus used for the transport of hawks by train or other wheeled conveyance. It is nothing more than a frame resembling the body of a box—very often a box itself—without the lid. The four upper edges of the sides are padded to form perches. Holes are bored in the sides an inch or two below, through which the leashes can be passed and made fast. In the bottom of the box is sawdust to catch the mutes ; and the hawks are put on, as naturally they would be, facing outwards, with their tails towards the inside of the box. You will be surprised, if you have never seen it tried, how small a box will accommodate six or eight great big hawks sitting in this simple fashion. By the bye, the box-cadge should be heavily weighted, to prevent upsetting or jolting, in case any hawk should unluckily bate off.

The writer of these pages has invented an apparatus which may be called a pole-cadge, and will attempt to describe it, because in his own experience he has found it very useful and

CADGE WITH PEREGRINES

handy, especially for small hawks. It consists of a plain pole
—a broom-handle does very well—over which a single or
double fold of green baize is stretched and fastened. About
nine inches from each end of the perch thus formed, stout
wire is firmly twisted round it, and the ends of the wire are
allowed to project at an angle of about 90, from one another
downwards. When the perch is being carried, it is simply
grasped by the middle in one hand ; and when it is desired
to put it down, the four ends of the wire are rested on the
ground, or pushed into the earth if it is soft enough. The
hawks are, of course, attached by leashes tied round the pole,
as if they were on the screen-perch; and four can be accommodated with the greatest ease on a short stick—one near the
bearer's hand on each side of it, and one near each end of the
pole. A long stick would hold six or eight hawks. There is
no reason that I can see why a stouter pole should not be used
for big hawks. The advantage of this over the ordinary and
time-honoured cadge is that all the hawks, if properly placed,
must necessarily face the wind, and need never stand sideways
to it. The pole-cadge can also be picked up and set down
much more quickly. And for carrying hawks when driving in
a dogcart or riding on a bicycle — a not impossible feat in
these days—this form of cadge is, I think, unsurpassable.

Hawking-gloves, for wearing when a big hawk is on the fist,
are gauntleted half-way to the elbow, and made of buckskin or
very strong leather. They should, of course, be kept clean and
dry. For the smaller hawks a two-button dogskin glove is
strong enough, and preferable. Some hawks, when they are
very sharp-set, or fidgety and in a bad humour, will pick and tear
at the glove or perch in a tiresome way, and even tear it to
pieces after a while. A cure for this is to rub the exposed part
of the glove or perch with onions or a solution of alum, the
taste of which will generally soon disgust the offender with that
bad habit. Very often, however, it is good to provide such
a hawk with a very tough piece of "tiring," such as the
bare pinion of a goose or fowl, upon which to expend her
superfluous energy. Worn gloves should not be patched or
mended, but replaced by fresh ones. A glove which has
once become thoroughly greasy or sodden should be regarded
as spoilt.

Mews, or hawk-houses, are more particularly described in
Chapter XIII. They should be absolutely free from draughts,
and not liable to get too hot in summer or too cold in winter.

The doors should fit well, and be kept locked as a rule ; and the windows should all have well-fitting shutters.   They should be ventilated at the top, and be kept bare of furniture and rubbish of all kinds, and scrupulously clean.   The windows should by preference face towards east and north.   And in hot climates there should be a verandah outside, and double roof above.

CHAPTER IV

Eyesses and Hack Hawks

EYESSES, or young hawks taken from the nest, should not be taken until the latest possible day. If the captor can defer the moment until they are able to fly a little, so much the better. He may then possibly snare them by some means or another. But this is an exceedingly difficult job, as the newly-fledged hawk is for a considerable time fed by her parents, and does not prey for herself. Consequently, she will not come to any live lure or baited trap, and, being very distrustful of men, cannot easily even be approached. Thus it is rarely that even an experienced falconer can lay hands on a wild hawk after it has once left the eyrie. The next best thing to be done is to catch the eyesses when they are branchers, that is to say, when they are able to run and jump about on the branches of a tree, though not yet able to rise on the wing from the ground. In short, the longer they can be left in the natural nursery under the care of their natural guardians, the better they are likely to turn out, not only in their bodily condition, but in temper and disposition. Very often, however, the young birds will come to their trainer when there is a good deal of the white down of their infancy still clothing their unwieldy bodies, and only partially replaced by the brown feathers of their first plumage. At any rate the flight feathers of the wing will not be nearly down to their full length. The outer ones will still have some inches to grow; and those of the tail will be short soft things, with flabby shafts, and not much shape or strength.

It is for many reasons desirable that the trainer should go personally to the place where the eyrie is, and either himself assist in taking the young birds, or at least be ready to receive them within a few hours, and give them their first feed. Unfortunately, most hawk-dealers and many gamekeepers have a rooted objection to this plan, and prefer to muddle about with the hawks themselves, not sending them off to the purchaser until they have already unwittingly done them more or less injury, in one way or another. They either are, or pretend to be, unable to understand or to believe that an eyess delivered immediately into the trainer's hand is worth at least 25 per cent. more to him than one which has been messed about by unskilled hands, and racketed about in a train for several hours. This stupid prejudice of the captors and vendors is often productive of the deplorable blemish called hunger-streaks, which weakens every important feather in the hawk's body, and to some extent checks and stunts her whole bodily growth and energy, just at the time when it is most desirable that they should be steadily maintained and developed. A hunger-streak is caused whenever a young hawk has been allowed to grow unreasonably hungry. The result is that that part of the whole web and shaft of each feather which is growing out of the body at the time is deformed through want of proper nourishment, and bears on it ever afterwards a cross line like a blight, so that the feather looks as if a sharp razor had been passed lightly across it. As the feather grows down this line comes down with it, and may be seen in all its hideousness, after the hawk is summed, if any big feather is examined carefully. A fast of more than fifteen hours—in the daytime—will generally cause a slight hunger-streak ; but the night hours do not count for much ; so that hawks which have to travel far before getting into the trainer's hands should be taken late in the day and started at once, so that they may be met as soon as they arrive on the following day.

If the falconer cannot attend personally at the capture of the eyesses, he should at least send to the captor a suitable hamper in which to pack and send them. This should be roomy and round in shape, having its sides and top lined inside with sacking, matting, or other soft material. In the bottom of it a good thick layer of straw should be lightly strewed, for the hawks to rest upon ; and the lining should fit well enough to exclude almost all light. Even with all these precautions there is some risk of breaking feathers, and still more of bending them and deforming them with dirt. On railways the guards may generally be cajoled into taking special care that the hamper is not turned upside down or banged about. But I have more than once known of valuable hawks arriving dead from a short sea voyage—killed by the evident ill-treatment to which the padded hamper has been subjected on the way.

Once arrived at the trainer's quarters, the hamper should be opened in a darkened room, with doors and windows closed, in which has been got ready another straw-lined hamper, this time of an oblong or square shape. Each hawk in her turn will be gently taken out of the soiled travelling hamper, of which the lid can be shut down between the times of removing the several inmates. Unless these are very young, a rufter-hood can be slipped on the head of each one, and the jesses and bell at once attached to her. If they have come far, a few morsels of food may be given even before the new-comer has been deposited in the second hamper. But, if too young to be able to move about much, they can all be transferred directly to the new quarters, and the lids left open. In every case the operation of feeding should be at once undertaken. And a much more troublesome thing this operation is than the unlearned may suppose. In the first place, there must be in readiness a good store of fresh, tender beef or sheep's heart, cut into small strips and slightly warmed. And of this the new-comers must by some means or other be induced to swallow at least a small quantity. If care has been taken from the very first not to alarm them, they may possibly take the morsels of meat quietly and naturally, when offered to them gently on the end of a small stick. If so, an important point will have been gained. But it is much more likely that at the sight of their new and awful-looking foster-parent—when a subdued light has been let into the room—they will draw back their heads, open their mouths, and hiss indignantly. Still, if the meat is very slowly and quietly obtruded towards the open mouths, there is always a good chance that one of them, bolder than the rest, will strike at it, half in anger, and half with the idea that it may be good to eat. And, if such a youngster should happen at the first shot to catch hold of the piece she aims at, she is quite likely to swallow it, in which case the rest of your task becomes easy. If things do not go quite so smoothly, and a hawk which has seized the meat flips it scorn-fully away, there is no need to give up the attempt. She may do this a dozen times, and at the thirteenth time of ask-ing may swallow the food and begin feeding readily. Or, whilst pupil number one is thus making a fool of the teacher, number two may take heart and come up to the attack, with a more practical result. Even at the expense of much time and patience, it is worth while to get the youngsters to conform from the first, and take their rations willingly and amicably. As soon as one has done this the others will follow suit, some quickly and others grudgingly.   If all such efforts fail, or if the hawks, being nearly grown up, bate and begin to dash about, you must, of course, use rougher measures.   To starve them is worst of all.   There is no harm, if all modes of persuasion fail, in " stuffing " a young hawk.   Let her be held firmly, and as she opens her mouth in defiance at the meat offered, let the falconer push it inside her beak, and then, if she will not swallow it, push it down with the small stick into her throat.   I have known an eyess hobby which had to be " stuffed " with all her meals for eight days !   And afterwards she became a fine hawk and a very strong flier.

When all the hawks have taken a half-crop or so, they should be left in peace in the darkened room for two hours at least. It is a good thing, by the way, to put on each of them different-coloured jesses, so that from the first they may be easily known apart.   Brown, yellow, white, orange, and black are perhaps the best colours—not red, or pink, or green.   Notes may also be made from the first in a hawk-book or falconer's diary.   As, for instance, " June 10—Eyess peregrines arrived ; No. 1 : small falcon ; fed readily, and had nearly a full crop ; seems strong and active ; outer wing feather about half down ; brown jesses and hack bell.   No. 2 : big tiercel or small falcon (uncertain) ; fed with difficulty ; half a crop ; seems timid and rather dull ; black jesses."   Of course, if the hawks are to be turned out as soon as they can fly, no slits will be made in the outer end of the jesses.   Another thing which may very probably have to be done is to clean the hawk's tail-feathers, and possibly the tips of the wings, if soiled during the journey.   This is done with warm water, soap, and an old toothbrush.   If the dirt is allowed to get hard on the feathers it will be almost impossible to get it off without fraying the web.   The feet of each hawk should also be well washed and brushed with soap and warm water ; and it is always as well to do the same with the nares, or else brush them and the beak with a brush dipped in a solution of tobacco. A fresh feed should be given at intervals of not more than five hours between sunrise and sunset, *i.e.* three at least in the day. In fact, young nestlings can hardly be fed too often or too much, when they seem ready to eat.   But the food should not often be as heavy as beef.   Young pigeons, young chickens, bullock's heart, and rabbits may be given to the big hawks ; small birds—fresh-killed always—and sheep's heart to the small ones.   Old pigeons are rather too heating, and old fowls are too tough.   Whenever butcher's meat is given, it should be slightly warmed first, but not dipped in water.   The hawks must be kept quite dry, and in a moderately warm but airy place, away from all draughts. Very young sparrow-hawks must be kept in a specially warm and well-sheltered place, or they are pretty sure to develop a fatal attack of cramp. Whenever it may be necessary to move a young hawk or meddle with her, the room should be made as nearly dark as possible.

After a few feeds, administered quietly and patiently, the young hawks will begin to lose their distrust of their new surroundings ; and first one and then the others will begin to take their meat eagerly, stretching their necks out, and perhaps pushing their way towards the feeder's hand. When this is the case they may be indulged with a few tit-bits on the fist or on the lure. If the lure is used, the pieces of meat should be merely laid upon it, so that at first the hawk may pick them off quite easily ; and by degrees they may be made to walk towards it from their artificial nest along a causeway roughly constructed for that purpose. If it is preferred to get them to feed on the fist, as it probably will in the case of short-winged hawks, they must first be made to pick pieces off the gloved hand. Then hold in the gloved fist, between the outer part of the thumb and the end of the forefinger, a very tender piece of meat or wing of a small bird. As the hawk takes hold of it, and finds that it cannot be taken up without a pull, she will, at once or after a while, give a tug at it, and afterwards probably put out a foot and seize the glove, using her foot as a leverage, just as an oarsman uses his stretcher. A little encouragement will make this easy for her ; and by a little management it can be so arranged that she gets both feet upon the fist. Thus by degrees she will be induced to stand on the back of the hand, and in that position tear up her food. The next step is to raise her slowly up on the fist, while busy at her meal. In like manner, when pulling at the lure, she may be lifted bodily on it, and thence shifted adroitly on to the fist, while the garnished part of the lure is still kept under her.

With a little luck this stage of the young bird's education may have been reached at almost the same time when the feathers are nearly down and they are ready to fly. In such case the sooner they are turned out to hack the better. When they have grown so accustomed to feeding on the lure or on hand that they will run to it as soon as they see it, they may be let loose in the hack field, with a man to watch them, having a lure with him to entice them if they stray away. Most of the popular books dealing with hawking complacently assume that here no difficulty arises. Unfortunately for the beginner, such difficulties will occur, even in the best-regulated establishments. For instance, the hawks may begin to fly the very day after they arrive, and before they will feed willingly. What is to be done in such a case? Well, each hawk must be made to the lure or the fist before she is turned out. She may be brailed and kept in a spare room, with or without her sisters and brothers. Or she may have slits cut in her jesses, and be attached by a leash to a block, for all the world like a trained hawk, and thence enticed by degrees to run to the lure for her food, until she is keen for it. She should at least know what the lure means before being let entirely loose. But it is generally sufficient that one of a lot which came from the same nest should be made to the lure. The rest, when turned out, will find their way, when hungry, after her to the feeding-place. Some special caution should be observed with hobbies. I know of two which would come to the lure in an outhouse, but only reluctantly. They were turned out one morning to hack in a quiet place, and, though they had never flown more than a yard high before, went up into tall fir-trees. And there they remained, staring at the well-garnished lures which were laid out underneath, declining to go down, taking short flights from tree to tree, and cruising about in the air. This state of affairs continued for about three days, after which it was discovered that the two youngsters —who had never been seen to chase anything, far less to kill it—had become wild hawks! Some falconers habitually carry their eyesses, break them to the hood, and partially reclaim them, before turning them out to hack. But the more natural and promising system is never to confine them at all until they are taken up at the end of the period of hack. The youngster, when thus treated, has become, by the time she has to be put in training, as like a wild hawk as a tame one can be. And, as the haggard is better than the red passager, and the passager than the soar-hawk, so by analogy it may be assumed as a rule that the hack hawk which has never been handled is superior to the eyess which has. Sir John Sebright's plan of putting out the young hawks in a hamper hung against a tree-trunk, with the lid of the hamper turned down as a platform by day, and fastened up at night, will answer with orderly, well-behaved hawks. But it will be wise to keep a close watch upon the artificial nest, in case of a hawk jumping off when it can run but cannot fly. It might stray for ever so far, and hide in bushes, or be devoured by a cat or fox.

We suppose now that the eyesses are at hack. Even yet their outer wing feathers will not be fully down; and the sails, even of those which will ultimately be the longest winged, appear rounded at the ends, like those of a sparrow-hawk. But they will very soon learn to fly quite well, with a rather gliding movement, the tips of the feathers bending upwards as they strike the air. They will not go far from the spot where they are turned out. What sort of place should this be that is chosen for the hack ground? That depends upon the facilities which the trainer enjoys for selecting a country. None perhaps is better than a large park, with fir-trees in it, or an open moor with a few stone walls. If the falconer is nervous about turning out a whole nestful at once, he may tether one of the most backward at a block in the middle of the hack field, with a "tiring" to amuse her, and place some garnished lures on the ground near to her, to which the liberated hawks may come when they like. There should also be spare blocks put out in the field, upon which the hack hawks may jump if they like after feeding. Of course, if the weather is very wet, the commencement of hack should be deferred till it is more settled, and the hawks brailed and let loose in an empty room or loft. If they have been "manned" pretty well before they are turned out, and will allow themselves to be taken up when feeding on the lure, they may be taken in under shelter the first night or two. But if it is fairly warm and fine they will be better left out. They will generally at or soon after sunset go up into pretty tall trees to roost. If they stay too long on a block or a gate or post, it is as well to drive or take them off, and see that they are perched up somewhere aloft, out of harm's way. By the bye, hawks, as a rule, should be turned loose in the early part of the day, after a light feed, so that they may be sure to get hungry again by the middle of the day. Jubilee, the best hack hawk I ever had, when he was let loose at 7 a.m., having never before flown two yards, spread his wings, and at the first start flew softly but steadily away across a small river, and, rising easily, took perch 300 yards off on the top branches of an elm 70 feet high. He afterwards flitted about from one high tree to another within a range of 500 yards, and only at midday came down to his sister, who was eating her luncheon at a block in the hack field. He spent that night in a tall elm, not far off, and did not go more than half a mile from the hack field until he was taken up nearly a fortnight later.

If the falconer can hack his own hawks, so much the better. He will learn during the process much about their individual characters and aptitudes. Often he will name them in accordance with their peculiarities or the adventures which each may meet with. It is, however, generally possible for him to get his hawks hacked by some other person, or to purchase fully-hacked hawks after they have been taken up. The worst of it is that unless you know a good deal about the deputy hawk-master, you have no guarantee that the month's hack which they are supposed to have had is real or imaginary.

On the first or second day of hack the falconer should make up his mind whether he will hack his hawks to the lure, to the fist, or to the board. For short-winged hawks the fist or the board is preferable. For gers, peregrines, and hobbies, the board or the lure. For merlins, the lure and the fist, combined in such proportions as seems to be most suitable ; generally more of the lure than of the fist. Each of the systems has its merits, and each its defects.

If the board is chosen, it must be substituted at once for the lure which was used on the first day. It consists of a plank or log of wood, the lower side of which rests on the ground, while to the top side is attached the food for the expected guests. One ration should be provided for each hawk out—at intervals of two feet or so all along the board. It is very important that the meat should be so attached that it cannot be pulled off and carried away, but must be, strictly speaking, consumed on the premises. When the feast consists of rabbits' legs, fowls' wings, or the like, it can be firmly tied by the bone. But, when meat is given, much care and ingenuity is required to make it fast. Perhaps the best plan is to tie the piece tightly by the two opposite corners. If it is possible for a hawk to bolt with a substantial piece, she is quite likely to do so. And, having done so once, she will try to do it again, especially if she happens to be a shy hawk, and afraid of her stronger sisters who are beside her at the board.

It must be confessed that hawks at hack exhibit a good deal of perversity in their dealings with the hack board. Theoretically, each of them ought to come down punctually at meal-time, and take her place at the *al fresco* table, where she can eat up in peace and quiet the portion set out for her, without interference by or with her neighbours. But, as a matter of fact, I regret to say that, instead of adopting this rational and orderly course, hack hawks are often no better behaved than an American traveller at a roadside feeding-place, or a dowager at a ball-supper. As soon as the first comer has settled down to that part of the board to which chance or choice has brought her, the next comer will make straight for the same spot, taking no notice whatever of the dainty morsels with which the rest of the board is bedecked. Thereupon, of course, squabblings and bickerings, and probably a scuffle, in which the weaker or less greedy of the rival gluttons is driven off. Sometimes there will be three hungry young ladies at the same piece, and a sort of battle ensues. Fortunately the quarrel does not end in blows, nor in broken feathers, unless the edges of the board have carelessly been left square and sharp at the upper edges. The disadvantages of the board-school system, as it may be called, are thus considerable. It leads to rivalries and jealousies, and sometimes to free fights, among the school-children. These are not birds which, in the words of Dr. Watts, "in their little nests agree." Moreover, one bad habit at least is very likely to be learnt. It is impossible always to fix on the rations to the board so that they cannot be pulled off until finished. Suppose, now, that a tiercel, having eaten half his ration, finds that the remainder has come loose. And suppose that one of his sisters, having made a joint meal farther down the board with another falcon, happens to want some more. She may turn a covetous eye towards the tiercel's portion. Upon which exit the latter, food in hand, closely followed by his big sister, who gives him a hot time of it, chasing him about the hack field, and probably catching him. Then follows a tooth-and-nail encounter, in which the male, or unworthier sex, as it is with hawks, gets the worst of it. Few things can be more conducive than this to the tiresome vice of carrying. It is for this reason that, in the case of merlins, which are especially addicted to this fault, I do not much believe in the board system. On the other hand, it has its advocates and its advantages. Hawks which are so hacked soon become much wilder than when treated in another way. And wildness, at this period of a hawk's life, is a thing to be desired. Board-school hawks, when taken up, are found to more nearly resemble a wild-caught bird. They seldom or never scream. They have none of the namby-pamby, molly-coddle habits of the fist-fed or lure-fed eyess. They do not hang about round the trainer, or follow him like spaniels. On the contrary, they often will not come down to the board unless he retires to a respectful distance. They are unapproachable by any louts or strollers who may come in sight, and, being shy, take wing very readily, and generally get more flying, and at a better pace.

If the lure system is chosen, the trainer goes to the hack field at feeding-times with as many lures as there are hawks at hack. Each lure must be so heavy that the hawk cannot move it at all, and the food must be attached so that it cannot be pulled off while uneaten. To the first hawk which comes up the first lure will be thrown out; to the second comer another;

and so on till the last is served.   Fighting will occur, no doubt, as it is impossible to prevent two hawks from coming down to one lure.   But, then, the master of the ceremonies is at hand to separate the combatants, and keep each to her own lure, whereas at the board they have to just fight it out.

It is much the same thing with the fist-feeding system.   But this can hardly be attempted with success when many big hawks are at hack together.   As the trainer comes to the hack field, the hack hawks will come up, taking perch on his hand, his head, his shoulder, or wherever they can find a place.   Two or three may generally be accommodated on the left forearm and fist.   From his meat-box or feeding-pouch the trainer will take out with his right hand the prepared mouthfuls of food, and distribute them impartially among the hungry claimants.   But if there is more than one hawk out, it will be found almost necessary, and certainly convenient, to use lures as well.   After a few morsels have been distributed, these lures can be thrown down for all the hawks except one, which may finish her meal on the fist.   One day one hawk may thus be retained, and another day another may take her turn, so that all keep up their habit of feeding freely there.   Sparrow-hawks which are to be hacked on this system may be coped a little before they are turned out, for they have a way of digging in their claws to any soft place. But a goshawk can only be hacked to the fist if she or he is the only one out.   The spectacle of a falconer (or ostringer, to use the correct word) with a goshawk's claws firmly fixed in his head or shoulder would be a rare subject for a serio-comic portrait !

Meal-times for the hack hawks should be pretty punctually observed.   Otherwise the hawks will become irregular in their habits, and the falconer will be compelled rather to dance attendance on them than they on him.   The food may be left out on the board for an hour each time, and then removed, before it has become fly-blown or soaked with rain or frizzled in the sun.   6 to 7 a.m., noon to 1, and 6 to 7 p.m., are very good hours.   And each time when the board is garnished and the food in readiness, the trainer may blow a whistle, or ring a bell, or sound a gong, to give notice from afar.   At each meal there must be " calling over "; and if there is any absentee a mark must be recorded against his or her name.

A bath or two must be set out in the hack field.   From about 9 to 11 a.m. it should be kept pretty full of clean fresh water ; but it should be removed or emptied before noon.   Most hawks are very capricious about bathing ; and hobbies, which want it most, will seldom bathe at all.   The others should be accus-

tomed to bathe early in the day, so that when they are old they
will not depart from this godly habit. Plenty of blocks should
stand around, on which the bathed hawks may stand to sun and
air themselves.

The longer the period of hack can be safely protracted the
better for the hack hawk and her trainer. All the while she is
learning to fly. During the latter part she is also learning to
chase and to stoop. Here it is that the danger comes in.
For in that ardour of youthful chase what kills may come!
At first the random shots made from tall tree-tops at passing
swallows will be wide enough of the mark. Even the young
missel-thrushes or wood-pigeons which have frequented the
hack ground will make light of the clumsy efforts made to
cut them down; and the house-pigeons from the nearest dovecot will treat with supreme contempt the well-meaning but
awkward stoops made at them. But every day finds the
young hawks more expert, as well as stronger on the wing.
The long feathers are now all down. The shafts harden, and
no longer bend perceptibly as the wing-tips strike the air.
Presently the flights at wild birds are no longer mere child's
play. The fugitives have to exert themselves to save their
skins. Very likely the young hunters of the air are not at first
altogether in earnest. Secure of their food at the hack board
or lure or fist, and trusting to it for their subsistence, they are
merely "having a lark" with the intruders on what has begun
to be their domain. But it is increasingly difficult to know how
much of their endeavours is play and how much real business.
Be sure, however, that when any stoop, whether playful or not,
proves successful, and the unfortunate victim is in the pursuer's
clutch, there will be no more play; and on some lonely patch
of ground not fifty miles from the hack field there will be left
a litter of feathers, the mortal remains of the first quarry killed
by hawks of the year.

Let me here quote from my hawk diary: "12 noon; out
to hack field, and follow a blackbird down Butt's orchard hedge.
Nearing the corner, blackbird (young cock) takes across the
orchard. Drop him, winged, as he goes over the front hedge;
and he falls in the hack field. Jubilee [eyess male merlin] is
on a block in the middle of it, 90 yards off. It is his third
day out. As the blackbird falls, he starts, and, stooping at it
as it runs, takes it, kills it, and begins to plume it like a wild
hawk before I get up." Pretty sharp work this for a little
hawk that had never used his wings till the day before yesterday. But this capture of a winged bird was not counted as a

"kill"; and Jubilee was left out for a good eight days more, and might probably have been left a few longer. Hack hawks know no sentimental scruples about taking their prey on the ground. Here is another extract from a hawk diary: "6.30 a.m., out and fed hack hawks on lure. 'She' not visible. At 7 saw her on wire fence, half-way across park. As I got near with lure she started, and, flying low over the ground away from me, turned suddenly, and dropped on some bird in the grass. Was pluming it, when heifers came right up to her. Then lifted, and carried into the lower belt. Quarry looked like a missel-thrush." The same day "She" was taken up. It is a risky thing to leave hawks out after they have once begun serious and successful chasing. Yet it is a thousand pities to take them up too soon, just when they are improving most rapidly. Peregrines may be left out, with heavy hack-bells, for four weeks or occasionally more. Merlins seldom more than three weeks. If the hack place and its neighbourhood are very open, and the wild birds about are few, there is less danger, and less need for hurry. But when the trees and bushes are well stocked with wood-pigeons, thrushes, and small birds, beware.

It is now that the advantage will be seen of putting distinctive jesses on the hawks. The trainer must watch the board carefully. He may not be able to get within 80 yards of it. But from his hiding-place, be it far or near, he must tell over the number of his charges every morning, noon, and evening, so as to see that all have been down. A field-glass may be necessary to identify each visitant. Brown-jess may come down at 6 a.m., take a light breakfast, and be off. White-jess may not appear till 12; and even then no signs of Black-jess. The case begins to look serious. But at 12.50 at last a hawk comes down. Is this the truant? Or is it Brown-jess again, with her luncheon appetite come on? The glass will tell you quickly if the colour of the jesses worn corresponds to the one name or the other. But if both hawks wore the same coloured jesses, you could not say. If the last comer is Black-jess—only delayed till so late by mere want of appetite—she may be left out, perhaps for some days longer. And the extra days' exercise will undoubtedly make her a faster and stronger hawk. But if you cannot tell one hawk from another, it will be impossible for you to know when one has missed two successive meals or not. If Black-jess absents herself all day until the evening repast, the inference is strong that in the morning she killed something for herself. If she keeps away for a whole day, that conclusion becomes almost a certainty. She must be taken up when the first chance occurs. Here, however, arises a fresh difficulty. If it is a tiercel who so absents himself—especially a small tiercel—the presumption that he has killed for himself is pretty well conclusive. But what if it is a falcon? Her brother may have chased and killed; and the sister—a slow hawk who could not catch anything for herself—may have seen the flight, or seen the tiercel pluming his dead quarry, and then come up, and by her superior strength driven him off, and pirated the spoil. You, wrongly inferring that it was she who killed the quarry, will take her up the next day, quite prematurely, and leave the real captor, who is much more worthy of bonds and imprisonment, to remain in dangerous liberty. The same doubt may arise when the absentee is an extra strong and extra greedy bird of either sex. That she or he has breakfasted or dined out is, of course, equally clear. But was it the captive of her own wings and talons that she devoured, or that of a weaker, but cleverer, hawk? These are questions impossible to answer, unless some person has actually seen what occurred. The safest plan, though not the most magnanimous, when such evidence cannot be got, is, when one hawk has clearly been killing, to take the whole lot up.

Hack hawks are as various in their habits at hack as they are at all other times. Some are lazy, some active, some both by fits and starts. One will be playful, and find a childish delight in chasing butterflies or falling leaves. Others, surly and ill-tempered, ready on slight provocation to make vicious stoops at their brethren or sisters. Some will sit for hours sullenly on a post; others will fly long distances for their own amusement, and soar aloft to a good height. These are the most promising. The falconer, if he keeps his eyes open, will have learnt before hack is over pretty well the relative speeds and particular dispositions of his wards. Rarely are these early indications falsified in after-life. But a backward hawk is not necessarily a bad hawk. During quite the last days of hack a hawk which had seemed rather dull and slow will sometimes wake up, and put on pace in an astonishing way, until from being a member of the awkward squad she comes to rival the leaders of the whole school in activity and speed. But a sulky and moping hawk seldom turns out first-rate.

Speed is the great desideratum in a hawk. It is like the "big battalions" in an army; like a good eye to a cricketer. When people complain about bad-tempered hawks, it is often the trainer who is to blame. But in the matter of speed, as shown at hack time, the trainer is hardly, if at all, responsible.

Bad temper is a nuisance, no doubt, and a difficulty.   But want
of speed is worse.   It is incurably destructive of good sport.
And here, speaking of the relative speeds of hawks at hack, I
will ask leave to relate two anecdotes.   Queen, a powerful and
speedy, but not very brilliant flier, went off with a rabbit's head,
pursued by her sister and two brothers.   Winding about along
the side of a long hedge, now one side and now the other, she
evaded all their stoops, and, after reaching the end of the hedge,
where there were some elms and oaks, dodged rapidly in and out
among them, loaded as she was, throwing out all the pursuers,
and finally conveying her booty to a safe corner, where she
discussed it all by herself in peace.

On his eleventh day of hack, Jubilee, the male merlin already
referred to, was sitting with his two sisters and one brother in
the branches of a fallen tree in the hack field, under which I
was seated, garnishing the lures for their delectation a little later
on.   Suddenly the little hawk started at his best pace right
down the field.   I supposed that he was after some blackbird
in the far hedge.   But before reaching it he turned, and began
mounting as he came back towards me.   I looked round, and for
the first time saw that a wild kestrel had come over into the
field, and was dodging the stoops made at him by the remaining merlins.   Now this kestrel was one of a brood which had
been flying at hack under their parents' care in a neighbouring
field.   They were already strong on the wing before the merlins
were turned out ; and I had been rather fearing, when I discovered their near presence, that they might do the young
merlins a bad turn.   No encounter had, however, as yet occurred
between the two families.   The kestrel had at first little difficulty in eluding the stoops of the three merlins, who seemed
not much in earnest.   But when Jubilee came over, at some
height in the air, there was a different tale to tell.   With his first
stoop he made the wild hawk cry out ; at the second he almost
feathered him, and made him shuffle off to the orchard near
at hand, where, swirling round the tree-trunks, he threw out
his assailant, and made off to a tall elm.   Here, no doubt, he
fancied he was safe, especially as the other hawks, on Jubilee's
appearance, tailed off.   But not a bit of it.   Throwing himself
well up above the elm, the little jack dashed down at the enemy
in the tree, dislodged him, and with a back-handed stoop drove
him down to the ground, hunted him all across a meadow,
grazing him at every shot he made, and lost him in a big
orchard farther on.   The pace of the wild hawk was very poor
in comparison with that of this half-tame lure-hacked merlin.

It seemed as if the latter could have given him ten yards in a hundred. In straight-ahead flying, in mounting, and in throwing up, the kestrel was completely outpaced. Yet before now trained merlins, as I have heard tell, have been outflown and chased by a wild kestrel. I should not like, and do not ever expect, to own such a trained merlin.

The day comes—all too soon—when the falconer dares to keep the hack hawks out no longer. The decree goes out for one to be taken up. If this one has been hacked to the fist the proceeding is simple enough. As she stands complacently breakfasting on the fist, the jesses are grasped in the fingers of the left hand. A couple of snips with a sharp pair of strong nail-scissors make a slit in the two jesses. And through these a spring swivel is deftly slipped. Attached to the swivel is a leash, the end of which is wound round the little finger, while the button of it is grasped in the palm of the left hand. As the hawk proceeds with her meal she is taken quietly to a darkened room, where a rufter hood is slipped on her head. Five minutes' carrying, and she is placed on a mound of turf, food and all, while the leash, unwound from the little finger, is fastened to a peg strongly planted in the ground. If the hawk has been hacked to the lure or to the board, the process is a little more complicated, but presents no real difficulty. A bow-net must then be used. This instrument is more fully described in the next chapter. It consists of a hoop of metal on which a light net is stitched. The ends are fixed down; and the hoop is so set that a pull on a long string will bring the rim up and over any object which may be near it on the near side. The object, of course, in this case will be the lure, or the piece of food with which the hack board is garnished. When the hawk is feeding, the string is pulled. The net swings over, encompassing both meat and hawk. Up runs the falconer, to secure the captive, who is made fast, hooded, and taken home.

Even if a hawk has begun to prey for herself, she can still often be captured with a live lure, that is, a live bird attached to a light cord. Once find the hawk, and let the live lure fly, and she is pretty sure to take it. Then she may be snared in one of the ways described in the chapter on Lost Hawks.

A hack hawk, once taken up, is treated in very much the same way as a wild-caught hawk. The process of reclamation begins at once. And this process will be found described at length in the succeeding chapter.

CHAPTER V

PASSAGE HAWKS

A LL big hawks captured after they have begun to prey for themselves are now commonly called passage hawks, although the name, strictly speaking, may not be at all correct. Wild-caught is a more inclusive term; and it is often used in the case of sparrow-hawks, merlins, and hobbies, when casually caught by bird-catchers or gamekeepers, and not killed in the process. We have seen that passage hawk means properly a hawk caught during the period of her first migration southwards. It is, however, of course, possible to capture her either in early autumn before the migration has commenced—in which case a peregrine is more properly called a slight falcon or slight tiercel—or late in the winter, when she has become a lantiner, or in the spring migration, when she is travelling north. But if she has begun to moult before she comes into man's possession, she is correctly described as a haggard. If gamekeepers were a little more alive to their own interests they would often catch sparrow-hawks, and sometimes merlins and peregrines, alive, and dispose of them at a very remunerative price, instead of killing them, often in a most barbarous way, by means of pole-traps and other snares, which destroy or cripple them after hours of torture, and render them almost valueless. But for generations past no systematic attempts have been made in this country to snare wild hawks in an uninjured condition ; and if a falconer should be able to obtain any hawk so taken he may consider himself exceptionally lucky. Several such hawks have indeed been caught in England, and, getting rather accidentally into good hands, have turned out very excellent performers. Occasionally a sparrow-hawk or merlin is saved alive out of the nets of a bird-catcher ; and these, if heard of before their plumage is ruined, are prizes for which many a falconer will gladly give something like their weight in silver.

But, as a rule, the full-grown hawks which come into the market are captives which have been taken on the autumnal passage by the professional hawk-catchers of Valkenswaard, in North Brabant. The sons of Adrian Möllen, formerly falconer to the famous Loo Club, still carry on this business of snaring peregrines on the great open heath, which for many centuries has been resorted to for a like purpose, and which, of course, takes its name from its renown as a place over which the migrants must often pass. Anyone who wants a wild-caught peregrine should write beforehand to one of these gentlemen, who will probably not fail to send him what he requires. They go out every year, in the months of October and November, and lie in wait daily in their cunningly-constructed huts until they have secured as many captives as have been ordered in various places. A dozen or more are annually required for England, and sometimes a few for France. The variety most in demand is the red falcon, that is to say, the female peregrine in the nestling plumage, not yet moulted. But blue falcons are also sometimes wanted, and of late years there has been some considerable demand for tiercels, both red and blue. Merlins, sparrow-hawks, and an occasional goshawk may be taken, and, still more rarely, a ger. The price for a falcon is four to five pounds, and of a tiercel from three to four. But a special apparatus is required for catching the smaller hawks, which will not usually come to the same lure as a peregrine. If the captured hawk has to be kept for any length of time in the captor's hands before being fetched or sent away, an extra charge is made for her maintenance.

The device whereby the wild hawk is caught in Holland is somewhat elaborate. It has more than once been described in print, and may be briefly noticed here. A hut is first built up with sods of turf in an open part of the plain. It looks from outside like a mere knoll or rising in the ground. A nearer inspection shows a small opening in front, through which a man, or at a pinch two men, can crawl. It is fitted with a low seat inside, and at the back, behind and above the seat, is an aperture something like the small port-hole of a cabin, which can be opened by pulling out a sod of turf, and closed by replacing the same. This is to enable the hawk-catcher to spy out at a hawk which is coming up from behind his back. Outside the hut and in front of it is a sort of small altar or table of turf, on the flat top of which is pegged down, by means of a short creance and jesses, a butcher-bird or shrike. Scraps of meat are set out for the delectation of this feathered watchman, who is also indulged with a miniature hut of his own, into which he may retreat when terrified, as it is hoped that he soon may be. The eyesight of this tethered spy is so keen that he can descry his enemy the hawk at an incredible distance in the sky. Whenever one is approaching, though far out of range of the sharpest human eye, he begins to exhibit signs of alarm. As the hawk comes nearer he fidgets more and more, glancing nervously—or pointing, as they call it—in the direction of the foe. If the latter still comes nearer, he will cry out in his terror, and finally run cowering under the shelter of his hut.

Meanwhile the falconer has not been idle. Snatching the turf shutter from the little window behind him, he takes a look through his field-glass in the direction to which the shrike is pointing, searching for the coming hawk as an astronomer does for a lost star. If, on espying it, he judges that it is a peregrine, he sets to work seriously about the main business of the day.

At some distance from the hut is fixed up a pole with a line—we will call it A—running from the top of it to the hut. To this line, at some yards distance from the pole, is attached a branch line, after the manner of the paternoster used in angling, at the end of which is a live pigeon in jesses. When the line A is slack, the pigeon rests on the ground, or in a hut to which he is at liberty to resort when he likes. But if, by a pull in the falconer's hut, the line A is pulled taut, up goes the pigeon in the air, and flutters about at the end of his branch line, conspicuous from afar. Often there is a second pole at a like distance from the big hut, but in a rather different direction ; and to this a second line, B, is attached, with a tame tiercel or peregrine of some sort, rigged out in the same way as the pole-pigeon. This hawk may have a handful of straw or worsted fastened to one of his feet, so that he may look as if he had some dead quarry in possession, and serve the better to attract the wild passager. As the shrike points, and the wild hawk is coming up, the falconer works with a will by the two strings A and B at the pole-hawk and the pole-pigeon. But as soon as the passager is nearly overhead, and the shrike has hidden himself, it is time to let loose the pole strings and let the very live lures attached to it also bolt into shelter.

We now come to another component part of the Dutch hawk-trap. A third line, C, leads from the hut to a small ring-peg in the ground sixty or eighty yards away, passes through it, and a few feet farther on, but at the side, is attached to a live pigeon in a box, out of which it can be pulled by drawing the line. One more particular, and the whole apparatus is complete. On each side of the ring-peg, and about two feet from it, are pegs which hold down the hinges of a bow-net, something like that which was used for catching up the hack hawks. The usual and best way of making a bow-net is to take two equal lengths of strong wire, five or six feet long, and bend each into a nearly semicircular arch. The two ends of each hoop are twisted up into a ring, and the two hoops are joined together so that a sort of easy hinge is formed at the ends. A net of fine but strong string is stretched over the whole circle formed by the two hoops. When it is set, one-half of it is pegged down flat on the ground and the other is folded back over it. To the middle of the upper hoop is attached a fourth long line, D, by which it can be pulled over, so that when the line is taut the hoops form a circle, with the net covering all the space between the hinges. This will explain how the falconer, ensconced in his hut, can, by a pull at the long line D, passing through a ground peg to the arch of the bow-net, pull it over the ring through which the line C passes. Thus there are four lines of which the ends lie in the floor of the hut, each marked with a different colour, and each requiring to be worked with prompt and accurate skill at the eventful moment.

We can now understand the whole process of entrapping the passage hawk, and shall find that it includes the following movements :—(1) Pointing of the shrike ; (2) removal of the turf shutter, and observation of the coming hawk through the field-glass ; (3) pulling of the lines A and B, by which the pole-pigeon and the pole-hawk are made to flutter or fly about and show themselves ; (4) slackening of these lines and escape of the pole-pigeon, pole-hawk, and shrike, under their respective places of shelter. By this time the wild hawk ought to be close at hand, and eagerly looking out for the pigeon which has so mysteriously disappeared. Then (5) tightening of the line C, by which the hitherto unseen pigeon is pulled out of his box, and displayed to the expectant hawk above ; (6) capture of this pigeon by the hawk. Next (7) a much stronger and steadier pull is given to the line C, by which the far end of it is dragged —pigeon, hawk, and all—towards the ring between the horns of the bow-net. As soon as the pigeon, with the hawk upon it, has got to this ring, a piece of tape or ribbon fastened on to a particular place on the line C will have been pulled to a certain place within the hut, and will warn the falconer that he need pull it no farther, as all things are now ready for the next and most critical move. Then, holding the line C still tight in one hand, the operator (8) will, with a quick well-sustained effort, tighten the line D, and pull the net over hawk and pigeon. All that remains now for the falconer to do is (9) to make fast the end of the line D round a peg fixed in the hut for that purpose, and then (10) to run out, with his best leg foremost, and take the captive out of the net.

The reader may think this rather a needlessly elaborate and complicated device ; but it is a very sure one, when the operator does not bungle. It has stood the test of many centuries, and is as good now as it was in the days of Alfred the Great. There is no doubt that by means of such an apparatus—slightly simplified, perhaps—wild peregrines might be taken on the Wiltshire and Berkshire downs. Lord Lilford once had a hut or huts out in England with some success. A similar apparatus, with a less elaborate hiding-place, would enable keepers or shepherds to catch many a sparrow-hawk and some merlins. For the former there is almost always a good demand. So far is it from being true, as many books assert, that "sparrow-hawks are easy to procure," there are always half a dozen falconers in England who are vainly wishing that they could lay hands on one.

To extract a wild hawk of any kind, but especially a ger, peregrine, or goshawk, from the bow-net is sometimes no laughing matter. To set about it with thickly-gloved hands involves much awkwardness, and is not unlikely, in the case of an inexperienced man, to end in the loss of the hawk. There is also the danger of breaking feathers, or even a bone in the wing or leg. On the other hand, to go to work with even one hand ungloved exposes you, unless you are adroit beyond the average of human beings, to some particularly painful punctures and gashes. There are eight talons or claws, each as sharp as a needle, awaiting your attack, and it will not be the hawk's fault if she does not maul you with them. As, for the beak, it is well-nigh sharp and strong enough to nip a piece clean out of the back of your hand. Yet the prisoner must be got out somehow, and moreover must be held quiet while a pair of jesses and a hood or sock are put on. A sock is an article of unpretentious but sterling value to the hawk-catcher. Sometimes it is not a real sock, but a strait-waistcoat of more artificial kind made to serve as an improved imitation of the homely article of clothing originally used by the old falconers. But the common and unimproved sock is quite good enough for the hawk-catcher's purpose. It is turned inside out, in the way familiar to washerwomen, so that at the heel there is an open end, while the toe and top of the sock form the other end.

Into that open heel is pushed the head of the captured hawk. The sock itself is then drawn bodily on to and over the hawk's shoulders. The beak, being hooked downwards, will not interfere with the operation. The soft covering is pulled down right over the back, chest, and thighs of the victim, until nothing but the tail and the tips of the wings protrude. If it fits tolerably, the hawk will be effectually strait-waistcoated, and may be laid down on its back like an overturned turtle. A man's sock, big or little, fits a falcon or tiercel fairly ; and a boy's or child's sock may be used for the smaller hawks. Before the sock is used a couple of tapes may be sewn across it, one three or four inches from the toe, and another five or six inches farther back, so that when it is on the ends of one tape may be tied—not tightly, of course—round the throat of the captive hawk just in front of the shoulders, and the ends of the other tape round the back, just above the tail. The toe of the sock may then be cut off, so that the hawk's head is left free.

The first captive, once reduced to quiescence for the time being, will be laid out on the floor of the hut or near it, while the falconer returns to his watch-place. For there is no reason why he should not effect another, or even more captures, in the same day. Climatic influences or mere chance may have ordained that for a week or more he should have had no chance, and yet now the hawks should come fast and furiously to the decoy. Long-winged hawks, unlike woodcocks and many other migratory birds, travel with the wind in their faces ; and they by no means hurry on their way, pausing, sometimes for some days at a time, at any place where quarry is abundant, where the bathing is good, and where, perhaps, there are other attractions which we dull, earth-treading mortals cannot understand or appreciate. As night comes on, the captives are carried home in their socks, and a rufter hood is put on, after which the socks are cut off, and they are set down on a hillock of soft turf, or, if they show no signs of violent uneasiness, on the screen-perch, the leash having, of course, in either case been attached and made fast. From this moment the person for whom the hawk is intended should by rights assume the ownership and charge of her. It would be absurd to suppose that the hawk-catcher, however good a falconer he may be, should act as trainer too, when he has to go out on the morrow, and perhaps for many days afterwards, to entrap other hawks.

Before bedtime, in the long evening of late autumn, a grand attempt should be made to induce the newly-caught hawk to eat. If she was caught early in the day, and had not already breakfasted, it is possible that the attempt may succeed, especially if she is of a placid and philosophic turn of mind. But do not think that success will, even then, be easily achieved. You may very likely have to wait a long time. Different men, of course, have different methods of persuading a newly-caught hawk to feed ; but all agree that it is a very difficult job. Many of the books advise the drawing of meat across her feet as she stands on the fist, and repeating this until she begins to pick at it. Perhaps I have never sufficiently tested this plan. I do not think I can honestly say that I have ever drawn the seductive morsel of meat more than a hundred times successively over the feet of the unwilling feeder. But I must confess that the process, even when protracted to this moderate length, is a little tedious. For my own part I have found that, if she is touched lightly on the shoulder with a finger of the right hand, she will generally strike out with open beak in the direction of the offending finger—not, of course, with any idea of eating any-thing, or even any very defined intention of biting her assailant, but in a mere spirit of anger and defiance. If, then, between the moment of touching her and that when the blow with the beak is struck you can substitute in the place of the finger a juicy slice of raw beef, there is quite a good chance that she will seize it. At the first trial she will not swallow it. Probably she will bate off and make a scene. Nevertheless, a certain taste of very delectable food will linger in her mouth, and when peace is restored she will take note of this. At the second trial she may possibly retain the meat a little longer, and make less ado. By and by a small scrap of it may be torn off before she gets rid of it ; and this, if it is at all sticky, and cannot be flipped off with a shake of the head, will be swallowed. Now, if everything is done very gently and quietly, there is a chance that she may strike out again with some real notion that there is food to strike at. Directly she takes the meat and gives anything like a pull at it, let a morsel come off. If the meat is really quite soft it will be quite easy to manage this. By degrees she will, if hungry, begin to take more kindly to the lesson. As often as you can get a small morsel seized by her, however unwittingly, she will, if only to get rid of it, pull it with her tongue down the natural lane where it is intended to go. And at length she will voluntarily pull through the hood the viands which are so very ready at her service.

Let her then take as much as ever she will. It is not likely to be very much. Keep her either on your own fist or on the fist of some assistant all through the first night, without allowing her to sleep a wink. And until she has fed keep on at times tempting her to do so. Wild-caught hawks may quite well be kept nearly twenty-four hours without food. Eagles may be kept even for two or three days without much injury; and goshawks for a day and a half. But twenty-four hours is too long for a very small hawk, which must have been already hungry when she came to the decoy. And if you can feed any hawk soon after her capture, so much the better. Anything like starvation is now completely tabooed by falconers pretending to any knowledge of their art. To reduce a hawk while in process of reclamation is no more than you will be obliged to do. For it is hopeless to expect to keep a passager, or indeed any trained hawk, in quite such high condition as a wild hawk keeps herself. But a thin hawk is a disgrace to the trainer. If you cannot reclaim your hawk without submitting her to such hunger as will make her weak and poor, you had better abandon falconry and try some less difficult form of sport.

Possibly before your hawk will feed, and while you are carrying her, you will find that she wants to cast. With her last meal eaten in freedom, she is pretty sure to have swallowed some castings. Ten to one she has thrown these up before she came to your decoy pigeon. But it is possible she may not. Moreover, if the first hood she wears is an easy one, well cut away at the beak opening, she may cast through the hood. But if she is seen making efforts to cast, and is prevented by the hood from doing so, take her into a nearly dark room or passage. Remove the hood with the fingers and teeth, and, when she has thrown up her casting, slip it on again. Otherwise she may possibly choke herself in the vain attempt to cast. Of course you will not dream of allowing her, for days to come, to eat anything anywhere except on the fist.

If a wild-caught hawk is so rampageous from the first that she will not stand on the fist at all without jumping off, she must be left on the turf mound, but by no means be allowed to go to sleep. An attendant must be at hand who will effectually prevent this by touching her whenever she seems to be dozing off. A few hours of this stirring-up will make her ready enough to keep quiet on the fist when she has a chance. And a few hours more will make her willing enough to stand still there, even when the fist is moved unsteadily about.

We will suppose now that the passager has at last fed moderately but unstintingly through the hood upon the fist; that she can be carried about on it without much risk of bating off; and that she has had no sleep since she was brought in. She may now be stroked gently with an uncut pencil or short stick, first on the back, then on the breast and legs. Some writers advise doing this with a feather ; but the stick is far preferable. The time has now arrived for releasing her for a while from the hood. But before this is done, she must be taken into a room which is nearly dark, so that on the removal of the hood she can hardly see her way about. The time chosen should also be when she is sharp-set; and a tempting piece of food should be under her feet at the time. As she pulls at it, more light may be let in; and possibly she will keep at her meal quietly until it is nearly or quite broad daylight in the place. But most falconers first unhood their hawks by candlelight. Then one candle may be first lighted at one end of a long room, when hawk and man are at the other. If all goes well, a second may be lighted, and then the man, keeping a sharp eye on his hawk, may walk slowly towards them into the fuller light. Thus by degrees, taking care not to proceed too fast, or ever alarm the pupil, she may be made tame enough to feed bareheaded even in the open air.

The old falconers used to "seel" their wild-caught hawks, stitching up the eyelids so as to make them blind ; and anyone who is neat-handed enough to be able to seel a hawk without causing her any pain or injury may find it a good plan now to adopt this system. Then, suppose there are four stitches in each eyelid, on the first day of unseeling the pair nearest the beak may be removed, and one more pair on each succeeding day, till the whole eye is free. But seeling, as a matter of fact, has now gone quite out of fashion in this country. Many modern amateurs also seem to disbelieve in the expediency of waking wild-caught hawks, *i.e.* preventing them from sleeping. And true it is that this expedient is not absolutely necessary. But one may safely say that a hawk which is waked well directly after it is captured will be reclaimed three or four times as soon and as easily as one which is not.

I have spoken of slipping the hood on and off a hawk as if it were a thing that the falconer, whether experienced or not, could accomplish without bungling. But it must not be inferred that the operation is easy. Probably it is the part of a falconer's first duties which is more difficult than any other. Even amongst expert falconers it is not altogether common to find a really good hooder. The knack of hooding is only to be acquired, like other fine arts, by long and assiduous practice. For this reason, if for no other, every beginner should try his 'prentice hand on a kestrel before he aspires to a peregrine or merlin. If he can by any means make acquaintance with a graduate in the art of falconry who is known to hood well, let him observe minutely his method and manner, and after each lesson practise on the *corpus vile* of the " knave's hawk " to acquire the same facility which he has seen his senior to possess. Example in this case is more valuable than precept. But do not, by any mistake, become a pupil of a bad hooder! In the hands of a bungler no hawk can well be good-tempered, whereas in the hands of a first-rate master she will stand to the hood as if she rather liked it. When Adrian Möllen was with the Loo Club in Holland one of the king's brothers came to him for a fortnight, for an hour every day, simply and solely to learn how to hood. There are various manners of putting the hood on. Some hold the base of the plume between the right forefinger and thumb, and, passing it slowly up the breast of the hawk, pop it on quickly over the beak, and with a tap on the forehead push it back into its place. Others hold the hood by the plume between the fore edge of the palm and the inside of the base of the thumb, and, presenting the palm of the hand right in front of the hawk's face, push it forwards, and cause the beak to pass through the opening, raising the wrist afterwards so as to force the back of the hood down on to the nape. In any case there must be an appearance of quiet deliberation about the movements made, combined with a certain amount of actual quickness.

The hood used in learning to hood should be an easy one, very much cut away at the beak opening. And the hawk herself must be first so far manned that she will allow the intending hooder to pass his hand over the crown of her head, and to stroke her on the back without making any objection, or exhibiting any uneasiness. She should be accustomed to the sight of the hood, and have often been allowed to pick nice little morsels of meat from the outside of it. Then she may be allowed to pick a clean piece or two from the inside of it ; and from the beak opening, under which, as the hood lies upside-down in your hand, you hold the seductive morsel. If a hawk is so treated as to become the least *afraid* of the hood, it will be a work of dire difficulty, and almost impossibility in awkward hands, to break her to it, or cure her of the vice. And hawks are sometimes to be seen so mismanaged by their owners that they get into a " state of mind " at the mere sight of the obnoxious head-dress. A hood-shy hawk is not only a nuisance, but a discredit to her trainer.

When the hawk has once gone so far as to dip her beak

into the hood in search of a scrap of food, it requires no great dexterity to slip it over her head.   While doing so the knuckles of the left hand should be turned slightly outwards, so that the hawk's head is naturally projected forwards towards the hood, and cannot easily be drawn back ; whereas as soon as the hood is on the same knuckles should be turned a little inwards so that the head is held up.   The braces can then be seized, one in the right finger and thumb, and the other by the teeth, and pulled tight, before the wearer can jerk or shake it off. Merlins are of all hawks the most difficult to hood, owing to their extreme vivacity and the quickness with which they discern and anticipate any movement of the trainer.   But then their amenability to kind treatment is also so great that they can be handled, like a horse or dog, without offence, if a little patience is exhibited.   And, once well broken to the hood, they will stand to it as well as peregrines or goshawks.   Gers have a reputation for often being hood-shy ; but perhaps the proper treatment of them, in this as in other respects, is now imperfectly understood.

The early steps in the process of reclaiming passagers were so well described four centuries ago by Turbervile that I cannot do better than quote, on this subject, his exact words.   After giving instructions for seeling the captive, and putting on of bells, jesses, and swivel, he continues : " Being thus furnished you shall go about to man her, handling her often gently, and both to avoide the sharpnes of her beake as also the better rebuke her from biting and nipping, you shall have a straight smoothe sticke, as bigge as your finger, and halfe a foot long or more, with the which you shal gently stroke your hawk about the pinions of her wings and downwards athwart all her train. And if she chance to knap or byte at the sticke let her bite hardly, for that will rebuke her thereof, whereas your hand being twitched away fearfully would make her proceed the more eagerly.   To man her well you must watch all the night and keepe her on your fist, and you must teach her to feed seeled ; and having a great and easie rufter hood, you must hood and unhood her oftentimes, seeled as she is [here we see the advantage of seeling], handling her gently about the head, and coying her alwayes when you unhood her, to the end she take no disdayne or displeasure against her keeper.   And also to make her plume and tyre sometimes upon a wing, and keepe her so on the first day and night without perching of her, untill she be wearie, and suffer you to hoode her gently and stirre not ; and correct her of her ramage toyes, especially of snapping and biting, stroking her evermore as before said with your sticke. But if it happen (as it doth sometimes) that your chance be to have a Falcon so ramage and shewde-mettled, that she will not leave her snapping and biting, then take a dose of Garlicke cleane pilled, or a little aloes cicatrina, and when she byteth or snappeth at your hand or stick, offer her the Garlicke or aloes, and let her bite it, for either the strong sent of the Garlicke or the bitter taste of the aloes will quickly make her leave off.

"And here I thinke good to expresse mine opinion, that hee which taketh in hand to be a Falconer, ought first to be very patient and therwithall to take singular delight in a Hawke, so that hee may seeme to bee in love (as it were naturally) with his Hawke. For hee which taketh not that delight, but doth rather exercise it for a pompe and a boast, in mine opinion, shall seldome prove a perfect Falconer, but a mar-hawke, and shall beare the bagge after a right Falconer.

"When your Hawke, being so seeled, doth feede well, and will abide the Hoode, and to be handled without striking or biting at your hand, then in an evening by candle light you shall unseele her, and when you have hooded her take her on your fist, and holde her so all night untill day appeare againe, doing off her Hoode oftentimes, and handling her gently with your hand, stroking her softly about the wings and the body, hooding and unhooding of her and giving her sometimes to feede, a morsell or twain, or sometimes tyring or plumage. But above all things you must watch her on the fist so many nights together without setting her downe on any pearch, that shee may be wearie and suffer you to hoode and handle her gently without any manner of resistance, and untill shee have alto-gether left and forgotten her striking and byting at your hand; but some hawkes will be long before they leave that fault, as the more coy or ramage that they be, the longer they will retain all those ill tatches, and will not peradventure be wonne from them in three, foure, or five dayes. When she is well reclaymed from it then may you let her sit upon a pearch to rest her. But every night you shall doe well to keepe her on the fist three or foure houres, handling her gently and stroking her gently and causing her to tyre or to plume, alwayes making much of her, and hooding and unhooding her oftentimes, as before said. And the like you may doe also by daylight but in a chamber apart where she may see no great light, untill she feed surely and eagerly without dread.

"If your Hawke be thus in foure or five dayes manned so that she begin to feede eagerly and boldly, then you shal first begin to make her know your whistle or the chirping of your mouth, and afterwards your voice." And he goes on to advise the giving of a live pullet in a place where there is just enough light for the hawk to see it, and then to "chyrpe with your voyce and use those other sounds which Falconers do to their hawks"; and recommends for the ordinary feeding of the haggard falcon, while being reclaimed, "pullets not very old, and calves' hearts, weathers' hearts, and hogs' hearts," and, if she is not eager for her food, to wash the meat either in cold water or wine, and occasionally to give her, fasting, "as much sugar candy as the quantity of a small nut."

The duration of the process of manning varies greatly, according to the breed and individual character of the pupil. Wild-caught merlins can be reclaimed by a skilled man in a few days, whereas if you can reclaim a haggard peregrine in less than a month you will have something to boast of. Short-winged hawks, if not well waked at the first, generally require a long time, although this is not invariably the case. Every falconer is familiar with the story of Sir John Sebright's historic sparrow-hawk, which killed a wild partridge on the tenth day after it was caught. But some few sparrow-hawks are as good-tempered, if skilfully treated, as others are rebellious and obstreperous. Waking will enable the most unamiable pupil to be manned in much less than half the time which would be otherwise required. A judicious use of the hood is also essential. While the hawk is still feeding freely, unhooded, and with a good appetite, she should be hooded up before she begins to be at all satiated. For "bating on a full crop" is to be particularly avoided at all times. The remaining part of the meal can be pulled through the hood. When a hawk eats readily on the fist indoors, she is not yet more than half reclaimed unless she will do the same in the open air. There is a vast difference between the one thing and the other. First take her out a little way in the twilight, or in an ill-lighted place at night, with food in her foot, on the fist. Then in the same place when there are men about. By degrees she will begin to think it natural enough to feed on the hand; and a tiring, tougher and tougher every day, may be substituted for the succulent viands by which her attention at first had to be kept up. Beware at the first, however, of carrying a hawk bareheaded, unless she has something to amuse herself withal. The chances are that you may rather make her more wild than more tame, if she feels that nothing but the jesses and leash confine her to her new perch.

Throughout this period and during all the early stages of

training, the grand secret of discipline is carrying. It would perhaps be difficult to say why the mere transporting of a hawk, hooded or unhooded, upon the glove from place to place should have so great an effect; but the experience of centuries has shown that it does, and this ought to be enough for the beginner. When he has carried hawks for some hundreds of hours, he will acknowledge the truth of the old theory; then possibly he will be able to explain it to others or to himself. In the meantime he will do well to take it on trust, and adopt the practice without question. If, as he walks about or rides or sits—for the ambulatory part of the process is not compulsory—he is amongst other people, it will be all the better. The sound of the human voice, naturally and instinctively trying to all wild creatures, will by familiarity with it become less alarming. And with the diminution of the uneasiness originally caused by the voice will come a lessening of the distrust felt for the man who owns the voice. It is almost needless to say that the falconer's voice, especially at times when the hawk is unhooded and in sight, should be soft and soothing in tone. We modern trainers do not use the voice much, as the old falconers did, in educating and directing our pupils. And therein, probably, we make a great mistake. But, however incredulous anyone may be as to the charms of the "falconer's voice" for which Juliet so prettily sighed, it is at least natural to suppose that the harsh tones of an angry or peevish man must give any intelligent animal a bad notion of his character, and, by analogy, of that of the whole human race.

The actions of the trainer should, like the voice, be gentle and conciliatory. In fact his whole behaviour, when in his pupil's presence, must be, as Turbervile recommends, friendly, lovable, and free from offence. "Sit procul omne nefas: ut ameris, amabilis esto!" And the hawk should not only like the trainer, but also respect him for his equanimity and self-control. Do you not want to convince your disciple that you are wiser as well as stronger than she? and yet that you are ready to pay respect to her own pride, and even some of her prejudices? "Maxima debetur *falconi* reverentia"; and if you exhibit petulance and ill-temper yourself, how can you expect that she will be amiable in return? Rough and sudden movements must never be made in the near neighbourhood of an unhooded hawk. Nay, they must be very watchfully guarded against, or they are nearly sure to be involuntarily made. Has a gnat got into your eye, as you are walking about with an unhooded hawk? Your natural impulse is to raise the right hand quickly to brush it away. But that abrupt movement, so natural and almost instinctive on your part, is not at all expected by the hawk, as she stands close by. A catching of the breath and a half-spreading of the wings, if nothing worse, will very likely show you that you have made a mistake; and, if the hawk is a shy one, you will be lucky if the little incident, trifling as it may appear, does not lead to a bout of bating and a feeling of resentment and suspicion for the future. When walking along with an unhooded, half-broken hawk, be on the lookout for everything that may by any chance cause alarm. Women are more to be dreaded than men; children more than women. Dogs are the worst of all, especially if they bark and rush about. Steer clear of them all at first; and in passing them keep them always on your right hand, so that they are never behind the hawk's back. Getting over a gate or stile, be careful how you step down. The sinking of the left hand always annoys the hawk standing upon it. Very naturally; for she feels that her perch is, as it were, dropping away from under her. Do all descents, therefore, even down an easy flight of steps, with as few jerks as possible. When riding or driving with a hawk on the fist, accommodate the whole left arm to the movement of the horse or the vehicle. A skilled falconer will hold his hand almost still while his whole body is being jogged about in a jolting dogcart or wobbling railway carriage. Just as you may sometimes see a hawk with her eye fixed steadily on some spot, and her head in the same place, like a fixed star, while her whole body is moved up or down by an independent action. Beware also of getting near any obstacle against which your hawk may by any sudden movement strike the tip of a wing. In passing through a gate or door, for instance, or under a small archway, give the gate-posts and walls a wide berth. Never wear a hard-brimmed hat yourself, nor go near any person who has a stiff hat or anything stiff about his clothing. In short, never risk the accidental breakage of a feather.

Carrying is therefore not quite such a simple matter as it at first appears to be. But it must be persevered in without any intermission until the hawk is thoroughly manned. For, all the time the hawk sits contentedly on the fist, she is learning a lesson that must eventually be taught her. Hawks are amongst the creatures most easily taught. They learn any lesson skilfully and diligently taught them with an ease that often astonishes the trainer himself; and, having once learnt it, they are in no hurry to forget. The artificial habit, once grafted on their nature, becomes almost a component part of it. But, as they learn quickly to do well, so they also learn quickly how to do otherwise. If you do not make a friend of your pupil, she will soon begin to regard you as an enemy. And then farewell to any hope of making a good servant of her.

"Manning" includes, of course, habituating her to the company not only of men, but also of dogs, horses, and all other animals and things which she is at all likely to meet with in her artificial existence of the future. She must be gradually introduced into society; and, like a young lady of fashion, her début will probably be made at nighttime. Streets more or less frequented may be visited with advantage by gaslight, or under the rather weird rays of the electric light. The extent of the publicity courted must be graduated according to the progress made by the débutante. If the main street is found too noisy or exciting, walk away down the side street. If that is too monotonous, stroll into an inn-yard or a billiard-room. When my lady shows signs of shying at an approaching object, sheer off a little, and create a diversion of some kind, perhaps by giving a pull at the meat under her foot, or by stroking her gently on the breast with the forefinger or a stick. If she strikes at the finger, do not snatch it away, but let her see that no harm is meant. You may even tell her so in a reassuring voice. She will partly understand. Then, when she can be taken without trouble through a pretty well-filled street, or amongst a group of people, she may be brought out by daylight. She may be carried through the stables and across a courtyard in which dogs are chained up. Then past a group of stable-boys, and along the side of a kennel. Meal-times are the best for all these early lessons, which must be advanced by easy stages. First the under-falconer will stand by, perhaps with another hawk, as the pupil takes her dinner. Next day he may be accompanied by a horse or a hound—of undemonstrative and unemotional temperament. On the third day a group of children may be playing at a short distance. Then the tutor himself may be mounted when he takes off my lady's hood and produces the day's ration. At each sign of real alarm the irritant object should be eliminated. If the stable is found too trying, step aside into the harness-room. If the children make too much noise, or begin to stare too impudently at the scornful beauty, get away to a safer distance. Tempt her forbearance as far as you safely dare, but not an inch farther. *Festina lente* is a capital maxim for the impatient trainer.

Should a half-trained passage hawk ever be pegged out at

the block? Many falconers will answer Yes. But I am of a
different persuasion. A man who is over-hawked, or has too
few assistants, may think it almost a necessity to weather his
hawk at the block. But even in such a case I would advise to
weather her in her hood. The proper way, however, to weather
a hawk, when she is in course of being manned, is surely on the
fist. If a man has so many hawks and so few falconers that he
cannot spare one of the latter to carry each of the hawks for
some hours every day, he is going about his business in an
unbusiness-like way. What good can a passage hawk possibly
get from standing as a prisoner on a block of wood, tempted
continually to jump off, and jerked back as often as she does so
by a rude pull on to a damp plot of grass? The fashion now
so prevalent of pegging hawks out on the lawn by themselves
seems to me, if the truth is to be told, to have originated in the
laziness of the falconer or his subordinates. It is manifestly
much easier and simpler to tie a hawk to a block, than to roam
about with her on the fist. But is it equally beneficial? Is
it even advisable at all? It is argued that a hawk, while so
pegged out, is breathing the fresh air and getting manned, if
there are, as there should be, people passing to and fro before
her eyes. But, on the other hand, she is all the time plagued
by a feeling of discomfort and discontent, which cannot be good
for her. Her position is not natural to her. It is not the one she
would choose of her own accord. Every bird which flits across
within her field of view, every cloud which passes over head,
almost every breeze which whispers in the tree-tops, suggests to
her a longing to take flight. A dozen places invite her to leave
her humble perch and go to them and obtain a better view.
Four out of every five wild-caught hawks, unless their spirit has
been half broken by fasting or persecution, will be found to
bate off constantly when pegged out. And bating off cannot
do them any good. It must remind them painfully that they
are now captives and slaves. Moreover, it is impossible to
properly arrange their surroundings. Either there will be too
many or too few people about. And whoever there is about,
whether man, child, or dog, will either be too near or too far
away. The background will not arrange itself with a due regard
to the happy medium between distant reserve and vulgar familiarity. On the whole, there are very few passage hawks that
I should like to peg out bareheaded before they have arrived
at a much later stage of their education than we have yet
reached.

FALCON AND TIERCEL WEATHERING

CHAPTER VI

Training and Entering

WE have traced the history of the wild-caught hawk from the moment of her misadventure in the bow-net to that in which having been introduced under good auspices to the society of her new friends she has learnt at least to tolerate their presence, if not to rejoice in it. She can be taken amongst men, women, and children, dogs, horses, and carriages, without feeling uneasy. She has, in fact, now been manned. When we took leave of our eyesses they had not yet arrived at this stage. They were only just taken up from hack. But the manning of the eyess is accomplished in no different way from that of the passager, except that the more vigorous parts of the discipline may be omitted or modified. Waking is not necessary for eyess merlins, hobbies, or kestrels. It may often be dispensed with altogether with eyess peregrines, even after a prolonged hack. Carrying and handling are with them, as with their wilder brethren, the simple but laborious methods whereby they are tamed. But manning is only the first step in the reclamation of a hawk. She must be made also to come to the fist, at least to a certain extent. If, indeed, she is a short-winged hawk, this lesson of coming to the fist may be considered the principal part of her training. But all hawks should be taught and accustomed to jump a short distance on to the fist, whenever it is held out invitingly towards them. Nor is there any great difficulty about this, if a right beginning is made. As the falconer stands with his hawk bareheaded on the glove, he should get her first to reach forward with her head when he offers a morsel of food on the end of his short stick. Then by degrees he may induce her to step an inch or two sideways towards his wrist for the same purpose. Next, to walk a little way along the screen-perch. And, when she will do this, he may set her down on the perch, and, touching it with the open fingers of the gloved left hand, invite her to step on to them and to the knuckles. The next short step is to get her to jump from the perch to the hand. When once she will do this, even if the jump is one of an inch only, the distance can soon be made much greater. But in order to succeed with this lesson she must not be tantalised. It is no good to stand for five minutes with the left hand outstretched and a piece of meat on or near it within six inches of your hawk, when she is in no humour to make the leap which seems to her so perilous. When she will not come, humour her, and put the meat nearer, so that she can get it without jumping. Sooner or later she will find that the meat so placed before her is not a trap or a sham, but really meant for her delectation, and that she can get it a little quicker if she chooses to go for it. There is no use in telling her the story of Mahomet and the mountain, but you can illustrate the theory by a sort of practical dumb-show. If a more advanced pupil is placed on the perch next to the slow learner, the latter will see how much quicker her sister gets the proffered delicacies by jumping for them. As soon as she will come a little way from the screen-perch, try her from a block, and then from a gate-post out of doors. Keep her at this exercise for some days, but do not make a toil of it to her; merely let her know that if she comes for it, she will get the tit-bit at once, whereas, if she does not, she will get it all the later.

Next comes the lure. Passage hawks are notoriously and naturally bad at the lure. Nothing in their previous experience at all leads up to it; and you have to teach them an entirely new lesson. Consequently, you must take pains about it, and be prepared for disappointments and delays. The lure is as important to the falconer as a hook to a fisherman, or a bridle to a rider. To take a long-winged hawk out to the field without a lure would be almost as silly as to go out shooting without any cartridges. When first introduced to the pupil the lure must be well garnished with attractive and palatable viands. It is by no means enough to throw down a freshly-killed pigeon in front of the hungry hawk. She is quite likely, if a passager, to stare at it absently, and apparently without any very defined belief that it is at all good to eat. After a minute or so she is not unlikely to look the other way, and pay no more attention to your well-intended bait. But you must not then be surprised, or begin exclaiming at her "stupidity." If the passager will not come to the dead pigeon, take a lure and cover it with chopped meat. Give her pieces off this, and presently let her pick them off it. Then let her walk towards the lure to get the pieces, as she has already learnt to go to the fist. When once she has walked even three inches to it she can soon be made to fly to it right across the lawn.

Prolong these lessons, therefore, till your hawk is well "made to the lure." Each day at feeding-time make her come a longer and longer distance to it for her dinner. After a while she will be flown to it in a creance, that is, a line attached to the end of the leash, or, better still, to the swivel, from which the leash has been detached. The best way to give the lesson is to get an under-falconer or assistant to hold the hawk on his fist in an open piece of ground, and then, going a little way off, to show her the lure, on which she knows by experience that her food is fastened. In the case of eyesses which have been hacked to the lure they are of course well habituated to the business in hand. But all hawks, if properly treated, will after a time learn to look with some eagerness, at the dinner hour, for the appearance of the lure. Peregrines and all the bigger hawks will be hooded up before going out; and when the hood is taken off they will glance around in search of the trainer. As soon as they discern him swinging his lure, they should jump off and fly towards it, and, when it is thrown on the ground, alight on it. Merlins and sparrow-hawks may generally be set down on a post, and lured from it by the same person who took them out, without the need of an assistant. Or, when they know the lure sufficiently, it may be attached to the far end of the creance, and, after being swung once or twice, thrown to a short distance, and the little hawk thrown off at the same time, when she is pretty sure to go straight to it. These exercises at the lure should be continued till there is no longer any reasonable doubt that the pupil will come as soon as she has the chance; and, in order to make sure, the length of the creance may be increased from a few feet to at least a hundred yards. It will be a proud moment when first you trust your passage hawk entirely free, and, detaching the swivel from her jesses, abandon for the moment all actual control over her. On this occasion you will probably take extra precautions, making sure that no intruder will interrupt the operations, and that your hawk is undeniably sharp-set. But in order to make certain of this, do not dream of starving her; merely put off the feeding-time for an hour or so. Hawks in captivity should commonly be fed, as will be seen later on, at about 11 a.m. When you first fly your passage hawk free, wait until past noon. The small extra delay will have put an edge on her appetite. If all goes well she will not notice or suspect that anything unusual is occurring. Very likely, if a light line has been used, she may have supposed for days past that she was flying free. Possibly she has never once suspected the existence of the creance.

It is well to make all hawks to the lure, even if afterwards you should have no use for it. A lost goshawk will very often come to the lure when she will not come to the fist. As a rule, it will be seen that short-winged hawks in the field should not be called to the lure; they are "hawks of the fist," and should be taught to come to it whenever they have the chance, in default of wild quarry. It requires some faith to believe when the wild-caught sparrow-hawk is first taken in hand that she will ever do this. Nothing will seem much more unlikely than that this fierce, restless creature, a feathered termagant, would ever so lay aside her innate wildness as to come contentedly out of the free air, and, disdaining all other resting-places, take perch by preference on the hand of her once detested captor. Yet so it is. Goshawks and sparrow-hawks can all be brought to come habitually to the fist, and remain there willingly at all times except when there is quarry to be pursued. In their case the calling-off to the hand in the open field is only a prolongation and extension of the early lessons in which they were taught to jump to it from the perch, as already described. After the creance is no longer necessary each kind of hawk should be called off for two or three days at least, the one to the lure and the other to the fist, one man holding the hawk, while the other swings the lure or holds out the fist. And here ends the early drudgery of reclaiming the wild-caught hawk.

The education of the eyess, whether flown at hack or not, must, of course, be brought down to the same stage. If they have had no hack at all they will have been manned very early in life and habituated to come to the fist. If they have been well hacked, they will have become in many respects very like wild hawks—possibly "more so." Anyhow, they will be full summed and full grown in all respects before they come to be put in actual training for the field. We took leave of our eyesses in the third chapter, soon after they had been taken up; and we must now assume that by a modified application of the régime prescribed for the haggard they have been manned and taught to come to the hand or the lure, or both. The time occupied in this process will of course have varied according to the disposition of the individuals. A well-natured eyess merlin hacked under the lure-and-fist system will be manned in two or three days. A goshawk, or a peregrine of an independent turn of mind, hacked at the board, may resist for the best part of a fortnight the best-intentioned efforts to subdue her wild instincts. It will be well in all cases, and will save an immensity of time and trouble, to reduce the eyess to some extent as soon as she is taken up. For my own part I incline to doing, even at this early stage, a bit of mild physicking. Half a Cockle's pill for a peregrine or one-eighth for a merlin will do no manner of harm. At all events the allowance of food must be cut down. Hack hawks, when taken up, should be as round as balls and as bumptious as undergraduates. They know not what it is to be really sharp-set; and unless dosed they make quite a favour of eating at all during the first two or three days of real captivity. Continue feeding them at the rate they have been accustomed to, and you will lose patience before you can bring them under any sort of control. In fact, you will not do so at all. Yet I do not mean that they should be made thin. There is, it is true, no longer any fear of hunger-traces, but a thin hawk is a weak hawk, and sometimes even a spoilt hawk. Her small feathers lose their gloss; her flight feathers grow weak and brittle, and are ready to break on slight provocation; her nares lose colour, and begin to harbour mites. In short, a thin hawk is an abomination and a disgrace. She must therefore not be either over-fed or under-fed, but just made hungry enough before each meal-time to be really keen after her food. And as she has accumulated during her probationary time of adolescence more or less internal fat, the quickest and easiest way to get rid of it is to give her a mild dose or two of purgative medicine, and some rangle, as recommended in the chapter on ailments. Hack hawks and all other eyesses must be taught to jump and fly to the fist. If long-winged, they must be made to the lure. And in all cases they should be thoroughly broken to the hood.

Thus we have arrived at the same stage with our eyesses and with our wild-caught hawks; and the subsequent stages are very nearly the same with each. Carrying (on the fist—I do not mean the vice of that ilk) is still a *sine qua non*. No hawk can have too much of it. I have read in some hawking books a reference to hawks being "too tame." The phrase, as applied to a trained hawk, is not very well chosen, and might mislead a beginner. Some of the most deadly hawks ever flown have been as "tame as parrots." When a very tame hawk flies badly it is not, as a rule, because she is too tame, but because she is too fat, or, more likely still, because she is not properly sharp-set at the moment of flying. Some remarks on the conditioning of hawks will be found later on. In the meantime let not the beginner be afraid of getting his hawk too fond of him. She should "rejoyce in him," as the old falconers expressed it, and at sight of him be all excitement to come to him, not only for food, but for the chance of a flight, which she will soon begin to think that he alone can procure for her. Even wild hawks will sometimes wait on upon their known enemy, man, on the chance of his putting up game, and so "serving them," as the saying is. How much more should a trained hawk do, who is beginning to know that the falconer is a good friend?

Our charges must now be classified in a different way. The distinction is not now so much between eyess and passager, as between long-winged and short-winged—between those which are to be flown at one or other sort of quarry. Thus, short-winged hawks of both kinds, eagles, merlins, and all the long-winged hawks which are to be flown at rook, heron, kite, or gull, are flown from the fist, whereas hobbies and all the long-winged hawks which are destined to fly either at game or duck are allowed to mount to their pitch before the quarry is sprung, and from thence descend upon it. We may first speak of the first-mentioned category, premising that as far as safety is concerned the flight from the fist is preferable.

We assume that the hawk will come readily to the lure or the fist as soon as she has a chance. Now contrive, if you can, that your assistant, having her hooded on his fist, shall stand on an open ground at a distance from you of some two hundred yards, and that somewhere between you there is a live bird or beast of a suitable kind on the ground, or in a very small bush. In the case of a merlin a wild lark may very possibly be marked down in such a position. So may a blackbird for a sparrow-hawk, or a rabbit for a goshawk, or even a young partridge for a peregrine, ger, or lanner. If you cannot manage to make this arrangement with a wild creature, you must employ a bagged one for the nonce as a substitute—a poor one, no doubt; but it may serve the turn, if used in the way to be presently described. Now let the assistant unhood the hawk; and make sure that somehow or other you can put up that marked quarry when you like. As soon as the hawk has had time to look round and has looked towards you, let the man walk in the same direction, and walk in yourself to put up the quarry. When you are close upon it and are sure that it is about to rise, you may show the lure for a moment, quickly hiding it again. And, as the hawk starts towards you, put up the quarry with a shout. If you are quick enough, it will rise just as the hawk is approaching the spot where it was, and the temptation to her to pursue it will be strong. If the hawk yields to the impulse, you are in luck. She is already "entered." If she takes it you are still more fortunate, for the hawk is "made" at the first trial. But very possibly she may refuse. No matter, take her down to the lure, and try her again another time—perhaps an hour later. Possibly you may possess or borrow a make-hawk which is already *au fait* at the quarry—a sister or brother of the tardy learner, which has already taken more kindly to the business—maybe a last year's hawk, which is now coming into action again. If such a pupil-teacher is thrown off as the quarry starts, the force of example will pretty surely lead to imitation. Rook-hawks are very often entered in this way. But the plan is advised for the nobler races only, for short-winged hawks must not be slipped together, for fear of "crabbing" or fighting.

A propos of bagged quarry, which are an abomination to all right-minded falconers, it should be said that whenever they are turned out great care should be taken to deceive the hawk into the idea that they are not bagged. With this intent dig a small hole in the ground, just large enough to accommodate the bagged quarry comfortably. Over the top of the hole and the quarry inside it place a flat board of the same colour as the surrounding surface, green, brown, or as it may be. Let the board be sufficiently heavy to prevent the captive from escaping, as long as it remains over the hole. Then attach a string of the required length, and coloured like the board, to one of its corners. When you want the quarry to bolt, pull the string and thus uncover the hole. When the liberated prisoner comes forth, the hawk will be too intent upon looking after it to inquire why or wherefore it appeared on the scene. If, on the contrary, you throw it up out of the hand, or let it out of a bag, the case will be different. Most likely the hawk will see that it is no chance quarry, but is expressly thrown out as a sort of animated lure, and pursue it as such. When afterwards you try her at a really wild quarry, she may refuse, just as if you had given no bagged quarry at all. Hawks, like other creatures, are averse to hard work when they think it unnecessary; and when they are accustomed to easy flights—such as are always afforded by birds thrown up from the hand—they are apt to shirk the more difficult job of catching a wild bird.

Many hawks are, of course, entered without any such manœuvring as above described. An eyess, for instance, which has begun to chase birds freely at hack may often, when properly reclaimed, be taken straight out into the field, and thrown off at the sort of quarry which it is ultimately intended to pursue. Perhaps two out of every three eyess merlins may, in skilful hands, be thus dealt with. But they will perhaps not begin at once. I remember well the first day when Princess was taken out, as the first of a nest of four merlins intended to be entered. It was on the open down, where the larks were very strong. She refused eight in succession, merely making a pretence of following, and sometimes not even that. But at the ninth, which got up very near her, she flew with the utmost pluck and skill, and, after at least half a dozen good stoops, put it into a potato patch, where it could not immediately be found. She then refused three more, and ultimately, thinking perhaps that it was long past dinner-time, caught the thirteenth lark in good style. Another year Colonel Sanford and I took out two jack-merlins—the advance-guard of the hack hawks—very early in the season, to be entered at the same time. We threw them off at the same lark. The hawk which was nearest to it refused: the other went on and killed the quarry. Sparrow-hawks will generally fly, if in yarak, without being entered artificially. With peregrines there is generally more difficulty. As for those of them which are intended for game or duck, they belong to the other category, and will be referred to later as hawks of the mountee. But passage peregrines, coming to the falconer as they do late in the autumn, will first be flown at rooks or gulls from the fist. With each of these quarry there will probably be trouble. For the wild hawk does not, as a rule, fly at rooks, unless when hard driven for food, nor is she much addicted to gulls, except at breeding-times, when she has many mouths to feed. If, when the time comes for her to be entered, she is started straight away at a rook or gull, without a make-hawk as companion, she is almost sure to refuse, or take no notice at all of it. Possibly, if she is first flown at a white pigeon, in the same place and way as afterwards a gull is sure to be found, and flies well at the pigeon, she will afterwards go for the gull. But for entering rook-hawks, where no make-hawk can be used, a bagged quarry or two is generally found necessary.

When once a hawk has taken one of the quarry at which she is intended to be flown, she may be allowed to eat it if it is to her taste. But if its flesh is not of an appetising or palatable kind—as, for instance, rook or gull—a ruse should be adopted to induce her to believe that the prize is more valuable than it really is. A freshly-killed pigeon, or part of one, should be smuggled under the hawk's foot as she is pluming the dead rook or gull. There will be no difficulty in practising this innocent deception. Hawks, while pluming their quarry, keep a firm hold of it with the inner talon of one foot, and often of both. But it is easy to contrive that the outer talons of one foot shall get hold of the pigeon, and afterwards to shift the inner talon on to it. Then, as she goes on feeding, the other foot can be shifted, and the real quarry stealthily withdrawn from underneath. As there is nothing that peregrines like better than pigeon, your newly-entered hawk will, after a meal presented to her in this fraudulent fashion, take a new view of the merits of a hitherto despised quarry.

It remains now to warn the beginner in the process of entering to beware of the hawk's carrying, that is, lifting or bolting with the quarry. Unless you have very good reasons to suppose that she will not do this, you should specially guard against it from the first. When bagged quarry is used, attach a short light string to it, such as will not materially impede its flight. After the hawk has made a capture allow her to come with it quietly to the ground. This she will do if accustomed always to feed on the lure upon the ground. You will also, of course, be in a place where there is no temptation, and, if possible, no reasonable chance, of her taking it up into a tree. Then approach her very gently and cautiously until you are near enough to take hold of the end of the string. Having secured this, you can prevent all attempts at carrying. Do not, however, on that account hurry up. There is much art in "making in," as it is called. You will have plenty of time ; for the mere plucking or depluming of the quarry (always nearly completely finished before the meal is begun) will last several minutes at least. Still holding the string, go up very slowly, advancing a few inches when my lady is intent on her booty, and stopping when she looks up. Above all things avoid staring at her, which hawks greatly dislike. Look any other way than towards her, and walk rather obliquely towards her than in a direct line. When you are nearly within arm's reach bend down. You may kneel or even crawl along like a snake. When you begin to reach out your hand towards her let it be garnished with a well-looking piece of food. Get it gradually within reach of her ; then close to her feet ; then near enough to touch the real dead quarry. When you have hold of this you have gained another point. But be patient and wary still. If you alarm the hawk, even a little, it will throw you back terribly in your progress towards making her. It may lead to the abominable vice of habitual carrying, than which nothing is more annoying and more dangerous. If by mishap the hawk should bolt, hold on gently but firmly to the string, and give her still more time before again approaching her. The art of "making in" should be studied and practised from the first. You will afterwards be amply repaid for all your trouble. See the important remarks made on this subject in Chapter IX.

When you have secured the quarry, keep down for at least two or three minutes more, and let the hawk begin feeding at her ease on it, or on the pigeon which you may have substituted. Help her to find the best pieces. You may talk to her in encouraging words, if such is your habit, while she is eating. Then slowly get up, lifting the food, and the hawk upon it, without any haste or jerking. Let her have nearly a full crop —the reward of good behaviour—and subject her to no chance of annoyance or interference all the rest of the day.

These instructions may seem lengthy and needlessly minute. If they are, it is a fault on the right side. You are at a critical stage now in your pupil's education. You are "making" her to the business which is henceforth to be the business of her life; and a little extra precaution is justifiable in order to ensure that the lesson you are teaching shall be well learnt. As the hawk finds by experience that you approach her with no predatory intentions, but rather to help her and add to her enjoyment of her meal, she will gain confidence, and be less and less inclined to misbehave herself by bolting. And as her mistrust diminishes so will your trouble be lessened, until at last you will be able to make in without any of these precautions and delays. Whereas, if you are negligent or over-confident at first, you may end by not being able to make in to her at all, and may have the mortification of having been for some weeks the owner of a fine hawk which could fly admirably, but which, after one of her first few flights at wild quarry, literally "vanished into thin air."

The training required for hawks which are to "wait on" is different. It has already been said that merlins and the short-winged hawks cannot be taught this accomplishment. A merlin which will wait on even for half a minute is rather a phenomenon. I have had such an one, it is true, but only one. The thing is not impossible in all cases, but so rarely practicable that it is needless to speak of it. Nor is it advisable to teach the art of waiting on to any hawk which is intended to be flown at rooks, gulls, heron, or the like. But all long-winged hawks intended for game should wait on well. The whole race of peregrines and their cousins, gers, hobbies, sakers, lanners, and the humble kestrel, can all be made to wait on beautifully. Soaring (to which waiting on is so nearly similar) is the natural exercise of all these hawks. In the wild state they spend hours almost daily at it. But if they are to wait on in the rather artificial style required by the falconer, nature must be aided a little. When they are keen at coming to the lure, you should call them off, and, as they approach, jerk the lure away off the ground in front of them. When they have missed it, their impetus will carry them on beyond the place where it was, and they will rise in the air, partly turning round to see what has become of it. Then after a very short delay you may throw the lure down again, and let them have it. At the second lesson it may be hid for a longer time, and the hawk allowed to make one or two circles in the air before it is produced. At each fresh lesson make the interval of waiting longer, hiding the lure as long as the hawk is circling round within a short distance of you, but producing it when she strays away, or gives signs of being tired out. By this means she will soon learn that patience is not only a virtue, but a profitable, and even a pleasant one. For if the wild hawk soars from choice for the mere pleasure of stretching her wings, it must be natural for a trained hawk, which has so much fewer opportunities of doing this, to take a delight in it. Eyess peregrines are very unlike one another in their aptness for waiting on. Some are very slow to learn it, and can hardly, by the greatest efforts, be got to go up any height, or even to keep on the wing at all. Some few, on the other hand, take to it quite readily, and, after a few days, of their own accord mount to a great height. Of course the higher a hawk can be induced to go, the better game-hawk she will turn out.

As for passage hawks, you must remember, when teaching them to wait on, that there is much more danger than there is with eyesses. The longer they are kept on the wing, and the higher they go, the more chance there is of their espying some bird passing — perhaps some old familiar quarry, of which they have struck down scores for themselves—and making off after it. The very fact of being in the air, and feeling the free breeze as it lifts their wings, must remind them forcibly of old days of liberty, and slacken the ties which bind them to their new master. Be extra careful, therefore, in the case of all passage hawks, and most of all with the haggard, to watch for any signs of returning native wildness. Fly her in a country where chance quarry are not likely to appear. If she "rakes away," or wanders far from you in making her airy circles, call her back before it is too late. Fly her always when she is quite sharp-set, even if you have to give her little or no exercise on some of the intermediate days between one lesson and the next.

You may diet her now upon "washed meat." This is meat washed in cold water and squeezed dry, so that a part of the nutriment originally contained in it is lost. It is, of course, less palatable and less sustaining. But it should be used in moderation. The old falconers seem to have given it much more often than we do now. But for some reason or other the nineteenth century hawk, if at all habitually dieted on this distasteful food, seems to lose pluck and power as well as weight.

There is another mode of flying hawks to the lure, which is a sort of combination of the first-mentioned process of "calling off" and the last-mentioned "waiting on." This is the practice of "stooping to the lure," which is certainly an excellent means of exercising a hawk, although some very good falconers object to it on other grounds. For merlins and kestrels, however, it may be recommended without any reservation. To teach it, begin, as before, by calling your hawk off to the dead lure, and jerking it away from the ground in front of her. But instead of afterwards encouraging her to mount and wait on, produce the lure, and repeat the same trick by jerking it away. In order to make the most of this exercise you should rig up a soft lure, which can be struck in the air. Take a stout bag, padded on the inside, and into it put a smaller bag, with as much sand or shot in it as will three-quarters fill it. Sew up the mouth, and attach to it a strong leash or cord. The whole apparatus must weigh about two-thirds as much as the hawk which is to be flown to it. At the juncture of the leash and the bag attach on each side the wing of a bird, choosing by preference for each hawk a bird of the kind which is to be her particular quarry —a rook for a rook-hawk, a lark for a hobby, and so on. These appendages will have to be often renewed; and it is well to keep a stock of old ones, pickled or peppered to keep out the moths. There will be strings, of course, as in an ordinary lure, for attaching the food; and particular care is required in garnishing this kind of lure, as with the hard usage to which it is subjected, any food which is at all insecurely fastened on may come off; and if the hawk bolts with it a terrible disaster may be the result.

At this padded lure the hawk may be allowed to strike freely in the air as it is swung. Gers and merlins are all very clever at this work, and often seem to enjoy vastly this opportunity of exercising their muscles and their intelligence. Some of them are amazingly clever in getting hold of the lure. Not only do they foresee exactly where the swing you are giving to the lure will bring it the moment when they pass; but, if you are in the habit of interrupting that swing by giving it a particular jerk or twist in another direction, they will discount, as it were, this trick, and anticipate your little plan. Considerable adroitness is required on the part of the falconer also. By the employment of some cunning, he can encourage his hawk to great exertions, and can very greatly increase both her speed and her footing powers. If the stoop is very narrowly eluded by this dead lure, working under your guidance, the hawk is not unlikely to think that it was her own slowness of flight which made her too late. If you can encourage this idea, she will strive to improve her pace, and fly to the lure almost as hard as she would at a wild quarry. I have repeatedly seen merlins with their mouths open after five minutes of this work. The best plan is to let the hawk touch the lure whenever she specially distinguishes herself, whether by a very hard down stoop, or a high throw-up, or as it may be. Let the lure be as small as it can be, consistently with sufficient weight and softness, and whenever the hawk touches it, whether by your leave or without it, immediately let it fall on the ground ; and let the hawk come down to it, if she did not bind when she touched. This is a very important particular in the case of eyesses. It teaches them that a swift stoop which even grazes the quarry is better than all the slow ones which miss it. As for passage hawks, they need not to be taught this. But for them, in consideration of the hardness of their stoop, I have sometimes found it well to use a modification of the soft lure. I have diminished its weight and bulk, so that it can be struck without any fear at all of hurting the hawk's feet ; and at the end of the cord or leash to which it is attached, I have fastened the solid weight which is necessary to prevent carrying. This weight may be held in the left hand, while the lure is swung by the right ; and when the successful stoop has been made, both can be allowed to fall on the ground.

I have said that some great authorities disapprove of this method of exercising hawks. They say that in the case of game-hawks it spoils them for waiting on, and that in the case of rook-hawks and gull-hawks, the habit of looking for the lure makes them less keen at sighting their wild quarry. There is a great deal in these objections; and I shall not presume to decide between the advocates and opponents of the practice. As regards game-hawks, however, where a hawk has once taken to mounting well, I should certainly not advise any stooping to the lure, for fear of spoiling her pitch. As regards other hawks, I think some part of the force of the objections is removed if the place where the hawks are stooped to the lure is altogether different from any place in which they are likely to be flown at wild quarry. In lark-hawking it is certainly very essential that the hawk should get sighted at once. But though I have habitually made my merlins stoop at the lure in the early morning, I have not found them in consequence slow in starting at quarry in the afternoon. It cannot be denied that, as far as the hawk's condition is concerned, stooping at the lure is a grand resource. If you were always quite sure of giving your hawk a hard flight at wild quarry every day, that would doubtless be the best thing for her. But who can be sure of this? Bad weather, scarcity of quarry, and several other causes make it only too certain that there will be many interruptions. But even when you cannot give your hawk a real flight, you can generally stoop her to the lure, and ensure that she has at anyrate had a "breather" during the day. It is very rarely so windy during a whole day that a trained hawk cannot be put on the wing. A peregrine in good condition ought not to be excused by anything short of a whole gale from daily exercise, even if it amounts to no more than calling off or stooping three or four times at the lure.

It is a good thing, even after a hawk is fully made and is flying wild quarry daily, to call her off occasionally to the lure, though you have no need to do so. Sometimes a hawk will have a long run of kills without a miss. I have known such a run to last with a merlin to over thirty. During all the time while such a score is being made, there will have been no occasion to use the lure, except perhaps when a quarry has put in and has had to be routed out. She runs a risk, therefore, of forgetting all about that humble apparatus, to which a few days ago she trusted so confidently for her food. Let her memory, therefore, be refreshed occasionally, by interpolating a fly to the dead lure amongst the long series of uniformly successful flights. Otherwise, at the first unsuccessful one, you may find that the once loved object has lost all its attractions.

CHAPTER VII

ROOK-HAWKING

EYESSES, as well as passage peregrines, may be flown at the rook; but this quarry is more suitable for a falcon than a tiercel. Mr. O'Keefe used eyess falcons for this flight, and once killed with them on the Curragh of Kildare as many as 117 in three weeks. William Barr had an eyess which, when entered to rooks, took as many as seven in nine flights. Comet, belonging to Mr. Brodrick, took many rooks. It is only rather exceptionally that a tiercel can be got to fly them. But Mr. Newcome's passage tiercel, Will o' the Wisp, took them very well. The difficulty which is generally experienced in entering falcons to rooks is much greater in their brothers' case. And the superiority of the passage hawk over the eyess is more marked in this flight than in game-hawking. Besides peregrines, several other kinds of long-winged hawks may be trained to take this quarry—gers of both sexes, lanners, and perhaps some lannerets, and the shaheen falcon, both black and red. No doubt the saker of both sexes would afford excellent sport with rooks. I am not aware that the training of any of these hawks for such a flight differs from that recommended for the peregrine.

For a rook-flight very open country is required. It would be no use to attempt it in what is called a well-wooded district, or where hedge-row trees grow as they do in the far greater part of cultivated England. A single tree, or even tall bush, will ruin a whole square mile of otherwise suitable ground. Nor is it sufficient that the land should be clear of trees and buildings. Many other obstacles, such as tall, stiff hedges, wire railings, and even sheep-folds, full or empty, are detrimental to the sport. A flock of sheep, a drove of pigs, or even a herd of cattle being driven along, is quite enough to utterly spoil a good flight. Thus in all England there are but few places where you can carry on this sport with success. Amongst them are parts of the Berkshire and Wiltshire downs, and some of the South-downs, though these are usually too undulating. Parts of Norfolk, especially near Lakenheath, are good ; and so are portions of the fen country, where there is not too much water. In the North of England and in several counties in Ireland there are moors and open spaces which do well.

It must not be supposed, however, that the passage pere-grine, or any other of the big long-winged hawks, any more than the eyesses, take kindly to rook-flying. Some have so little fancy for this unattractive quarry, that they can never by any skill be induced to fly them with any zest. Generally it is necessary to use either a make-hawk or bagged quarry for entering the beginners. The way in which such quarry are used has been sufficiently explained in the last chapter. But, as everyone does not know how to catch a rook, a few hints borrowed from the sister art of bird-catching may not be out of place. The commonest way of entrapping a rook is to send a boy up to the top of a tree in a well-frequented rookery with the end of a string, with which he can make a noose or nooses, and set them on the old nests to which the birds resort before roosting for the night. At the moment when the noisy crowd come back to the rookery and settle on their accustomed perches, a simultaneous pull at several lines connected with properly-laid nooses will generally secure a victim or more. Another plan by which a rook is made to look even more foolish is to go round with a plough in a field where rooks come to pick up the worms which it turns up. The rook-catcher must be provided with a number of paper hoods made like large extinguishers, and these he will place upside down in the furrow with a tempting bait—grain, worm, or meat—in their inside. The rest of the inside of each cap is well smeared with bird-lime or some other very sticky matter ; and the rook, in picking at the food, may be hoped sometimes to hood himself. Then while in his astonishment he struggles to get rid of this blinding fool's cap, he may be picked up and carried off into captivity.

When the newly-entered hawk has taken his bagged rook, you must get up as quickly as you can and make in at once. Then seizing the "pelt," or dead body of the quarry, you must contrive so that the hawk, instead of breaking in upon that unsavoury morsel, shall proceed by mistake to begin her meal upon a pigeon which you have just before killed, and which you surreptitiously substitute for by holding it side by side with the dead rook. The object, of course, is to induce in her ladyship's mind the belief that she is eating what she has killed, and finds it uncommonly good. Eyesses are naturally deceived very easily into this fallacious notion. As for passage hawks, it is quite possible that many of them have no more idea than eyesses what a rook tastes like. Unless they have ever been hard pressed for a meal, it is more than probable that they have never condescended to dine off a rook. Anyhow, they will not be at all unwilling to lend themselves to a deception fraught with such gratifying results. "Dear me," may be the haggard's inward reflection, "what a goose I have been all this time never to pay any attention to these vulgar black birds! Why, they taste as good as pigeon!" And the next time she has a chance of paying attention, she will. This "personation trick" is invariably used by Indian and Asiatic falconers in kite-flying with sakers. It is necessary, or at least advisable, in entering hawks at herons, gulls, and other coarse-fleshed birds. In the case of rooks it may be discontinued after a short while, if it is found on a cautious trial that the hawk will eat rook with any relish. Many falcons, when flying rooks almost daily, are habitually fed upon the last victim they have killed in the day. But it is not to be supposed that any hawk will be very fond of such coarse viands ; and some will not eat them at all.

Supposing now that the rook-hawk is safely entered, and a suitable country found, the next thing is to also find a wild rook in a suitable part of that country. And this is not altogether an easy matter. In some very excellent districts, where the rooks are flown at every year, they become excessively wary, and quite clever at avoiding the chance of a good slip at them. The old birds, who have been spectators of many a battle in the air in which one of their comrades was worsted and lost his life, or who have perhaps even themselves done battle, and escaped with great difficulty, become suspicious of all mounted men. They remember very well and with a fluttering heart the appearance of the little squadron of horsemen which once brought with them Lady Long-wing, who made such a dreadful example of poor papa Caw-Caw. Who can say that they do not remember the very faces and the green uniforms of the murderous men to whom Lady Long-wing belonged? Anyhow, as they strut on the hillside or pick about along the furrows, they are on the alert directly a detachment of irregular cavalry comes in sight, which looks at all as if it might be accompanied by hawks. Very often their sentinels incontinently give the signal of alarm, and the flock scuds off summarily to safer feeding-grounds. At all events they do so long before they can be approached within what a beginner would consider a reasonable distance. The result is that in order to get within reach of such quarry it has sometimes been found necessary to resort to stratagem. Rooks have been stalked by a falconer on foot creeping along behind the shelter of a waggon, or actually disguised as a farm labourer. Sometimes the hawking party will lie concealed under the lee of a rick, waiting for a distant rook to cross within range, or to be driven by mounted beaters in the direction of the ambush. And after all precautions have been taken it is often useless to wait for a short slip. The distance at which good passage hawks are now thrown off at Wiltshire rooks will astonish a person who has never seen anything better than a moderate eyess. A quarter of a mile is not considered at all too long a start when a hawk is a fast one and in good flying order. But the longer the start the better the country must be if you are to score a kill.

A falconer on the look-out for rooks will often have to get over a good deal of ground in the day. Twenty miles—without counting in the flights—is probably rather under than over the average distance when any considerable number of hawks are to be flown. It is, of course, almost a necessity to be mounted ; and it is well to have a horse under you which is not new to the business, especially if you are to carry a hawk yourself, or may be called upon to take one up. A horse which has never been out with the hawks before is likely to be very much put out by the ringing of the hawk's bell, and still more if she also flutters her wings in a high wind. While following a ringing flight your eyes will naturally be directed more towards the realms above than to the ground over which you are galloping ; and, as many of the downs on which this sport is most often pursued abound in ant-hills, if your animal stumbles over one of these obstacles you are likely to pay for your inattention by a severe cropper. If it falls to your lot to take up the hawk after she has killed, you must, of course, dismount. To enable you to do this and devote your whole attention to it, a special apparatus is provided. To the outside of your saddle will be attached a pocket, within which can be fitted a leaden weight secured by a leather, the other end of which can be attached to the horse's head, so that by merely throwing the weight on the ground he is at once tethered. No one of course presumes to take up another man's hawk unless it has been so arranged beforehand, or in case of urgent necessity, as for instance if the owner is not in sight, and there is danger that the hawk may be attacked on the ground by some deadly enemy. Of course rook - hawking may be attempted on foot. But unless markers are posted skilfully at the places where a hawk is likely to go out of sight, there is great risk of losing her. Moreover, it is impossible to see much of the best flights. A great deal of time will be wasted in moving about between each flight ; and still more in shifting the markers from place to place, as well as in finding the hawk after a long flight which has ended in a kill. The rook-hawker on foot comes back footsore, and very weary. And he is lucky if these are the only ills of which he has to complain.

Rook-hawks which have been brought out to fly, but are not for the time actually engaged, either because their turn has not come, or because they have already flown and been fed up, are either carried about by a cadger on the cadge, or made fast to a field-block in a well-sheltered place, or consigned to perches rigged up in the inside of a van, which can be drawn by a cart-horse. The latter plan is adopted by the Old Hawking Club, by which more hawks are usually taken out than could be accommodated on one cadge. It has the great merit of serving to protect the inmates from the bitterly cold winds which often prevail in the rook-hawking season, and also from the rain. Such a van should be well provided with springs. Otherwise the jolting, while it passes over rough ground, as it needs must, would do almost more mischief than the wind or rain. In any case, whether you go singly with a single hawk on your fist or with a whole cadge full or van full of hungry peregrines, the hood will be worn. Nor will it be removed until the moment arrives when the wearer is to be thrown off. But when any hawk is being carried with a view to a flight the swivel will be detached from the jesses and the latter held tightly in the fingers of the left hand. Some falconers who use ring swivels in the field, take them off directly the hawk is taken on the fist for the purpose of being flown, and then slipping the leash through one ring of the swivel and afterwards through the loops in the two jesses, are ready to pull it out quickly when there is a rook in sight and it becomes possible that they may have to throw off at any moment. Some also, when a flight is pretty sure to begin shortly, loosen the hood's braces without taking it off, so that there may be no delay in whipping it off at exactly the right moment. No one has ever been able to explain how it is that peregrines can emerge suddenly from utter darkness into the full glare of daylight, with eyesight as good as ever, ready in the very first moment to catch sight of a distant rook and to begin the chase. That they have this faculty everyone knows who has ever seen a rook flown by a trained peregrine. Fortunate for the falconer that it is so, as he can choose his own moment for the throw-off.

If you are intending to fly a hawk for the first time at a wild rook, get some other person who is out with a made hawk to be also ready with her. Then, if the first chance at a rook is not an easy one, let that other person throw off his hawk and keep yours for a less difficult flight. Wait, if possible, until you can find a quarry which is not too far off and not high in the air. If you can get up within a hundred yards or so of one on the ground to windward of you, so much the better. The moment he jumps up, off with the hood, and with a steady movement of the left arm forwards, something like that of a left-arm slow bowler, launch your hawk into the wind. Use whatever cry of encouragement you like, or use none at all ; at anyrate, not any cry which you may have used in calling off. And if, in the excitement of the moment you should not throw away the hood, but stuff it into your pouch or pocket, that will also be satisfactory. If you drop it you are not likely to find it on the open down without some hours' search, if at all. Such presence of mind is, however, I am aware, rather too great to expect.

A rook with any self-respect about him will begin to mount as soon as he is aware that he is being pursued. And of this fact he will not be long in ignorance. Seldom does a trained hawk make half a dozen strokes of her wing before the quarry espies her and knows exactly what she means. With this knowledge the black-a-moor of the air wakes up, and then, if never before, he is on his mettle. Few people know how a rook can fly until they have seen him in front of a peregrine which means business. His wings are broad and strong, and not much worse shaped than a hawk's. His muscles are good ; and by reason of much daily exercise in all weathers he is in good condition — better far, perhaps, than your passage hawk, which was cooped up inactive for weeks, and only during the last fortnight or so has had a modicum of exercise while flying to the lure. The two birds will breast the wind as they mount ; but not necessarily taking the same line. Sometimes the two lines will diverge so much that from your point of view behind, the birds seem to be flying away from one another. Generally speaking, the better the hawk the less slavishly will she follow the course taken by the quarry. She flies " with her head," and, trusting for victory to the long, powerful stoop, concentrates her efforts on attaining to a position from which she can deliver it to best advantage. Thus if, the wind being north, and the safest shelter west, the rook shapes his course to the north-west, the falcon may very probably steer due west. By doing so she makes sure that she will soon be almost between the quarry and that desirable place of refuge. To make it he must come right past her and under her. Or else he must keep away and make for another covert, and in that case he will have a long way to go; and there will be time to catch him up, and get between him and that other haven. To passage hawks, especially haggards, this finessing is the A B C of scientific flying. Moreover, an experienced hawk does not always choose to stoop exactly up-wind, but prefers, for some reason of her own, to come at her victim sideways. There are mysterious laws and principles of aërial steering, which no man understands, but which sometimes make a stoop more telling when made in a direction unexpected by the riders down below. Eyesses are generally some time before they learn the art of utilising the wind to increase the force of their stoop, and of using their heads to help their wings. Some, it is true, seem to be born good tacticians, or at least to have instinctively learnt to be so while flying at hack. But these are quite the exceptions. Not only do eyesses as a rule begin with an inferior style, but very few of them ever attain to the perfection of form which long practice in all weathers at all sorts of different quarry has taught the old wild hawk.

As the two birds mount, the hawk naturally gains on the rook. She is the quicker flier; sometimes, perhaps, by a hundred per cent., but generally much less than this. Going down-wind there is not so much difference between them, when both are at the same height. But the start at a rook should always be up-wind. To throw off at a down-wind rook is bad falconry. When a rook means to "keep the air," or beat the hawk in fair flying, he will, after a while, begin to ring, that is, to ascend spirally in circles. Why he should do this, instead of continuing in a straight line, no one, I think, has properly explained. But the road upwards for most birds when they are exerting themselves—be they kites, herons, rooks, or larks —is in spiral circles more or less regular, a very obliging dispensation of nature for those who want to look on at a high flight! For while the ringing lasts the horsemen down below need not hurry themselves. Only, if there is anything of a wind they should always keep moving, so as to be well to leeward of the flight, shifting their ground to right or left according as the circles seem to tend in one or the other direction. The higher the quarry goes the faster and farther will be the headlong dash down-wind if he is beaten in the air. After a while, if the hawk perseveres, her superior flying powers will take her above the quarry.   At what time and height this desirable result is brought about depends, of course, partly upon the speed of the one bird and partly on the speed of the other.   There is a saying among falconers that a good hawk makes a bad quarry, meaning that a rook or other bird which might give a fine flight when only a moderate hawk was behind him very often makes quite a poor show against a first-rate performer.   It may also be said with some truth that a good quarry makes a bad hawk, inasmuch as hawks which have flown many a good flight and killed many a fairly fast-flying rook may sometimes find themselves pitted against such exceptionally strong ones that they seem unable to get above them, and give to the stranger an appearance of being slow themselves.

A good and experienced falcon or other rook-hawk will not be content with merely getting above her quarry before she makes her first stoop.   She will go on ringing until she is so far above that the first stoop will be a good one.   That is to say, that she may be able to get such an impetus upon her in the dash downwards as to rush up to the rook hand over hand, or, as the racing men say, as if he were standing still.   And, having so run up to him, that she may, if she misses him, utilise the remainder of her impetus in shooting up again in preparation for a second stoop.   The rook, on his part, when he finds the falcon above him, has to choose between two courses.   Either he will persevere in trying to keep the air—and in that case must trust to quick turns and twists to elude the foe—or he will adopt the less valiant but almost equally dangerous alternative of a race to the nearest covert, with the necessity of eluding a certain number of stoops on the way. In the first case the flight will become a sort of improved version of coursing.   Improved, because a bird has so much more varied chances of throwing out his pursuer than the hare, which can turn only either to the right or the left.   He must always be on what the mathematicians call the same plane. The rook, on the other hand, may, if he likes, double simply to right or left.   But he may also, if he prefers it, duck downwards or shoot upwards, allowing the hawk to pass over him or under him.   Or he may turn partly upwards or downwards, and partly to either side.   Thus there are an unlimited number of angles at which he can swerve away to avoid the stroke.

The art and science of "shifting" is indeed one of the most elaborate that is possessed by the dumb creature.   Almost all birds cultivate it to a certain degree.   Instinct suggests it to them; but many birds improve upon their natural powers by frequent practice. Who has not seen one rook chasing another, either in sport or in a petulant humour, and the fugitive evidently enjoying the fun of throwing out his persecutor? In the tropics there is nothing that a crow likes better than stooping at kites; and nothing that the kite takes greater pride in than showing how easily he can elude the shots so made at him. I have seen pigeons, when a slow or lazy peregrine is in the air, deliberately hang about within reach of her for the express purpose of enjoying the amusement of successfully shifting when she makes a dash for them. Indeed, it will be seen in Chapter XIX. that I saw this game played rather too rashly by a house-pigeon with a trained ger-tiercel. It has been said that the rook in full plumage is no mean flier. He has also a good head on his glossy shoulders, and he shifts cleverly enough while his lungs and muscles hold out. He does not often lose his head, in the metaphysical sense. Sometimes, when particularly close shots graze him, or even feather him, he is frightened into wasting a little breath in an angry complaining croak. But this is almost the only piece of stupidity that can be alleged against him. Usually, however hard pressed, he keeps all his wits about him; and when he is beaten in the air, it is oftenest from sheer want of speed and want of wind. The violent effort required to escape by shifting a good stoop of a first-rate peregrine takes it out of him terribly. The whiz of the falcon as she rushes by is enough to make the stoutest heart quail. But cowardice is not the weak point of the rook, who, for the most part, has a determined and fair struggle for his life.

Of course the stoop takes it out of the hawk also. But then the hawk has two great advantages. She is the faster bird, and she is better at the "throw up." This is the counter-move by which she responds to the shifts of the quarry. A good long-winged hawk, after an unsuccessful stoop, immediately shoots up to a great height above the place where the stoop was intended to take effect. She rebounds, as it were, from the rapid descent, glancing upwards with wide open wings to a new position of advantage. And herein she has the advantage of the greyhound. The farther the dog is thrown out, the more laborious is the work of getting into position for the next attack. But a falcon may come past her quarry with as much way on as ever she can command. That impetus need not carry her away to a disadvantageous position, but, on the contrary, to one where she is still admirably placed for a fresh stoop. By throwing up well and with good judgment, and sometimes a little luck, a

E

good hawk after once getting well above her rook will keep the command of the air for the rest of the flight. The quarry may throw up too ; but if his pursuer makes the most of her first advantage, he will always find her above him after he has done so. It may be that she will be very wide of him. But distance calculated in mere length counts for comparatively little. It is the distance in height from the earth below that makes all the difference.

Consequently, if the rook persists in trying to keep the air, and Lady Long-wing has the pluck and the condition to keep up the chase, the time comes sooner or later when the shift is not strong enough or not quick enough. Then as you watch the two birds—or the two little specks, as they may by that time have become—the lines along which they are moving will be seen to converge and not separate again. There will be a shout of jubilation from below. "Who-whoop": it is the death-cry. One of those eight sharp talons which, half hid by feathers, arm the lower side of the hawk's body has hooked itself into some bone, or at least some fleshy part, of the victim's body. Then from the under side of the slim falcon, as she spreads her wings and sinks nearer into sight, will be seen hanging a confused mass of black shiny feathers. As the two birds—victor and vanquished—come down to earth, the former will sometimes be seen tightening her grasp or catching hold with the second foot. At anyrate, within less than a second after they have reached the ground, the deadly clutch of the conqueror will be on the head of the conquered. In another second or two the point of her beak will have broken the victim's neck at the top of the vertebral column. No man can encompass the killing of a rook so speedily and neatly as can a peregrine. Within a marvellously short time after the last stoop was delivered, the head of the captured bird droops inert from the dislocated neck. and life is completely extinct.

Such is the finish of a ringing flight flown out on both sides with unflagging courage—the sort of flight which every true sportsman would like to see often in the hawking-field. But much more often the rook, when getting the worst of it in the air, abandons the hope of beating his foe in fair mounting and fair manœuvring. Taking advantage of some moment—perhaps after an ineffectual stoop—when his foe is a trifle wide, and on the side farthest from a covert which he has marked as a possible place of refuge, he turns tail, and makes off—down-wind if possible, or if not, across the wind—to that seductive shelter. A wood or spinny is what he would prefer, but a tree

Death of a Rook

of any kind will do—the taller the better. A farmyard or a flock of sheep, even a hedge or an empty sheep-fold, or a waggon —anything behind or around which he can save himself from the dreaded stoop. In any, even of the least effective refuges, there will be at least a respite. And if that very poor stronghold is found untenable, he can begin a fresh retreat to a more promising place, with recovered wind, and perhaps better luck. Often a rook will make for a rather distant plantation, with a nearer shelter of an inferior kind in view as a *pis aller*. The hawk, of course, knows as well as he what he is after, and follows at her best pace. Now is the time to ride hard. Even with a moderate wind the birds will be travelling over a mile a minute. Ride as you will, they will be over your head long before you are near the covert, if it is at all distant. Lucky if you are even in time to be near when the first down-wind stoop is delivered. The down-wind stoop of a peregrine is terrible. It is often avoided, no doubt, but the impetus, if she misses, carries her on right ahead of the rook, over the place where he must pass if he goes on. And there she is, blocking the way to the desired haven. She can poise herself steadily for the next shot, choosing her own time for it, and will have every possible advantage over the rook, which has to run the gauntlet of those eight dagger-like talons. The last stoop before reaching covert is very often fatal. The hawk knows that probably it is her last chance of catching hold, whereas in the open she is aware that a very fast stroke, though not quite accurately aimed, will do a great deal towards taking the nerve and strength out of her quarry, and make him easier to hit later on.

If the rook once makes a plantation of any size, he is safe. No human power can drive him out. Peregrines, of course, will not go into cover after their quarry. Now and then a young hawk at hack will try to do something vague in the way of cutting down or dislodging a bird which has put in ; but such attempts are dismal failures, and are hardly ever even thought of by " grown-ups." If the rook has put in to a very low tree or a tall hedge, he may often be dislodged by throwing sticks and stones at him, or sending a boy up. Sometimes snapping a cap on a pistol, or cracking a whip, or making any other sudden and loud noise, will put him on the wing again. But before going far, he is only too likely to put back to the same place, or to a neighbouring tree, if one is near, or to another part of the hedge. Even when the shelter is only a low line of hurdles, it is quite difficult to hustle out a rook so that the peregrine, waiting on above, may have a fair shot at him. A big tree is generally a safe refuge. If you send anyone up, the refugee will only shift his quarters to another branch. And all the time while you are trying to get him out, the hawk will be circling above—if, indeed, she does not get tired of waiting, and start after some other quarry. With a passage hawk which has not long been at work, you cannot risk keeping her long in the air on the chance of your routing out a rook that has put in. She may check at a passing pigeon, or at a quite distant flock of rooks, or any other bird which she was once wont to kill, and then, even if you are well mounted, you will have great difficulty in keeping her in sight. If, therefore, you are hawking with a passager, and cannot get your rook out quickly, take her down with the lure, and have a try later on at another rook in the open.

If the hawk kills, the falconer will get up at once, and " make in " in the manner described in the chapter on Entering. There is not much danger of any attempt to carry when the quarry is as big a bird as a rook. But caution should be observed, nevertheless, as, if you are rough or in a hurry, you may induce in the hawk a disposition to carry, which on some future occasion may cause no end of trouble. Do not even now let your hawk feed upon the rook, unless you are quite sure that she likes such food. Take care that from the first she shall be well pleased with having taken this quarry, which is not the one she is predisposed to fancy. If in doubt about her liking for rook's flesh, substitute a pigeon. And it is as well to be contented with one kill on the first day. A fresh flight might not end so happily, and would then partly annul the good effect of the one that has succeeded. Besides, you want to reward your hawk for her victory by giving her a good feed at once, which of course you could not do if you intended to fly her again. Be well satisfied, therefore, that the first step has been made towards making a good rook-hawk. After a few more flights, if even a moderate percentage of them end well, your pupil will begin to take a delight in the business. Sometimes she will become so keen at it that you can freely let her feed upon the last rook she kills in the day. Only do not give her too much of this food. It would be a thousand pities if, after having acquired a liking for this flight, she should, for the sake of a small economy to her owner, be allowed to become disgusted with it.

Rooks may be flown as soon as the passage hawks are trained. Old peregrines can of course be flown at any time (except when there are young rooks in the nests). But the winter and early part of the year is the best time, as later on

the young crops preclude the possibility of riding over arable
land; and it is impossible to ensure that the area of a flight
shall be confined to the open downs. It is on some broad
expanse of turf, however, that the quarry should be found, if
you are to enjoy a good gallop and a proper view of the flight;
for if you have to jump fences, you must needs take your eyes
off the birds, and it may then be difficult to catch sight of them
quickly again. You should not fly at a rook if there is any
tolerable covert within half a mile down-wind, or a third of a
mile on either side. The distance up-wind to the nearest covert
need not be so great. When a rook is just rising off the ground,
you can of course give him more law than when he is already
on the wing. For, as has been said, height in the air counts
very much more than distance along the flat. Even the small
elevation from which a hawk starts as you carry her on horseback gives her a certain advantage over the rook which is only
just off the ground. Rook flights often end more than a mile
in a straight line from the start. But generally this is equivalent
to saying that the distance flown has been more than double as
much, by reason of the doublings and up-and-down dashes which
both birds have made. In following a flight, it is best to keep
about a quarter of a mile to leeward, or as near this as you can
get, while keeping a good view of the scene. As the rook gets
higher, still keep well to leeward, until you are pretty sure what
covert the rook will ultimately make for. A little practice will
generally enable you to make a pretty good guess, although
perhaps for a while the rook may be heading a different way.
If you are wrong, and find yourself thrown out, perhaps the best
plan is not to ride hard in the vain hope of getting nearer, but
take out your field-glasses, and watch the flight from about
where you are. Each man out who knows enough about hawking to be able to take up a hawk, should carry a spare lure, so
that, in case of a lost hawk, he may try for her in his own
direction, while others are engaged on the same task in theirs.
Agree beforehand, however, with the owner of the hawk, that if
you find her you may take her up.

Falcons are generally flown single at rooks, except at the
time of entering them with a make-hawk. In a double flight I
think that the rook is as a rule a bit overmatched, that is, if
the hawks are in proper fettle. But for entering a backward
hawk, or encouraging one which does not take kindly to this
flight, it is very useful to use a make-hawk, that is to say, one
which is already keen in the cause. Most hawks are very
strongly influenced by example; and a young eyess particularly,

recognising as she does the superior style of a haggard or passager, will readily imitate her, and join in a chase upon which she sees that the other has embarked. A double flight is very pretty, and very effective. The way in which the two hawks assist one another, waiting each for her turn to stoop, and making her plans so as to profit by the action of her comrade for increasing the force of her own strokes, is interesting even to the most careless observer of animal life. But the double flight is better reserved for such more arduous undertakings as the pursuit of kites, herons, and gulls. A few words will be said in a later chapter about these quarry and the sport they afford. But in all the main particulars it resembles that which has been here described. The rook flight is at once the commonest and the most typical form of sport when the hawks are flown out of the hood ; and he who has successfully trained a peregrine to this business should have no great difficulty in making any other of the large long-winged hawks to such other quarry.

CHAPTER VIII

GAME-HAWKING

PARTRIDGES, pheasants, and other game birds may be killed with several kinds of hawks. In ancient times it seems that the former were taken in England with the jerkin, or male ger, and occasionally with the gerfalcon,—though this was mostly reserved for much bigger quarry,—with the peregrine falcon and tiercel, the lanner and lanneret, the barbary falcon and tiercel, the male goshawk, the female sparrow-hawk, and sometimes even the tiny merlin and almost equally diminutive hobby. In our times most of these varieties have been almost disused for the flight at game birds, for various reasons, the chief of which is that peregrines are found to be more useful at it than the other sorts. It is true that goshawks have been flown quite lately both at partridges and pheasants, and with some success; and it will be seen in treating of the sparrow-hawk that she has also done some execution amongst the denizens of the swedes and stubbles. Even merlins have been found occasionally to take a young partridge in September. But goshawks and sparrow-hawks are seldom speedy enough to catch many full-grown partridges, unless they can be approached nearer than is usually the case nowadays. Probably not more than one merlin in fifty could be induced to fly partridges with any zest; and not one in a hundred could hold a full-grown one on the ground without great difficulty and risk to the tail feathers. And, as merlins will not wait on, the flight with them at partridges, if it were to be accomplished, would lack the chief attraction of game-hawking, and not be much worth seeing. The lanner and the barbary, as well as the ger-tiercel, would still certainly show good sport with game; so would the two kinds of shaheen, and very possibly the saker. But the supply of these hawks is extremely limited; and the climate of England does not suit them so well as the peregrine. Moreover, the

115

mode of training and flying them does not materially differ from that of the commoner and hardier bird. It may be assumed, therefore, for the purposes of the chapter, that game-hawking means, what falconers generally understand by it, the flight with peregrines at grouse, black-game, or partridges. Pheasants, snipe, hares, and woodcocks will be dealt with in another chapter.

Grouse and black-game hawking differ in no important particular from partridge - hawking; and, generally speaking, what is to be said about the latter may be said with equal truth of the other two. It should be mentioned, however, that falcons, from their superior strength, are much to be preferred for the flight at the bigger quarry. Although there have been cases where tiercels have done well at grouse, these are exceptional. Usually they are averse to tackling so heavy a quarry, and, of course, still more reluctant to take the field against blackcock. They are, however, perfectly equal to the flight at partridges. Some falconers have even professed to prefer them for this flight to their sisters. This, however, was not the view taken in the classic age of falconry; and if a fair comparison is made the falcon will be found to be at least as good for the stubble-fields, while vastly superior on the moors. Here again the method of training and working, whether the one sex or the other is used, is identically the same.

In game-hawking, the eyess is much more on even terms with the passager than in the flight out of the hood at rooks and larger quarry. In fact, some of the very best and deadliest grouse-hawks in modern times have come from the nest to the falconer's hands. The records of the Old Hawking Club show a quite exceptionally brilliant score made by one of their eyesses, Parachute, who took no less than fifty-seven grouse in one season, heading the list of that year's performances on the Club moor. In the same year, 1882, Vesta, an eyess of her first season, killed as many as forty-three grouse. Yet it must not be inferred from this that every nestling is as likely to kill grouse or partridges as well as a passage hawk. It is rarely that the latter does not fly at least creditably, when trained, whereas with eyesses the general rule is rather the other way. A really first-rate performer is amongst eyesses the exception, however well they have been hacked and trained. On the other hand, the making of the eyess to this flight is beset by few of the difficulties which trouble him who would train a wild-caught hawk to it. It has been said already that a passage hawk, waiting on at any height, must naturally be more apt to check at passing birds than an eyess. The latter has been, or ought to have been, reserved, from her youth up, for the one flight for which she was specially destined by her owner; whereas the other, from her youth up, until captured, has been accustomed to fly at whatever happened to be most ready to hand. There is, too, generally a special reason why the passage hawk should be apt, when expected to wait on for game, to check at any rook which may be in sight. As a rule she has come into the trainer's hands in the late autumn, has been deliberately entered by him at rooks in early spring, and has flown them with his entire approbation for some weeks. No wonder, then, that if on the twelfth of August a rook comes past she should think it her duty to go for him.

Let us, however, speak of the eyess first, and we can see afterwards what modifications are to be made in the case of the older hawk. When your pupil will come well to the lure do not keep her long, if at all, at work in stooping at it. On the contrary, let the interval between the time when she is thrown off and the time when she is invited to come down on the lure be as long as possible. Keep her on the wing as long as you dare. But you must not at first go too far in this direction. If you wear out her patience she may go to perch, either on the ground or perhaps in a tree half a mile away. Take her down, therefore, if you can, before she is too much tired. But if you should make a mistake, and the inapt pupil goes to perch, do not hurry after her, unless there is any special reason for doing so. Stay where you are if she is well in sight; or, if not, move to a spot where she can easily see you, and do not have the air of pursuing her. Make her understand that, in this case, it is she who must come to you, and not you to her. When she finds after a long sojourn in the tree or on the ground, that after all, she has either to trouble herself to come or else go without her food, she will be less likely to be troublesome next time. She will think to herself, "What was the use of all that delay? I might as well have kept on the wing and had my dinner sooner." Such reflections are very salutary. You do not want to be beat by your pupil, but your pupil to be beat by you, and to learn that your way of doing things is the best both for her and for you. She will learn it, too, if you go the right way to work and persevere. With an eyess you have the whip hand. She cannot easily feed herself without you; and she knows it. For weeks she has been indebted to you, directly or indirectly, for her daily rations. Even in her wildest days at the end of hack, when she would let no one come near her, she was often watching you with eager eyes as you put out her meat on the hack board, and since that, have you not always either given her her food on the lure, or at all events taken her to a place where she could fly and kill a quarry which you had put up for her?

Have patience with her, therefore, and induce her by slow degrees to go up higher and higher. You must use all imaginable devices to accomplish this main object. Try to make her understand that the higher she goes the more chance there is of your producing the lure. Thus, suppose she has made three or four circles without going more than forty feet high, and in the next goes to fifty or sixty feet, bring out the lure and let her have it. Here is another device. Two men go out, each having a lure. One stands on higher ground than the other. Then call off the hawk alternately, each man showing his lure in turn, and hiding it as the hawk comes up. But let the man on the upper ground never indulge her with any success. When she is gratified let it be when she comes from above. She is not unlikely to associate the idea of success with that of toiling upwards and then coming more swiftly down. This is, moreover, a view of the matter to which the minds of all hawks are naturally prone. The flesh is weak, particularly in eyesses, but the spirit knows that the proper way to earn a living is to mount and then stoop down.

It is not good to defer needlessly the moment when you give your hawk a flight. Flights at quarry, even if it is bagged quarry only, almost always improve the mounting of a hawk. Why? Because first nature and then experience teaches her that from a height she has more chance of catching a live bird. It is not a bad plan, if your hawk mounts badly, to start for her (from a place of concealment, of course) a fast house-pigeon at a distance of five or six hundred yards up-wind from a thick covert. She will have plenty of time to make a stoop or two in the open. But she will almost certainly fail, and the pigeon will get off easily into shelter. Then if your hawk comes back to you at a good height, give her a much worse pigeon, which she will have a good chance of taking. If she comes back low, take her down to the lure, and save the second pigeon. The next day you may take out two pigeons —a good and a bad. If your hawk mounts better give the bad pigeon ; and if not, give her again the one which she will not be able to catch. These are not infallible methods ; but they may succeed, and they are worth trying, when a hawk is averse to mounting naturally. In the lone hours of darkness, when her hood is on, such a hawk may fight her battles over again, and inquire seriously of herself what was the cause of her ill-success. And, reflecting on the experiences of hack, she may very likely conclude that she could have done better if she had started in pursuit from higher in the air.

The old falconers had a device which is not often adopted now, but which seems to have been effectual, at least, in some cases. They "seeled" (see Chap. v.) the bagged quarry,—usually a duck or a pigeon,—and the effect was that, when so blindfolded and let loose, it flew upwards, like a towering partridge, avoiding the risk of striking against obstacles which it could not see. The hawk flown at such quarry was naturally induced to keep high when waiting on. The objection to any such flight is that the quarry has not a fair chance of shifting from the stoop when it comes.

The giving of bagged quarry is not a thing to be encouraged or continued for any length of time. Bagged game never fly well, seldom passably even ; and they demoralise a hawk. Bagged house-pigeons fly admirably ; but then they are not the quarry you want your hawk to pursue. On the contrary, you are particularly anxious that as your hawk is waiting on for a covey to be put up she shall not start off in pursuit of a chance pigeon. Be very stingy, therefore, with your bagged pigeons ; and if you give any at all, leave off directly your hawk has begun to mount at all decently.

Eyesses of all kinds are often given to raking away, *i.e.* wandering away from the falconer to inordinate distances, when they ought to be waiting on nearly over his head. And these aberrations are generally in a down-wind direction. It is fortunate, therefore, that in game-hawking the quarry is usually put up by walking down-wind. Otherwise many young hawks would have little chance of coming up with them. For it is a curious thing that, as compared with game birds, the speed of a peregrine is greater when going down-wind, whereas in rook-hawking she gains more rapidly when both are flying up-wind. On the troublesome habit of raking away, some observations will be found in the chapter on "Vices." Practice is usually the best remedy. A hawk generally has gumption enough to see that by constantly waiting on down-wind she puts herself at a great disadvantage for killing her bird if it goes up-wind ; and when she has come to understand that the bird is going to be put up by you, and not accidentally, she will begin to place herself willingly in such a position over you as to be ready for the stoop when the birds are flushed. "Why loe !"—a cry with a rather Chinese sound about it—was the shout used for calling in a raking hawk. Of course, while flying her at the lure you may do something towards habituating your eyess to keep up-wind, by rewarding her when she stoops from there, and not from the other side. So also, in actual flying, keep still, and let the game lie, while she is wide; and move on when she is in her proper place. If she can get a kill or two from a pitch over the falconer's head it will be better for her than any number of kills made when she was waiting on wide.

The glory of a falconer who goes in for game-hawking is " a falcon towering in her pride of place"; and her "place" is some hundreds of yards above her master's head. A high pitch is the beauty of a game-hawk. It is what enables her to kill, and to kill well. The best game-hawks go up until they look quite small in the sky. A thousand feet is often attained. When a peregrine is as high as this, it matters comparatively little whereabouts the game gets up. She can come down upon them nearly as easily at an angle of 70° or 80°, as at an angle of 90°. Sometimes even more easily. The time occupied in coming down is a mere nothing compared with the time which would be occupied in flying along the level to the same spot. When once, therefore, you see your hawk at a good pitch, use every effort to get up the game. When she sees the men running she will very likely be all the more ready to keep in a good place. After a week or two's practice she will know well enough what the whole show means, and will play her part in it *con amore*.

If your hawk will not mount properly, but potters about in a useless way at a mean height, you may try other plans. You may call her off half a mile or so from the lee side of an open moor, and, as she comes across it up-wind, let beaters from each side try to drive grouse inwards towards her line of flight. If you can once enable her to take a grouse there are hopes of her yet. You may even fly her from the fist at a grouse if you can get near enough to one to make it at all likely that she will catch it. I have seen this done with a backward young falcon, which would not wait on. There ensued a stern chase all along the ground for at least half a mile, both birds flying at almost exactly the same pace. The sight was ridiculous enough; but in the end the falcon managed to catch the grouse, and was allowed to take her pleasure on it. The success, small as it was, saved the hawk at anyrate from being disgusted with grouse-hawking, as she would otherwise very soon have been. It is wonderful what good is done to a young hawk by catching a difficult quarry by her own unaided efforts. The encouragement she derives from it is occasionally so great that she seems suddenly to develop her latent powers beyond all expectation.

You must not, however, expect that every young falcon will be a good grouse-hawk. Indeed, you must not expect many to be so. The quarry is a difficult one, and until you have trained a good many partridge-hawks you are not likely to make one for grouse. In partridge-hawking no very great speed is wanted, if only the hawk will mount well and throw up well. Partridges can be flushed much nearer, as a rule, to the hawk than grouse. Although they are fast, especially up-wind, they are not as fast as grouse, nor as wild. Nor perhaps, I may add, as perverse in getting up at the place and time you like least, though both are clever enough at choosing their time for making off. In an enclosed country, if you do not kill your partridge at the first shot, he will often put in at the next hedge, and there you may mark him and get him out. But on an open moor the grouse generally go so far before putting in that you cannot mark the place near enough to get them out quickly. Thus out of a hundred eyess peregrines, probably more than 70 per cent. will, in good hands, fly partridges very fairly, whereas out of a hundred eyess falcons—leaving tiercels out of the account—you will not find anything like fifty which are really good at the bigger quarry. Of tiercels it would be rash to say that even 1 per cent. would fly well at grouse. Of the falcons which fail some appear to be too lazy, and others too slow. A good deal depends on the first few flights. If a hawk has good luck on two or three occasions when she is first taken out, and a young grouse gets up well within reach, the young hawk will take heart, and, feeling assured that she can take the quarry, will try hard and will improve. Choose, therefore, for a hawk that is of doubtful courage the flights which seem likely to be the easiest. Remember that an immense deal depends upon the conditions under which you call upon your hawk to make her first flight at a grouse.

There are still some places where you can shoot grouse over dogs. If it be your good fortune to have access with your hawks to a moor where this can be done, you are in luck. As soon as there is a steady point (you are, of course, on open ground), unhood and throw off your hawk, which has already learnt to wait on. As long as she is moving upwards, making each circle a little higher than the last, stand still and let her go on, or, if the point is far off, walk steadily towards it. The grouse will have seen the hawk, and be in no hurry to move while she is mounting; but presently they will be aware also of your approach. Then there will be a small debate in their minds— or rather in that of their papa—whether it is best to keep still and eventually be shot at, or to start off at once and at once be stooped at. The nearer you approach, and the farther the hawk rakes away, the more does the decision incline towards making a bolt of it; but papa grouse is not going to make a fool of himself by bolting at the moment which you would prefer. Your programme, of course, is to wait till your falcon is heading in towards the dog, and then rush in upon the hesitating assembly. Unfortunately, this plan does not fit in with the views of the worthies in question. They have also been waiting till the hawk's head was turned away, and now, as she is near the outer part of her circle which is farthest from the quarry, up they get, and off they go, whizzing along the top of the heather.

At this stage of the proceedings the modern falconer does, for once, find the use of his voice. He shouts loudly to call the hawk's attention and to cheer her on. " Hey, gar, gar, gar ! " or " Hoo, ha, ha ! " are old-fashioned cries for encouraging a falcon to stoop from her pitch, and are still often used. There can be no doubt that a shout of some kind, or a blast on the horn, if you prefer it, has an inspiriting effect on hawks, and that not only when they start for their first descent, but at each successive stoop. I almost fancy that I have actually seen them cheer up as they heard a loud " Bravo " come from the field far beneath after a brilliant stoop or a masterly throw-up ! It is with grouse and black-game, more than with any other quarry, that you see at once when they get up the immense advantage of a high pitch. When the falcon is some hundreds of feet high she commands a wide area below. At the height of a quarter of a mile it matters little whether the range of her circling flight takes her a hundred yards to one side or the other. She can come down with equal ease upon any one spot in an area of thirty acres.

No one knows how the speed and force of a falcon's stoop are gained. All we can say is that it is the fastest movement made by any living thing in the world. It is not flying, and it is not falling, but a combination of the two, with some other impulse which we do not understand. Mere weight must be at least a most important element, for a heavy hawk seems always to come down quicker as well as far more forcibly than one of the same species which is lighter. But weight is only one factor in the agglomeration of influences which make the stoop of the peregrine and the ger so swift. It must be seen to be believed in. There is no conceivable way of measuring its speed, but it is such that the momentum of it alone carries the hawk with half-closed wings right past a grouse at his best pace, making that pace appear absolutely slow by comparison. The descent from above is often made so that the hawk is at the end of it a few feet or yards behind the grouse, and nearly on a level with him. Hence the course of the pursuer bends forwards horizontally, but with such deviation from the straight line as is necessary to correspond with the flight of the pursued. It is so regulated that it may pass through that part of the air where the quarry is expected to be. Of course the expectation may be falsified. The hawk may suppose that the grouse will swerve to the right, whereas he may swerve to the left. But, just as a fine fencer will divine by some subtle skill whether his adversary is going to parry in *carte* or *tierce*, or to make a single or double disengagement, so the good game-hawk judges from some slight movement or attitude where the grouse intends to be at the moment when she rushes past. This power is not so surprising in a haggard, but some eyesses seem to be instinctively gifted with a share of it. Others acquire it rapidly both in stooping at the lure and in their actual flights. But with eyesses it is rather the exception to be really good footers, whereas with haggards and many red passage hawks it is almost the rule.

Passage peregrines are, of course, much more likely to succeed with grouse and black-game than eyesses. Out of a dozen falcons skilfully taken in hand, and kept specially for game-hawking, it would not be unreasonable to expect that eight or nine would take their quarry well. By rights a passager which is intended to be flown principally at game should be captured in the spring. There is no use in keeping her all the while idle from November to the next August. If taken in April she would be well fit for flying on the twelfth of August. There would, it is true, be some trouble about the moult, but this might often be deferred till very much later than it can be with eyesses. According to modern practice, which is to catch no wild peregrines in spring, the passager has almost always been more or less flown at rooks in the early part of the year. She has accordingly to unlearn a good deal that she learnt then, and be introduced to the much more risky and artificial accomplishment of waiting on. That she should take kindly to this habit is not a thing to be anticipated. It would be going rather too far to expect her to moon about overhead humbly waiting till the falconer below pleases to throw out for her a morsel of cold and uninviting food. You will generally find it best to employ with her rather different tactics from those which served for the eyesses. Thus you may call her off to the lure from the other side of a wide moorside, and, as she comes across the heather, contrive that there shall get up out of it a very fast pigeon. On the first occasion it is ten to one that she will start at this from the very moderate height at which she was flying towards you ; but whether she takes the pigeon or not, she will know very well that she ought, for her own advantage, to have been higher when he got up ; and the next time you call her off at a similar place and in a similar way, the odds are that she comes to you higher in the air. A third trial will probably find her higher still, and you may let her make a circle or two before starting the pigeon. When she has once flown a grouse in a somewhat similar way the effect will be still more marked. Do not now dream of lowering her pitch by ever letting her stoop to the lure. Indeed, after the passager is once made to the dead lure, it need scarcely be used at all, except to call the hawk back after unsuccessful flights.

For the first twelve months you must still be mistrustful of your passager. Some of the old writers advise not to try her at waiting on until she is intermewed. But when once she can be trusted she will do better than almost any eyess. To begin with, she can kill from a much lower pitch than the latter. She is swifter on the wing ; she is a better footer; and she knows much better how to play her cards. And one of the best cards of a game-hawk is a high pitch. Why should she not play it? Has she not already done so to perfection long before you had the honour of her acquaintance? How often, in far northern lands, has she from above the highest mountains come down like a thunderbolt upon the fast-flying ptarmigan or shifty rock-pigeon? Does she not know that it is this altitude which gives power and success? When she has begun killing grouse she will soon enter into the spirit of the thing. Every bird—and a hawk not least—knows that what has happened once or twice may happen again. She was thrown off; she saw no lure, no rook. (For we took care, did we not, that none was in sight?) After a while you put up a grouse for her. And now, on another occasion, to the same beginning will there not be the same end? She will almost certainly think it well to be prepared for such a contingency; and the only way to be prepared is to get up a bit, and to remain pretty near the falconer. As soon as her pains have been rewarded she is "made." The mischief of it is that you cannot, with grouse, make sure of giving her these fair trials just when you wish. Grouse are such "contrairy" birds, that you cannot always find them when you have the best right to expect that you will. You must, however, do your best; and I, for one, verily believe that the hawk knows when you are doing your best. Otherwise, what is the moral of that pretty story, so well told by "Peregrine," of the falcon which, finding the pointer rather slow in putting up the covey, made a stoop at him by way of a gentle hint, and then got up to her pitch again?

Black-game are still more difficult to take than grouse. An old cock will hardly be taken unless from a good pitch and under favourable circumstances. Grey-hens, however, have a way early in the season of sometimes lying very close; and when this happens, and the hawk happens to be waiting on near, she will cut the poor wretch down easily. With black-game the first stoop is generally the most deadly, but it must be made from a high pitch. A gerfalcon or tiercel stooping at an old blackcock in a really open place is the perfection of game-hawking, and from certain points of view—that of mere speed, for instance—the *ne plus ultra* of all hawking.

Partridges, on the other hand, are easier in all respects—easier to find, easier to approach, easier to kill. The *modus operandi* is exactly the same as for the larger game. If you can work with a pointer or setter, so much the better; the hawk will generally know after a while what the dog means and where the birds are likely to get up. An old game-hawk will often display marvellous intelligence in waiting on in the right position. When this is the case, and the country is good, the bag fills rapidly. No sooner is there a point than off goes the hood. After a short delay the hawk is at her pitch, and you can walk or ride in. Any partridge must be clever which avoids the first stoop of an old peregrine. Even if he does, except in a country where there are thick covers, the fatal blow is merely deferred. Putting in at a thin hedge is only a temporary escape, for you can mark the place. The hawk will mark it also, by making her point, *i.e.* throwing up into the air over the spot, and she will wait on while you beat. A spaniel or retriever will generally rout out the fugitive. The orthodox cry for encouraging the hawk when the game is so routed out is "Howit! howit!" Sometimes the partridge which has put in is, as an old author says, "so surcharged with fear" as to be caught by the dog or picked up by the hand. It should then generally be thrown out for the hawk to take, especially if she is a young one, and the dog admonished by the cry of " Ware, hawk ! ware !"

If you use no dogs, mark down a bird or a covey, and put your hawk on the wing to windward of the place, then, as she waits on, walk or ride down-wind towards the spot. If the hawk flies wide make a halt till she is coming up, and then go on at full speed again. As long as she is facing the birds, and not down-wind of them, you have a good chance of a kill. When you are quite sure that there are birds on a ground you need not wait to mark any down, but beat the ground down-wind, keeping the men in line, with the hawk in the air. When the birds are wild this is often the only way in which you can get a flight. The worst of it is that the first bird which gets up may get up a quarter of a mile ahead, though there are plenty of nearer ones on the ground. Of course the hawk will go at the first which gets up, and there will be a long stern chase, with small chance of a kill, and perhaps a long delay before the hawk is got back. If you have to go down-wind after her —which ought not to be the case, but often is—you must make a dead beat in coming back so as to get up-wind again, and begin afresh to drive to leeward.

Such, as far as the aërial part of it is concerned, is game-hawking. A much more complicated affair than rook-hawking, as the hawk has to be trusted all alone to mount to her pitch, and stay there sometimes for many minutes without raking away, and, above all, without checking at other quarry. The hawk, moreover, is not the only actor in the play. You must arrange your beaters and markers properly, even for partridge-hawking, and much more for moor-game. If you intend to hawk over dogs, which you should certainly do if you have the chance, the hawk, while being manned and entered, must be induced to make friends with them and they with her. In the nature of things a hawk mistrusts a dog, even if she does not actively dislike him, and you must get rid of this mistrust. Your pointer or setter, and your retriever too, or whatever dog you intend to use for any purpose, must often be present while her ladyship is being fed and carried. First, of course, at a respectful distance, but by degrees nearer and nearer, until the pair of them are on quite good terms with one another. A few raps over the nose will teach Ponto not to be too familiar ; and a nice wing of chicken offered to Stella within a foot of that same nose will do wonders in reconciling her to its proximity. A long step will have been gained when you can let the dogs play about on the lawn while the hawks sit still on their blocks, watching with contemptuous eye movements which are clownish and undignified as compared with their own in the air. But the real triumph will come when they have all been out for a day together; when, with Ponto standing at the point, Stella has glittered high above him in the sunshine, circling gracefully with expectant eye turned down; when Ponto, downcharging humbly, has seen the lightning-like stoop a hundred yards ahead; when the partridge, shifting cleverly, has put in to a hedge; and when Pompey the retriever, tugging at his leash, has been led up to the spot and has enjoyed the felicity of putting out that same partridge for Stella to finish off with another dash from the sky. Then it will be a pretty sight, if you have time to enjoy it, to see the hawk, with the pride of victory in her eyes, pluming the dead quarry on the ground, while the two dogs, stretched at length close by, look on contentedly, conscious that part of the credit for the whole performance is due to them.

Even if there are no dogs, the falconer must have a watchful eye on his company in the field, especially if it includes new hands at the now unfashionable sport. These must be warned mildly, or it may be reminded sharply, to maintain that repose of demeanour which befits the sport of kings. To keep still as the falcon mounts is quite as essential as to press on when she has got to her pitch. If a kill occurs it is lawful enough to join in the death-cry, but not to hurry up. Such ill-timed zeal might cause an infinity of mischief, and even, in the case of a falcon or ger, the loss of her then and there. Everyone present should stop fifty or more yards from the fatal spot, except the one man who is authorised to take her up; and while he makes in, no noise or violent movement should disturb the solemn scene. Cigars may be lighted, and the incidents of the flight may be discussed; but it is only when the falconer, rising from his knees with the victor on his glove, gives the signal to come on, that curiosity may be gratified by a good look at the vanquished.

There is some variety in the mode employed by hawks in taking game. In rook-hawking they all "bind" to the quarry, that is, they clutch it in the air, and retain their hold as they come down to earth. I think I am right in saying that when a hawk strikes and does not hold a rook, it is almost always either accidentally or because her talon has not held fast. Many peregrines—perhaps all eyesses—begin by binding to grouse and partridges. But the tremendous speed of the stoop in game-hawking often carries the stooper so fast up to her quarry, and onwards after it is struck, that the talon will not hold. Something in the body of the victim gives way—the skin, or maybe a bone or two. Moreover, the strain upon a falcon's foot, if she dragged along with her a heavy bird flying only half as fast at the moment as herself, might be painful and even dangerous. Consequently a hawk which has a very "hard" stoop, as all passage gers have and many wild-caught peregrines, will sometimes not endeavour to catch hold or bind. They then "strike" in the truest sense of the word. They deal a blow, either downwards or forwards, using the two hind talons for it, and either break some bone or knock all the wind out of the victim struck. The jar of the blow as they rush by tells them that it has come home, and instead of throwing up high, as they would if they had missed, they check their flight quickly, and, swinging round in the air, descend rapidly on the panting or dazed foe. Instances have been known when a stoop has cut the head clean off from a grouse, and one of Mr. Freeman's falcons cut through several ribs of a partridge as she hit it down. And yet the ger's stoop is accounted much "harder" than the peregrine's.

Game-peregrines, when well entered, may very well be flown four or five times a day. Some of them, when in good fettle, more. Six kills in one day is a decided feat for a peregrine ; though it has been accomplished in modern times, and probably surpassed occasionally. But it is unwise to overdo the thing, and so tax the hawk too severely. If you have a very high-mounter, you may as well remember a piece of advice upon which D'Arcussia insists. This is to fly her not many times in any one day. Her high mounting is such a grand thing in itself, he says, that it is better to maintain it, even if your bag and your score suffer, than by letting her kill more—which she could undoubtedly do—to run the risk of lowering her pitch. If, however, a hawk has had bad luck, and still seems "full of flying," you may go on after several unsuccessful flights in the hope of rewarding her at last. It is a very good thing in all sorts of hawking to "leave off with a kill." Accordingly, if the third or fourth flight is successful, the wise falconer will often feed up and leave well alone. I should like to go a little further, and say that at any time after a very hard flight, in which the hawk has triumphed over exceptional difficulties and greatly exerted herself, it is a wise thing to feed up. "Oh, do fly her again," is a seductive cry which some friend is likely to raise. But though next time she could not fly better, she might perhaps fly worse. I should be inclined to tell such

enthusiastic friend that I would wait until the morrow. I would
let that hawk go to rest with the memory of that one big flight
in her mind. It will be a pleasant memory, embittered by no
thought of subsequent failure. One really severe flight, after a
good bout of waiting on, is a fair day's work for any long-
winged hawk, unless she is owned by a mere pot-hunter. It
may be the first flight of the day, or it may be the fifth—perhaps
the sixth or seventh; but I think it will be well to finish up
with it.

I am glad to be able to give here some actual records of the
performances of game-hawks, which have been most kindly
given me by Mr. St. Quintin, whose skill in this department of
falconry, as in many others, is second to none.

1881

September 24	Partridges	Pheasant
Belfry	2	...
Butcherboy	2	...
Parachute	3	I
Vanquisher	I	...
Mosstrooper	I	...
	9	I

September 30	Partridges	Rook
Aide-de-camp	I	...
Belfry	I	...
Butcherboy	2	...
Heroine	...	I
Parachute	3	...
Vanquisher	2	...
Mosstrooper	I	...
	10	I

1882

August 16	Grouse	Hare
Parachute	I	I
Angela	2	...
Creole	3	...
Aide-de-camp	I	...
Amesbury	2	...
Vesta	I	...
	10	I

August 19	Grouse
Parachute	5
Angela	2
Aide-de-camp	I
Amesbury	2
Vesta	2
	12

August 25	Grouse
Parachute	4
Angela	I
Aide-de-camp	3
Amesbury	2
Vesta	2
Virginia	I
	13

In the season of 1882 Mr. St. Quintin and Colonel Brooks-
bank, on a moor which they took in Sutherland, took with the
hawks 200 grouse, besides three blue hares, killed by the eyess
Parachute, and one wild duck. After returning to England,
Parachute killed no less than seventy-six partridges, besides five
pheasants.

On the same moor, in 1884, the same gentlemen killed in
one day (August 18) five grouse, four black-game (greyhens and
young blackcock), and a hoodie crow; and on another day
(August 20) eleven grouse.

CHAPTER IX

LARK-HAWKING

THE merlin, the lady's hawk, has always been the hawk *par excellence* for larks. Hobbies, no doubt, have taken them in the old days, though they were used more often for "daring" them by waiting on above, which so terrified the larks that they could be picked up by hand. They take them now constantly in the wild state. But when reclaimed, they have for many years past proved complete failures in the hands of our modern amateurs. The late Lord Lilford made several attempts to get work out of them, but with hardly any success. Mr. George Symonds obtained a large number when he was in Italy, but out of the whole lot could only get one to fly wild quarry. The writer has twice attempted to train a male hobby for larks, and on the second occasion enjoyed the advantage of valuable assistance and advice from Colonel Sanford, who was at the same time training a brother of the same bird. Great pains were taken with both of these hawks, which were in perfect plumage and condition, and had been well hacked by no less able a falconer than Mr. Newall. They were well broken to the lure, and thought nothing of waiting on for a quarter of an hour or more at a vast height. Yet it was found impossible to induce either of them to make any serious attempts at a flight. I started mine on one occasion at least twenty times at various small birds, sometimes putting them up underneath the hawk as he was waiting on, and at other times throwing him from the fist at them. These were skylarks, woodlarks, pipits, and other small frequenters of the turnip-fields. When they were put up under the hobby, he seldom took the smallest notice. When thrown off at one, he would generally make a show of pursuing, but give up before he had gone fifty yards. One lark put in in front of him to a small heap of hurdles. But instead of being "surcharged with fear," and allowing himself to be picked up, he seemed to have as much contempt for his pursuer as the latter deserved, and went up briskly again before there was any chance of even trying to pick him up.

The other hobby, which I trained some years before, did a little better. He once made two or three rings after a wild lark. The rings were very pretty, and the style of flying most correct. But there was one thing wanting, the pace was insufficient. To tell the truth, it was poor; and at the risk of being denounced by all ornithologists and most falconers, I venture to express a doubt whether the hobby is really a fast hawk. To support the common theory that he is exceptionally fast we have, no doubt, the fact that he kills swallows and swifts. But then he has the advantage of them, owing to his habit of constant soaring at a great height. From this vantage-point, if he killed one swallow out of a hundred aimed at, it would not be a conclusive proof of any great speed in flying. Much more difficult to explain are the passages in Latham and other old writers to the effect that hobbies, and especially female hobbies, have "plenty of courage," and will well repay the trouble of training. Blome, in the *Gentleman's Recreation* (1636), is especially loud in his praises of this hawk. After declaring that she is very amiable, bold, and daring, and will make a hawk of great delight, he adds that she may be left out in the field after being fed up, and will come back home to the place where she was hacked (except at migration times); and ends up by affirming that she is "in all respects, according to her capacity, as bold and hardy as any other hawk whatsoever." Either the training of them has become a lost art, or the hobby has changed his nature entirely since he was thus eulogised.

Very different is the account to be rendered of the merlin, so inferior in external appearance, so vastly superior in courage and energy. This, the smallest of the true falcons, has not yet been persecuted out of existence in England with gun and snare, though the days of its disappearance are doubtless not far distant. Of this little hawk I speak perhaps with undue enthusiasm, having made them an object of special care. But the merlin has had admirers amongst some very illustrious persons. Louis XIII. kept hundreds of big hawks. He could have a good day's hawking whenever he liked at cranes, kites, or herons. Yet he did not disdain, amidst all these temptations, to devote a whole morning to lark-hawking with merlins, and was overjoyed at killing one lark with a cast of them. It is true that this was a winter lark, but it was only a lark for a' that! One of the greatest falconers that modern times have produced, Mr. E. C. Newcome, declared that after heron-hawking, already extinct in England in his day, the flight with the merlin at larks excelled all others in this country. Catherine II. of Russia was also an ardent admirer of this diminutive squire of dames.

The training and entering of the merlin, eyess or wild-caught, differs in no important particular from that of the peregrine which is to be flown at rooks. Only the reclamation is much more speedily effected. Often it can be completed, even in the case of an adult jack, in less than a fortnight—with the exercise of diligence, of course. An eyess, well hacked, can be manned in less than a week. This, however, does not mean that they can be trained to larks in that time. Writers on falconry sometimes inadvertently lead their readers astray by declaring that the merlin is easily trained. What the writer means is probably that they are easily manned and made to the lure. This is so ; but the preparation for flying in the field, at least at larks, is quite a different matter. Merlins, like all other hawks, differ greatly in temperament. Occasionally you will find a whole nest of them quite free from vice. Such hawks are all easily trained for the field. But more often these little creatures are imbued from the first with a disposition to carry. And to fly a merlin at larks before she is cured of this weakness is to involve yourself in endless trouble. Eyesses are as bad as haggards—often worse. Consequently, when the hawk is manned and made to the lure, more than half your work is still before you. A non-carrying merlin can be trained in less than a week after being taken up from hack, whereas a determined carrier will hardly be safe to fly in double that time.

There is another respect in which doubts may be entertained as to the truth of the opinion that merlins are easy to train. If by training is meant merely the qualifying them for driving moulting larks into covert, and killing them there, the saying is true enough. You may go to an enclosed country full of moulting larks. You may put one up and start the hawk. The lark, after a short flight, will go into a hedge ; and there, if the merlin does not take him herself, you can either pick him up with the hand or drive him out for the hawk, which has taken perch on the fence ; and he will be counted in the bag. But if by training you mean making the hawk fit to take ringing larks in open ground, the case is different. To do this a merlin must be in the pink of condition—quick, long-winded, persevering, and a good footer. How will you make her so ? She will not wait on ; no exercise is to be got that way to bring

TRAINED MERLIN

her into condition. If an eyess, she has had no practice at footing. How is she to learn that art? Then the dieting is a matter of extreme delicacy. If you give butcher's meat, she will become dull and heavy; pigeon's flesh will give her a sort of fever; in sheep's heart, the food which most amateurs recommend, there is but poor nourishment; and she must be strong enough to go up half a mile, if required! Again, how are you to measure out the exact quantity that is good for her? If you give a peregrine or a goshawk an ounce too much or too little, the mischief done is slight. But give even half an ounce too much or too little to a jack-merlin, and he is straightway wrong in his condition. A big hawk is fed only once a day; there are about twenty-four hours on an average between each meal. If you fly the big hawk on a fast of twenty-two hours or of twenty-six, it matters little. But between the feeding-times of a merlin there is only an average of twelve hours. Therefore it matters a good deal whether you fly her early or late. She may be either too hungry or not hungry enough to do herself full justice.

The trainer who aspires to make a good score with ringing larks, and not to be content with mere hedge-row pot-hunting, must work pretty hard. He must not make many mistakes. He must observe very strictly the instructions already given for guarding against the besetting vice of carrying, never allowing a piece of food to be negligently fastened to the lure, or giving any bagged quarry that can be taken into a tree. He must find freshly-killed small birds almost daily for every merlin, so that her digestion and strength may be unimpaired. And in order to keep his hawk in wind, he must give her plenty of exercise. He can hardly do this without stooping her often to the lure. Ten minutes of this work, if the hawk is going all the time at her best pace, means a good many miles flying. Then the merlin must be taught to look principally to the fist for food. When feeding on the lure, whether it is garnished with a newly-killed sparrow or with a tiring, she must be provided with tit-bits from the hand, until, instead of fearing the approach of the falconer, she looks for it with pleasure. She must constantly be called to the fist. If there is a good-sized spare room available, she may be exercised there in coming often from one side of the room to your fist at the other. Some falconers advise keeping merlins loose in an empty room, where blocks and perches have been placed; and this is, no doubt, a very good plan when you have or can build for yourself the right kind of room. The sort of place recommended later on for moulting purposes will sometimes do well enough.   I have found that the roof or ceiling is the great difficulty, as the hawks, constantly flying round just underneath, rub off the outer web of the long flight feathers.   Of course the windows must be guarded with vertical bars, upon which the little hawks can find no foothold.

For the worst cases of carrying I must refer the reader to the chapter on "Vices."   But even with a well-behaved merlin the trainer must be constantly on his guard, at least for a fortnight after the hawk has begun work in the field.   He must beware, when she has killed, of shepherds' dogs, of wandering crows or rooks, and of the fowls which are now often found colonising the open fields, far away from a village or farmhouse.   All or any of these may attack the hawk, and by inducing her to carry away the lark, sow the seeds of the vile habit.   "Once a carrier, always a carrier," is not an entirely true maxim, but it is not far from the truth.   I have known merlins carry badly, and afterwards abandon the practice; but such cases are not common, and the trouble involved in effecting the cure is sometimes more than the merlin is worth.   Prevention is many miles better than cure ; good, honest miles, too, measured over the stony hillsides of Wilts!   As you approach your merlin on the ground, remember not to stare at her, and to give her plenty of time. On the first few occasions you must exercise the patience of a veritable Job.   She is now, after her victory, more apprehensive than ever that her hard-earned meal may be ravished from her. As you walk about, pretending to look at anything rather than her, she is all the time wondering whether your intentions are honourable or the reverse.   Instinct tells her that they are base. Her previous experience, on the other hand, is reassuring to her. Your attitude, as you stroll about, is indicative of no sinister design.   "When in doubt do nothing," is a hawk's maxim, as well as a diplomatist's.   Meanwhile there is the quarry to be plumed.   So with many lookings round, and many pauses, and with a rather misdoubting mind, she falls to at the work of picking off the feathers.   Not greedily—unless she is a greedy hawk, or too thin—but with a provoking deliberation, and with intervals that seem interminable.   At last the feathers are off ; and the warm food — the best she has ever had — begins to engross more of her real attention.   Now she is ten times easier to approach.   If, thinks she, you had been going to claim the quarry for yourself, surely you would have interfered before this. When she is fairly busy, you may by degrees get nearer, but keeping a keen look-out, and on the least show of alarm retreating quietly, but quickly.   At length you will be able to get your hand, well garnished with a tempting morsel, within reach of her.

With a troublesome merlin you may employ, if you are sure of not bungling it, a very admirable device. You may resort to what may be called the "fishing-rod trick." You will take with you into the field two joints of a fishing-rod, not including the top joint. On the thin end of the thinner of these joints, which must be stiff and stout, you will have fitted a brass hook or tooth, with its sharp point standing out an inch or so at right angles from the rod. This apparatus is sometimes invaluable. You may use one or both joints, as you find you can get nearer or less near. When you begin to be afraid to go any nearer, slide the thin end of the rod along the ground as you kneel until it is quite close to the dead quarry. If your hawk has had any decent manning at all, she will not be alarmed at it, even if she notices its stealthy approach. Having got the point on the lark's body, steering clear of the hawk's feet, turn the point downwards on it, and firmly but gently press it down and in. If you bungle, and the point slips, you are probably done; but if it holds you are safe. Proceed then with your making in, just as if there was no rod in the case. Always endeavour to take up the hawk with the hand alone, retaining your hold by the rod only as a last resort, in case of mischief. Each time that you can take her up without any trouble occurring, the easier the job will become. And even an attempt to bolt, which your firm hold with the rod renders unsuccessful, will tend to convince the evil-doer of the futility of her proceeding. Beware particularly of making in if a bagged lark is the victim. With bagged larks, easily taken, hawks are always inclined to bolt. On the other hand, if the lark has flown well, and the hawk is winded, there is less to fear.

When you have taken up your hawk, if you intend to fly her again, contrive that the body of the lark is held in the palm of your hand, and the neck alone protrudes between the forefinger and the base of the thumb. Then, when the brain has been eaten, and you have thrown away the beak and as much of the rest of the head as you conveniently can, let her think, or try to think, that there is no more to be had. If, on the other hand, you intend to feed her up, let her eat the rest of the lark, or almost all, and, as she finishes it, slip on the hood, and let her pull through the last few mouthfuls. Or, as the remains of the lark may be too bony to pull through easily, you may substitute a morsel of sheep's heart, which she can more easily dispose of. A jack which has had half a lark in the morning, and three or four heads already in the afternoon, will be generally too much gorged if allowed to take the whole of his last lark. And some female merlins may, under like circumstances, be considered to have had enough before they have quite finished their lark. I have generally found that about a three-quarter crop in the evening is as much as it is wise to give.

Larks should always be flown up-wind ; that is to say, when they get up to windward, and not to leeward of the hawk. A down-wind slip is very seldom satisfactory. If the lark is good you see nothing of the flight, and are dependent on your markers for finding the hawk, if she kills. The time lost is also often regrettable. It is not likely that with the first lark flown by any trained merlin you will have a kill. Only twice, I think, do I remember such a thing to have occurred. But the escape of several larks at first will do you no manner of harm. Even if your merlin refuses, you need not be at all discouraged. One of the most deadly merlins I ever had, when first taken out, refused seven larks in succession, and did not kill till her twelfth flight. But after that first kill she never refused again. If a trained hawk persists in refusing, or leaving the good larks, in hopes of getting a bad one, the case is serious. Possibly the reason may be that she is out of condition. But if it is her pluck that is wanting, you cannot expect to make much of her. In any case physic her, and give her two days' rest. And the next time, if you can, fly her in company with a better merlin. If you should lose such a hawk for three or four days, and then take her up again, you may take her up cured. But you may take her up confirmed in her bad habit. When I took up Ruy Lopez, after three days out in a gale, he would not fly any but bad larks.

If, in the early days, your merlin puts in a lark, mark the place very exactly with your eye. You must consider whether you will drive him out for her or not. If the place is a thick hedge or big bush, I should be inclined not to attempt it. But if it is a place where you have a good chance of a second flight, as under the side of an isolated rick, or under a hurdle where there are no sheep, I should gratify the hawk by assisting her in the moment of need, when you can be so useful to her. If you can see the lark crouching and hiding himself, do not pick him up with the hand, but drive him out with your foot or the end of your rod. And do so when the hawk, from the top of the hurdle, or rick, or wherever she has taken perch, is looking the right way. A kill on such occasions will encourage her to wait on another occasion till you can help her in the same way. The form shown by a lark that has been put in and routed out is generally not so good as before he put in. But there are many exceptions. A lark got up in the open down before Eva, probably the best hawk I ever had. But before she could get to him, he fell without a blow, right in the open. Eva was then young, and rather fat, and wanted a hard flight, so I was in two minds whether I would not leave this weak-spirited lark, and go on and find a better one. Either the lark got up of his own accord before I had decided, or else I resolved to fly him; anyhow, when he started for the second time he went right up into the sky. There was a ringing flight of immense height; and after a great many stoops the lark was bested, and came down into a field where there were stooks of wheat. Eva sat on the top of a stook with her mouth open; the lark underneath, doubtless in no better plight. I might have walked miles and not found a lark which afforded me so much sport, and the hawk such a lung-opener.

The first time your merlin puts in a lark, do not take her on your fist, unless she goes away from the spot. Let her take perch close at hand. Be very careful indeed to drive out the fugitive towards her, so that she sees it go away. By this means she will see that there is no deception; that it is really the same lark; and that you have done her the service to rout it out. But on subsequent occasions it is best always to call the hawk to the fist before you put up the quarry. Otherwise he may very possibly go off when she is not looking, especially if the hawk is on the ground, as she will be if the lark has put in to a tuft of grass, or in clover, or, as they will when hard pressed, in stubbles. *A propos* of putting in, remember always that the country for lark-hawking must be, if you are to have good flights, even more open than that necessary for rooks. It requires so small a shelter to conceal a lark. Even the high grass which often fringes a road across the downs, a patch of nettles or thistles, an old stone wall, or a waggon, will tempt a faint-hearted ringer to come down. He comes down to almost certain death; for the man is there, in alliance with the hawk. But the ringing flight is spoilt; and that is what you do not want to occur. The better the hawk, the more ready the lark is to put in. So that the mere length of flight does not prove much as to the excellence either of pursuer or pursued, unless you know from experience what is the ability of the former.

Larks, for hawking purposes, may be divided into three kinds. First there is the "ground" lark—generally deep in moult—who does not mount at all, but makes off as hard as he

F

can fly towards the nearest place where he thinks he can save himself. These larks are sometimes pretty fast, and take a good deal of catching, dodging the stoops by shifting to right or left, and sometimes avoiding a good many. But more often, especially in an enclosed country, they are wretched creatures, taken easily by a fast hawk, either in the air or by being driven into insufficient cover. These are the sort of larks that beginners are sometimes very proud of killing. The true falconer detests them as a sad nuisance. It is true that when they are fast and clever, they improve the hawk's footing powers, and give her a sharp burst of hard flying. Such a flight serves as a short gallop at full speed does to a horse in training. But from the sporting point of view it is objectionable. Fortunately, on the open down, it is not common.

Secondly, there are the "mounting" larks, which go up and try to keep the air. The original ambition of these larks is to fairly out-fly the hawk, and never let her get above them. But at moulting-time they can seldom hope to accomplish this if the hawk is a fast one in really good condition. Sometimes, going wide of them, and making an upper-cut, she will bind to them at the first shot. But this is rare. Generally there are several stoops ; and the whole business very accurately resembles a coursing match. The stoops are made from all sorts of distances,—short and long, upwards and downwards, with the wind and against it. I have seen a stoop by a trained merlin—a jack, rather—which was 300 yds. long, measured along the ground, to which must be added something for the height. Very often, when the lark has escaped one stoop by a hair's-breadth, and feels a conviction that next time he will not escape at all, he drops headlong towards a place of supposed shelter, with the hawk close at his heels. The harder he is pressed, the more indifferent will be the hiding-place with which he is fain to be content. Before a first-rate hawk he will go to a bare hurdle, a flat-sided rick, or a tuft of grass, whereas if he has less trouble in shifting, he will pass over all these attractions, and continue to throw out the pursuer—though with exhausting efforts—till he can get to a thick hedge or a substantial spinny. With this kind of lark you may have more flights, more running, and more excitement with a moderate merlin than with those of the very first quality. The latter are a bit too good for the work, and make the flight too short. Strangers who come out hawking and see a mounting lark so taken, are apt to say: "What a bad lark to be caught so soon !" It is often not the badness of the lark, but the goodness of the hawk, which makes

short work of the flight. The mounting lark would always be a
ringer if the hawk was not fast enough to get above him quickly.

The third sort of lark is the veritable "ringer." With the
start he has, he keeps ahead of the hawk, climbing up in spiral
circles. Why not in a straight line? I believe no one can tell
the reason. Possibly he finds that he can get on more pace by
having the wind now in front, now at the back, and between
whiles at the side. The curious thing is that the hawk adopts
the same tactics. The one bird may be circling from right to
left, and the other in the contrary direction. Neither seems
to guide the direction of his rings by any reference to those
which the other is making. It is now a struggle which can get
up the fastest. And it is astonishing to what a height such
flights will sometimes go. Not in a bad country; for there
there will always be cover available after the quarry has gone
up a little way. And he will not be such a fool as to stand the
racket of a shot in the air, when by dropping into a stout hedge
or plantation he can make sure of his escape. As soon as a
lark is 800 ft. high, he can drop, almost like a stone, into
any covert within a radius of 200 yds. from the spot just
under him—allowance being made, of course, for the effect of
wind. But 800 ft. is not high for a ringing flight. At least
there is nothing at all unusual in it. A lark does not go out of
sight until he is much above that height; and it is no extraordinary thing for him to do this. I have heard it said that
merlins go up after larks till they are themselves lost to sight.
But it is very seldom that any man is directly below the hawk
at the time when she is highest. I know one case, however, in which a jack-merlin came right over the markers as
they were running down-wind, more than half a mile from the
start. He must have been very nearly over their heads when
he went up out of their sight. But that hawk was never seen
again. It is, of course, quite possible that such a thing should
occur. But I have never seen any country in England where it
is at all likely. For from such a height—nearly half a mile
high—there would always be a safe place into which the quarry
might drop. And if hard pressed, he would do so. When a
lark keeps up as long as this, it is generally because he knows
that he is the better man of the two. And before that time the
hawk will also have found this out.

Larks are in moult from the beginning of August, which is
the earliest time that an eyess merlin can fly, till the middle of
September—in some years till nearly the end. During this
time, easy ones will mostly be found in the stubbles from which

the corn has just been carried. Stronger and older larks may
be found on the open down, but not in any great numbers. In
years of drought, many will get to the fields where roots are
growing. At these moulting larks, a merlin may be flown six
or eight times in an afternoon. But what was said in the
chapter on "Game-Hawking" about leaving off with a hard flight
and a kill, is still more applicable to merlins than peregrines.
These little hawks can in addition be flown in the early morning. But though I have done this occasionally, I doubt its
being a good practice, and should prefer, if the weather is
settled, to give stooping at the lure before breakfast, and wait
till past midday for the field. But when the weather is bad
you must go out when you can. The biggest score that I know
to have been made in a day, flying both morning and evening,
is ten, which Colonel Sanford killed with one of his merlins.
I have myself killed ten in a day with a single hawk ; but one
of them was taken by her in a double flight, and therefore
counts only for a half. Each of these hawks was a specially
good-tempered and well-mannered hawk. For any merlin to
take six larks single-handed in one day is a decided feat. The
most I have known to be killed in any one year by a merlin
single-handed is 106, the score of Jubilee in 1897 ; and the
highest average I have known made is fifty-nine out of sixty-
five flights—a percentage of more than 90 per cent. This
was achieved by the merlin Sis, which made the extraordinary
score of forty-one out of forty-two successive flights, the one
miss being a ringer at which she was thrown off when the head
of another lark was hardly down her throat—before she had
shaken herself, or had time to look round.

As soon as the larks have moulted, they become practically
all ringers. Such larks have never yet been taken regularly.
Usually the merlins begin to refuse them in the latter part of
September. The latest lark I have killed was on a 7th of
November. To take winter larks it would be necessary to have
a cast of very first-rate merlins, which had never, upon any
pretext, left a moulting lark. With these it is possible that a
few might be taken ; but after very long flights. And what of
the unsuccessful flights? They would go so far that I fear the
hawks must certainly be lost. A merlin which is good enough
to take even one moulted lark is good enough to find her living
anywhere ; and I doubt if she would trouble to come back
after a long unsuccessful flight for any reason, sentimental or
otherwise !

Double flights at larks are very pretty, and also very deadly.

If you throw off together one merlin which mounts quickly, and another which is a good footer, you will rarely be beaten during the moulting season; and when you do meet with a first-rate ringer, will see as real a bit of sport as man can imagine. Occasionally you may have a double flight without intending to do so. Eva had made two stoops at a very high ringer, and brought him down some yards, when a wild female merlin joined in. Stoop for stoop they alternatively played their strokes, as if they had been trained together. After some twenty of these alternative shots, the lark was taken, high in the air. But not until we picked up Eva on the dead lark, half a mile away, did anyone in the field know whether it was she or the wild hawk that had made the fatal stoop. In other years I have had many joint flights in the same way; and on one occasion two wild merlins joined forces with a trained one, and the lark ran the gauntlet for quite a long time of the three chance allies. I confess, however, that there are objections to the double flight with merlins. It may be from stupidity, but I have never been able to keep the peace between the partners. After the take, but before you can possibly get up, there is a scrimmage on the ground, even if there has not been a chevy in the air, which is not only undignified, but also most trying to the temper of the hawk which has footed the lark. Of course when you do come up you can separate the combatants, and reward the one which has been worsted in the squabble. But in the meantime, how much mischief may have been done to the feathers? In heron-hawking, where two falcons are always flown, the empty-handed one is taken down to the pigeon, and, with good management, she accepts the situation pretty cheerfully. But merlins in high condition are exceedingly hot-tempered, and often violent. No doubt the double flight can be accomplished with them by the aid of patience and tact. Mr. Freeman was able to fly his merlins well in casts. And it is only with a cast that winter larks could be attempted. Any falconer who could succeed in taking them right through the winter would have accomplished a greater feat than that of which Louis XIII. was so proud.

CHAPTER X

Gulls, Heron, Kite, Duck, etc.

THE flight at gulls is so similar to that at rooks, although much more difficult, that I should be tempted to say no more concerning it, were it not that I have been favoured by Mr. St. Quintin, who is the great authority on the subject, with some most interesting details of this sport. There can be no doubt, I think, that of all flights in which peregrines can now be flown out of the hood in England, gull-hawking is the best. It requires a cast of hawks; and these must be of special excellence, and in the height of condition, if any success is hoped for. Tiercels may be used as well as falcons; eyesses as well as passagers; but of course the probabilities of success are less with the smaller and less-experienced hawks. In the case of the herring-gull, indeed, the quarry falls so heavily, when taken, that a small hawk is apt to be badly shaken, and may thus become disgusted with the whole business.

Of the three kinds of gull, the largest, the herring-gull, is also the least difficult to take. He makes something of a fight of it on the ground when taken, and can, of course, bite hard if the hawk gives him a chance. Next to him in order of difficulty comes the common gull; and last in order is the black-headed gull, which will hardly be vanquished except by a cast of very first-rate hawks, and then on a calm day. All gulls have a great advantage when the wind is high, and usually escape, so that it is best not to fly them at such times, for fear of discouraging the hawk. Peregrines must be entered at bagged gulls, and fed after a kill on pigeon, or some very palatable food. It is also very advisable to use a make-hawk when available. On a very still day it is possible that a single hawk in good practice might take a common gull at the first stoop, if she had a good start; but if that failed, the quarry would most likely escape.

142

The best idea of gull-hawking will be given from a few quotations from the diary of Mr. St. Quintin, who considers it a very good day's work to kill two such quarry. On one occasion an old tiercel, Destiny (who was flown for no less than eight seasons), was taken out with a very fast eyess tiercel called Kismet. Thrown off at a gull "on passage," that is to say, passing on the wing, the hawks rattled off high in pursuit, when a flock of starlings got up under them, and Destiny, turning over, picked up one, while Kismet, getting above the gull, killed him at the first stoop. Later on Kismet was flown single-handed at a flock of gulls with a long slip, and again managed to kill with his first stoop. Destiny was also slipped single at a gull, but, after putting in stoop after stoop for at least three-quarters of a mile, was fairly beaten, the quarry apparently reaching the river Derwent. As the party hurried after him he came back quite flown out, and was, of course, not flown again that day. These hawks were at the time in first-rate condition. Another year, Gulliver, a very fast eyess tiercel, belonging to the Old Hawking Club, was taken out to be flown with Starlight, who had more experience and was a very high flier. The gulls were spread along a long furrow, and the two hawks went for different ones. After Gulliver had fetched his quarry and put in two stoops, Starlight, leaving his gull, came to the assistance of the other hawk, and went at the quarry with a smashing stoop. This, however, the gull avoided; and a long bout of good stooping followed, the eyess sticking to the work pluckily, but showing signs of fatigue, while the other hawk mounted high for a decisive shot. This, however, also failed, and the gull, showing once more above both hawks, went off scathless, leaving them both with "bellows to mend." Destiny and Kismet on another occasion were thrown off together at a mixed flock of gulls. They again divided, Kismet singling out a very large but immature herring-gull, which he hit hard several times, and finally brought down almost on his owner's head, while Destiny took after a common gull, and killed him three-quarters of a mile down-wind. In the winter of 1889-90 Mr. St. Quintin was so successful as to take forty-three gulls in seventy-seven flights.

Heron-hawking is a subject which, as far as England is concerned, belongs rather to history than to practical falconry. A great deal of nonsense, as well as a good deal of truth, has been written about it, but those who feel interested must be referred to the excellent account given in the work, already referred to, by Schlegel and Wulverhorst, of the proceedings of the Loo

Club in Holland.[1] I have talked with Mr. Adrian Möllen, the falconer of that club, and heard from him that the sport differed in no respect from rook-hawking, except that the heron was always flown "on passage," when already high in the air, and that two passage falcons were flown together. He told me that he had very seldom found any real difficulty in entering a passage falcon, and never lost one of his own training by any accident except once, when the mischief arose in a strange way. The hawks were mounting, when the heron disgorged a good-sized fish. At this one of his falcons stooped as it fell, took it, and made off to an inaccessible place, where she devoured almost the whole of it, and afterwards died of indigestion. In India heron-hawking is still practised, but there is not the same enthusiasm about it as there was in Europe some centuries ago, or in the days of the Loo Club.

A much more favourite and exciting sport in India and other parts of Asia is the flight at kites. In England the fork-tailed kite was flown from very early times, and it is not a century ago since one afforded a flight six miles in length in the Eastern Counties. For this very fine flier gers were commonly used in the Middle Ages ; and the kite was enticed within range by turning out an owl with a fox's brush tied to its feet. In India the Brahminy kite and the brown kite are both very common, and are taken with sakers, as well as peregrines, and occasionally by shaheens. I hear that eyess sakers are preferred, and that they are never allowed to fly any other quarry until they are slipped first at bagged kites. It is also necessary to make sure that the hawk shall never taste the flesh of the kite when taken ; as if once this has occurred the saker is useless ever afterwards for this quarry. It appears, however, that not many sakers are good enough to take the kite, even when physicked and flown two together ; and when they have been made to it they command a very high price.

We must also now go to foreign countries, and especially to India, to see duck-hawking, which was formerly so favourite a sport in the British Islands. Duck are not now plentiful enough in England to induce one to keep a hawk for them alone, although occasionally one is taken by a game-hawk during the season. Hawking "at the brook," as it was called, was conducted on very much the same principles as game-hawking in

---

[1] This famous society was started by the Duke of Leeds and Mr. Newcome, with the assistance of the Dutch falconer Bots, and had as its president Prince Alexander of the Netherlands. In 1843, with forty falcons it took about two hundred herons, almost all of which were released with rings round their legs.

our own times. The hawk was thrown off and waited on at a high pitch, while the duck were put up by water-spaniels working in the water in concert with beaters on the bank. Much pains were taken to drive the quarry in the right direction. The first stoop would of course be the most dangerous to the rising duck, and if he avoided this, there would often be a fine chase, as the duck, when once fairly on the wing, is very swift, and severely taxes the powers of the best peregrine. Peregrines are very keen after this quarry, and indeed in some countries are commonly known by the local name of "duckhawks." In India the peregrine and the shaheens are both used for this flight, which is highly esteemed, and, no doubt, quite as good as grouse-hawking. It is certain that it was also a favourite sport in China and Japan, where it may still be had by any adventurous sportsman who travels so far.

A very lively and amusing flight is that at the magpie, which was largely practised in Ireland until the middle of the nineteenth century, and is still occasionally to be seen. It partakes of the two characters of sport described in Chapters VII. and VIII. In fact, just as the magpie is a parti-coloured bird, neither all black nor all white, so the pursuit of him is neither wholly by flying from the fist nor wholly from the pitch, but by a combination of the two. The magpie is seldom to be found in very open country. You must therefore get at him as you best can. A cast of hawks is flown ; and often it is an even chance that their wide-awake quarry will get off to some shelter before either hawk has even had one shot at him. Then both hawks will wait on, when they have become *au fait* at the game, so as best to cut off his retreat to another covert. The falconer meanwhile has to use his best exertions to dislodge the fugitive from his place of rest. He should be assisted by a large field, which must hurry up with all speed to the spot, and by every imaginable device endeavour to rout out the quarry. Sticks and stones are discharged. Hunting - whips are cracked. Pistol-shots are even brought into requisition, and boys are deputed to climb the trees. The tiercels—for tiercels are most commonly used for this flight — wait on knowingly in advantageous places,—one sometimes close to the covert, ready for a sharp, quick stoop ; and the other at a higher pitch, hoping for a long shot. The magpie is not a fast flier ; but he uses his head as well as his wings, and is ready whenever a chance occurs to get back to covert. The beaters have often more to do than the hawks, with shouting, running, pelting, and contriving by their joint efforts to make the fugitive take to the open, where one of the hawks can get a fair shot at him. But the latter must be staunch at waiting on, good footers, and quick to take advantage of the efforts made by their friends below. There is not much in this business of what may be called the nobility of the noble sport,—none of the long dashing stoops out of the clouds which you see in grouse-hawking, or of the laborious mounting and ringing which you had with the gull or rook. It rather resembles the hedge-row driving described later on in the chapter on Sparrow-Hawks. But for those who like bustle and excitement, and hard exercise for the legs and voice, few things will beat magpie-hawking. And few things will demonstrate more clearly the marvellous adaptability of the peregrine to the exigencies of the case. A wild hawk would have no chance with a magpie, unless he caught him unawares, crossing from one bush or plantation to another. But the trained hawk, knowing that the men are working with him, joins his efforts with a good will to theirs, and does exactly that which you want him to do, and which it is best for him to do. As an example of co-operation between man and hawk, a magpie-worry is not to be excelled. Neither of the actors in the scene is any good without the other ; and if either fails to do the right thing at the right moment, the whole play is spoiled, and both players disgusted. Tiercels, well assisted, and well worked at their quarry, make very good bags. Mr. St. Quintin and Colonel Brooksbank, with two tiercels, Meteor and Buccaneer, killed forty-five in one campaign ; and several other capital scores have been made within recent years.

The green plover is such a common bird, and so easily found in open ground, that it is a pity, in one sense, that he cannot be flown. The unlearned may ask, Why not? The answer is, Because no hawk is good enough to take him. By which I do not mean that no peewit is ever taken by a peregrine. The wild peregrines take them not unfrequently ; and trained ones have now and then succeeded in cutting one down. But the attempt to make trained hawks take them regularly, or even fly them for any length of time, has always failed. John Barr, amongst others, trained some picked tiercels specially for this quarry. When I saw him some time after he had made this experiment, he assured me that to kill peewits with trained hawks was impossible. Of course plovers of all kinds are not more exempt than other creatures from the ills that flesh is heir to. In fact, to judge from the tone of their cry, and considering the way they have of sitting in wet feet without changing their stockings, it may be supposed that they are often out of sorts. Sometimes, doubtless, like other birds, they are infirm and old. When labouring under any such disadvantage, even if it be only rheumatism or a cold in the head, a chance peewit may be cut off and reckoned in the hawk's score. Otherwise these birds are too clever for even the best trained hawks. I have seen even bagged peewits make such a complete fool of a falcon that she was ashamed of herself. They did not exactly "fly round" the hawk, as the saying is, but they did almost as much. They made rings underneath her as she was ringing up, keeping in exactly that position where she could never get her head towards them at all. Then if the hawk did manage to put in a stoop they would face about so as to avoid the shot, and, with a great flop of one wing, start away like phantoms in an unexpected direction. If the hawk contrived to get at them from behind, they would take a sort of header downwards, and, making a kind of somersault in the air, come up behind the hawk with a manifest smile on their usually daft countenances.

On the downs in Wilts and Berks you will sometimes see a rook-hawk, or, for that matter, a game-hawk, when coming back from an unsuccessful flight, make a dash at a lapwing as he flounders about below. But the creature generally shifts from the stoop with almost contemptuous ease. Only in rare cases is he too slow. Mr. E. C. Pinckney once took a lapwing with a very young eyess tiercel; that is, the hawk put him in after a good flight, and he was picked up. But I do not think that tiercel ever took another. There is therefore a chance for anyone who wants to beat the record in the matter of plover-hawking. With two very first-rate passage tiercels, or, perhaps, better still, two shaheens, the attempt might be made again. Whoever succeeded would thereby have carved for himself a prominent niche in the falconer's temple of fame.

The Norfolk plover may be taken with a falcon or tiercel, generally without great difficulty. Golden plovers would, I think, always escape, unless they could be put up just under a hawk waiting on. Curlews and several of the common sea-fowl might also be taken, if found at a sufficient distance from the sea. The wild goose was formerly flown with success in England by gers. Landrails, if they can be got to rise, will, of course, fall an easy prey, and quail can also be taken, though the sparrow-hawk or the merlin is the right hawk for them. They are fast, but do not shift well. The jackdaw is faster than the rook, and a better shifter. He is sometimes killed by a rook-hawk, and may afford a very good flight. Pheasants, of course, will be caught by a falcon when they get up in open ground. Colonel Sanford knocked down a full-grown pheasant with a tiercel; but the little hawk could not hold him on the ground.

Woodcocks have been flown with a great deal of success in comparatively recent times, and have shown very excellent sport, requiring quite a first-rate peregrine to take them well, and that usually after a long and often high flight. Between 1823 and 1833 Mr. John Sinclair flew woodcocks regularly in Scotland, and captured in one season as many as fifty-seven with a falcon. Before this the Renfrewshire Subscription Club did good execution with the quarry, and Colonel Thornton also had some splendid flights. Sir Thomas Brown (cited by Harting, *Bibl. Acc.* p. 27) says that a hawk, probably a peregrine, made a flight at a woodcock nearly thirty miles in one hour. The mention of so long a time suggests the inference that the quarry "put in" several times, and was routed out. A famous account is extant in print of a woodcock very well killed after an unusually high flight by one of Major Fisher's peregrines.

Snipe are occasionally taken by peregrines that happen to be waiting on when they rise. The first stoop is, of course, dangerous for the snipe, but if he eludes that, a cast of the best tiercels will hardly catch him. I have seen a female shaheen hawking at snipe for her own pleasure, and saw her knock one down very close to me in the long grass, but she could not find it. Waiting for me to serve her, she remained for a while very near over my head, and even took a dead snipe which I threw up for her, but finding it cold dropped it after a yard or two's flying. Mr. St. Quintin once flew a snipe hard with a good game-tiercel of his, which bested it in the air, but it got off by means of continually putting in to a deep ditch.

Many other birds are taken occasionally by peregrines when they get up under the hawk, either while waiting on or coming back from an unsuccessful flight. I saw a male kestrel taken in this way—and very easily too—by an eyess game-tiercel of Major Fisher's. Larks, too, are now and then taken when the dog stands to them, and they are put up. Major Fisher had a long flight once with a peregrine at a wild merlin, which was very hard pressed, and at last put in to a thick hedge.

In some Oriental countries peregrines are commonly flown at hares; but the sport is not one which would ever be popular in highly civilised countries, for the falcon, or falcons, do not bind to the animal like a goshawk. They deliver repeated stoops at the head of the unfortunate creature, which is, of course, no match for them in speed, and thereby in the long-run deprive it of what little wits it had to start with.   In course of time this repeated buffeting reduces it to a state of utter bewilderment and exhaustion, so that it can be held by the falcons, or seized by the dogs which sometimes follow the flight as their allies.   In England, of course, a hare may be put up by accident, and a falcon, waiting on, may stoop at it instinctively.   Parachute, the very excellent eyess falcon already named, killed three hares in 1882.   At one of these she was flown intentionally, to show what she could do with him.   She kept striking him on the head till he was so exhausted that she thought she could safely catch hold.   But when she did so a rough-and-tumble occurred, as it will in hawking with the goshawk ; and before it was ended, the very steady setter which was out thought it time to run in and give the *coup de grâce*.   These were all Scotch hares ; and the last-mentioned of them weighed a full 6 lb.

CHAPTER XI

The Goshawk

NO distinction was made when we were talking about hack and the manning of hawks between the different species to which they happen to belong. Nor is it necessary to insist much upon the distinction even down to the time when they have been reclaimed and are on the point of being entered. But whereas all those which we have been considering are "hawks of the lure," we have seen that the short-winged hawks, which remain now to be dealt with, are "hawks of the fist." Let us see what modifications must be made in the system of training when it is the latter that we are preparing for the field.

In the first place, some authorities question altogether the utility of hack for eyess goshawks or sparrow-hawks. Others maintain that it is quite sufficient to let them loose in a shed or empty room until their feathers are strong. This latter plan seems a very poor sort of compromise between hack and no hack. The eyesses so turned loose get no real liberty, and nothing at all like the amount of exercise which they would if they were in the open. Yet as compensation for what they thus lose they get no advantage that one can easily understand. Without pretending to decide the point in question, I may perhaps venture to say that any hawk's muscles and eyes, as well as her general health, are more likely to be improved by a free life in the open air than in a sort of big cage. If they are not hacked at all they may of course be very early made to the fist and the hood, and will be manned and in flying order much quicker than hack hawks. Whether this will be of advantage or not, circumstances alone can decide ; but a short-winged hawk can generally be allowed a fairly long hack, and yet be ready for her trainer's use as soon as the latter requires her services. Of course it is not safe if there are other hawks out at hack to let goshawks out anywhere in the vicinity ; and I should be very doubtful about the expediency of hacking sparrow-hawks in the same place as merlins or kestrels. In fact it is not safe even to peg out a goshawk in any place where hack merlins can come. I remember an unfortunate jack—the smallest I ever saw—to whom his owner had given the not very classical name of Jones. This hawk was out at hack in a rather promiscuous way, killing sparrows for himself occasionally, and at other times coming to the lure. I think he knew we laughed at him, and thought that life in general was a sort of joke. But one day the fancy seized him to go and fraternise with a big young goshawk which was out on her bow-perch, duly secured by the leash. The owner was absent at the time; and when he returned there was nothing left of poor Jones other than the feet and a sad litter of pretty brown and white feathers round about the bow-perch.

When your short-winged hawk has been taken up from hack, or at anyrate when she is to be taken in hand, her trainer must set to work very seriously and very promptly at the business of reclamation. This is not, it is true, different at first in character from that required for the long-winged hawks. But it is often different in degree; for personal attention and almost perpetual care are a necessity. Unless you can contrive to have her "waked," you will have a tough job with her. Anyhow, she must be carried almost all day. Whether eyess or wild-caught, she should be treated very much like a haggard peregrine. Almost superhuman efforts will be required in some cases before she can be manned; yet manned she must be, and that more thoroughly than a long-winged hawk, before you can hope to do much with her. It required a Sir John Sebright to kill a partridge with a sparrow-hawk ten days after she was caught; and it would be still more difficult to kill a blackbird in that time. That is, at least, to first kill it, and then take up the hawk! For carrying is a vice to which the short-winged are naturally disposed, though they are not so bad in this respect as merlins or hobbies. In manning a short-winged hawk it will generally be found better to work very hard for a few days than to work only moderately hard for a much longer time. In fact, a less amount of attention, if concentrated upon the pupil at first, will do more than a much greater share applied to her in smaller doses.

It is not usual to hood sparrow-hawks much after the time when they are being reclaimed. But they should be kept, like all other hawks, accustomed to being hooded, and not by any means allowed to become hood-shy. And while the business of reclamation lasts it is a good plan to tie the tail. This is done by making a half-knot round the shaft of the outer feather, nearly half-way down, passing the ends over and under the tail, and making a double knot of them on the shaft of the outer feather on the other side. When the hawk bathes the thread is nearly sure to come off; and when she is dry you can put on another. If it stays on, no harm is done. This simple device ensures the tail feathers against any accident which might otherwise occur while she is being handled by the trainer, and perhaps by more or less incompetent assistants. Later on it will be tried hard enough! Some falconers—and good ones, too—despair of saving it for long; but you need not sacrifice it sooner than you have any real occasion. The tail is just as much—or as little—use to the hawk while she is being manned —or, for that matter, when she is flying to the fist—whether it is tied up or not; and in the former state it can come to no harm. Let the hawk at least take her first quarry with un-damaged feathers. A moderate degree of coping will be found permissible for short-winged hawks, although it is hardly ortho-dox to say so. No doubt blunt claws would be detrimental to these hawks in the field; but between bluntness and the needle-like sharpness of the uncoped claw there is a world of difference. The uncoped goshawk not only ruins the best glove in double-quick time, but sometimes in starting from the fist does not completely disengage all eight needles immediately from the buckskin, and so is impeded, and flurried, and vexed in that short temper of her own.

The strength of a goshawk's beak and feet is almost in-credible; and, this being so, it is well to be provided with good store of useful tirings. Heads and necks of fowls will be acceptable; and the more elderly and bony these creatures are the better for the purpose. For during the long process of carrying you will want to give your goshawk plenty of hard morsels to pull at; and none but the toughest will withstand for long the attacks of her sharp-pointed beak. The frequent discussion of bony tirings will wear down that sharpness a little, but I think not quite enough. Goshawks should not be allowed to get at all thin, far less weak; on the other hand, they should not be too freely fed. Half a crop a day of beef or good fowl, or a little more of rabbit, is a very fair allowance, if she has once a week, or rather oftener, a good gorge, with plenty of castings, and the next day very short commons. As soon and as much as possible she must be made to work for her food. That is, she must earn it by showing every day some improvement in her behaviour. If yesterday she bated off twenty times in ten minutes, you may call it an improvement to-day if she bates off only ten times in the same space of time. So when she has walked even two inches for her food, it is an improvement when she will walk four or five. Step by step you must coax her to do more for you, rewarding her the moment she has given way. And all the time you must be making friends with her. Stroking with the stick or a feather is always to be recommended. But you must be able also to stroke her with your hand as you like without any remonstrance or fear on her part. It is a troublesome job, do what you will, the manning of a short-winged hawk. But the harder you work, and the more patience you can exhibit, the better and quicker you will succeed. It is best to be content at first if very slow progress is made. In the later stages, if you make no mistake, there will be days of much quicker improvement, such as may even sometimes surprise your too desponding mind. Thus though it may be days before you can get her to exchange her walk to the fist for a jump, yet this feat once accomplished, you may have quite a short time to wait before she flies to you the length of the room. On the other hand, a hawk which has come well to you indoors will perhaps not come a foot, or even look at you, when first called off in the open air. Of course for all the early out-door lessons the hawk will be secured by a creance. It is well even to be a little extra-cautious in dispensing with this safeguard, for if a goshawk when only half trained does once make off, it is rather a chance if you ever come up with her again.

In time your goshawk will be manned, and at least partly reclaimed. She will look gladly on you when you come near, and jump or fly to you on small encouragement for a small reward. If you tease her with a morsel of meat, she will perhaps make that quaint crowing sound which sounds like a mild protest against your hard-heartedness. When you hold out your fist temptingly with a nice piece of food in it, she will fly fifty yards to you at once. If now you have carried her sufficiently throughout the process of reclaiming, she will not need much to bring her into "yarak"; that is, into a state of eagerness for killing quarry. A small dose of purgative medicine may be given, and after twelve hours' fast, a small feed of very good food, without any castings, and on the next day she may be entered.

Female goshawks are now usually trained chiefly for hares or rabbits. Males should always be tried first at partridges or pheasants; and if they are not good enough for such quarry, may be degraded to water-hens and the like.   The bagged quarry for entering should, in the one case, be a rabbit, and in the other, a partridge or house-pigeon.   When a rabbit is used, a short, tough cane may be attached crosswise to the end of a very short creance, which will serve to prevent the quarry from disappearing bodily down a burrow.   The partridge or pigeon should not, of course, be a first-rate flier ; or, at least, he may have a longer creance to carry.   Let the hawk take her pleasure on the first live quarry killed ; and next day give a very light feed, not later than noon.   On the third day she may be flown either at a better bagged quarry or at a wild one.   She should have a very good start for her first real flight, and in a country free from burrows or impenetrable covert.   Then, if she only starts, she ought to kill in the case of a rabbit.   Nothing is more bloodthirsty than a young goshawk in yarak ; nor, in proportion to its size, has so much strength in its grasp. When once the four long daggers with which each of her feet is armed are imbedded in the head or neck of a rabbit or leveret, it is generally all up with that unlucky beast.   He may jump and kick and roll over in his frantic efforts to escape.   He may by the latter tactics force the hawk to let go for a time, though this is by no means always the result even of a complete somer-sault.   But if the grip is thrown off, the respite is short.   Before the quarry can make use of what wits are left to him, the pur-suer is on him again—this time probably with a still firmer hold than before.   Though a rabbit is fast for a quadruped, and the goshawk slow for a hawk, yet the advantage in pace is always with the latter ; and though she may be thrown out again and again by the doubles of the quarry, yet in an open space speed must tell, if the pursuer is in condition.

Nevertheless, as it is often difficult and sometimes impossible to find rabbits in open places, it is advisable to let the first flight for your beginner be as easy as you can.   When she has taken an undersized rabbit or leveret, she may be advanced to a full-grown rabbit, and thence, after a few kills, to a full-grown hare, if your ambition is to fly hares.   Very possibly it may be neces-sary to throw her off at the quarry and not expect her to start of her own accord.   She may also refuse more than once, and yet be in the mind—that capricious and wayward mind of hers —to fly.   I have seen a young goshawk, only just trained, taken out and thrown off at three or four hares in inviting places, and have seen her refuse them all ; and yet, ten minutes later, I have seen her go at one like a whirlwind, and have it down and helpless within sixty yards from the start.   The flight at hares rather overtaxes the powers of any except the strongest female goshawks; and many people think that the flight at rabbits is preferable, even in the quality of sport afforded. In fact, the difference between the two is not so much one of speed as of brute strength; and in quickness the rabbit will be found generally superior. A goshawk which will take hares is the more valuable; but it is doubtful if she shows any better sport. Gaiety Girl, whose portrait is given, changed hands at £20, and was well worth the money. This hawk, trained by Mr. A. Newall on Salisbury Plain, killed no less than fifty-five hares in one season, besides other quarry. Of course if goshawks are to be flown at hares, they must be left strictly to this quarry as far as possible, and not encouraged to ever look at a rabbit.

The goshawk has one great advantage over her nobler cousin, the peregrine; she need not necessarily stop when her quarry has gone into covert. Provided only that the covert is thin enough for her to see the quarry, and to get along, she will stick to him there as pertinaciously as in the open. She will naturally not be so likely to succeed; trees and bushes will impede her stoops, and give the quarry a far better chance of doubling out of the way. But it is astonishing how clever even an eyess goshawk can be in threading her way through covert, and choosing the moment when a dash can be made. The hare is not as well able to use her natural cunning in front of a hawk as in front of a hound. The whole affair is so rapid, and the danger behind is so pressing, that there is hardly time to devise, and still less to put in practice, those tricks which are so successful in hare-hunting. If one could only see it all, possibly the flight at a hare in a thin covert would be better worth seeing than a flight in the open. At anyrate, the skill exhibited by the hawk must be greater. For she not only has to keep the quarry in view, and to make straight shots at him, but also in doing so to avoid breaking her wing tips, or even her neck, against an intervening tree.

The wild rush of the falconer—or ostringer—and his friends after a flight at a hare in covert is also a thing to be seen. It is unique of its kind. In magpie-hawking there is a lot of hurrying up, much tumbling about, much laughter, and any amount of shouting and noise; but there is not the same necessity for headlong racing through the thicket. If you want to be "in it" with a goshawk, you must go at a break-neck speed over or through all obstacles; you must be able to see through screens of interlacing boughs, and dash through almost impervious places. You must cut off corners by instinct and follow by inspiration.

There is something in the impetuosity of a goshawk which is contagious; and the ostringer, who has perhaps not marched at the double for years farther than the length of a platform to catch a train, may sometimes be seen tearing along with his very best leg foremost, through bramble, thorn, and quagmire, in hope of being in at the death. The whole sight is certainly worth seeing. Artists are fond of depicting the goshawk as she stands with outspread wings and half-open mouth with the hare paralysed in her terrible foot. No better personification could, indeed, be found of the pride of victory. The hare weighs commonly three times as much as his captor; yet the victor hawk must not only vanquish the hare, but also hold him fast. It is almost as if a strong man were expected to hold a wild zebra in his clutches. But the strength of a goshawk's grasp, like that of the eagle's, must be tested by experience to be properly understood.

The female goshawk, besides being flown at ground game, may be trained to take many other quarry, both big and little. At pheasants she may be expected to do good execution. Partridges will sometimes be captured in fair flight when a good start is made. Herons may be caught before they have gone any distance on the wing. Wild geese, wild duck, and wild fowl of various kinds in the same way. Land and water rails are available; and water-hens are perhaps the favourite objects of pursuit by a hawk that is not quite first-rate. Stoats, weasels, and squirrels may be taken; and the harmful, unnecessary rats will be picked up almost as fast as they can be driven out. When ferrets are used there is a danger that one of them, emerging from below, may be nailed and finished off by his winged ally. In the old days goshawks were generally assisted by spaniels; and it was pretty to see how eagerly and cleverly the dogs backed up the chief actor in the play, while she in turn trusted to them to drive the quarry in the right direction. The conditions of modern game-preserving do not lend themselves much to the use of spaniels; and perhaps they are not so often of service to the gos, but they are frequently used. A good retriever is often useful, especially if you are flying pheasants, and the hawk should always be on the most amicable terms with him.

Male goshawks are thought by some to have more speed than their sisters. When they are good, they will take partridges, with a good start, but not otherwise; and many of them will tackle a pheasant. It is said that in some countries quails are taken with the male. Very strong males will sometimes hold a full-grown rabbit; but the effort is rather beyond their strength. The flight of a gos is very peculiar. After a few fast flaps of the wing she often spreads them a moment or two, and sails along, giving to the falconer, who is accustomed to long-winged hawks, the appearance of having left off. Almost immediately, however, she begins moving her wings with greater vigour than ever, and, gaining quickly this time on the quarry, comes at him, sometimes with an upper-cut, if it is a bird, before you think she can have had time to reach him.

Goshawks may be flown repeatedly the same day. In fact, it is almost difficult to say when they have had enough flying. But in this, as in all kinds of hawking, it is well to remember that an extra good flight with success means an extra good reward. If, therefore, after some indifferent or unsuccessful flights, the hawk has flown hard and killed cleverly, I should advise feeding her up, and not flying her again merely for the sake of making a bigger bag. Under this system she may go on improving indefinitely; and you will be rewarded for your pains and labour at the beginning by possessing a hawk which perhaps for years will give a good account of herself. I have said that a goshawk which is intended for hares should be kept to them alone. So, likewise, a male which is meant for partridges should not be thrown off at pheasants or anything else. But, as a general rule, there is no such necessity with the short-winged hawks, as there is with the long-winged, of keeping them from checking at odd quarry. The bag of a goshawk has often been known to include four or five very different items, such as a rabbit, a rat, a weasel, a pheasant, and a water-hen. These sanguinary creatures are not particular as to what they kill when they are in the humour for killing. They commit murder, as foxes do, for the mere pleasure of it; and this you may easily prove if you put out a number of fowls where a gos can get at them. If you keep one in the same room where other hawks are, and by any mischance her leash comes unfastened, she is as likely as not to go round and massacre the whole lot.

Live fowls should never be given on any account to a goshawk. If you can, you should prevent her from ever supposing that they are good to eat, otherwise she may take a liking to poultry, and seize every opportunity of helping herself to the hens and chickens of your neighbours. The attraction of poultry-yards is a great objection in places where there are many of them, and some very good falconers have actually felt themselves obliged on this account to discontinue keeping hawks.

I am indebted to Mr. John Riley, of Putley Court, Herefordshire, for the following most interesting records of scores with trained goshawks, and the notes which are annexed. They illustrate this department of hawking in the most vivid and practical way:—

Enid (eyess female goshawk)—
  In 1888–89, took 82 rabbits.
  „ 1889–90,   „   59 rabbits, 1 pheasant, 1 water-hen.
  „ 1890–91,   „   67 rabbits, 1 water-hen, 1 partridge,
          1 stoat, 1 mole.
  „ 1891–92,   „   52 rabbits, 1 mole.

Isolt (eyess female goshawk)—
  In 1885–86, took 110 rabbits, 2 pheasants, 13 water-hens,
          5 ducks, 1 rat.
  „ 1886–87,   „   130 rabbits, 1 pheasant, 4 ducks, 3 water-
          hens, 1 stoat.
  „ 1887–88 (to 26th Dec.), took 70 rabbits.

Sir Tristram (eyess male goshawk)—
  In 1886–87, took 26 partridges, 10 pheasants, 16 rabbits,
  5 landrails, 12 water-hens, 1 stoat.

Geraint (eyess male goshawk)—
  In 1888 (to 4th Oct.), took 11 partridges, 5 pheasants,
  2 landrails.

Tostin (haggard male goshawk), caught 15th July, flown 9th September—
  In 1891 (to 17th Oct.), killed 21 partridges, 3 pheasants,
  1 landrail, 1 leveret, 1 wood-pigeon, 1 water-hen = Total,
  28 in 38 successive days.

Mr. Riley trains his own hawks, and, for convenience and for saving time in an enclosed country, has sometimes used a lure. He keeps them as hard at work as he can. He has much difficulty in finding enough quarry for them, and is much troubled by poultry. But for these causes the bags made would have been even much larger than they were. He has a great preference for haggards, whose style of flying he considers very far superior to that of the eyesses. Tostin, especially, used to shoot up some feet when he left the fist; and this seemed to have a demoralising effect on the partridges. He hit them so hard that the blow could be heard a long way off.

TRAINED GOSHAWK "GAIETY GIRL"

When he was unsuccessful, instead of coming straight back, he would throw up two or three hundred feet, moving his head from side to side as he flew. Sometimes he would come down upon partridges on the ground, so as to put them up all round him, and then, if there was no friendly hedge at hand, he was pretty sure to have one. It was no doubt a great feat to get him fully trained in so short a time after his capture as fifty-six days. Pity his brilliant career was so soon ended by death! Almost all the partridges taken, by one hawk or the other, were captured in fair flight, without any routing about in hedges or other covert.

To show what goshawks will do when well worked, I may mention that Mr. St. Quintin's falconer (now the head falconer of the Old Hawking Club) took out his female goshawk in November 1885, and gave her seventeen chances at rabbits lying out in the grass. She caught them all, but being a bit blown, let the last one go. Sir Henry Boynton's goshawk, Red Queen, on 2nd December 1895, killed as many as twenty-four rabbits in one day.

The illustration is a portrait of " Gaiety Gal," the goshawk which, while she was owned by Mr. Arthur Newall and flown by him, killed in one season fifty-five hares, nineteen rabbits, two pheasants, one partridge, one wood-pigeon, one Norfolk plover, one landrail—total, eighty head. This fine hawk was afterwards sold for £20; and the vendor always considered that he had been a loser by the bargain.

CHAPTER XII

The Sparrow-Hawk

THERE is so little difference between the training of the goshawk and that of the sparrow-hawk, that it is unnecessary to give any special directions for the latter. But, just as the merlin is a more delicate feeder and a more delicate subject than the peregrine, so it must be remembered that the diet and treatment of the smaller short-winged hawk must be more *recherché* than that of the larger. This is more especially true of the musket, or male sparrow-hawk, which is very much smaller than his sister, and is in many respects a kind of miniature hawk. Nothing in the shape of hard or tough meat must ever be given to him. No long fasts, no hardships. He must be always something of a spoilt child. And after he has once been manned, the more he is petted and pampered the better in most cases he will become. As far as my experience goes, he has a better temper, and is more easily reclaimed than his bigger sisters; but I have heard other falconers express a contrary opinion. Both the ladies and gentlemen, however, excluding exceptional cases, are, for a time at least, about as troublesome creatures as ever wore a good pair of wings. For the first few days after they are captured, or taken up from hack, it seems quite impossible to make anything of them. The beginner, unless he is of a most sanguine temperament, may be excused for despairing of the prospect of ever reducing them to obedience, and far more of ever using them profitably in the field. And, to tell the truth, if he has had no previous experience with a more docile kind of hawk, he seldom does succeed.

Yet an old hand will tell you that, when taken properly in hand, the sparrow-hawk becomes as trusty and hard-working a servant as man can well wish to have. She will combine the tameness of a parrot with the courage, and even ferocity, of a tiger, and will learn to treat her master to the amiable side of her character, and the quarry to the other. She will go on flying almost as long as you like to fly her, and start at one sort of bird almost as readily as another. She will work in any kind of country to which you introduce her; and if she does not make a good bag it will not be for want of will on her part, or for not doing her best. It seems almost that in proportion as the difficulties of training are great, so is the result the more gratifying when they have once been overcome. Mr. Riley, who has flown both goshawks and sparrow-hawks with the greatest ardour and success, is of opinion that from the point of view of mere sport, the latter are even superior to the former.

In the good old days partridges seem to have been taken pretty commonly with the female sparrow-hawk. But when I say taken, I do not mean that many old birds were actually caught in the air by the hawks. This would imply that the old-fashioned sparrow-hawk was faster and stronger, as well as better trained, than those of our own time. What often occurred was no doubt that the partridge was pursued by the hawk, and taken by the men or dogs. For the sight of this hawk, when she really means business, is quite enough to take all the courage out of even a bold partridge, and induce him to lie close in the hedge or thicket into which he has been put, when he can be grabbed by a spaniel or retriever, or even sometimes picked up by hand. I make no question that the old-fashioned falconers, by the aid of their drugs and nostrums, kept their hawks of all kinds—and especially hobbies—in better condition than we do. But even then it would probably have been considered quite a feat to take old partridges on the wing with a sparrow-hawk. And now, when the stubbles can only be called covert by courtesy, and to get within fifteen yards of a bird is a rare thing, it is certainly more difficult for us than it was for them to get a fair start at one. But a time often comes in a day's shooting when the birds, having been shot at a good deal, and scattered like sheep without a shepherd, lie very close in a patch of clover or thin roots. This would be the time for one of the guns, who had brought out his falconer with a sparrow-hawk in reserve, to call the latter forward. The rest of the guns—or some of them at least—would probably be glad enough to see so unusual a sight as a flight with a sparrow-hawk at a partridge. Anyhow, the interruption to the business of the day, while the little hawk was flown, would be very slight. Of course a sparrow-hawk which is intended to fly partridges should be kept, as Turbervile recommends, as much as possible to "big fowls." And there would always be more or less a risk, unless the hawk was in first-rate condition,—in what is called "screaming yarak,"—that she would refuse at the critical moment the carefully marked bird, and put her owner to an everlasting shame. A falconer who is afraid of this, however, is not the sort of man who will ever do much good with any kind of hawk nowadays.

The quarry *par excellence* of the sparrow-hawk is a blackbird. Every female which is sound in wind and limb, and also most males, ought to be able to take blackbirds, whereas it must be an exceptionally strong and bold female which will be good enough for the much more difficult flight at partridges. The hawk referred to in the *Merry Wives of Windsor* seems to have been an eyess musket. Unless, therefore, the falconer is particularly ambitious and confident in himself and his hawks, he had better lay himself out for blackbirds as the *pièce de résistance*, with the chance of a few thrushes, starlings, water-hens, and small birds to make up the bag. Peter Gibbs the falconer told me that he had taken thirteen head of quarry, varying in size from a partridge to a wren, in one day with a female sparrow-hawk.

One advantage of the flight at blackbirds is that the quarry is easy to find. Few enclosed countries in England are without a good supply of them; and it is seldom that their haunts are so secure that they cannot be dislodged so as to afford a flight. Only a man must not go out blackbird-hawking all alone. He should rather get as many people to join in the business as he can. There is nothing unsociable or exclusive about a blackbird-hawking expedition. The gardener, and the gardener's men, as well as the keepers, the boys home for the holidays, and in short everyone who is available, should all be encouraged to volunteer as beaters, and help in the campaign against the plunderers of the raspberry bushes. Formerly this sort of hedge-hunting was a very popular amusement. Although in the fantastic apportionment of hawks to different ranks and degrees, the sparrow-hawk and musket were appropriated to ecclesiastics, it was a common thing for yeomen and small landowners to keep and fly this familiar and serviceable little creature. When Mr. Page says that he has a "fine hawk for the bush" (*Merry Wives of Windsor*, Act iii. scene 3), he means that he has a sparrow-hawk which will afford sport for a whole company of country-folk; and when he and his friends go out the next morning after breakfast

" birding," they may safely be supposed to get a morning's sport very much of the sort that is now to be described.

Ruby looks very murderous as she sits with her thin yellow fingers gripping the arch of yew which forms her bow-perch on the lawn. The warm autumnal sun lights up her feathers in their true colours of slatey brown on the back, and barred white on the breast. Very keen and pitiless is her yellow eye as it turns quickly towards each spot where the slightest unusual movement attracts her notice. Presently, however, all her attention is concentrated on one object, as her master steps across the lawn. In a moment she is on to the outstretched fist, where a well-known reward is almost always found. The leash is untied ; we are beckoned to come on, and we start at once, accompanied by the terrier Sandy, with a knowing look on his shrewd face. It is a warm still day, and we go straight to the big meadow, where in the bottom hedge we put out a thrush. Ruby is off the fist like lightning, and gains fast on the quarry. Just as he turns to get into the hedge the hawk makes a dash, which very nearly succeeds, but the thrush has just managed to swerve out of the way, and, running along and through the hedge, escapes on the other side, while Ruby betakes herself to a tree hard by. Before she is called down a blackbird is sighted near the same tree, and we form a line so as to drive him towards the hawk. This, however, does not accord with the views of our black friend in the bush, who resists our well-meant endeavours, and tries to work his way past us away from the tree. Fortunately there are enough of us to frustrate his efforts, and prevent him from shirking along the hedge. He is obliged to take a line across the field, and as soon as he is well away from the fence Ruby is up to him. In shifting from the stoop he dashes himself against the ground, and even by this violent effort does not wholly escape, as the hawk hits him hard as she passes overhead. He picks himself up at once and makes for the hedge, but is just too late, as Ruby grabs him just as he is entering.

Passing on to another long hedge we soon get a flight at another blackbird, which puts in before the hawk gets up. Ruby will not wait, but goes on to an oak at the end of the hedge. We beat on, with a view to drive him towards the hawk, and find that there is more than one blackbird in front of us. One of these is driven out, and Ruby makes a fine stoop at him out of the tree, but fails to hit him, and he puts in. After several tries he is persuaded to fly out into the open, and make for some bushes that are not far off, but as he goes the hawk knocks him over with a severe cut, and though he gets up again and staggers on, she has him well before he can reach the bush. With the next blackbird we have no end of excitement under and round a tree in the fence, the fugitive several times baffling us as we are driving him along towards a bare place in the hedge, and compelling us to hark back and begin driving him up again. Once he comes out a yard, and whips back again instantly. The hawk goes again up into an oak-tree near the gate. Now we drive on furiously, hoping that at the gate, anyhow, he will take wing. Some time before we get there he loses patience and ventures a flight across the field. Ruby gets a poor start, but the blackbird makes a bad use of his chance, allowing the hawk to recover lost ground rapidly, and makes such a weak attempt to get inside a brake that he is taken on the top—perhaps dazed with all the noise and hustling in the fence.

The next is a very plucky young cock, found in a short piece of hedge by a wire fence. In and out of the wire fence he shifts very cleverly, and only just saves himself in a holly bush. Here he establishes himself in a nearly impregnable fortress, made up of an earth-bank, with some tangled roots, and an infinity of quickset, wild rose, and bramble. The yapping of Sandy, the shouts of the beaters, and the howls of an under-gardener, who in the ardour of pursuit has torn his cheek open with a briar—all are unavailing to storm the citadel until some-one with a well-directed thrust nearly pins him by the tail. Then at last he is off in real earnest towards a thick brake. Before he can get there Ruby compels him with a knock on the back to drop down on the ground, and though he gets up and shuffles into the brake, he is evidently the worse for wear. It takes ten minutes' hard work to dislodge him again, and even when dislodged he dodges back after going a few yards. At last, as it is getting dark, he happens to go out just under the spot where the hawk is sitting, and she collars him above the ditch, dropping into it with him. A flight of half an hour, "including stoppages," and hard work all the time—for the men !

Another day we are out with Lady Macbeth, a young eyess with broad shoulders, large feet, and a very small head. The luck is against us at first. We are foiled by a blackbird and outflown by a thrush, and have failed to find any water-hens. At length a blackbird is marked down in a field of swedes in the open, and we adjourn there, full of hopes. The tactics adopted by this blackrobed gentleman are simple, but ingenious and effective. They consist of flopping down, as the hawk gets quite near, into a thick bunch of turnip leaves, and, when once on the ground, doubling round the stalks so as to elude the hawk, which, of course, dives into the damp covert at the same place where the quarry disappeared. Then when the hawk's head is safe behind the leafy screen of verdure, the chance comes of jumping up and slipping off unseen. Twice does Lady Macbeth detect him in the act of thus slinking off; but she is thrown out again by the same stratagem, and on the third occasion the fugitive gets off unseen by his persecutor, though in full sight of us, and also of Sandy, who yelps demoniacally, either from pure vexation, or perhaps in the hope of attracting the attention of his friend and ally. Well, of course, we lose that fellow, who goes off joyously over the hedge and the next field, glorying, like Ulysses, in the success of his wiles. More valuable to magpie and blackbird than the rather limited allowance of wing-power with which Nature has provided them, is the considerable supply of brains by which the balance is made up.

At last, however, we get a bit of luck, which indeed makes it rather a red-letter day for Lady Macbeth, for as we beat along one of the least likely-looking hedge-rows, more for the sake of doing the proper thing than with a hope of finding anything, there is a huge flurry and bustle almost under the feet of our falconer, and up gets a single partridge, beating the air noisily with broad, round wings as he gets clear of the overgrown ditch. When he is once fairly on the wing he will soon put on a pace nearly, if not quite, equal to any that our hawk can attain to. That is, he "would" rather than he "will," for we have not been idle all this time. On the contrary, Lady Macbeth, somewhat startled at first, spreads her wings, and at once shoots upwards, as if with a view to see what is the matter. Then, pulling herself together as she takes in the situation, she makes a sort of half-turn in the air, comes down in a slanting course, half stooping and half flying, and before the partridge has gone forty yards, strikes him full on the back with both feet. One, at least, of the eight sharp claws hold, and down they come with a whack on the brown earth of the ploughed field, where they seem almost to roll over one another in the excitement of the fray which has still to be fought out. For a real set-to it is, of the rough-and-tumble order. The hawk's claws, long and sharp as they are, do not penetrate to any vital part of the partridge as they do when a sparrow is the victim. Nor do her long spindle-like legs look as if they could do much service in a wrestling bout, when opposed to the short, stout, and very muscular understandings of the other. But Lady Macbeth makes play with her wings and tail as well as her feet and legs, otherwise she could be upset and shaken off in no time. Half a dozen long feathers pressed down into the ground on each side prevent her from being thrown to right or left; a dozen almost equally long and elastic feathers behind steady her still further, and act as a sort of drag if the struggling partridge tries to rush forward and so free itself. So, though the encounter is fierce, as the two feathered bodies sway about spasmodically over the rough surface of the furrow, the assailant keeps the upper hand; and soon the allied forces come up in support. The trainer, joyous at the tardy success which has crowned his afternoon, gets hold of one of the partridge's wings and holds it down, so that the kicks and scratchings to which he now resorts are wasted on the insensible clods beneath. The hawk now shifts one foot from the shoulder to the head ; two claws imbed themselves in the face and neck. A third, sad to say, pierces the falconer's unguarded thumb ; but though he moans with the pain, he does not withdraw his hand till he has cleared it from the hooked claw. Then, with sharp knife, he severs the partridge's jugular vein, and, opening the skull, allows the hawk to pick out the brain. Lady Macbeth will now be fed up; she has had some work and some encouragement, and we shall next time try to find her another short start at a partridge.

One of the merits of "birding" with a sparrow - hawk is that everyone out is always busily engaged. Everyone thinks that he has marked the exact spot where the fugitive put in, and can lay his hand at once on the place where his cunning head is hiding under the ferns or leaves. And yet when the hedge is reached these boastings are all falsified, and the hiding-places seem all to be bare. "He never stopped in the hedge at all," says one. "Yes he did. He doubled down to the right." "He climbed up into the middle." "Hark, there ! I heard him flutter." "You make such a confounded row with your argumentation ; no one can hear anything." "There he goes !" "No; that's Sandy." "I see him now." "To the left !" "Keep him back." "Cut him off." And so the chase goes on. Lady Macbeth, or Ruby, sits quietest of all on the commanding bough, though her yellow eyes glitter with excitement, and her legs and wings are ready for a start the moment that a black feather shows itself. It is equally hard to grab an old cock blackbird in the hedge, or to drive him out of it far enough to give the hawk a chance of a fair shot. As for the thrushes, they seem to puzzle a sparrow-hawk more even than the wiliest of their black cousins. They have more wing-power, too, and are apt to distance her in fair flight. A starling is, I believe, not an easy bird to take if he has anything of a start. Wood-pigeons, when taken by wild sparrow-hawks, must probably be caught unawares.

A small wiry-haired dog which is not afraid of thorns will often be useful. Sandy is not without his honours in the hawk-ing-field. Many a blackbird has he snapped up in his mouth within a yard of his formidable ally, in whose presence the quarry thinks that almost anything is preferable to a flight across the open. Then the victim is, of course, taken from him —often unhurt—for Sandy is too well bred and too well trained to injure it if he can help doing so ; and with the orthodox cry of " Ware, hawk! ware!" is thrown out to the hawk. Water-hens are a rather favourite quarry for the female sparrow-hawk, as well as for the goshawk, when she is not a very distinguished performer. A water-spaniel which knows how to work with a hawk is in each case very useful. Landrails would afford a capital flight if they were plentiful enough, and could be induced to give themselves a fair start, instead of waiting to be kicked up when the hawk is close upon them.

But perhaps the best flight of all, next to partridges, is at the quail, and it is one in which the musket can be employed as well as his sister. The Italian authorities, upon whom Turber-vile draws for the chief part of his treatise on falconry, speak of the quail as the special quarry of the sparrow-hawk, and give minute directions for this flight, which could, of course, be had in perfection in the Egyptian paddy-fields, and in other parts of the East. It is said that some of the tribes tributary to the Grand Turk, who had to pay their tribute in quails, used to provide themselves by means of sparrow-hawks alone with the neces-sary number of birds. The African falconers, when in pursuit of quails, take the sparrow-hawk round the body in their right hand, and as the quarry rises throw her at them like a round-hand bowler, thereby giving her an initial impetus, of which she seems fully to understand the advantage. In some places they surround the neck of the hawk with a *halschband*, or linen collar, which serves to steady the flight.   The Besra sparrow-hawk, as has already been said, is used as well as the common species.

A quotation from the last-named author will here, perhaps, be found to the point.   "Set your sparrow-hawke," he says, "every morning abroade in the sunne two houres, or neare thereabouts, and set her to the water twice in a weeke at the least, and especially nyasses, for they covet the water more than the rest.   Soar sparrow-hawks should not be flown withal too soone in a morning, for they soare willingly.   Take your sparrow-hawke from the pearche alwayes with somewhat in your hand, to make her love you, and be fond of you, for that is a thing of no small importance and consideration.   And also to make your sparrow-hawke foot great fowles, to the end that she may not learn nor be accustomed to carrion.   And as touching mewing of a sparrow-hawke, some use to put her in the mew as soon as they leave fleeing with her, cutting off both her bewits, lines, and the knots of her jesses, and leave her in the mew until she be cleane mewed.   But if you will have her to flee at partridge, quail, or the feazent poult, then you must draw her in the beginning of April, and have her on the fist till she be cleane and thoroughly enseamed.   And they which delight in haggarts must take great heede that they offend them not, but rather coy them as much as they can, with all devices of favour and cherishing.   For they will remember favor or injurie much better than any kind of hawke.   And he which hath a haggart sparrow-hawke must above all thinges take paines in weyning her from that vile fault of carrying : and that shall he do by serving her often with greate pullets and other great traines, the which she cannot carry, and thereby she will learne to abide upon the quarry."

Mr. Riley has given me some extracts from his hawking diary, in which the following scores are recorded :—

Blanche (eyess female), 1885–86—44 blackbirds, 13 thrushes, 1 partridge, 2 small birds.

Lady Mabel (eyess female), 1887–88—56 blackbirds, 5 thrushes, 4 water-hens, 3 partridges, 1 pheasant, 2 small birds.

Faerie (eyess female), 1889–90—64 blackbirds, 3 thrushes, 4 water-hens, 1 partridge, 4 small birds.

Ruby (eyess female), 1894–95—106 blackbirds, 1 partridge, 1 starling, 1 small bird.

G

Sparrow-Hawk and Partridge.

Princess (wild-caught female), 1895–96 (Nov. 11 to March 24)
—39 blackbirds, 1 thrush.

Of these the wild-caught Princess, though injured in the leg by a trap, was very superior in her style. Ruby at the end of the season flew very like a wild hawk. This Ruby was wonderfully fast and clever, and an excellent footer. The number of blackbirds she killed stone dead by stoops out of trees was astonishing. In size she did not exceed the average. Speaking from an experience of a great many years, and with an authority which everyone must acknowledge, Mr. Riley declares that "no sport with a female goshawk can touch that to be got with a good female sparrow-hawk."

CHAPTER XIII

HOME LIFE

PROBABLY the commonest fault in young falconers of the modern school is that of keeping too many hawks. Almost every writer on the subject has warned them over and over again against this rage for being "over-hawked"; and yet it is still the cause of endless failures, disappointments, and disasters. "Don't you know, if I lose one I like to have another to fall back upon." Such is the excuse, and a very bad one it is. If a beginner can manage to keep one hawk of any kind in flying order he may consider himself exceptionally clever; and the sole charge of a cast of hawks is quite as much as any amateur ought to undertake, unless he is blessed with a great deal more leisure time than is usually the case. An experienced professional falconer, with a boy to help him, and with nothing else to occupy his time, may manage an establishment of three short-winged hawks, or about five long-winged, or one of the former and three of the latter, short-winged hawks, when in flying condition, requiring about twice as much attention as their nobler cousins. But if it is desired to keep up a larger establishment, there should be, counting in the head falconer, one man, or at least one boy, to every two hawks.

A falconer who attends properly to his charges will find that they monopolise a very large portion of every day—at any-rate, from the time when the eyesses arrive, in early summer, to the end of the rook-hawking season in spring. His duties may be divided into those which we may call normal or permanent, and which relate to the hawks which are already in flying order, and only require to be flown and kept in working condition, and exceptional or special duties, such as the hacking of eyesses, and the manning and reclaiming of hawks which are newly caught, newly taken up, or newly removed from the moulting-place. Thus, as in other professions, there are

170

times of extra pressure, when every hour in a long day has its full complement of busy work, and times of comparative rest, when the labour is a good deal lighter. But at all times the falconer, if he is to excel, must be possessed of certain qualifications, either innate in him or carefully acquired, which will enable him to become a favourite amongst his winged pupils and servants.

Among such qualities the foremost is prudence. A moment of carelessness, or even inattention, may almost every day entail the loss of a valuable hawk. A knot insecurely fastened, a door inadvertently left open, a leash or jess that has become unsound,—all these are examples of small imprudences, some one of which many a falconer will bitterly remember to have been the cause of a catastrophe. Cleanliness and tidiness are virtues none the less desirable in a professional falconer because they were, and still are, a little rare. It is not so easy a matter as it may at first be supposed to keep a hawk-house clean and neat; and the very first aspect of many such places speaks volumes for the character of the owner or his servants. The person who has to manage hawks should be gentle in all his dealings with them. He should have the touch of an organist rather than of a pianist; the hands of a sculptor rather than of a wrestler or quoit-player. Any hurried or sudden movement is offensive and alarming to hawks; and rough treatment of any kind disgusts and makes enemies of them. Patience and a good temper are quite as necessary to a falconer as to an angler—probably more so, as the difficulties and injustices with which the falconer is confronted under modern conditions exceed those which are met with in any other kind of sport. He must be a good judge of the characters of animals, and of their moods and fancies, for there is as much difference in the dispositions of hawks as of human beings, and no two of them, except by a rare accident, can be treated successfully in exactly the same way. His sight and hearing must be good, for much depends upon his ability to keep a long flight in view, and to distinguish the sound of a hawk's bell in a high wind, amidst the rustle of leaves and grass, the murmur of a stream, or the pattering of rain.

In the golden age of falconry great weight was attached to the possession of good lungs. The "falconer's voice," for which Juliet fondly wished, was used not only to lure the tassel-gentle back again, but to encourage him in his efforts, and to cheer his successful or brilliant strokes. A modern trainer is not so demonstrative. We have—wrongly, I think—almost abandoned the use of calls and cheers to animate our winged friends in the air. But even now a loud voice is a merit in a falconer, if only as enabling him from afar to warn the field and any chance intruders not to meddle with a flight or run in to a hawk that has killed. Those few who still make a practice of "giving their voice" to their hawks are, I think, well repaid for their trouble. For no one can doubt how attentive hawks are to sounds, especially of the human voice, or how thoroughly they become convinced, when well handled, that they and their followers on foot or horseback, and the dogs, when there are any, are all friends and comrades engaged, each in his different way, in the same campaign against the same quarry.

As the huntsman in his kennels, and the trainer in his stables, so the good falconer should take a pride in his mews, or in the place, whatever he calls it, where his hawks are lodged. We have abandoned for the most part the old name of mews—long ago degraded to a new signification—and with it the fashion of building proper quarters for the accommodation of our feathered friends. The modern hawk-house is often a poor substitute for the substantial buildings which our ancestors called mews. Nowadays almost any outhouse seems to be thought good enough for the purpose ; and the trained hawks of several amateurs who are justly reputed good falconers are housed in what are little more than shanties, barely able to keep out the rain and wind, and not at all proof against that insidious enemy, the damp. There can be no doubt that the excessive prevalence in our times of the horrible disorder called "croaks" is largely due to the want of care with which our hawks are housed in winter.

A hawk-house should have solid walls, and a floor well raised above the ground, so as to be impervious to damp. It should have a loft or room above it, which will help to save it from extreme variations of temperature by day and by night. In such a place all hawks, except merlins and those which have come from any hot climate, may be kept through all ordinary weathers, care being taken, of course, that the ventilation is sufficient, but in winter not excessive. In times of severe frost or excessive damp a very moderate amount of artificial heat should be introduced. A very good arrangement, when it can be adopted, is for the back wall of the hawk-house to be also the back wall on the other side of a warm conservatory or well-heated room. In such cases it is unnecessary, unless in exceptional winters, to have any heating apparatus in the hawk-house itself. Merlins and the tropical hawks, such as shaheens, barbarys, and also the desert falcons, should, in cold or damp weather at least, be placed in a room which is over a very well-warmed apartment, and has the flue of one chimney at least running along one of its sides. A room immediately above a kitchen is pretty safe in all weathers for all hawks if the fire is kept up all night, but not otherwise. Where the room is unavoidably isolated, there must be a stove or some heating apparatus ; but the heat thrown out must be very moderate indeed, or the hawks when taken out for weathering, or even when left stoveless by day, are nearly sure to catch cold. Changes of temperature in our islands are sudden and severe enough when due to natural causes only, but if they are produced by artificial means no hawk can be expected to endure them with impunity, and least of all gers, merlins, and the denizens of the sunny south. The hardiest hawks are peregrines and hobbies, but these, too, must be given a fair chance, even if it entail upon their owner some inconvenience and expense. Whenever the weather is very wet or damp, with penetrating fogs, opportunity should be taken, when the hawks are all out on their blocks or being carried, to warm the hawk-house thoroughly by artificial means, and purge it of all suspicion of damp.

Adjoining the hawks' apartment should be another small room, where lures and spare "furniture" can be kept. Meat and food of all kinds should be rigorously excluded from the first-mentioned room, but may be kept, if it is quite fresh, on an emergency in the other, where blocks and bow-perches when taken in out of the rain can be deposited. On the walls in either room may be hung on small pegs or nails the hoods for each kind of hawk ; but it is well to mark clearly above each peg a description of the sort of hood which is intended to be there hung, so that in a case of hurry one may not be mistaken for another, and a tiercel's hood crammed on to a falcon, or a female hobby's be found wobbling about on the head of a jack-merlin. Every falconer should have in his cupboard a tin box containing a supply of imping needles suitable for the hawks which he keeps, and some spare feathers ready for imping. The same box will hold other small paraphernalia and odds-and-ends, such as waxed thread, pincers for "coping" or blunting the beak and talons, tweezers for putting on jesses, punches for making holes in leashes, scissors, files, and a scrap of thin leather for making jesses and bewits. Or there may be a compartment where ready-made jesses, bells, swivels, and spare leashes are stored. The lures, well cleansed from all food that has been attached to them, and the hawking gloves, can have their proper place in the side-room.

If the building inhabited by the hawks is large, the upper part may be used as a loft wherein to moult them. If there are hawks of different kinds to be moulted, it must be divided into separate compartments, so that no two of very different size may be together. And each individual goshawk must have a room for itself. It would not be safe to turn falcons and tiercels loose together, nor a female with a male sparrow - hawk. Merlins and jacks may be left together, and in the same place with male hobbies ; and probably peregrine tiercels with female shaheens, lanners with lannerets, and perhaps barbarys. But it is not very wise to risk the chumming together of any dissimilar hawks at a time when they are all kept in specially high condition, with no work to do, and ready for the mischief which Dr. Watts assures us is a natural concomitant of idleness. Of course if there is a living-room above the hawks, or above the furniture - room, it may serve most conveniently for a falconer's or under-falconer's bedroom, enabling him to be at hand by night as well as day in case there should be anything wrong, such as a hawk hanging by her jesses from the perch, or a scuffle amongst hawks moulting in the same compartment.

At six o'clock in summer, and as soon as it is light in winter, the falconer should be in the hawks' room. If newly-caught hawks are there, they will be in a compartment from which all daylight has been excluded. Taking them one by one on the fist, he will put on their hoods, and then, lighting a candle, or admitting enough light, he will search for their castings under the screen-perch. If any one of them which has had castings the day before should not have yet cast, he must either put her back on the perch in the dark, or else, if she is far enough advanced in training for this, hand her over to an under-falconer to be carried till she has performed that operation. Under the place occupied by each hawk the pellet should be looked for and examined before it is thrown away with the sweepings of soiled sawdust collected under the perches. As the falconer ascertains that each hawk has cast up a healthy pellet, well-shaped and free from oily mucus, he will be doing no harm if he presents her with a mouthful or two of food, by way of a morning salutation, and just to show that there is no ill-will.

Then if it is a fine morning, there will probably be a hawk or two which may with advantage be pegged out, either in the sunshine, if she is fond of it, or under the cool shade of a tree. At anyrate, there will be a hawk which will be none the worse for half an hour's carrying; and if there are merlins, it will be none too early to fly them to the lure. Every falconer, each time he rises, ought to take note of the weather, marking especially the direction and strength of the wind, and should do his best to forecast how the day will turn out. If he sees reason to expect a stormy afternoon, he will prepare to fly the hawks as early as he can; whereas, if it is already blowing or raining hard, he may think it best to provide for the possibility of a late start, taking the chance of an improvement in the weather at midday, or later. He should decide betimes which hawks are certain not to be taken out to the field, and make sure that their allowance of food is ready to be given them early in the day. Such hawks may generally be put out early in the morning, and provided with tirings, at which they may pull away contentedly on their blocks till it is time either to fly them to the lure, or to give them their ration on the fist. In the game-hawking season there will be a consultation with the keeper as to the country to be visited and the dogs to be taken out; and the falconer, having an eye to the direction of the wind, will plan out provisionally the sort of tactics which it will be best to adopt in beating the ground. Beaters and markers should also be secured, and directed as to the order of the day's proceedings, whether the business in hand is grouse-hawking, lark-hawking, or any other form of sport for which these attendants are required.

After breakfast, on sunshiny days, there will generally be candidates for the bath. Fresh water must be brought; and in very cold weather a cup or two of hot water may be added, to take off the chill. Each hawk, after bathing, should have an hour at least to dry and air herself in the sun and wind. In emergencies, on cloudy days, the old falconers used to dry their hawks after bathing by holding them with their backs to a fire. Hawks do not usually care to take a bath much before eleven o'clock; and they should not be indulged with one after half-past twelve. Those which have bathed will, of course, not be ready to fly till well on in the afternoon, especially as they will have had a very light feed in the early morning, as it is not good to let a hawk bathe on a quite empty stomach. The falconer will generally like to be present while the hawks bathe, so that he will not be ready to start for the field, even with those that have not bathed, much before noon. This hour, moreover, is full early for peregrines and most of the larger hawks, which are apt to be slack in the pursuit of their quarry when they have, or at least think they have, the best part of the day before them in which to provide themselves with their one daily solid meal.

Hawks which are not yet thoroughly accustomed to the hood should be hooded up with care, so as to avoid any trial of their temper just as they are about to be called upon to do their best. Hawks, of course, ought always to be good at the hood ; but some manifest an obstinate repugnance to it, as for instance Vesta, the very excellent game - falcon trained for the Old Hawking Club. The duties of the falconer in the field are referred to at length in the next chapter. As soon as he has returned—which will usually not be much, if at all, before dark —he must be satisfied that each hawk has had the full allowance of food which he had decided to be good for her, that her beak and talons are fairly clean, her feathers in good order, and her swivel and leash properly attached. Then each will be put in her accustomed place on the screen-perch, the leash being securely tied round the perch itself, as described in Chapter III., and the hood, if she is hooded, removed and hung up.

As for the hawks, if any, which, not being destined for the field, have been left at home, either at blocks on the lawn, or indoors, some person will have been left to shift their blocks as they become exposed to the sun, to carry them for a specified time, and perhaps to fly some of them to the lure. Every trained hawk, unless she is put down to moult, or is being flown at quarry, should be exercised daily to the lure or the fist —merlins twice, and all others once. The methods of giving exercise have been already described; but it must be remembered that when once a hawk has been entered the more real flying in the field she gets the better. Otherwise you are between the horns of a dilemma. If you give no exercise the hawk grows heavy, stale, and lazy. If you fly her too much to the lure she may grow too fond of it, and less keen at wild quarry. Good practical falconers are thus rather averse to a too free use of the lure with peregrines and lanners. On the other hand, I have found that merlins cannot well have too much stooping at the lure. Rook-hawks, and others which are never expected to wait on at a height, may often be made to do a large amount of pretty fast flying when stooping at the dead lure. This sort of practice is of course not to be encouraged in the case of game-hawks or duck-hawks, as tending to lower their pitch, which it is the chief desire of the falconer to keep as high as possible. But long-winged hawks, even in the mere act of waiting on, especially in a strong wind, get a good breather and a good stretching of their wings, if they are always allowed to be uncertain in their own minds whether in the end it will be a partridge or a pigeon that they will have to come down for, or merely the dead lure.

As for the short-winged hawks, and for such others as will not keep on the wing willingly without going to perch, they must be exercised chiefly by the device known as calling off. The most effective plan is that mentioned in Chapter VI., where two men go out, and, standing at a distance from one another, alternately bring the hawk across the intervening space by showing the lure or the outstretched fist. If two men are not available the hawk may be deposited on a railing, gate, or post, and the falconer may walk away, hiding his hands, and when he is as far off as he likes, or as the hawk will allow him to go, may call her and reward her with a few morsels, and then put her down again for the operation to be repeated. A trained hawk will often follow the falconer about for a long time, as he walks along, waiting a while in expectation of being called, and, if disappointed, flitting to a nearer resting-place, or coming right up to him on the chance that his hand will be held out; and if it is not, betaking herself to a neighbouring tree or other convenient place. Such excursions as these, in a park or on the downs, with a favourite hawk always in sight, either in the air or on a conspicuous perch of her own choosing, afford an opportunity of indulging her with the best possible sort of weathering. It is the nearest approach which can safely be made to giving trained hawks their liberty.

It is a common thing with writers on hawking to recommend their readers, when a trained hawk is out of sorts, to put her on a pair of hack-bells, and turn her out to hack for a while. I desire to speak with all respect of a practice which has doubtless been often attempted with success; but I am compelled to say that my own experience is altogether unfavourable to any such experiment. Attempts that I have known made to keep trained hawks at hack have not only failed, but have over and over again entailed the loss of the bird operated upon, sometimes for a time, and sometimes permanently. A strong and clever hawk, even if she is a bit unwell, and even if she is weighted heavily, will manage to kill something, if she has a real mind to it ; and even if she does not, her wanderings may lead her first out of sight, and then into some neighbouring field or place, where a stray gunner may make an end of her. I am not able to advise beginners to turn their hawks loose for any longer time than they themselves or some agent can be near at hand, unless it be in the case of a kestrel or hobby, or other hawk which has never killed wild birds regularly in fair flight.

No ordinary bad weather should deter a falconer from taking his long-winged hawks out to exercise. Rain, unless it is very heavy, will do a hawk no harm during the short time she is flying to the lure or being called off. Even if the rain is heavy, an umbrella can be held over the hawk as she is carried to the exercise-ground and back. Wind must be very high indeed before the trainer should hesitate to fly his hawks at exercise. When they are to be merely called off, they will, when sharp-set, if in good condition, face half a gale of wind. But the two men should, in this case, post themselves rather across wind, and not one exactly down-wind of the other ; otherwise the hawk of the up-wind man will have her head always turned directly away from the other, and moreover, if she comes fast towards the latter, may be carried so far past him that she will not take the trouble to fetch up again, and struggle up-wind to a lure of which she has once been disappointed. A game-hawk, especially if it is a passager, should not be kept waiting on very long on a boisterous day. Should she, while in the air, catch sight of a wood-pigeon or house-pigeon down-wind, and give chase, she may be out of sight in a moment, and, if the quarry takes the air, may go miles before you can run or ride five hundred yards. The best hawks rather enjoy flying in a very high wind, and seem to take an obvious pride in exerting their mastery over it. Their stoops at the lure in such weather are often exceptionally fine ; and the tremendous pace at which the wind enables them to come down, evidently affords them much inward satisfaction.

In hot and sunny weather some caution is advisable in flying hawks to the lure, as well as in the field. For when in high condition, even if they are hungry, they are sometimes disposed to go soaring, and, as it were, forgetting all about mundane affairs, disappear in airy circles down-wind. Eyesses will, it is true, generally come back when they are tired of soaring. They are reminded, sooner or later, by an internal feeling that there is such a thing as a garnished lure in the foreground. But suppose a passage peregrine, after stretching her wings for five minutes at a height of a thousand feet, to catch sight of a wood-pigeon crossing the open down. It would be almost too much to expect that she should resist the temptation. In the cool of the day, morning and evening, hawks very seldom soar if they are sharp-set, and have had the chance of a bath most fine days. It is from nine to four o'clock in summer that there is the most risk of it; and hobbies, which are greatly addicted to the habit, should not be flown during these hours in fine weather, unless the owner is prepared to wait twenty minutes, or even longer, for my lord or my lady to finish airing herself in the sky. Very special care must be taken of all hawks during the migration season—that is, for some weeks after the latter part of September and the beginning of April. At the former period, indeed, it is barely safe to let hobbies wait on at all; and the steadiest peregrines and merlins are apt to feel more or less strongly the restlessness born of migratory instincts. Many favourite hawks which seemed a few days ago to be as safe as tame cats, have been known at migrating time to develop quite suddenly an ungovernable wish to travel, and have cleared for foreign parts when they had an opportunity, without a moment's warning or a word of leave-taking.

Each hawk, after flying to the lure, will be immediately fed up, usually on the way back to the hawk-house or the lawn. As a rule, the earlier a hawk can be fed up the better, for she will be the sooner ready for the field on the next day. Moreover, she will fly better, probably, to the lure if she is aware that that ordeal is often the precursor of a solid meal. The rather common practice of feeding all the hawks at about the same hour—generally late in the day—has nothing that I ever heard of to recommend it. How can a hawk which habitually dines at six o'clock or later be expected to be keen or to fly well when thrown off at her quarry at three or four o'clock? If a peregrine, when it has been finally decided not to fly her in the field that day, is fed at about eleven o'clock, she will be fit to fly on the morrow at any time after noon. The falconer should note in what order his hawks are fed, so that on the next day, unless any special circumstances prevent it, those which have been fasting the longest should be flown the first.

No hawk, after being fed up, should be disturbed, frightened, or shaken about. If the return journey from the field or exercise-ground is long, and the hawk inclined to bate off the fist, she should be hooded just before or after she has finished her meal ; and on returning home she should be put in a quiet place —either on a block where nothing can interfere with her, or on the screen-perch ; and if given to bating off, she should remain hooded, or else in a darkened room, till nightfall. No hawk should be allowed ever to finish her meal within sight of another that is still hungry, or to be in a place where she can see a lure or any sort of food without being able to get at it. At no time should a hawk be pegged out in a position where she is exposed to a strong wind, or to a hot sun, except just before and for a while after her bath. Never should food be dragged or pulled away forcibly from a hawk, leaving her hungry on the fist or perch with nothing to eat. The falconer must play the part of a friend, and of a generous friend, not of a niggardly and tyrannical master, who makes use of his superior strength to rob his servant of the good things which she expected to enjoy.

In summer, when the weather is fine and the ground tolerably dry, peregrines, hobbies, and some of the hardiest of the big hawks may be left all night at their blocks on the grass. But the advantages, if any, resulting from such a plan are, I think, more than questionable. It is argued, of course, that wild hawks sleep in the open air, and therefore why not trained ones ? But the wild hawk chooses his or her resting-place—almost always a tall tree or rock—far out of reach of the dews and mists which belong to the grass and the lower air. If the wild hawk gets wet, or feels cold at midnight, she has only the elements or herself to blame. If the trained hawk suffers, will she not blame the man who tied her down in a position where she could not escape from these discomforts ? A perfectly clean and well-aired hawk-house is, to my mind, as good a place for hawks to sleep in as the finest lawn on the fairest night of the year. What good does a hawk get from bating at the block on to the wet grass from 3 or 4 a.m. till the falconer appears ? If wild hawks did this, instead of keeping aloft in the clear air, would they not be likely sometimes to get the croaks ?

I have reserved till as late a place as this the question of dieting, the most difficult, if not the most important, part of the falconer's art. Condition in a trained hawk, as in a trained horse or hound, is the most essential requisite for really great success. Without it the very best hawk will make but a poor show ; and with it even a naturally slow hawk can be flown with pleasure and credit. Condition must always depend chiefly upon two things, exercise and dieting. Now, as regards exercise, it is impossible for a falconer to err on the side of excess. Wild hawks in their airy circlings, and in pursuit of their daily subsistence, traverse an almost incredible distance in the course of a year; probably fifty times as many miles as the most active of trained hawks can be expected to travel in the same period. Let the trainer, therefore, make it a simple rule to give his charges as much exercise as he can—not all at racing pace, of course, but in using their wings. He need not be afraid of overdoing the thing, as long as he leaves off when the hawk has made too violent an exertion in an actual flight at quarry. I have seen a hobby, waiting on in a high wind, refuse to come down to the lure, though quite sharp-set, and, for the mere pleasure of flying, remain on the wing for twenty-five minutes. The distance flown through the air in the time—counting only that in which his head was to the wind—amounted to a great many miles; and so far was he from being tired at any time, that he would stoop at and hit the lure, and yet refuse to hold it, and go up again to the soar. Few hawks will do this willingly; they must often be induced by some device of the trainer to keep on the wing; and it is impossible to fly such hawks too much.

With respect to food, the matter is altogether different. It is just as easy to overfeed a hawk as to underfeed her. But what trainer can ever be sure that he has always exactly hit off the golden mean? Gers, peregrines, and all the hawks which resemble the peregrine, desert-hawks, hobbies, eagles, goshawks, and female sparrow-hawks, are fed, as a rule, once a day—peregrines well; eagles, goshawks, and the desert-hawks more sparingly. Merlins of both sexes and male sparrow-hawks twice; but lightly on one at least of the two occasions. Raw beef is generally the staple food of the big hawks; but it should not be tough, and should be often varied by a rather lighter diet of bullock's heart, rabbit, fowl, or pigeon. Merlins and sparrow-hawks should be fed chiefly on small birds, and in default of these on sheep's heart, rabbit, young fowls, or exceedingly tender mutton or beef. This sort of diet will also be good for hobbies and kestrels; but it is not necessary to be so nice with them, and they can be regaled with coarser food, as long as it is not tough. But they must also have a freshly-killed small bird occasionally. Goshawks will thrive upon rats, weasels, squirrels, rooks, and, in short, almost any kind of bird or animal, except water-hens, which are indigestible and apt to bring them out of yarak. But a goshawk in good flying order should not be kept for long upon coarse food, but indulged now and then at least with viands of the best quality. Mice are capital food, not only for kestrels and hobbies, but for merlins and sparrow-hawks, and may be given whole to any kind of hawk by way of castings. Eagles are not particular as to diet; but they should have plenty of tirings, and their meat will be none the worse for being a bit tough.

Eagles and all short-winged hawks should have a gorge, that is to say, as much as they choose to eat, about three times in a fortnight, and on the following day should be very sparingly fed. Eagles, indeed, and some female goshawks need not be fed at all, if they are to be flown at wild quarry on the second day after their full meal. But none of the smaller hawks will stand anything approaching to starvation; and to leave a male sparrow-hawk or merlin without food for twenty-four hours would probably do him a permanent injury, or at all events ruin his chance of doing himself any justice in the field for a long time to come. In the case of these, and indeed all the long-winged hawks, when in constant exercise at wild quarry, I am not quite sure that any good is done by giving any gorges at all. I never do so with merlins in the lark season; and yet I have killed with one of them over thirty larks in succession without a miss. Granting that in their wild state all hawks occasionally gorge themselves, it must be remembered that trained hawks are not in a wild state. The analogy is not a just or true one, any more than it would be to argue from the habits of Red Indians to those expedient for a white man in training. However, there can be no great harm, even if there is no great advantage, in giving a gorge to a peregrine once a week. It is a practice consecrated by old tradition and precept: and it is not for us degenerate modern amateurs to lightly discard the maxims of the age of chivalry.

In saying that peregrines and other big hawks are fed once a day, it is not meant that they should never taste a morsel of food except their one solid meal. Small tit-bits will be forthcoming at odd times, as for instance in the early morning, when they are moved from the perch to the block, or taken to bathe, or to be carried. They will pick a little from the tirings at which they are almost every day set to work. There is no need to be stingy with these odds-and-ends; indeed, the old falconers would very often give their falcons quite a small meal when they hooded up for the field, or a little before. One ancient writer declares that a falcon will eat the wing of a fowl, and two hours afterwards be quite fit to fly. Another recommends his readers always to feed eyess peregrines twice a day, but of course moderately. The exact amount of food which it is proper to give to each hawk cannot be specified even very approximately. For amongst the same class of hawks, nay, amongst hawks which actually came from the same nest, will be found individuals with quite different sorts of appetites. One of them will grow too thin upon rations that make her sister, or even her brother, too fat. Nevertheless, taking the average of a number of hawks of the same species, it is possible to arrive at a rough estimate of what is usually required. The allowance always prescribed for a peregrine falcon is one-third of a pound of beef. Tiercels, therefore, will require about a quarter of a pound; and other English hawks must be provided for on about the same scale, *i.e.* the amount of food, if very solid, should weigh nearly one-seventh of the total weight of the bird fed. The desert-hawks, however, are much smaller feeders. A saker, for instance, looks about as large as a gerfalcon. But it was computed that a trained ger would eat three times as much as a saker. The power of fasting of these hawks is naturally very great; and they should have great gorges, with intervals of very spare feeding. On the other hand, the small hawks eat a great deal more in proportion to their size than the large ones. A whole skylark, of average dimensions, given freshly killed, with all the blood warm in it, is not quite enough for a merlin's daily ration, but would be about right for most jacks. The ladies, when doing hard work, require about four larks in three days. A starling or blackbird is about the right daily meal for a female hobby, but rather too little for a female sparrow-hawk, and decidedly too much for a "musket" or "robin." A sparrow without its feathers weighs an ounce, as nearly as may be; and two whole sparrows a day is a very ample allowance for a merlin, even when flying both morning and evening. Probably this would be about the fair quantity to keep a female hobby in good condition. A sparrow and a half would be about sufficient for a jack, a robin, or a musket. An ounce of beef is of course a heavier meal than an ounce of sparrow, but it may be doubted whether it will give a small hawk more strength or courage, though it will sustain him longer.

It is needless to say that the apportionment of food to each individual hawk becomes a more difficult matter in proportion as the hawk is smaller. A mistake of an ounce, one way or the other, is no great matter in the case of a ger or a falcon, but give a jack-merlin an ounce too much or an ounce too little, and you may very soon find out your mistake in a most practical way. Sometimes a jack will eat more—and need more—than his own sisters or any merlin in the establishment. Sometimes, but more rarely, a single merlin will want nearly as much as two jacks. Tiercel peregrines, barbarys, and others, sometimes, but rarely, require almost as much as a falcon. A hawk which has throughout her life never known what it is to be thin can generally be kept in high condition on less food than one which has once been below par. Fortunate is the man who has been able to train his hawk without ever putting her on short commons, and has always been able, by skill or luck, or both combined, to fly her just at the time when she was keen enough and yet not over-hungry. Such hawks have the best chance of turning out well; and among them may probably be numbered many of those whose names are glorious in the annals of the sport.

A hawk's condition may be tested to a certain limited extent by passing a finger down her breast-bone, and by feeling the broad pectoral muscles on each side of the breast between the forefinger and thumb. Some indications may also be got by gently pinching the muscles of the leg, to ascertain whether they are full and hard. But these are very rough tokens to judge from. One hawk will fly her best when almost as fat as a wild one, and when the sternum is hardly more prominent than it is in a partridge; whereas others, when fed up to this condition, will do no serious work, but go off soaring on their own account, or take perch in a tree or rick, and stare unconcernedly at the lure as if they had no conception that it had any attractions for them. The experienced falconer will form a better judgment as to the condition of his hawk from the manner in which she flies. There is a power and ease of motion about a full-fleshed hawk, a force in her stoop, and a sort of pride about her every movement, which one looks for in vain in a hawk in poor condition. Thin hawks fly in a laboured way against a strong wind, instead of facing it easily and appearing to rejoice in their victory over it, utilising its very opposition to lift them up, and sailing on it like a stiff yacht in a gale. Weak flying may result from overfeeding as well as underfeeding. But in the one case the style appears too heavy; and in the other, too light.

It is, however, very easy to mistake the symptoms, and to imagine that a hawk wants reducing when in fact she wants feeding up. The result, of course, of such faulty diagnosis will

be that the treatment applied as a remedy aggravates the mischief already done. It is much easier to reduce a hawk than
to get flesh on her again. The beginner should therefore be
very sure that his hawk has been overfed before he shortens her
daily supply of food. By making a mistake on the other side,
and feeding up a hawk which is already a bit above herself, the
worst inconvenience that is likely to follow, in the case of an
eyess, is a little delay in getting her down to the lure. Passage
hawks, especially for a while after they have first been reclaimed,
are of course liable to be lost if too highly fed, for when dis-
inclined to come to the lure or fist they are apt to rake away
after chance quarry. But they may be full-fleshed and strong,
and yet be eager for their food. It is a great mistake, though
a very common one, to suppose that a thin hawk is necessarily
a hungry one. Whether a hawk is fat or thin is a question of
days, whereas it is a question of hours whether she is hungry or
not. For instance, a peregrine may have had nearly a full crop
every day for a week, and yet if on the eighth day she has only
a very light feed in the morning she will be as hungry as a
hunter on the ninth day in the afternoon. The tendency nowadays is rather to overfeed hawks, and to forget the old maxim
about a fat hawk making "a lean horse and an empty purse."
The amateur has been so loudly warned against keeping a thin
hawk that in avoiding this reproach he falls into the other
extreme, and attempts to fly his hawk when she is really not
sharp-set at all.

Washed meat—so commonly used by the old falconers, that
it may almost be said to have been a normal daily diet—is now
but rarely given, unless, indeed, where a parsimonious or careless owner has neglected to provide fresh meat, and tainted beef
is soaked and squeezed so as to make it available as food. The
proper mode of preparing washed meat is to take it when quite
fresh and immerse it for a while in cold water, and then dry it
in a warm place. Part of its nutritive power—of its goodness,
in fact—will then have disappeared, and what remains will digest
quickly, leaving the hawk more keen and sooner hungry than
if she had swallowed the same quantity of unwashed meat. For
the smaller hawks it is less suitable than for the larger; and if
it is desired to take them down a peg or two, it will generally
be found best either to resort to a diet naturally light, such as
rabbit or sheep's heart, or to reduce a little in quantity the
accustomed allowance of their usual food. When a merlin is a
bit bumptious, independent, and disobedient, her morning ration

may be curtailed, or in feeding up after the day's exercise she may be indulged only with a good half-crop, instead of the habitual three-quarters. When a peregrine or hawk of similar habits is inclined to be uppish, and to disdain the dead lure, it is a good plan, besides being a shade stingy at dinner-time, to fly her each day at least an hour later than the day before. When, in this way, her time of flying has got to be so late that it cannot be deferred till later on the following day, give her a gorge, or at least a very full meal, when she has done flying, and on the next day, an hour after she has cast, give her quite a light feed, and do not fly her at all till the day after at noon. Sakers, lanners, and that class of hawks must be rather sternly treated if they get above themselves, for their nature is to support long fasts without much trouble. And eagles, of course, must sometimes be almost starved a little.

Remember always that the food given to a trained hawk belongs to one or other of several categories, which rank differently as regards nutritive power. Highest on the list is the flesh of birds or other animals eaten immediately after they are killed, while the life-blood is still warm within them. The meals of wild hawks are, as a rule, of this description; and these accordingly, by virtue of their diet, as well as of their habits, are the most vigorous and healthy of all. Next in order comes the flesh of such creatures as have been killed long enough to grow cold. And in the last rank must be placed washed meat—artificially reduced to its least nutritive character. When it is desired to improve the condition of a hawk, food of the first class will most quickly and most surely effect the object. Any hawk which is found to be below par should have at the first opportunity at least one "bloody crop," *i.e.* should either be allowed to take her pleasure on some quarry which she has herself killed, or be indulged with a pigeon, duck, fowl, or other animal which has just been killed. The flesh of animals, whether freshly killed or not, differs a good deal in quality. Pigeons, duck, plovers, and sparrows are about the most nourishing; chickens, rabbits, quails, larks, and mice, somewhat less so. The flesh of rooks, gulls, magpies, water-hens, and coots is not very palatable; and some trained hawks will not touch it. None are likely to improve in condition if fed upon it. There is nothing a trained hawk likes better than good tender beef, especially if it is slightly warmed before being given. It is also very sustaining, and will increase a hawk's weight rapidly, when a generous allowance of it is made. It is, however, much heavier and more solid than the natural food of any hawk, and therefore apt, if freely given, to make her dull, slow, and sluggish. For sparrow-hawks and merlins it is distinctly bad, if often taken, and in large quantities at a time. These latter, when in flying order at the right season of the year, are, of course, almost always fed up in the field on the quarry they have last killed before finishing their day's work, and the next morning have a few mouthfuls of similar food which has been killed the afternoon before. When a rook-hawk will readily feed up in the same way on her vanquished quarry, it will be convenient, occasionally at least, to let her do so. Game-hawks should also be allowed sometimes to take their pleasure on their own grouse, partridge, pheasant, or even woodcock ; but in practice they are seldom lucky enough to get more than the heads and necks, though modern falconers who fly mostly for sport, and not " for the pot," are often more liberal in this respect than their predecessors of the Middle Ages.

Goshawks, when kept to hares, or indeed to any quarry which taxes their utmost powers, should often be allowed to finish their meal on one of their victims. Between whiles they may often with advantage be regaled with washed meat only, or some not very appetising food. It is well to induce all hawks to believe that a kill after a hard flight means an extra good feast. But merlins and male sparrow-hawks must very seldom, if at all, know the taste of washed meat, or of any third-rate diet. Some of them, when in first-rate fettle, are very dainty, and will lose the pink of their condition if not indulged with their favourite food. These little hawks are exceedingly fond of swallows and some other very small birds ; and although few people would be barbarous enough to deliberately kill any small bird except a sparrow, yet if a young martin should be picked up under the nest from which it has accidentally fallen, and given to a merlin, it will be odd if that hawk does not fly unusually well when next put on the wing. In the lark-hawking season, one of these active workers will not only keep herself in food, but often supply enough extra victims to provide a daily meal of the very best kind for a tiercel, or even a falcon, which happens then to be in moult. The short-winged hawks will also sometimes in one afternoon kill more than they could themselves eat in a week.

A not unimportant item of the commissariat is a supply of good tirings. A tiring may consist of anything tough which is appetising enough for a hawk to keep pulling and picking at it to satisfy her hunger. For tiercels and all hawks of about the same size, rabbits' or leverets' feet, with the lower part of the leg, make capital tirings. So do the necks of fowls and ducks, which a falconer should always cause to be reserved for him when any poultry is slain for the kitchen. The foot of an old hare is not too tough for a strong falcon. The small hawks will generally be kept employed for a good many minutes by the two outer joints of a duck's or old pigeon's wing. These tirings should be given whenever a hawk is short of exercise, or fidgety on the block or perch. Their effect is not only to strengthen all the muscles—for it is quite hard work picking the scanty scraps of food off the bones and skin amongst which they lie hid —but also to engross the attention of the hawk, which would otherwise very possibly be pining more or less sadly for freedom, and often jumping off in the vain endeavour to attain to that blessing. The frequent picking of bones also keeps a hawk's beak from growing down at the point to an unnatural length. A man who tells you that he often has to cope his hawk stands detected of being in the habit of not giving her sufficient tirings. Another most valuable use of these tough morsels has been already referred to. It is discovered during the first period of manning the hawk, when the necessary job of carrying is found to be ten times more agreeable and better performed if, while the pupil has perforce to stand on the fist, she has some induce-ment to do so in the shape of a fowl's " drumstick " or the wing of a goose, off which almost all the meat has already been picked. No better advice is given by Mr. Freeman—though every one of his counsels is admirable—than to prolong as much as possible the meals which a half-trained hawk takes on the fist. Often the delicacy on which you are regaling her will be tender in one part and tough in another. For instance, it may be the full-fleshed leg of some fowl, off which the meat can easily be torn, with a part of the back, consisting chiefly of skin and bone. If your rather shy pupil takes kindly to the least manageable part of her appointed dinner, let her pick at it, and laboriously polish with many applications of her beak the ill-covered bones of the back, stroking her from time to time with a pencil or with the right hand. Possibly she will not yet stand such acts of fami-liarity, but bate off. When she is on the fist again, let her recom-mence operations without taking any liberties with her. Reserve your attentions with the stick for the time when she will be busy discussing the more succulent morsels in the *menu*, and when she is more likely to submit, without much protest, to the indignity of being stroked. So also, while she is pulling contentedly at the juiciest parts of the joint, you may take her more freely into the presence of men, horses, dogs, and children—in fact, introduce her to more society. The bolder you become the more inclined she will be to let her mistrust prevail over her fondness for the feast, and the less exclusively she will confine her attention to it. Thus a pigeon's wing, which it would take a fully-trained tiercel less than five minutes to dispose of, may, with a falcon caught only a fortnight ago, engage her attention for nearly half an hour.

With tirings there will often be a small quantity of castings which will be swallowed with the pickings of meat. The trainer must judge for himself whether enough of them has been thus taken during the day to form a proper pellet, or whether more should be given in another way. In feeding up upon quarry which they have themselves killed, whether on the fist or on the ground, hawks will almost always naturally take castings enough. But when the meal consists of beef, or of anything that has been skinned or plucked quite bare, it will be necessary either to add some feathers or fur, or the like, scattering it about on the meat which the hawk is about to swallow, or else the casting may consist of a strip of skin with fur or feathers left on it, and a piece of meat at one end. While swallowing the meat the hawk will gulp down the skin attached to it, and thus with one or two mouthfuls give herself the required quantity of castings. Some falconers make up the casting into a sort of pill, and cram their hawks with it ; and I believe this plan answers the purpose very well, though I have seldom if ever tried it. It is not, of course, necessary to give castings every day. But they are generally beneficial, and always, as far as I know, harmless. Some of the old falconers advise not to give castings on days when a hawk has bathed ; but I am unable to give the reason for this. Castings are taken daily by wild hawks, which certainly have less need of them than tame ones. And if, through laziness or any other cause, the falconer omits for days in succession to give any, it is pretty certain that his hawk's crop and stomach will become clogged with a sort of mucus, which will either make her dull, sluggish, and morose, or otherwise impair her general health. Castings should be given rather late in the day than early ; and after they have been taken the hawk must always be kept unhooded at about the time when she may be expected to throw them up, *i.e.* from about the fifth hour after she has swallowed the casting, until she has cast. For this reason, if for no other, when it is intended to train passage hawks in any place, it must always be possible to darken artificially a part of the room, so that hawks can sit there bareheaded on the perch after castings have been given.

Another article which may in a sense be included in the category of diet, is one which will somewhat surprise the reader who has heard nothing about falconry before. This is "rangle," which is nothing more nor less than small stones or pebbles, swallowed after the manner of castings, and with a similar purpose and effect. After being taken into the crop these exceedingly indigestible delicacies—popularly supposed to be dear to ostriches only — collect around themselves by some special process of attraction a quantity of that same mucus which is apt to accumulate in a hawk's internal organism. When afterwards they are thrown up—for not even the greediest goshawk will actually assimilate stones—they come up with this oily coating adhering to them, having operated as a sort of emetic, without any of the disagreeable concomitants of physicking with drugs. Why the purpose for which rangle is given cannot be as effectually accomplished by simple castings of feather or fur, I am afraid I cannot explain ; but these latter do not appear to be able to clear the hawk's inside of the particular kind of superfluous humours which are extracted by the harder substance. Possibly the weight of pebbles causes them to descend farther into the crop, and thus clear it more thoroughly than any such light material as can be given by way of castings. For the small hawks rangle may be given by scattering a few pinches of rather fine gravel on the meat at which they are picking. It is a good plan also to scatter about, close to the blocks of any hawks for which a dose of this kind is thought good, a few stones of a round smooth shape, varying in size from that of a horse-bean for a falcon, to that of a sweet-pea seed for a jack-merlin. The patient often knows instinctively when such a dose is likely to do her good, and swallows one or more of the stones voluntarily. If she does not, and it is thought advisable that she should be dosed whether she likes it or not, the hawk may be cast, and the tasteless pill slipped into her mouth, and pushed down with a small stick. Latham, who was a great stickler for rangle, tells a quaint story of a hawk which he owned. He stuffed her with sixteen stones, which she threw up in due course. The stones were picked up and washed, and put down again near the hawk's block on the following evening. And every day for a month successively this very accommodating hawk voluntarily picked up and swallowed some dozen of the stones, which were daily collected, washed, and put down again. When a hawk, after moulting, is taken out, or "drawn," as the old writers call it, from the mews, it is generally beneficial to give her rangle. Hack hawks, when taken up, are often all the better for it ; and when a hawk seems dull, or displays dyspeptic symptoms, she may not unfrequently be cured off-hand by the same simple expedient.

Every evening the falconer, having fed up all his hawks (and possibly himself) and noted down in his register what has been killed or done by each of them, should collect all the bodies or pelts of the slain which have not been used as food, and bestow them in a separate place in his larder, so that the results of one day's campaigning may not get mixed up with those of a previous day, and it may be known how long each unfortunate has been killed. In hot weather no small bird, and very few other things, are fit to be given to a hawk if they have been dead more than twenty-four hours. In the tropics, of course, meat goes bad still more quickly ; and at about tiffin-time everything which has been killed earlier than on the same day should be cleared out of the hawks' larder. If the falconer can get to roost soon after his charges he will think himself fortunate. For the making up of his diary is, on busy days, quite a business in itself. Then it is possible that some accident has occurred. If there has been a broken feather, the damaged hawk must be imped. If one is amiss, measures must be taken for applying the proper remedies. If a jess is worn, it must be replaced. But the worst trouble is if a hawk has been left out. Then the wretched falconer must make up his mind to set forth before daybreak on a long and weary search. But of these pains and griefs, to which the poor man may always be a victim, we shall have to speak in future chapters.

CHAPTER XIV

Hawks in the Field

HALF an hour or so before the time appointed for starting to the field, the falconer will begin to hood up those hawks which are to be taken out. Each of them, if in proper order, will jump from the block or the perch to his fist as soon as he extends it within reach. For some of them it will be a very simple matter to slip on a hood; and without further ado they will be placed on the cadge and the leash made fast to it. Others which have only lately completed their training, or which have not yet quite mastered a dislike to the hood, may be first indulged by the production of a tiring, and before or just after they begin to pull at it may be hooded with such dexterity as the operator can boast of. A good hooder is also a quick hooder; but nothing is more likely to make a man bungle his business than to set about it in a hurry at the last moment, just before it is time to start.

The cadge, if a cadge is to be taken out, being placed in a sheltered spot, with its occupants ranged along it and safely attached, all the requisite paraphernalia to be carried must be properly stowed away either in some vehicle or in the falconer's pouches or pockets. For every person who is to take any active part in the day's proceedings, it will be well to have a lure which he can easily carry. Each such man should also reserve at least one pocket, unless he wears a pouch, in which he can put a spare hood and a spare leash. When it is expected that a live lure may be required, the bird which is to serve the purpose should be accommodated with comfortable quarters in which he cannot be shaken or knocked about, or be cramped or short of air. The man who carries the cadge must be instructed or reminded as to his duties—how to set down the cadge under the lee of a rick or fence or other shelter, and, having done so, to keep his eyes open, and act as a marker. Some code of signals may

192

generally be agreed upon for informing the cadge man from a distance when he is to go forward with his burden and in what direction. If the party is to include any people who have never been out hawking before, they should be warned as to running or riding in, and requested to stand still whenever a rook or other quarry makes towards them as a shelter from the stoop. The falconer himself should carry a spare leash and hood or two, some string which can be unwound quickly without kinking, and a supply of small coins wherewith to reward farm-labourers or other rustics who, in case of a lost hawk, may give useful information. He should also have a field-block or two, or at least some pegs for pegging down a hawk by her leash, and a certain provision of food for feeding up hawks which may have failed to kill anything, or which are not to be allowed to regale themselves upon the quarry which they may take.

If the place where the hawks are to be flown is close at hand, and there are not more hawks to be taken out than there are men to carry them, a cadge may sometimes be dispensed with altogether, and the light blocks which have been described as field-blocks can be brought instead, taking care that there are enough of them for each hawk (except the one which is for the time being about to be flown) to be supplied with one when it is desired to put her down. In some cases the hawk or hawks may even be taken out bareheaded, as for instance when three merlins are carried by three men, each of whom knows how to manage his part of the day's business. But in most cases where more than two hawks have to be flown, it will be found best to hood up all except the one which is first to be thrown off. For a hawk which is bareheaded on the fist or on a field-block will bate very much if she sees a flight is going on in which she cannot take part. Moreover, the man who is carrying an unhooded hawk cannot follow a flight freely in which another hawk is engaged, and, after assisting at the start, finds himself obliged to see hawk and quarry sail away out of sight, while compelled to stand almost still, rendering no service even as a marker, and left in the lurch, with a toilsome walk or ride before him, which very possibly he may not accomplish before another flight starts, in which he will have even less part or lot.

In every kind of hawking the marshalling of the field is a most important matter ; so much so that success or failure sometimes depends upon the manner in which the quarry has been walked up or approached. For instance, in the pursuit of rooks, gulls, and larks, the chances of a kill are comparatively remote if the quarry is down-wind when the hawk is thrown off. On the other hand, in game-hawking, the pursuer has a much better chance if the first stoop is made down-wind. Consequently, in beating for grouse or partridges, the falconer will start proceedings from the windward edge of his country, and keep the game, as far as he can, always down-wind of his line of beaters ; whereas in the other cases the hawking party will begin to leeward, and proceed as nearly as possible with their faces to the wind. In other words, a hawk flown from the fist should be flown up-wind at her quarry, and one which waits on should start down-wind at it. So well established is this principle that when a rook is espied on the ground to leeward, a whole party of mounted men will sometimes make a circuit of a mile in length, in order to make sure of getting the wind of him and giving the falcon a fair chance. When there is anything of a wind, it is advisable for a lark-hawker, after making a beat to windward, to return on his own tracks, with what is called a dead beat, and start afresh on another march parallel to the first, so as to avoid putting up a lark while walking in the wrong direction, and being reduced to the alternative of either letting the merlin go on a sort of fool's errand, or disappointing and vexing her by holding on to the jesses when she jumps off.

The posting of markers is a matter requiring some skill and care, even in the case where the falconer is well acquainted with his country. It will be found of the greatest possible advantage to have plenty of markers, especially where, as is often the case in game-hawking, all or most of the men are unmounted. Before beginning to try the ground, the falconer should detach men or boys to post themselves down-wind in positions where they can command the most extensive view, and, as it were, guard the approaches to any covert for which the quarry is likely to make. Often it can be predicted with tolerable certainty which plantation a rook or lark will choose as his place of refuge, or at which thick hedge or piece of tall roots or of standing crops a partridge will try to put in. Often, of course, there are two or more spinnies or sheltering-places, either of which may attract the fugitive. If these places are within sight of any marker with a good pair of eyes, he will be able to tell the first comer-up whether the flight ended in either of them, or went on in another direction. Without such information much valuable time may be wasted in searching a covert where neither hawk nor quarry is to be found. Markers are more useful down-wind than up. For in all long flights where the quarry takes the air, he is pretty sure, when hard pressed, to turn in that direction, whilst in game-hawking it is always the object of the beaters to drive the birds down-wind. Any marker, upon seeing a kill or a put-in, should note as accurately as he can the exact spot, and then stand still at his post until he can communicate with one of the field. In open country all markers should remain at a distance of about half a mile from the man carrying the hawk to be flown, and should shift their position rapidly to another vantage-ground whenever the space between them and the hawking party is much diminished or increased.

In rook-hawking the lookers-on must be mounted; and their horses ought either to be very sure-footed or else well acquainted with the ground on which the flights take place, which is often covered with ant-hills, and in places bored by rabbit burrows. If the rider is to see anything of the longest and best flights, his horse must be able to step out in a gallop of a mile or so. In game- and lark-hawking it is less necessary, and often impossible, for the men to be mounted; but in these cases also it is of very great advantage for at least one man to ride, so that he may follow a very long flight with a better chance of keeping the hawk in view. The horseman has a double advantage when the country is uneven. He can go faster, and he can also from his place in the saddle see farther over the brow of a hill or undulation. But ground which undulates in long ridges and valleys is to be mistrusted by falconers. When a flight, commenced in one valley, goes over the ridge which separates it from the next, it is impossible, unless there is a marker on that ridge, to know where it may have ended. Here the falconer, for once in his life, may hope that the ground on the other side is not too open, and that there may be some small covert not far off in which the quarry is pretty sure to have stopped if he got so far. When a hawk goes out of sight over a ridge, the men following on horseback should begin to spread out like a fan, and ride on, keeping a good look-out for anything that may indicate the direction which the flight has taken.

When a flight ends successfully, every person in the field should halt at a hundred yards or so from the place where the hawk is on the ground with the quarry in her foot. The falconer, or whoever it was that threw off the hawk, will use his own judgment as to when he will make in and take her up, and must go alone about this business, which, as we have seen, is sometimes delicate enough. Although it is an unpardonable mistake to make in too quickly, so as to alarm the hawk, yet it is not wise to defer too long the business of taking up. For it is always possible that a stray dog may rush in, or some other accident occur which may frighten the hawk just at the time when you most wish to save her from any such alarm.

If for any reason you wish your hawk to eat her quarry where she has killed, attach the leash to her jesses and to a peg in the ground, or to a field-block, leaving a man to watch her and keep a sharp look-out against intruders. Although in the very open country, where alone the long-winged hawks ought to be flown, there are not many interlopers in the shape of stray dogs or tourists, yet it is wonderful how, with a little bad luck at his heels, the falconer may be annoyed by unexpected intruders. I well remember a valuable hawk being lost on Salisbury Plain, not far from Stonehenge, by the appearance on the scene of an object which one would hardly expect to see there, three miles from the nearest village. The hawk, which was a bit shy to take up, was discussing a well-earned meal upon a heap of stones by the side of a cart-road, when along this road came a nurse-maid with a gaudy-hooded perambulator. She got past the hawk, but not without exciting a large share of its attention. Unfortunately, however, she caught sight of the falconers hurrying up, and then of the hawk, and with that feeling of curiosity which seems to be strongly developed in the genus nurse-maid, turned the perambulator round, and began wheeling it straight towards the hawk. This was altogether too much for the latter. Convinced that some deadly mischief lurked in the strange machine approaching, she picked up the remains of her quarry, and, taking it off with her, could not be afterwards approached.

Only when the falconer is seen to have secured the victorious hawk, and attached the leash to her jesses, is it permitted to the field to go up. When time is precious, and there are a lot of hawks to be flown, the line of march may proceed, leaving the work of taking up the successful hawk to him who flew her ; and when the next quarry is put up, the next hawk in order may be thrown off by the man who carries her. Otherwise it is best to get one flight altogether done with before another is started. When the quarry has beaten off his pursuers and got away, a lure or lures must be put in requisition ; and one man, if he can be spared, should remain, with lure in hand, near the place where the hawk, if out of sight, was last seen. The others will follow on, more or less quickly, in the direction she seemed to take. All trained hawks have a certain inclination to return after an unsuccessful chase towards the place from which they started in pursuit; and the man to whom the easy duty of standing still is allotted generally has as good a chance of taking up such a hawk as any one of those who have walked or ridden forward.

When the quarry puts in, and the place is known or shrewdly guessed at, generally all the field may participate more or less directly in the work of getting him out. In magpie- and black-bird-hawking, this routing out of the quarry is one of the most animated parts of the day's proceedings. But everything must be done under the control and direction of the head falconer. An amateur may do more harm than good, nay, may spoil the whole job and disgust the hawk, by blundering on and driving out the half-vanquished fugitive in a wrong direction, or at an ill-chosen moment. The falconer himself learns by long ex-perience many of the little ways of birds that have put in—on which side of a fence they will most likely be found ; whether inside a hedge or in the long grass or weeds outside it ; which way his head is likely to be turned; and whether he may be expected to jump up readily at a man's first appearance, or to sit still and allow himself to be taken up in the hand or kicked up with the foot. After a hard flight, in which he was getting much the worst of it, the latter is a likely event ; whereas if the hawk was making a poor show, and did not press him hard, he will be more ready to start again with fresh hopes of escape.

Some judgment is sometimes required to decide whether in any particular case it is advisable to drive out quarry which has put in, or to pick him up with the hand, if he will allow this, or to leave him alone altogether. This last alternative is not so unlikely to be preferable as a beginner might imagine. Suppose, for instance, that a very good rook, after a hard flight with a young falcon, has managed to get to a small tree which stands by itself, at a distance of a quarter of a mile or less from a wood or big plantation. The hawk waits on, but rather wide. By sending a boy up into the tree, you think you may most likely get the rook out. Will you do so, or leave him alone, and take down the falcon to the lure ? If you rout the rook out, it is about ten to one that he will get safe to the big covert. The hawk, if at all wide when he makes his attempt, will hardly have time in so short a distance to make even one stoop, and far less a fatal one. You will have disappointed her, and perhaps disgusted her greatly with the job of flying at rooks, never the most attractive of quarry. Many a good falconer will prefer to call down the hawk, and, leaving the rook to congratulate himself on his escape, reserve her for a fresh start at a quarry which she will have a fairer chance of catching. In lark-hawking, unless the country is extremely open, cases of this kind often present themselves.

On the other hand, if there is a really good prospect of a successful flight when the fugitive is routed out, it is, of course, very encouraging to the hawk to put him up. Every effort should be made to do this when the hawk is waiting on in a good position, so that, having killed, she may be pleased with the whole performance, including the men's share in it, and may perhaps imagine that the reason the quarry was got out so conveniently for her was because she waited on well. Hawks, whether waiting on in the air or at perch in a good place, soon get to know very well what the men are about when hunting up a bird that has put in. In the case of merlins, which naturally stand by on the ground while a lark is being searched for, it is almost always better to take them up on the fist as soon as it is determined to pick up or try to capture the quarry. Otherwise the lark, having his wits about him, may take advantage of a moment when the hawk is looking the wrong way, and slip off unseen by her. Moreover, even if she sees him go, she will not start from the ground with so good a chance as from the elevation, small though it is, of your fist. As for sparrow-hawks and goshawks, they may, when a quarry puts in, either be called to the hand or allowed to wait close by at the standpoint which they themselves chose. Many of them prefer the latter plan whenever there is a tree handy, as from it they get a better view and more impetus for their stoop. Lanners, when flown at partridges in an enclosed country, may also be encouraged to go to perch in this way.

There are some occasions when it is quite permissible to capture with the hand a bird which has put in. Suppose that you are carrying a first-rate merlin which is short of work and for which you are particularly anxious to find hard flights and plenty of them. Now, when a lark gets up which is either so young or so deep in the moult that he cannot live long in the air before such a merlin, you are in presence of that very eventuality which you most wished to avoid. There is the prospect of a quick and easy kill, which is about the least likely thing in the world to encourage a hawk to a severe flight afterwards. The best that you can hope for is that the lark, seeing his inferiority, as he is sure to do,—for all wild birds are very good judges of such a matter,—will flop down in front of the hawk—or just behind her, if the first stoop has been avoided—in some place where there is just enough covert for the hawk to be unable to espy and jump upon him. Then, when you come up, the lark, which knows as well as you do what fate awaits him if he gets up again, will be very likely indeed to let you seize him in your hand. Will you, then, let that bad lark go before that good merlin? Not if you have any wish to keep up or improve the excellence of the latter. If you have in the background an inferior hawk to enter, or to encourage after an unsuccessful flight, you may start her at the captured lark, taking great care that she does not know that he has ever been captured. Or you may consign him to a safe place where he will not be damaged, and save him for a time when a bagged lark may be of invaluable service to you as a live lure for a lost hawk. Or what you will probably like best will be to let him go when no merlin is by. Similar cases will occur with other quarry and other hawks; but they are pretty frequent in the case of larks, which at moulting-time differ more than any other birds in their pluck and powers of flying.

When a hawk is new to the work of taking wild quarry she should be allowed to kill it and to break in and eat at least some part of it. But when she is *au fait* at the business the humane man will often be glad if he can save the victim's life, and this he will not unfrequently be able to do. Unless the quarry has been struck on the head or has a wing broken, no real damage is at all likely to have been done except in cases where the particular hawk has a specially hard stoop of her own, and is fond of cutting down her quarry instead of binding to it. For herons, gulls, rooks, and larks, after they have been taken, it is often pretty easy for the falconer, if he is up in reasonable time, to substitute the pelt of another bird which has been killed before. As I write this page I hear the singing of a lark in a cage before me which was captured by Jubilee after a long ringing flight, and saved from him while he was recovering his wind.

When it is found necessary to get bagged larks for entering a hobby—I have sometimes used one for entering merlins—they may be obtained in this way. Stick two wattled hurdles into the ground three inches apart and side by side in the middle of a very big field where there are larks. Stuff up the space between the two hurdles with loose straw, all except about a foot

H

at each end. Then take out a merlin and beat the field, driving towards the hurdles. When a lark gets up, if the hawk presses him hard, he will go to the shelter which is so inviting. Then taking down your merlin, and giving her a tiring to amuse her, go and pick out the lark from the straw near one end of the hurdles.

I am aware that some writers—and those of the highest authority—have recommended the use of bagged larks after ringing flights when the quarry has put in and cannot quickly be got out ; and that the plan is advocated especially in the case of merlins flown at larks. I venture to think, however, that it is a plan which must be resorted to with very great discretion, and only in extreme cases. The idea, of course, is that the bagged bird, let loose at the place where the wild one was seen to put in, is mistaken for the latter by the hawk, which consequently supposes when she has killed that her victim is the one at which she first started. But does the hawk ever make this mistake ? A lark, for instance, which has flown a ringing flight is necessarily a good one, whereas the bagged one—unless by a rare accident you have picked one up just before—is necessarily a poor one and generally a bad one ; especially if he has been dragged about in a bag or box for an hour or more. Will the merlin believe that this third- or fourth-rate performer is the same bird which a few minutes ago took her up after him into the clouds ? Would you yourself, if you had chased a pickpocket or a welsher for half a mile, mistake his identity five minutes afterwards ? And the difference between a good and a bad lark is much greater than the difference between a good and a bad pickpocket !

There are several other objections to letting bagged quarry go as personating the real. For instance, a bad lark is generally taken in the air, and taken easily ; and with a lark so taken merlins almost always fly a good way before coming down with them to the ground. There is then the risk of not being able to find them ; and at anyrate the hawk has learnt how easy it is to carry her quarry,—a species of knowledge which it is a main object of the falconer not to let her acquire. Of course a light creance may be attached to the bagged bird, and the carrying prevented, but this aggravates the dissimilarity between the sham quarry and the one which was put in. On the whole, considering the difficulties of carrying bagged quarry about, and producing them at the right moment in the right place, I doubt if, in the moulting season at all events, it is wise to attempt the stratagem at all. A hawk which is fast enough and clever enough to make a ringing quarry put in is generally able, in a good country, to take him when he has done so; and, except in a good country, ringing flights should not be attempted. When the moult is over, if any merlins continue to persevere at larks it is possible that the device might be adopted with advantage. The bagged lark would then be given, not with any idea that it will be seriously mistaken for the real quarry, but as a *bonne bouche* simply, to show the hawk that her prolonged exertions in bringing the quarry down have not been unprofitable to her. At this period the very best hawks, even when flown in casts, will put in ringing quarry in places where they cannot be found, and, if repeatedly so disappointed, will give up that sort of flight; whereas if, when they have beaten the lark in the air, and thus played their fair share in the game, the man can occasionally make a show of playing his part by producing a live quarry in the spot where the real quarry ought to be found, the hawks may accept the situation, though without being really deceived, and persevere. Unfortunately, in these cases how seldom it is that anyone can arrive at the spot in time to thus gratify the hawks! They will, after their intended victim has put in, take their stand close to the place, peeping and prying about, and perhaps trying to "walk it up"; and may there remain for a few minutes. Five minutes is as much as you can at all reasonably expect. How is the man, half a mile behind where the hawks came down, to find and get to them in five minutes? If he catches sight of them at all, it will often be by mere good luck. More often than not his first intimation as to where the flight ended is to be gained by noticing from which direction the hawk came to her lure. For as soon as the hawk engaged in a flight goes out of sight, either in the sky or over a ridge, or by reason merely of the distance to which she has gone, the lure should be produced, and kept in evidence as long as the search is continued.

In finding a hawk after a long flight it is useful to bear in mind a few hints which experience has taught. Of course in the case of the bigger hawks the bell is an invaluable guide. The hawker's ear should be always ready to catch the faintest sound of this well-known tell-tale. But merlins seldom or never wear bells in the field. It will be well, therefore, to give some brief directions as to finding these little hawks. These will be useful also in searching for others when not found by the bell. The person who was nearest to the hawk when she went out of sight will get on as fast as he can to the place over which he last saw her in the air, and may with advantage give notice to others following behind by holding up a hand or making any other signal that has been agreed upon. He will then, if there is a marker within hail, shout or signal a demand for information. If none is forthcoming, he will note with his eye the coverts or places of refuge on ahead of him, and consider which of them was most probably the destination of the quarry. The most likely is certainly the one which lies in a straight line with the course which the two birds were taking; and the next most likely is the nearest in an oblique direction on the down-wind side. If the place which seems most likely should be a plantation, copse, or spinny, let him then, by tracing an imaginary straight line over the intervening ground, decide which is the nearest part of this covert—irrespective of wind—to the spot whereon he stands. In this spot, and no other, the quarry will probably have put in. So constant is this choice by a lark of the very nearest bush in any thicket, that, after searching it thoroughly without success, I should be inclined to leave that plantation altogether and try some other place of shelter. If the hawk has killed, she will be either in the covert or somewhere not far off, where she may have taken her victim to devour him in the open, free from the danger of unwelcome intruders, who in any thick place might come up unawares. Such a spot will generally be tolerably conspicuous. A mound of earth, a heap of stones, a ridge of raised turf or ant-hill is often chosen. When the ground is wet, merlins and hobbies will sometimes carry their quarry a long way merely in the hope of finding a dry place whereon to deplume and devour it. I have known a merlin carry nearly half a mile on a very hot day in order to get under the shade of a distant tree.

Many minutes will elapse between the time when the quarry has been taken and the moment when the hawk has completely finished her repast. Accordingly, the search may be prolonged for at least half an hour before the chance of success is given up and the hawk pronounced "lost" for the time being. Some hawks when in high condition will not break in to their quarry or even plume it before their master or some other person comes up, but, after killing it, stand expectant, looking round about them, and apparently in a sort of brown study, forgetful that such a thing as hunger exists. Some are even so little eager to begin upon the excellent meal which is before them, that they will jump from it to the fist as soon as it is within reach. I have known a merlin fly her best at a mounting lark, take it after a hard flight, and descend with it to a heap of stones. Lighting a cigar, and sitting down beside a neighbouring rick to wait for her to break in, I have seen her presently go off unconcernedly to another resting-place with nothing in her feet, and, walking up to the heap of stones, have found the lark lying there, dead and unplucked. The hawk must have been flying almost uniquely out of love for the sport, and not with a view to satisfying any hunger which she felt at the time ; nor is this the only time that I have known such a thing occur.

As a rule, however, trained hawks in high fettle are very far from preferring a journey to the fist or the lure to devoting their attention to wild quarry. Much more often the difficulty is to persuade them that for the moment they must return to their place on the hand in order that they may be provided with what they are hankering after—another flight. Almost all hawks which are in the habit of constantly killing and being fed up upon wild birds develop a passion for sport, and will not easily, when once they have been thrown off, abandon the idea that they are to kill something before they come back. It is for this reason that I have advocated the frequent practice of flying merlins to the lure and sparrow-hawks to the fist, not only when the hawk is not to be used in the field, but when she is. Few things are more vexatious than the delay which occurs when a hawk, however good in other respects, is bad at the lure, and keeps the whole field waiting until it is her good pleasure to come down. Such performers as Queen and Sis, and the famous rook-hawk Bois-le-Duc, which fly for a week or more, killing daily without any miss, are in danger of quite forgetting what a lure is like, unless they are exercised to it for mere practice from time to time. Here, again, the question of dieting will be found to be of much importance. A hawk may be ready enough to fly wild quarry long before she is ready to come to the lure. An extra hour of fasting on the one hand, or an extra ounce of food on the other, may make all the difference in the alacrity of the hawk when required to come down.

In spite of all the falconer's care, there will be times when a hawk stands obstinately at perch, refusing contemptuously to come, or perhaps even to look, at the dead lure. On such occasions, if time is valuable, it may sometimes be expedient to resort to the live lure. This, however, should always be regarded as a last resource. If reserved for special occasions it will never fail to bring down the most disobedient offender, but if live lures are commonly used they lose part of their efficacy, and are apt to become almost as much despised as the ordinary dead ones. Of course when live lures are used pains will be taken to make the process as little disagreeable as possible to the creature whose life is risked. When a pigeon is employed, as it almost always is for any of the big hawks, a pair of soft and broad jesses should be attached to its legs, and the ends of those to a strong but fine cord or creance, or a noose of soft cord may be passed round each leg by means of the double-ring knot shown in Figs. 26, 27.

When the pigeon (or lark or other bird) is thrown up it should be allowed to fly a short distance, then gently stopped by the creance and allowed to alight on the ground. As the hawk comes at it, it can be jerked away with a steady pull, and, as the hawk throws up, it can be secured and hidden, while a dead pigeon of the same colour is thrown down in its place. No great amount of dexterity is required to execute this little manœuvre. The hawk will be taken up on the dead bird, and the live one liberated or returned to its dovecot none the worse for its perilous adventure. It is only when the falconer bungles his part of the business that the live lure is struck and either killed or hurt.

For sparrow-hawks or merlins, when they decline to come down, and stand waiting for the chance of another flight, another device may sometimes be employed with a view to saving time. There has been an unsuccessful flight, and the little hawk goes to perch upon a rick, neglectful of the proffered fist or lure. She came out, as she has made up her mind, to taste blood, and blood she means to have, if she has to wait for it till sundown. As you cannot afford to wait her good pleasure till then, you may settle the matter by a sort of compromise. Leave her to herself upon the rick, and walk the surrounding country until you put up the quarry of which she is so much in want. By driving the fields or hedges constantly towards her you may beat a considerable extent of ground. If you draw it blank go on a little farther. As the hawk sees you beginning to beat that farther country, ten to one she will come on after you and take up her position on a fresh resting-place nearer the scene of your operations. You may go on thus sometimes for quite a long walk, the hawk not, indeed, standing on your fist in orthodox style, but keeping in a place where she can start at anything you put up with a fair chance of overtaking it. As soon as anything so put up has been taken, you pick up your rebellious hawk in the same way as if she had flown from the fist, and, if you are wise, you do not give her a big crop. In the case of merlins there is another plan: you may fly another hawk while the first is sulking or fooling away her time on her self-selected perch. The latter will indubitably join in when you throw off the hawk on your fist, and you will have a double flight, after which, if it ends in a kill, you will be able to take up both hawks easily enough.

In theory, after every unsuccessful flight the hawk ought to observe certain fixed rules of conduct. Peregrines and almost all other long-winged hawks ought first to throw up over the place where the quarry has put in, and then wait on a while for the falconer to come up. Short-winged hawks, and often lanners, should take perch as near as they conveniently can to the quarry's place of refuge ; and merlins will get still nearer, very often waiting on the ground within a few feet of the hidden lark. From these various situations they ought, if in proper order, to be ready to come whenever the falconer wishes—to the fist if they are short-winged, to the lure if long-winged. It is also, alas ! possible that they may have failed through being outflown—beaten fairly in the air. Directly the falconer sees, by the spreading of the hawk's wings, that this sad event has occurred, he will begin to swing his lure, and in such case my lady ought—and generally will—at once rally to headquarters. The young falconer should endeavour from the first to keep his charges in such condition that they will always come to the lure. If, at the same time, they are keen enough to do this and high-fed enough to do themselves justice in a hard flight, they may be called really well trained. Here lies the real difficulty of hawking—to strike the balance justly between too servile obedience and too disdainful independence. Every day, and with every hawk, whether eyess or passager, the falconer is confronted with it, only in the case of passagers it is naturally more obvious. Wild-caught hawks are only brought by degrees, and with a good deal of trouble, to really like the dead lure, whereas to most eyesses their first notion of working for their living is connected with the slight trouble of flying either to the lure or to the hack board. Yet of the two it is much more essentially necessary that the passage hawk should come down quickly after failing in a flight, for if she does not, she will hang about for a more or less limited time near the spot where she lost her intended prey. And every additional minute that she stays out alone, especially if out of her master's sight, she is being reminded more and more of her old life at large. Then, if even she does not go soaring or prowling about in the deliberate search for quarry, she may espy some passing wood-pigeon or other too tempting bird, and be off in pursuit before any of the hawking party are near enough to keep her in sight. And a passage hawk which has flown and fed herself on her own account is, of course, much less likely to be recovered than an eyess, to which real liberty is a blessing hitherto unknown. With the latter the balance of danger lies often on the side of making them too fond of the lure.

The falconer should have with him in the field a pencil and small notebook, or at the least a card, upon which he can jot down a brief note or record of each flight, so that on his return home he can enter in his quarry-book a summary of the day's sport. The performances of each hawk should also be recorded in this book, as it is only by reference to this authentic volume, correctly kept day after day, that it can be known and remembered how she has acquitted herself. On the chance that it may be useful as a specimen, I give here an extract from the quarry-book which I keep, and which has been found to record pretty fully and in an exceedingly small space the chief points of interest in every day's proceedings. The first column gives the month and the name of each hawk, the second and following columns give the numbers of the days of the month and the scores made by each hawk. The units mean that a flight was successful, the zeros that it was not. When a fraction, such as $\frac{1}{2}$, occurs it signifies that the hawk flew double, in company with another, and that the flight ended in a kill. The sign $\frac{0}{0}$ stands for a double flight in which the quarry escaped. L means that a hawk was lost or left out, and C that she was recovered. At the foot may be a short note as to the day's weather.

September.	1	2	3	4
Eva	...	I I I	$0\frac{1}{2}$ I	I O I I I
May . . .	...	I I I	$\frac{1}{2}$ O I	$0\frac{3}{4}$ O I I
Ruy Lopez . .	O L	...	C I	$0 0\frac{1}{4}$ I
Wind . . .	Gale.	$\frac{1}{2}$ Gale	High.	Moderate.

It is convenient also, and not at all troublesome, to keep a daily record of the flights and kills up to date. Such a score will read as follows :—

1883.	EVA.		MAY.		RUY LOPEZ.		TOTAL.	
Sept.	Flights.	Kills.	Flights.	Kills.	Flights.	Kills.	Flights.	Kills.
1	43	34	51	33	40	28	134	95
2	46	37	54	36	40	28	140	101
3	48½	38½	56½	37½	41	29	146	105
4	53½	42½	61	39½	44½	30½	159	112½

Or the double flights may be recorded separately, which is perhaps a better plan. In the general score I mark ½ to each hawk which has done any work in a double flight, although in the individual score for the day the fraction set opposite her name may be a larger or smaller one, according as she has done a larger or smaller proportion of the work.

In the same book which contains such tables it is well to write down some account of any flights which seem to deserve particular notice, as well as notes as to the behaviour of the hawks, their state of health and condition, and any physic which has been administered to them. In fact the book may be made not only a bald record of mere results, but a running commentary upon your sport as it proceeds, to which you may refer not only for pleasant memories in the past, but for hints and warnings for the future.

In lark-hawking the character of the flights is so different, as has already been explained, that a record of them is hardly complete unless it contains some further indications than appear in the above tables. I add, therefore, a specimen of a score kept in rather fuller form, which, although it may seem rather elaborate in print, is simple and easy enough to keep when in manuscript. Here the lines reserved for each hawk must be somewhat larger than in the other table, so that each unit standing on a line with the hawk's name may have a letter or indication of some kind placed immediately above or below it.

The method of keeping such a record may be best illustrated by explaining it in detail.

1888.　Sept.	1	2	3
Pearl　.　.　.	G R R 1 0 1 p	M M G R $\frac{0}{8}$ 1 1 1 p a p	M M R RR 1 1 0 1 h a p p
Ruby　.　.　.	M　M G M $\frac{3}{4}$　0 1 1 a　p a pp	M M R $\frac{0}{8}$ 1 ? L a	(1)　c
Diamond .　.　.	M R　M R M $\frac{1}{4}$ 1　0 0 1 p p	G G R 1 1 0 a	R 1
Wind　.　.　.	Fresh.	Strong.	Moderate.
Weather　.　.　.	Cloudy.	Showery.	Hot.

Here, taking the first hawk's score, it appears that on the afternoon of September 1 she took one ground lark (G) (see Chapter IX.). Secondly, that she flew a ringing lark (R), which she beat in the air, forcing it to put in (p), and that it could not be found or got up again, and therefore does not count as a kill, but as a miss. Thirdly, that she flew and killed another ringer, and that after these two hard flights she was not flown again, but fed up. The next day, the wind being strong, she began with a double flight at a mounting lark, in which Ruby was her companion, and they bested the quarry, which put in, but could not be found; then flew a mounting lark (M), and took it in the air (a); and then a ground lark, which put in, but was routed up and taken. Finally, having killed a ringer, she was fed up and excused further flying. On September 3 the weather conditions were better, and in the afternoon Pearl flew a mounting lark, which put in, and was taken up by the hand (h). Had it been a good ringer probably it would have been kicked up instead, on the chance of a good flight; and if killed, the hawk might have been fed up. As, however, it was only a "mounter," it was thought best to keep the hawk for the chance of a ringer later on. The second lark, however, was also a mounter, and the hawk, having taken it in the air, was flown again

Then came a ringer, which was well flown, and bested in the air, but escaped by putting in. At length there was a successful flight at a ringer, which, however, was not killed until it had been routed out from the shelter to which it had put in, and afforded a second flight. The double RR over the record of this item in the score shows that at the second start as well as the first the flight was a ringing one.

Ruby's score begins on the morning of September 1 with a double flight at a mounting lark, in which he did most of the work, and took the quarry in the air. He is therefore credited with $\frac{3}{4}$ of the lark, to mark his superiority, whereas only $\frac{1}{4}$ is scored to Diamond, who was his companion in the flight. In the afternoon he puts in a mounter, which is lost, kills a ground lark, and then puts in another mounter, which is routed out, but puts in again, and is only taken when driven out a second time from his hiding-place. Having stuck to this lark well, and accurately marked the places where he put in, the little jack is excused from further flying. Next day he begins with the unsuccessful flight which he flew with Pearl. Then he takes a mounter in the air, and at the next attempt goes up so far after a first-rate ringer that no one can keep him in sight. As this lark was obviously making for a big plantation towards which the flight went, and as the hawk, though usually obedient to the lure, did not come to it or appear again, it is almost certain that he must have killed. The fairest way in such cases is to mark the flight by a (?), and not count it either as a kill or a miss in the general score. The L shows that Ruby was left out, and the (1) on the following morning shows that it was ascertained in some way that while roaming about on his own account he killed (and ate) a lark. The C indicates his recovery late in the day ; and the manner of his recapture, of course, is referred to in the notes.

Diamond's first item is the $\frac{1}{4}$ credited to him for the part he played in the double flight with Ruby. He goes on by killing a ringer in the morning ; and for his pains is rewarded with a good half of it, being then reserved for the last of the afternoon's flights, when the half-lark may have ceased to trouble his digestive organs. In the evening he puts in first a mounter and then a ringer, and then having with some difficulty and after a long flight killed a good mounter, is fed up just before it gets dark. On the morrow he falls in with two ground larks in succession, and kills them both. Hitherto, ever since the double flight with Ruby, in which he was outpaced, he has been doing well.

Though not a fast hawk he has persevered and bested all his larks in the air, though he has put them in so far off that it was difficult to find them.   But now he is to disgrace himself by showing the white feather.   He starts at a good ringer, but, finding it too fast for him, comes back humbly to the lure. The little (a), which is a mark of honour when seen under a kill, is a terrible blemish to a score when found under a " duck's egg"—showing that not the quarry but the hawk has been beaten in the air.   After this sad exhibition Diamond is fed up, and examined to see whether by some mistake he has perchance been allowed to get thin.   If he has, there is an excuse for his poltroonery.   Anyhow he will be well fed now, and if he does not fly better to-morrow physicking may be advisable.   A medical council must be held over his case.   On the next day, however, he re-establishes his character.   Lighting at the first trial upon a ringer, he sticks to it like a man, puts it in, and then takes it cleverly enough.   Of course after this success, following upon the fiasco of yesterday, he is at once fed up.   Peeping a little behind the scenes we may, it is true, suspect that the ringer, though quite properly marked so in the score-sheet, would not have figured as such if Pearl had had to deal with him instead of Diamond.   He would have tried to take the air, certainly, and mounted as if intending to go up in circles.   But Pearl would have been up to him before he completed the first ring, and from that moment, keeping the upper hand of him, she would have given him trouble enough to shift from her stoops without nursing any such ambition as to fly right away from her.

A score-sheet thus kept gives at a glance an excellent idea of the performances of the hawks referred to.   As their several scores are usually kept on the same page in successive lines, a comparison between them can be readily made at any time ; and if a period of two or three weeks is taken, the best average made in the time will usually belong to the best hawk.   If only a week or less is brought into the account, it may easily be that a very good hawk by a run of bad luck scores fewer kills and makes a lower average than a more moderate performer. The true test of merit is the ringing flights ; and if these alone are considered, the result of an analysis will infallibly settle the question which is the better hawk.   Thus in the score last above given, there is no difficulty in perceiving that Pearl, who killed three ringers out of five, and put in the other two, was a much better hawk during the short period under notice than

Diamond, who killed two out of four and failed once to put his ringer in. The mere number of quarry killed in a season is not a conclusive test of merit; for it is more creditable to a hawk to kill one ringer than half a dozen ground larks. The greatest number of larks I have killed in one season with any hawk in single flights is 106. But Jubilee, who accomplished this feat, was certainly not so good as his sister, Queen, who killed 95 in the same time. Nor was the latter—I think—as good as Eva, who killed only about 65.

The same method of scoring might be, with some adaptation, used for rook-hawks, and possibly for game-hawks. The short-winged varieties are usually flown at such a number of different quarry that another system would have to be employed. But in all cases the quarry-book should be a sort of diary in which may be traced the history of each hawk as she improved from time to time or fell off in merit. The less experience the falconer has the fuller he should make his notes. Both in making them and in referring to them questions will arise about which he is in doubt; and practice alone, or timely hints from a master in the art, will solve the difficulties. Any falconer who has kept diaries for any long period will find that at the end of it he has altered several of the methods which he practised at the beginning. It requires some time and trouble, no doubt, to write up the notes every day. But, as it has been before observed, no one can expect without a good deal of toil to become a successful falconer.

It will be seen by a look at the score-sheet, as well as by perusing any falconer's notes, that first-rate results are arrived at partly by the excellence of the hawks flown and partly by the activity and diligence of the falconer and his assistants. It is no use for a falcon to bring down her ringing rook from the clouds, or a merlin her lark from out of sight in the sky, if when the quarry has put in there is no man forthcoming to drive it out again. The sparrow-hawk will make but a poor show unless she is backed up energetically by an excited field of beaters; and tiercels will soon give up flying magpies with any zest if they find that their friends down below are slack or incompetent in playing their part of the game. You think yourself entitled to grumble at your hawk, and perhaps call her ugly names, if just at the moment you call upon her she does not fly her best. Do you not think that she also is aggrieved if you at the same time, chosen as it is by you, do not give her the necessary amount of help? Incapacity or laziness on the part of a man or a dog provokes the contempt and disgust of a trained hawk, who is often a much better critic in such matters than the ignorant may suppose. Be careful, therefore, if you want to retain the respect of your hawk, not to give her just cause to complain of you ; not to be slow when you should be quick, or hasty when caution or deliberation is needed ; not to seem inattentive to her fair and just requirements. And above all, not to commit in her presence anything which she knows is a gross mistake—in short, not to make a fool either of yourself or her.

CHAPTER XV

Lost Hawks

AFTER a day of unsuccessful flights the falconer returning sadly with his discouraged hawks may derive some consolation from the thought that he has at least brought them all safe back. On the other hand, the triumphs of the most successful afternoon are a good deal marred when one of the best performers has been left out, and the quarry-book has to be noted up, opposite her name, with the unpleasant word "lost." Foremost amongst the dangers and difficulties which beset the falconer, more plentifully than any other sportsman, is the risk which constantly hangs over him of losing the faithful ally upon whose service he depends for carrying on his sport. Every time that he puts a hawk upon the wing he has to face this contingency, which is more or less probable according to the nature of the flight which is attempted. No questions are more often addressed by the uninitiated to a falconer than these: "How do you get your hawks back?" and "Do they always come to you?" If he is rash enough to answer the last query in the affirmative he may be utterly confounded by having to confess that the very next time he flew his hawk she did not come back! Of course, in exercising an obedient hawk when she is sharp-set the risk run is infinitesimally small. But it would be wrong even then to say that it does not exist. And unfortunately the harder the flight undertaken, and the better the hawk, the greater is the danger which her owner has to face.

It is unnecessary to enumerate the many causes which may lead to the loss of a hawk. They have been mentioned incidentally in many of the foregoing pages. But it is well to remember that a very large percentage of the losses which annually occur is due to mere carelessness on the part of the falconer. As long as you make no mistake, and give your hawks a fair chance, the danger of an out-and-out loss is reduced to very moderate dimensions. The worst cases, as well as the commonest, are those in which the man is blamable for some imprudence, and not the hawk for any vice or fault. A much greater number of hawks annually get loose with the leash still attached to their jesses than anyone would be likely to suppose. Whenever such a mishap occurs a search should instantly be made for the fugitive, for every minute which elapses between the time of her loss and her recovery makes it more probable that she will not again be seen alive. The long tail of the leash becomes a sort of death-trap affixed to the hawk herself. As often as she takes perch in a tree, or flies over a telegraph-wire, or near to anything around which the hanging strap can coil itself, there is the chance of its getting entangled, in which case the hawk, hanging head downwards will, after many struggles, perish ignominiously, perhaps before the eyes of her helpless owner.

Even if the leash is not attached when the hawk gets away, or luckily drops out of the swivel, there is no little danger that the jesses, joined together at their ends by the swivel, will get hitched up, and a similar disaster result. All accidents which occur in this way are due to sheer carelessness. No hawk should ever be put upon the wing at all unless her swivel has first been detached. Even the jesses, if they have big slits in their ends, should be straightened out when they have been freed from the swivel, so that there is no chance of their getting hooked up on a nail or strong thorn.

On the first intelligence that a trained hawk has got loose, the falconer should start in pursuit, provided with a dead lure in any case, and, if the hawk was not sharp-set at the time, with a live lure also. The more searchers that can be sent out, the better; and these should make inquiries of every person they meet. Any of them who are not competent to take up a hawk themselves may carry a whistle, or pistol, or any signal agreed upon, by which they may call up the falconer if they get tidings or a view of the truant. In the latter case they must take care not to alarm the hawk or give her any inducement to move about, for each time she moves she runs a fresh risk of getting entangled and brought to grief. The search for a hawk which has a leash or swivel attached is not altogether the same as the search for one that has only her bells and jesses. For the fear is now not that the runaway, having tasted the sweets of liberty, will little by little acquire or resume the habits of a wild hawk, but that, being still as ready as ever to come to the lure or the fist, she will involuntarily commit suicide by hanging herself head downwards before you have time to find her and interfere. Thus the searchers will go about their work with all the speed consistent with thoroughness, visiting first the places where there is most danger of a fatal disaster, such as wire fencing, telegraph lines, and such bushy or thorny trees as the lost hawk has ever been known to frequent. In an open country loose hawks with their leashes on will sometimes escape with their lives for days together, and even kill quarry, and keep themselves in high condition. These, however, are the exceptions; and in a wooded country such a fortunate issue to the adventure would be unlikely.

When the loss of a hawk has occurred in consequence of her having killed out of sight, and gorged herself before she could be discovered, the chances are that she will remain for the night in the neighbourhood of the place where she flew the quarry upon which she dined. A visit will be paid, therefore, next morning at daybreak to this part of the country; and the falconer must not assume that if he fails to find quickly the object of his search she is to be looked for somewhere else. For it is unlikely, wherever she is, that she will pay any attention to him or his lure until she has cast. This she may not do, especially if it was late in the previous day when she was lost, until some hours after a spring or summer sunrise. Consequently, even if the searcher gets away from this most likely spot, and explores the plantations for considerable distances round about, he should return to it from time to time, on the chance that she has been there all the while, waiting till her appetite came before making her presence known. As the day grows older, the radius within which the search is continued may be indefinitely enlarged. Every labourer going to his work, every farmer going his rounds, every shepherd walking towards his fold, should be interrogated when met, and asked, if they see anything of the lost hawk, to report it in some way. The neighbouring keepers may be warned, although probably they will long before this have been informed that trained hawks are in the neighbourhood. A man will hardly fly his hawks in a part of the world where he does not know that the keepers are to be relied upon.

When the hawk has been lost through raking away or checking at chance quarry, the work of finding her necessitates often very great exertions and fatigue. There is nothing particularly unusual in the fact of a passage peregrine wandering off in an afternoon seven or eight miles from the place where she was lost sight of.   To explore at all thoroughly an area eight miles long and ten broad at the far end means, of course, a great many miles travelling, even if the country is exceptionally open and clear of trees.   Nevertheless, the dull and dreary journey must be undertaken if there is a real desire to recover the wanderer. The best hawk-finder is he who travels the farthest and sees the greatest number of possible assistants in his search.   If you make an excuse for shirking a visit to a particular copse or valley, it is as likely as not that you will hear afterwards, to your chagrin, that the missing hawk was seen there, and might easily have been caught.   If you will not walk a quarter of a mile out of the way to hail a passer-by who is going in what you think an unlikely direction, that will perhaps be the very man who, ten minutes afterwards, comes across the object of your pursuit.

There is not much to guide a man in choosing what direction he should prefer for going about his search.   But, other influences being equal, the truant is more likely to have gone down-wind than up.   Weak hawks especially, when they have no particular object in facing the wind, are apt to shirk the trouble of flying against it, and drift away to leeward.   Of course, if it is an eyess that has gone astray, and the place where she was hacked is within easy reach, there is a more or less strong probability that she may have gone towards it.   Eyess hobbies, when lost, are said almost invariably to go back to the hack place in this way.   Merlins have been known to do so, though not within my own experience.   But a really strong and fast hawk, in full flying order, seems often to assume almost at once the rôle of a wild one.   Such a hawk, especially if fond of soaring, soon sees that there will be little difficulty in finding her own living.   And she sets about it without any particular influence to guide her, starting in whatever direction chance may decide, and shifting her ground as capriciously as it is possible to imagine.   When Tagrag, already mentioned, was out, he would be reported one night in a certain plantation, and early the next morning would be seen three or four miles off on the opposite side of the small village where he ought to have been housed, and where his brothers were (or ought to have been) lamenting his absence from the screen-perch.

Farm-houses and all habitations near the spot where a hawk was lost should be visited without delay.   Not only are they generally frequented by either pigeons or fowls, towards which a stray peregrine or goshawk may well cast a hungry glance, but their shelter is always a tempting haven for any wandering house-pigeon which may have been chased and bested in the air. As the falconer proceeds from place to place, swinging his lure and calling or whistling, if it is his custom to use such means of bringing up his hawk, he should note the behaviour of the rooks and other birds within sight. The presence of any hawk, especially if carrying a bell, causes some excitement amongst the feathered world. The unwarlike wanderers of the air, when an armed cruiser comes in sight, exhibit some such signs of panic as might be expected of a fleet of merchantmen if a hostile battleship were viewed in the offing. The symptoms most remarkable are generally those observed in a flight of rooks, which often begins to whirl about in the air, as if it were composed of escaped lunatics, shooting up and wheeling suddenly in unexpected directions, filling the air at the same time with discordant croaks and screams, and with big black specks, which hurl themselves about as if driven by impulses which they themselves cannot understand or control. But many other birds, by their strange movements and queer attitudes, will betray the near presence of a hawk to whose visits they are unaccustomed. When a hawk has killed anything, and is pluming or eating it, crows, magpies, and jays have a way of sitting on the top of a neighbouring tree, craning their necks, and peering down with a morbid curiosity as they watch an operation of which they strongly disapprove.

Rooks, starlings, and small birds are all fond of mobbing a strange hawk when they think they can do it with impunity, and swallows occasionally indulge in the same rather adventurous amusement. It is therefore often worth while to make a *détour* and investigate, whenever any bird seems to be engaged in eccentric and unusual movements. Of the thousand and one causes which may have given rise to such vagaries, only the most practised eye can determine which are likely to be connected with the appearance of the lost hawk, and which are not. The safest plan is to go up and make sure that the commotion is not to be explained in this way. Of course when a hawk has been in the habit of flying any particular quarry, a disturbance amongst birds of that species is more likely to arise from her presence than in other cases. But most peregrines, when they are at large, are fond of taking occasional shots at lapwings, though very seldom with success. Merlins, though they are most partial to skylarks, will make stoops at any bird which they suppose they can tackle, from a wood-pigeon to a wren ; and the short-winged hawks are, of course, almost always ready for any bloodthirsty adventure.

Fortunately stray hawks, at least of the long-winged kinds, do not usually betake themselves to thick places where they cannot easily be seen. In open countries, where alone they should be flown, there is no great choice for them of convenient perching-places. Probably the most likely of all stations for them to take up are the tops of ricks ; and here a peregrine, or even a merlin, can be distinguished at a great distance by a pair of good field-glasses. As a rule, the best hawks like the highest perches, where they can command, as from a watch-tower, the farthest view of the country over which they hope for a chance flight. A hawk which takes perch on low railings or on the ground is not usually much of a performer. Some of these are very fond of perching on fallow-fields, where it is almost impossible for an unpractised eye to distinguish their plumage against the colour of the ground. A knowledge of their ways will make the falconer aware that in such a field, however apparently flat, there will be either mounds or small peaks and projections of earth where clods have been unevenly turned up, which a hawk is sure to choose as a resting-place in preference to the surrounding ground for some distance on every side. The predilections of each of his hawks for particular kinds of perching-places will generally have been noted to some extent by the falconer, who will naturally look for each of them on the sort of stand which he knows that she most often prefers. Trees, while still leafy, are some of the worst places in which to have to search, and of course they are very common resorts. A lost hawk may be watching her pursuers as unseen as King Charles in the oak, and not deigning to come down to the most enticing dead lure, until, having cast, she feels an inclination to do so.

When a lost hawk is not recovered early in the morning a very good plan is to fly another, either at the lure or at some quarry, in the neighbourhood of the place where the loss occurred, or where you have ascertained that the truant was last seen. And the higher the decoy hawk can be induced to go the more chance will there naturally be that the other may come up and join her. Whenever one hawk is on the wing for any length of time, there is a good chance that every other hawk within about a mile will catch sight of her, and not a bad chance that the other may come up. In case of a high ringing flight, wild hawks will come up from much farther than a mile. And lost hawks

will, of course, come and fraternise much more readily, especially
if the stable-companion flown as a decoy happens to have been
a comrade at hack or in some double flights. They will, however, do so quickly enough without any special inducement at
all. A friend of mine brought a hawk, newly trained, from a
distance to Salisbury Plain. She was lost in a very long flight
before she had passed a single night in the house to which she
was being taken, and was not even seen by her owner for two
or three whole days. One morning I was exercising a hawk
which the lost one had never seen, and suddenly there were
two hawks stooping to the lure instead of one. I had never
seen the wanderer, but understood at once what had occurred,
and tried to so arrange that the lure should be struck by the
new-comer. Either by accident or design she failed two or three
times in succession to do this, and I was obliged to take down
my own hawk and carry her in, and bring out a live lure for
the other, upon which she was quickly taken up. Both Tagrag, which had been out a week, and a merlin, which had been
out for nine days, were brought up from the unknown hack
ground to join in a ringing flight by another hawk, and recaptured in the same way.

A trained hawk will sometimes be taken off by wild ones,
with which she will go soaring and otherwise amusing herself
for a while. But the good-fellowship between them does not
usually last long. In the open places where long-winged hawks
are flown there are often a good many wild hawks about—
peregrines, merlins, and occasionally even hobbies, besides the
ubiquitous kestrel, with which the higher quality hawks disdain to associate. But each wild hawk, or at least each
pair or family of wild hawks, seems to have its own appointed beat, and resents the intrusion into it of a stranger.
Everyone knows that birds will frequently attack any interloper which comes with any intention of staying and quartering
itself in the country already appropriated by its own denizens.
Now the wild hawks, though they will often attack a trained
one as soon as they have set eyes upon her, yet will also often
go playing with her as long as their idea is that she is merely a
visitor, and will not permanently poach on their preserves. It
is when they find that the new-comer is really intending to
take up her abode in the neighbourhood, and appropriate her
share of the booty, which they looked upon as reserved for
themselves, that they begin to really make it so hot for her that
she is fain to get on into a less-favoured district which has not

been already effectively occupied. Thus the copse haunted by a couple of young peregrines, or the down quartered by a wild merlin every day, is not the best place to look for a trained bird of the same species which has been lost for more than twenty-four hours, although during the first period the tame and the wild bird may be seen stooping at one another or racing together in a most amicable style. If you have seen them together one day, and been unable to get down your own hawk, you will do well to seek her afterwards not on the same ground, but in a different, though not very distant, district.

As soon as you can get well within sight of your lost hawk, the live lure may be relied upon to effect her capture, until she has been out several days—in the case of eyesses for at least a week. But I should not advise forcing it upon her notice at a time when she has a full crop, if you can defer this at all safely until she has had time to get a bit hungry again. For though she will probably take and kill the bird offered, she may, if she is not hungry, refuse to stay on it while you can secure her; whereas when she is keen after her meal you will be able to wind her up as she stands over it on any reasonably level piece of ground. The process of winding up consists in merely dragging a fine line, the end of which is affixed to the quarry or to a stone or weight, round and round the feet of a hawk which is feeding on the ground. The difficulty is to pass the line under the tail, which, of course, acts as a mild sort of shield to keep the cord off. As the falconer walks round and round his hawk with the end of the line in his hand he must wait, as the line gets to the hawk's tail, for a favourable opportunity of pulling it under. If the hawk is fidgety and keeps disengaging her feet from the loops which have been already wound round her, it may be necessary to make many circles, and to begin the work several times all over again. But if the hawk is not frightened by any violent pulls on the line, or by unsuccessful attempts to take her up, the loops will sooner or later be so securely hitched round one or both feet that she cannot possibly escape. In the case of a hawk which has been out long, and is shy and suspicious, a long line must be used, and much care must be taken not to alarm her by jerking or tugging at it as you wind. Some hawks will, during a week's holiday, have retained a great many of the habits and much of the tameness which a course of training has deeply instilled into them, while others will in the same space of time have developed into almost wild creatures. This method of recapture is usually the simplest and handiest, when it is found impossible to take the hawk up by hand in the ordinary way. For no preparation or paraphernalia are required except a live lure and a long coil of string. If, however, you prefer to haul about with you a bow net with its pegs and rings, and do not mind the trouble and delay of setting the net, with the bait in the proper place, that will, of course, effect your purpose in many instances very well. But it is rather an intricate business compared with the other, and one in which an unpractised hand may easily make a mistake.

Another plan which has been recommended is to fly a bagged pigeon or other quarry in a light creance, and let the lost hawk take it. Then, as she is breaking in, walk slowly in and endeavour to take her up with the hand. If she objects and tries to carry, let her go, but keep hold of her victim, which she will be obliged to drop. Then, pegging that victim down firmly to the ground, take a few feathers and stick them up in the earth on every side of the body, the tips bending inwards, but not quite touching it. Round these feathers pass the loop of a cord with a running slip-knot in it, and carry the end of the cord right away to a distance, where you can hide, or where at least your presence will not prevent the hawk from coming back. As soon as she has come back pull the string, which will tighten the noose round her legs, and, keeping it taut, run in and secure your prisoner. The plan is ingenious and sounds feasible. I cannot doubt that it has been found so. Only— what if the hawk never comes back at all? You may sit for hours, with the string ready in your hand, waiting for her to reappear, and if she does not, will you not look rather small? Often, perhaps, hawks do so reappear. But sometimes I can affirm that they do not. A lost hawk in full condition and feather will, if scared away from one quarry, not always sit disconsolate watching for a chance of getting back to it, but go off simply and kill something else. A third-rate hawk may be so overjoyed at having for once captured some live creature, and so diffident about getting another before nightfall, that she will hang about and come back to her much-prized victim. But remember that it is the best hawks which run most risk of being lost, and which one is most anxious to get back.

Some hawks seem to have a natural aptitude for feeding themselves. They will do so at hack, before their sisters and brothers have even chased anything except in fun; and when left out for a night they may be seen in the early morning careering about after their favourite quarry, or some other. When tidings are brought in as to their whereabouts, the message is either that she was "see'd on a bird," or "very near got 'im," or at least was "chasin' of 'em like one o'clock." Such hawks are easier to track, no doubt, than the dull ones which sit still by the hour together; but on the other hand, more activity is required to come up with them and disabuse them of the idea that their rôle is now merely that of a wild bird. Liberty often acts as a wonderful stimulant to a trained hawk's energies. The same falcon which has persistently refused rooks, and can seldom score off a partridge, will perhaps after twenty-four hours' fasting in the tree-tops bowl over with alacrity whichever of these quarries first offers her a chance, and then, having been reduced again into bondage, relapse into the same indifference, and refuse to be induced by any amount either of feeding up or starving to fly a yard after one or the other. It is extraordinary what feats a bad hawk can be made to do by the schooling of the hard mistress Necessity. There was once a lame merlin which had injured her wing badly against a wire, and could only just fly at all, and that with a clumsy wobbling action. She was turned out loose in a place where some rebellious hobbies were being hacked, on the chance of her bringing them down to participate in her meals; but finding one day that her rations were not forthcoming until much later than usual, she wandered off in search of what she could pick up for herself, and was caught by a lad about three miles away from where she had started, on a small bird which she had actually killed single-handed!

It is a good plan, when a hawk is out, and there are more searchers available than one, for one of them to stay at home a good deal, so that if news of the truant is brought from any quarter he may at once set off with his lure, and hurry straight to the spot indicated. It is vexatious after a twenty-mile walk to find on returning that if you had saved your trouble and sat quietly at home you would probably have been by now in possession of your fugitive. The labourers and other people who are likely to catch sight of a lost hawk should be warned not to attempt to catch it,—which is a feat that yokels have an almost insuperable desire to undertake,—but to come at once and bring word to the owner or his falconer. Rewards should be offered and paid for any such information which results in the recapture, but not otherwise, unless there is corroborative evidence as to the facts reported; for otherwise the too generous falconer may find that whenever one of his hawks is lost several King Richards are reported in the field at the same time, though not at the same place.

After a hawk has been recaptured, it behoves the captor to consider what sort of preparation, if any, is required before she is flown again. Much will depend, of course, upon the character of the individual. A case has been very recently mentioned in print, where a falcon lost in a flight at rooks in the spring was only recaptured in autumn, after more than twenty weeks' liberty, and yet was then nearly as tame as when his holiday began. On the other hand, I have known a hawk in one week become so wild and shy that the manning of him and making him to the lure took nearly as long as if he had just been caught on the passage. A day, or even two, naturally has little enough effect in nullifying in an eyess the lessons which she began in early life. Two or three days' flying at the lure, and a slight reduction in the quantity and quality of her repasts, will generally make her obedient and reliable enough. But with a passage hawk it is quite a different story. Often you will have to hark back to some of the practical arguments which you used before, when she was being laboriously converted from a wild into a tame creature. Washed meat may have to be put in requisition, and when the moment does come to put her on the wing again in the field, great endeavours should be made to give her a good start at her quarry, so that she may again grow reconciled to her master's mode of operations, and not go off to commence a fresh campaign on her own account.

Very often a hawk, especially if not a very first-class performer, comes back from an outing a good deal improved, not only in health, but in flying powers. Occasionally, however, I have known it to turn out otherwise. The danger is with some hawks that while they are out they may learn to run cunning. This abominable vice is, I think, rare in hawks, especially in young ones. But I have known it in a jack-merlin —not of my own training—as early as in August; and it developed itself very badly in another jack which I lost for three days in September, and which before he was left out had shown no signs of it. The line adopted by the offender is to fly lazily after the quarry, waiting for it to put in, when he marks the place, and going straight to it jumps (if he can) upon the fugitive. Sometimes the offence originates in double flights, when an inferior hawk, having allowed her partner to do all or most of the work, cuts in at the finish and secures the quarry. But it is more rare in merlins than in jacks, which seem to me the most prone of any hawks to this vice. A game-hawk has, of course, little or no temptation to indulge in it, and a rook-hawk would spoil her own game by doing so, as she cannot follow into covert. The fault, when once developed, is difficult, or perhaps impossible, to entirely cure. Double flights should be entirely eschewed; and when the hawk has flown cunning and failed she may be left where she is, unlured and unfed, until later in the day, and then flown again and again until she tries harder. Wild hawks (and trained ones, if long left out) often fall into a habit of picking their flights, i.e. starting at a quarry, and, if they find it a good one, turning back and waiting for an easier chance. On the whole, therefore, if only for this reason, I am averse to leaving out a trained hawk longer than is absolutely unavoidable.

CHAPTER XVI

ACCIDENTS AND MALADIES

THE care of a hawk's feathers is a very important and elementary part of the falconer's duties. If he is naturally clumsy or careless, and yet hopes to do any good in this vocation, he must be continually on his guard against a mishap. Experience and persistent watchfulness will cure him of these defects, or at least deprive them of any very bad effects. But an innate adroitness is certainly much to be desired in any youth whom it is intended to train up as a falconer. The most important of a hawk's feathers are exactly those which are most easily broken. A single vigorous flap of the wing against any hard obstacle within reach of them may very likely knock off the end of one or two of the long flight feathers, or at least fracture the shaft where it is quite thin, so that the end below the injury has to be taken off and the feather mended. Great care must therefore be taken in carrying a hawk that no such hard substance is ever so near to her that by a sudden movement she can strike it with either wing. Narrow doorways should be avoided entirely, or never entered unless the hawk is hooded and quite quiet on the fist. When walking through a gateway or near an iron railing, stile, post, carriage, or branch of a tree, give it a wide berth. When mounting a horse with a hawk on the hand, get up on the wrong, *i.e.* the off, side—unless, of course, you carry your hawk habitually on the right hand, like the Indian falconers. Never wear a hat with a hard brim. It is impossible for you to be sure that at some unexpected moment a hawk, hooded or unhooded, will not by a sudden movement just touch the edge with a wing feather.

The wing feathers of the short-winged hawks are more yielding and elastic than the straighter ones of the long-winged, and will stand a greater strain. Worst of all are merlins, whose principal feathers are almost brittle, especially when the hawk is at all poor in condition. As for the tail feathers, although they are of less importance to a hawk's flying, they require almost more care than those of the wing. In this particular, short-winged hawks, with their very long trains, are more liable to injury than the others. A very common occasion of damaging a tail feather arises while a hawk is being broken to the hood. As the attempt is made to push the hood on and over the head, the patient flinches and draws back the upper part of her body, forcing the tail strongly against the wrist of the operator, if this is in the way. Those feathers upon which the strain bears hardest are very apt to give way; and even if the awkward falconer has succeeded in getting the hood on, he finds to his chagrin that he has done so at the expense of a damaged hawk. It is of course for this reason that I have advised the tying up of the tail whilst hooding lessons are being given. In actual flights there are certain risks of injury to tail feathers, although if they are all in perfect condition these risks are less than might be supposed. The struggle which occurs on the ground between the hawk and a robust quarry which is bigger than herself severely tries these feathers, as the former is obliged to make use of them to steady herself and resist the efforts of the desperate victim to upset her or drag her along the ground. The fight between a merlin and a partridge or pigeon is of comparatively short duration, as the little hawk, having her foot tightly clenched round the neck of her captive, is sure of its death within a minute or so. But a sparrow-hawk battling with a full-grown partridge has a tough job before her, and is sometimes forced backwards on to her expanded tail, so that it may give way at any weak spot, if there is one. A gos-hawk which has bound to a full-grown hare, or even a big buck rabbit, has even a hotter time of it.

In double flights, when both hawks have fastened on to the same quarry, and are dragging at it in the hope of obtaining sole possession, there is also danger to the tails. I must admit that I know of no case in which mischief has been done, but it is impossible to watch such a struggle, while hastening up to interfere, without seeing that it may be fatal to some of the feathers so roughly used. The arrival of the falconer on such occasions, in the rôle of mediator, must be welcome to both hawks; and he should at once catch hold of the quarry by one wing, and, holding it tight down, proceed to the work of separating the hawks. When the quarry is a large bird, he will offer to the hawk which seems to have the least firm hold a substitute for the real quarry, and get her to devote her attention to it until the arrival of the second man, when both hawks can be taken up. If both hawks and quarry are small, the first falconer to come up may catch hold of the pelt and lift it up, hawks and all, from the ground against which the tails are being pressed and bent. Once on the fist, the danger is past ; and one or other of the combatants may be handed over, with a tiring to replace the contested victim, to the next man who comes up. When double flights are the order of the day, every man who is likely to be up at the death should wear a glove and carry a spare leash, as well as a morsel of tiring for use in a possible emergency. He should also, if mounted, carry a weight and tethering rein at the side of his saddle, so that he may dismount at any time quickly and run in to the struggling hawks.

When a feather is bent, without any actual breakage of the shaft, it will come straight if dipped in very hot water, but may not improbably remain weak for some time at the place where the bend was. Very often such a bent feather will come straight when the hawk bathes ; but it is just as well to apply the hot-water remedy at once, and if it does not return to its proper position, there will be little doubt that the shaft is damaged. Whenever this is the case, the broken part should be cut neatly off and the feather imped. When the breakage is not near the end, and consequently in a very thin part of the shaft, the piece removed can be put on again by imping. But if it is the tip which has gone, as is only too often the case with beginners, the owner must make up his mind either to keep and fly his hawk in that damaged condition, incurring the jibes or pity of facetious or sympathetic friends, or to undertake the rather delicate operation required for grafting a fresh feather on the remnant of the old one. Possibly the novice may be within reach of a professional falconer, or an experienced amateur, who will come to his rescue, and perform this troublesome job. If so, he should certainly attend while it is being accomplished, and carefully note the manner in which the professor sets about it. If not, he must attempt it himself, and do the best he can by the aid of his own ingenuity, and perhaps of the following directions :—

Hood the hawk, and have an operating-table ready, on which you have placed a tolerably stout but soft cushion. Get an assistant to take firm hold of the patient with both hands round the body, over which may be previously thrown a silk handkerchief to preserve the feathers. The assistant should place his hands over the hawk's body with the palms downwards and the thumbs joined, the tips of his fingers being towards the hawk's tail, and the wrists over her hood.   Lowering them quickly and gently, and bringing the outer parts of the hands towards one another, he will get a firm grip round the upper part of the wings and the thickest part of the body, and will hold the hawk down firmly, but without unduly squeezing her, upon the cushion, her feet being pressed down underneath the body.   The falconer will thus be free to operate more boldly upon the feather to which he proposes to direct his attention.   The latter must have provided himself beforehand with a very sharp penknife, a small saucer of vinegar or strong brine, an imping-needle of the proper size, and a feather of the proper sort.   The imping-needle should be of iron or steel, filed down lengthwise to a triangular shape and pointed at the ends. It should be in the middle about two-thirds as thick as the feather at the place of breakage.   The new feather with which the damaged hawk is to be adorned must exactly match the one which it is to replace ; that is to say, it must have occupied the same place in the same wing, or the same side of the tail, in a hawk of the same kind as the one now under treatment. Before commencing operations, the imping-needle to be used should be immersed in the bath of vinegar or salt water.   With the forefinger and thumb of the left hand, take hold of the damaged feather just above the place of breakage, and separate it carefully from the adjacent feathers.   Then with the right hand pass the blade of the penknife obliquely upwards along the web of the feather on its thinner side till the edge touches the shaft just above the place of breakage.   As soon as it has done this, turn the blade so that the flat of it, instead of being inclined obliquely upwards with the edge pointing towards the stouter part of the feather, is directed downwards in a plane with the web on the broad side of the feather.   Having got it into this position, make a clean cut right through the shaft so that the portion of it below the blade falls off.   The next thing is to measure off on the loose new feather as much of the end as will, when fitted on to the other where it has been cut through, add to it the exact length which it originally had.   The shaft of the new feather must then be cut through at exactly the same angle or inclination as the other.

Now take an ordinary needle, and stick its point a little way into the pith of that part of the old feather which has not been cut off, and afterwards into the pith of the piece of new feather which is to be grafted on, taking care that the needle goes in straight down the middle of the pith.   Into the small apertures thus made, the imping-needle will be more easily passed in the proper direction than if there had been no such preliminary boring.   It remains only to effect the junction of the new and old feather. Before attempting this, dip the shaft of the new piece into the vinegar, and also moisten the end of the old feather just above the place where it has been cut.   Then taking the imping-needle, push one half of it into the pith of the new piece of feather, and the other half into that of the old.   By this means the two will necessarily become one and the same feather.   Be sure, as you push the two together, that their flat surfaces are level with one another, and not inclined at different angles.   When the new end is pushed home up to the old amputated shaft, it will fit on to it, and the web on both sides will meet and form a uniform surface.   Then release the hawk and replace her, still hooded, on the screen-perch, where she must be left quite quiet.   It is a good plan to do the imping in the evening, so that very soon afterwards the hawk will naturally be ready to go to sleep; and if the hood is to be left on, her last meal should, of course, have been without castings.   If not, the room where her perch is should be darkened.   She is less likely, when in the dark or hooded, to meddle with the mended feather; and when it has been left alone for twelve hours, the needle will have begun to rust in the pith of it, and thus be firmly stuck fast at both ends.

When skilfully and neatly performed, the operation of imping not only replaces effectually the part of a feather which has become useless, but repairs the mischief so thoroughly that no trace whatever remains of any injury having ever been done to it.   I have known feathers so imped that the eye could not discern the place of juncture, and it was difficult even to discover it by passing the thumb-nail down the shaft of the imped feather.   The tenacity of the rusted iron keeps the needle immovably in its place; and an imped feather, if it afterwards breaks at all, will break more readily in any part of it than near the place where the juncture has been made.   Of course the smaller the hawk the more difficult is the operation.   Merlins are particularly troublesome, owing to their vivacity and the smallness of their feathers.   It is, however, quite possible for an experienced imper to mend up one of these tiny hawks, even without an assistant to help him in holding her down.

The falconer should keep by him, in a box or drawer where they are safe from moths, a few feathers in readiness for imping the kind of hawks which he flies.   When he is in the habit of moulting them he will be able to supply his needs by saving up the long feathers dropped in the moult. These should be so stowed away that it is possible to identify the year in which they were dropped; for it is not advisable tc use a very old feather, as it may be brittle, and crack in pieces round the needle. A spare tail feather or two of any of the hawks which are most commonly trained may often be begged from a brother-falconer. But when a ger, saker, or one of the rarer falcons needs imping, it may be necessary to purchase a whole skin, which will entail some trouble and expense. It should be noted that there is one exception to the rule that a feather from any one kind of hawk must not be used for one of another kind. This is when the broken feather is to be imped merely for the purpose of the moult. Whenever hawks are moulting, the new feathers, as they come down, must be protected on each side by others of at least equal length to those of the natural plumage. But unless the hawk is being flown while she moults, it is immaterial whether the new feather matches the others in shape or colour. If it is long enough, and of about equal breadth, it will serve the required purpose. But every hawk before going into moult should be well set up in feathers of one kind or other, which are of a proper length and sufficient strength. A new feather, while growing down, needs more protection than any other.

If a feather is broken so high up that the shaft at the place of fracture is hollow, there are at least two ways in which it may be mended. The simplest is to slit the shaft on its under side, and then, cutting off the base of the new feather which is intended to be used, push the latter in bodily to the hollow of the old shaft. When it is far enough in, pass a small needle with strong waxed thread right through both quills, starting from below, and, winding the two ends of the thread round the quills in opposite directions, tie tightly together underneath the feather. When the feather is big enough there may be two such lashings of thread, one a little lower down than the other. A second plan, which is known as plugging, consists in first stuffing up the hollow quill, of the injured feather, above where it has been cut through, with a chunk of some feather which is not hollow, but has a solid pith. The plug thus inserted is firmly fixed in by means of some glutinous compound. When it has had time to become immovably settled in its place the imping can be done with an imping-needle in the ordinary way, the new piece of feather having been plugged also in a similar way if necessary. If a feather should have been pulled out, base and all, it is advisable to put some solid grease into the place, to keep it from closing up and preventing the new feather from growing down.

When only the tip of a wing feather is gone it would of course be only for the sake of appearances that it would be imped. Considering that wild hawks, and some trained ones also, kill quarry while they are moulting, and have four or more of their biggest feathers wanting, or only half-grown, at the same time, it would be a bad hawk which could not fly passably because she was short of an inch square of the sail area she ought to spread. Occasionally, as for instance when you have not long to wait before the moult will begin, you may leave a hawk unimped though she is very ragged. But the worst of allowing any feather to remain with its end off is that the next feathers to it, especially in the tail, are pretty sure to go too. The strain which the tail has to bear is such as it can just resist by the collective strength of all the feathers together ; but when one is unable to take its full share of the resistance, the others are unequal to the pressure, and give way. What difference in a hawk's flying power does the loss of a whole feather or half a feather imply ? It is, of course, quite impossible to say. But arguing from the analogy of pigeons, the tails of which are some-times removed in order to increase their speed, it would seem that in mere straightforward flying the tail is of very small assistance. I once had an eyess jack-merlin sent to me from the nest in a deplorable condition. The tail was clogged at the end with dirt, and so many of the tail feathers were bent and broken that he was at once christened " Tagrag " ; and while he was at hack was regarded as unworthy of much attention. By the time he was ready to enter, his tail, which it had not been thought worth while to mend, was reduced to about half its proper length, more than an inch having been knocked off every one of the feathers. This hawk developed later on into the fastest hawk I ever saw. When he was out on his own account, as he was once for seven days together, he could be distinguished from a wild merlin less by the stumpy tail than by the headlong speed with which he flew, even when not in pursuit of anything. When engaged in a double flight he would put in about three stoops to two of the other hawk ; and these were not only more quickly made, but were longer, straighter, and more tell-ing. This hawk was an exceptionally good one. He was the brother (though senior by a year) of Queen and Jubilee, which

I

between them killed 200 larks, in single flights, in one season. He was therefore no doubt naturally a very fast hawk ; but I mention him in order to show how little difference, in his case, was made in his flying power by the loss of nearly half a tail. I have also flown merlins at the lure, when in course of being broken to the hood, with their tails tied up, and noticed how admirably they stoop and throw up, without apparently being incommoded by the temporary inability to spread out their tails.

Much more serious and alarming than the breakage of a feather is the fracture of a bone.   When the hawk is a favourite, a cure is often attempted, and occasionally with success.   I have known a peregrine to be shot at and brought down with a broken wing, and to recover without any treatment at all; but this was no doubt a very exceptional case.   Usually any grave damage to the wing, whether by way of a sprain or a fracture, is incurable.   The bones of the leg are more get-at-able, more easily set, and subjected, when set, to less strain than those of the wing.   Splints and bandages should be applied (though it is very difficult to adjust a bandage to the wing) under the direction and advice, if possible, of some person who has a good practical knowledge of surgery.   The hawk, after being operated upon, should be placed in a sock as described in Chapter v., and fed by the hand with strips of washed meat or light food without castings.   Before the sock is put on it must be ascertained that the injured limb has been placed in the natural position ; and every precaution must be taken that the patient is left undisturbed, so that it is impossible, or at least unlikely, that she should displace the setting which has been attempted.

Hawks are sometimes troubled with a weakness in the outer joint of the wing, causing the outer part of it, where the primaries are, to droop.   The affection is more or less pronounced in different cases, sometimes being so severe that the wing seems to hang down powerless, as if merely hooked on loosely at the joint, and at other times merely to be a little out of place and to be carried slightly lower than the other.   Occasionally the weakness is so great that the hawk cannot fly, while at other times, after perhaps wobbling a little when thrown off, the hawk, once fairly on the wing, seems to fly almost or quite as well as if there was nothing the matter.   Generally a hawk which is so affected keeps hitching up the bad wing, as it were, into its proper place, only to find it droop again in a few minutes into its old position.   The old writers, who were well acquainted with the symptoms, say that the injury is one which must have arisen from a blow received by the hawk; but I have known it come on suddenly at a time when the sufferer could hardly have come by such an accident without its being observed. The following is a prescription given by Turbervile for curing the malady:—"Master Cassian (a Greek falconer of Rhodes) sayeth that yee must take Sage, Myntes, and Pela-mountaine, and boyle them all togyther in a new earthen pot full of good wyne, and when they bee well sodden, take the potte and set it uppon hotte imbers as close stopped as maye bee. Then make a rounde hole of the bygnesse of an Apple in the clothe that your potte is stopped withal for the steam to issue out at. Which done, take your Hawke upon your fiste and holde out hir hurte wing handsomely a great whyle over the hole, that it may take the fume whiche steameth up out of the potte. Afterwarde lette hir be well dryed by keeping hir warme by the fire, for if she should catche sodaine cold upon it, it would becomme woorse than it was before. Use her thus twyce a daye for three or foure dayes togyther, and shee shall bee recovered."

The beak and nares of a hawk should be kept clean, and a good falconer will, after she has finished her meal, wipe off any remnants of food or blood which may remain attached to the upper mandible. Unless this is done—sometimes, indeed, in spite of its being done—the nostrils and upper parts of the cere, where the feathers begin, may become infested with acari, or mites, which, unless destroyed, will eat into the horn and the flesh and cause great annoyance, if not actual sores and inflamed ulcers. Hawks which are in low condition are particularly subject to this pest; but at all times a sharp look-out should be kept, so as to detect the presence of the minute parasites, which may be seen running about somewhere near the nostrils. Fortunately it is easy to get rid of them. A solution of tobacco soaked in water should be made, and mixed with brandy or some strong spirit, and then applied with a small brush to the parts visited by the parasites. After a few applications they will be found to have disappeared.

Hawks will often get corns on their feet if allowed to stand constantly on hard blocks or perches. It is strange enough that there should be found any falconers who have so little thought for the comfort of their charges that they will use such resting-places. The screen-perch, at all events, which is kept permanently indoors, should have a padding of some kind—cloth, baize, or soft leather—underneath the canvas or sacking upon which the hawk has to stand. One of the cruellest of all the cruel things done in zoological gardens is the neglect to pad the miserable perches provided for the birds of prey, which are usually in consequence seen to have their feet adorned plentifully with corns and deformities. What with bad food, bad resting-places, and defective bathing accommodation, these poor captives are usually types of what the falconer should wish that his hawks may not become.

Of actual illnesses trained hawks undoubtedly have their full share. The old books devote many lengthy chapters to the description of these disorders, and of the remedies recommended for them. How far the elaborate concoctions prescribed by mediæval quacks and used, as it is to be presumed, by their very credulous customers, were efficacious in curing the evils for which they were prescribed, it is not easy to say. For in modern times we do not put much faith in nostrums of any such kind. But as the ancients certainly killed with their hawks several species of quarry which we hardly attempt in these days, it may not unreasonably be supposed that some of their medicines were at least useful in stimulating the energies of their patients, and inspiring them with a sort of artificial courage such as the Asiatic falconers still impart by the use of sal ammoniac and other powerful drugs. It is, I think, more than probable that the hobby, which has not for a long time past been successfully trained, was brought by physicking into such condition that she would fly keenly and well, and deserved the praises which some of the old writers lavish upon her. In the palmy days of falconry it was not only when a hawk was actually ill that physic was given. If she did not acquit herself in the field with all the credit expected by her trainer, he dosed her almost as a matter of course. Remedies of a more or less fanciful kind were supposed to exist for almost every failing which hawk-flesh is heir to ; and the medicine-cupboard of a falconer who professed to know anything about physicking his charges must have contained as many herbs, spices, powders, decoctions, and tinctures as would stock a small druggist's shop. As far as I know, no modern falconer has had the patience or temerity to test the value of these multifarious pills and potions.

The state of health of a hawk may be ascertained by various signs, more or less infallible. Mutes, castings, and the general demeanour furnish the most obvious symptoms ; but the books, which bestow a vast amount of attention upon the two former, are much too silent as to the latter and more subtle indication of an incipient malady.   The falconer should always observe the colour of every hawk's mutes.   If she is kept for any long time at a stretch upon a screen-perch under which the sawdust or sand is so thickly strewn as to absorb them altogether, a piece of paper must be placed occasionally under the perch, which will enable him to make the necessary inspection.   And at the first appearance of anything wrong the proper remedy should be applied.   The mutes of a hawk in good health should be' of an almost uniform bright white colour, and of the consistency of the whiting with which a lawn-tennis ground is usually marked out.   If there are specks of black in them there is no cause for alarm, but these should not be abundant or large in size.   If any other colour is to be seen there is something amiss ; and if the mutes are either watery or too thick the hawk is not in proper health.   The sooner these symptoms are detected and the right steps taken the easier will be the cure ; and in most cases a diet of freshly-killed birds given in moderation twice a day will set matters right without any resort to strong measures.   If, however, the discoloration is great, and appears suddenly, a dose should be at once given before the sufferer loses her appetite and becomes unable to retain food or anything else in her crop.

Castings are easily found under the perch or round the block, though when hawks are tied very near to one another on the same screen-perch it is sometimes difficult enough to know which of them has thrown a casting which is picked up between her and her neighbour.   The appearance of them should always be noticed before they are thrown away.   They should be more or less egg-shaped and compact, with no great amount of oily matter adhering to the outside.   The colour should be rather darker than that of the feathers, fur, wool, or whatever else has been taken to form the casting ; and if it is not so, it is a sign that the crop is foul.   A hawk in good health should also cast within a reasonable time after the casting has been swallowed ; and otherwise you may suspect that the gorge is clogged.   A hawk which has been fed late even in a summer evening should throw up her casting before eight at latest on the following morning.   When a hawk is slow at casting, she should be carried a bit, and will then often cast on the fist, or immediately upon being put off it on to the block.   A wild merlin will often eat the whole of a small bird between 8 and 9 a.m., put it over by about 2 p.m., cast, and then begin to look out for the evening meal.

A trained hawk may cast well and have fairly good mutes, and yet be all the better for a small dose. If she has a dull eye and stands stolidly on her block without taking notice of passing birds ; if she eats without zest, or flies without animation ; if, when standing on the fist, she takes a weak grip with her feet, or puffs out her feathers without cause, or folds her wings loosely together, she may indeed be healthy enough to get a doctor's certificate, but she is not in the sort of fettle to do herself justice in the field. In such case do not, like some falconers who ought to know better, begin calling the hawk names, and neglect her, while bestowing extra attention upon one which exhibits more aptitude. Remember that in the wild state there is no such thing as a bad hawk. All find their living, even in the worst weather, and find it although continually plagued and thwarted by the knowledge that if they go within gunshot of a man they will probably be murdered. Cannot a trained hawk, well housed and regularly fed, and freed from the constant fear of gun and trap, be made as fast and as clever even as the worst of her wild brethren? Falconers must be a long way behind the professors of other arts and crafts if they cannot make their trained pets at least nearly as good as the wild and untrained. There is perhaps more delight in flying a hawk which is never out of sorts and always naturally ready to do her best. But it is more creditable to the trainer, and a greater test of his skill, if he can impart excellence where he found little sign of it, and in short make a bad hawk fly well. The Indian native falconers—from whom, by the way, we have a lot to learn—habitually fly some of their favourite hawks, such as the saker, under the stimulus of strong drugs ; and there can be no doubt that many hawks of all species are bettered by frequent dosing, just as a Chinaman by opium, and certain literary celebrities by absinthe. In some cases these doses supply more or less effectually the lack of exercise from which a trained hawk suffers, and in other cases possibly they act as an antidote to the feeling of annoyance and discontent arising from captivity and confinement.

As to the particular remedy to be applied when a bird is thus out of sorts without being absolutely ill, I fear the reader must be referred to one of the old text-books, and not alarmed by quotations at length from their well-garnished pages. The mischief proceeds, of course, either from excessive cold or excessive heat in the system, which will require consequently either heating or cooling medicine. For the former purpose, spices and peppers will be preferred, with fatty substances, such as oil or bacon ; while for the latter, purgatives may be used, and meat washed in the juice of certain vegetable products, such as endive, cucumber, or melon. If the malady is so strong as to amount to fever, the hawk's feet may be bathed with water distilled from lettuce, plantain, or nightshade, or the juice of henbane. If, however, the earliest symptoms are noted, it will generally serve all purposes to give hot feeds, *i.e.* birds just killed, in the case of cold, and washed meat in the case of too great heat. Those who are not content to wait for such symptoms, but prefer a prophylactic treatment, may perhaps be satisfied with the following prescription: " If you intend to keepe and maintayne your Falcons and all other Hawkes in health, take Germander, Pelamountayne, Basill, Grimel-sede, and Broome flowers, of each of them halfe an ownce ; of Isop, of Saxifrage, of Polipodic, and of Horse-mintes, of each of them a quarter of an ownce ; of Nutmegges, a quarter of an ownce ; of Cucubes, Borage, Mummy, Mogemort, Sage, of the four kinds of Mirobolans, Indorum, Kabulorum, Beliricorum, and Embelicorum, of each of them halfe an ownce ; of Saffron, an ownce ; and of Aloes Cicotrine, the fifth part of an ownce. All these things confect to a powder, and at every eygth day, or at every twelfth day, give your Hawkes (the big ones, that is) the quantitie of a beane of it with their meate. And if they will not take it so, put it in a Henne's gutte, tied at both ends, or else after some other meanes, so as ye cause them to receive it downe ; and lette them stand emptie one houre after." A more simple preventive medicine is Aloes Cicotrine alone, given every eighteen days as an emetic, just after the hawk has cast, and followed in two hours' time by a warm meal.

Coming now to specific maladies, the commonest and not the least dangerous of the complaints to which trained hawks are subject is the " croaks " or " kecks," an affection of the throat akin to what is called bronchitis in the human patient. Its existence is betrayed by a wheezing or hoarseness, noticeable as the hawk breathes. In slight cases the sound is scarcely audible, and only very occasionally ; but when the attack is a bad one, the breath is impeded, and the invalid appears to be suffering from a sort of asthma. These severe attacks sometimes come on suddenly in bad weather, and generally prove fatal ; but the milder attacks, if attended to in time, may often be mastered and vanish permanently. The cause is usually the same as that which would in men induce a cold in the head or throat,—a chill caused by sudden changes of temperature, excessive cold, or, most frequently of all, excessive damp.   The remedy is to put the sufferer in a warm and dry place, and to give the most palatable and nourishing food in moderate quantities at reasonably short intervals, with a peppercorn or mustard-seed now and then.   Freshly-killed birds are the best diet; but if sheep's heart or butcher's meat is given, it should be first warmed a little. The hawk should not be left out of doors after midday, or in a place exposed to the wind.   Strangely enough, gers, whose habitat is in more northern latitudes than any other hawks, are the most susceptible of all to this malady; and special care should be taken, therefore, that they are not allowed to be in damp or draughty places.

Cramp is a terrible disorder, also caused by damp or cold. It is specially apt to attack the short-winged hawks, and is, I believe, always fatal.   Eyess sparrow-hawks taken too early from the nest are pretty sure to develop it when there is no maternal wing to cover them at night.   Possibly by keeping them in an artificial nest in a warm place the mischief might be averted; but the slightest chill seems to bring it on, and when once it takes hold of the feet and legs it appears to paralyse and permanently disable them.   Beginning with a mere stiffness in the joints, it increases in malignity until the sufferer loses the use of one or more limbs, and then often paralyses the muscles of the back.   When the very first symptoms of anything like stiffness appear in a goshawk or sparrow-hawk, no matter of what age, she should be taken at once into quite a warm place, and the affected limb fomented with hot water and embrocations.   Unless these remedies speedily give relief the most humane thing to do is to put the hawk out of her misery at once.   In this matter not only is prevention better than cure, it is the only means known of combating the dreaded disease.

Ague, or a low fever nearly resembling it, attacks hawks much in the same way as human beings.   There are shivering fits and alternations of hot and cold, which may be discovered by feeling the body with the hand.   The cause is often exposure to cold after becoming heated by flying or standing in the sun, or confinement in a draughty or cold place.   The sufferer droops her wings, and looks miserable generally.   She should be put in a sheltered place, rather warm than cold, and fed often, sparingly, on the best light food that is to be had. When the hot or cold fit is on she should be left as quiet as possible, but when it goes off she should be carried, and even flown a little, if she will; and she should by no means be left alone in any dismal place without company. When her attention is occupied she will have less inclination to mope or give way to the malady, and is much more likely to improve. If the affection is obstinate and the hot fits frequent, about two scruples of rhubarb may be given (for a falcon) in a casting of cotton wool, followed after two or three hours by a moderate meal of something freshly killed and light. If, however, the shivering fits predominate, or the hawk has become low in condition and has a poor appetite, the dose must be administered with caution and in moderation, and the patient should be coaxed and induced to take as much as she will, up to half a crop, of some heating food, such as freshly-killed sparrows, which are best of all, pigeons, or, in case of a goshawk, young rats; and if at a subsequent meal a sheep's heart is given (which such hawks can very easily pick at) it may be washed in wine in which has been boiled sage, mint, cinnamon, cloves, or some such aromatic herb. In all cases the invalid must be petted and made much of until she has regained her robust health and appetite.

Apoplexy is no doubt the disorder most commonly fatal to trained hawks of the short-winged varieties. It was called by the ancients the falling evil, and it has carried off quite suddenly many a first-rate goshawk almost without any warning at all. And it is probably more to be feared in these days when the use of washed meat has been so generally abandoned. The cause of this effusion of blood on the brain is over-fulness of body or an accumulation of internal fat; and in order to guard against it care should be taken to avoid overfeeding a hawk with strong, heating, or fattening viands. Merlins are also very subject to apoplexy when short of exercise, and peregrines are by no means exempt from it. When any hawk is fat or full-blooded, any exposure to a hot sun, or any violent or unaccustomed exercise, or bating off and hanging head downwards, may cause a determination of blood to the brain; and death will follow without the chance of even attempting a cure. It is well, therefore, especially when any hawk is not taking daily exercise, and plenty of it, not only to avoid overfeeding, but also from time to time to give a purge and an emetic. One of the simplest prescriptions is lard or butter, well washed, and then steeped in rose-water, and given with a little powdered sugar.

Apostume of the head is called by Turbervile a "monstrous accident," and a "very grievous evil," and said by him to be infectious. " It is discerned by yᵉ swelling of yᵉ hawke's eyes, by the moysture which sundrie tymes issueth and distilleth from the eares, and often eake by evyll savoure and smell of the apostume." The·invalid is inert, and cares little for her food, and will not pull at her tirings. The remedies he recommends are exceptionally commonplace. First, butter, well washed in rose-water, with honey of roses and powdered sugar. Then afterwards, for the relief of her poor head, rue, 4 grains ; Aloes Epatie, 2 drams ; saffron, 1 scruple, to be finely powdered and made into a pill with honey of roses. If the ear is stopped up, clear it with lint on a silver bodkin or needle, and, having infused warm oil of sweet almonds, stop it with another piece of lint. Which failing of success, he gives directions for cauterising, for which the original, or some surgeon, should be consulted.

Another sort of swelling in the head which affects the nares as well as the eyes, and is nothing else but a catarrh, may, it seems, often be cured by a pill made of agaric, 2 scruples ; cinnamon, 1 ; liquorice, 1, powdered and mixed with honey of roses. The sufferer should be made to sneeze by giving her—not snuff, as one might expect, but pepper, cloves, and mustard-seed, powdered, and blown into the nares through a quill, or rubbed on to the nares and palate. After these, or indeed any doses have been administered, it is well to carry the hawk on the fist till they have taken effect.

For suffusion of the eye a purge of aloes or agaric is recommended, and local treatment by blowing the powder of aloes and sugar-candy into the eye.

Frounce is a malady which will pronounce itself sometimes without much apparent cause. The mucous membrane of the mouth and throat is inflamed, and the tongue swelled and coated with a brownish white matter. This coating should be scraped off with a quill or silver knife, and the mouth dressed with burnt alum and vinegar, or a weak solution of nitrate of silver. The dressing may be done with a piece of lint on a small stick. Another lotion is made by taking the leaves of woodbine, with sage, honey, and alum, and seething them till the leaves are quite soft, and straining the decoction through a cloth.

Inflammation of the crop may be the result of bad food or neglect to give proper castings. The first signs of it will be in the castings themselves, which may be˙discoloured or misshapen, and sometimes charged with undigested food. In aggravated cases the mutes may be reddish, and the hawk may often throw up her food, and be unable to keep anything down. A purge and an emetic should be given before this stage is reached ; and great care must be taken not to overload the crop, or to give anything which will nauseate the hawk. If the malady has been neglected, it becomes dangerous and very difficult to cure. The hawk wastes away, and it may be a long time before you are able to restore her strength—if you pull her through at all.

Pantas is an old name given to a malady of the liver, when it becomes hot and dried up. The hawk is costive, and opens her beak often, as if gasping for more air. The mutes are blackish, thick, and scanty. Amongst numerous remedies in vogue are olive oil, oil of sweet almonds, and sugar-candy, with butter or lard, washed in rose-water. Of course no heating food should be given, such as sparrows, rats, or old pigeons. Powdered cloves and cubebes may be given in a casting every three or four days. The liver is almost as apt to get out of order in trained hawks as it is in untrained men. Green mutes, as well as black ones, betray the mischief, and warn the falconer. A purgative, such as those last mentioned, will be the first remedy ; but it must be followed by great care in the subsequent feeding. A more fanciful remedy consists of snails steeped in asses' milk, and used as a washing for sheep's heart, which is soaked in it.

Megrim, or palsy, is denoted by a shaking of the hawk's head. Pepper, aloes, and cloves may be given, with a little washed lard.

When a hawk is troubled with worms she is fidgety, and has startings and twitchings of the body, and falls away in condition. Mustard-seed, aloes, and agaric are prescribed, and cayenne pepper may be given with her food. Filanders are a sort of worm more difficult to suspect, and more difficult to get rid of. One remedy is garlic, long steeped in oil ; and if this fails, iron filings, with oil of bitter almonds, may be tried.

Hawks, if kept clean and frequently encouraged to bathe, are not much troubled with parasites. Young merlins from the nest are often infected with a flying tick, which does them no particular harm, and usually disappears when the little hawks begin to bathe. The way to get rid of them is to paint the body with a decoction of tobacco mixed with brandy. This is also the remedy for lice, which peregrines will sometimes get from a rook which they have killed. The same wash is to be applied to the nares and forehead of a hawk when troubled with mites. These very minute insects—otherwise called acarus or formica—sometimes establish themselves in and near the nostrils, and may be seen running about rapidly over the beak. They cause great annoyance, and if not put an end to will eat into the horn of the beak, and cause inflammation and other serious mischief. They dislike, however, the tobacco wash, and cannot keep their ground against it.

Corns and swelled feet are the result almost invariably of standing on hard and unpadded blocks or perches. They are, of course, both painful and also highly detrimental to the efficiency of a hawk, whose feet as a weapon of attack are only second in importance to her wings. The corn must be cut out, or the inflamed swelling lanced, and the foot must be bathed with some lotion, such as white of egg, vinegar, and rose-water, or with tincture of iodine. A very well-padded perch must be used afterwards, and a fortifying lotion frequently applied. Inflammation is sometimes set up by the prick of a thorn, when a hawk has trod upon a bramble, or grasped it when making a grab at a quarry which has put into a hedge. The worst form of corn is called "pin," and is pointed like a nail. Lancing and lotions may cure it; but it is an obstinate complaint, often incurable ; and the various unguents prescribed by ancient authors seem none of them to have been used with any great success.

When a claw or talon is broken by any accident, the falconer is advised to apply to it a plaster made of the gallbladder of a fowl, and to fit a sort of collar round the hawk's neck to act as a guard, so that she cannot touch the place with her beak. The same thing may be done when a hawk has a wound or sore on the foot, and keeps picking at it, a practice not uncommon with merlins, which will actually eat away their own feet.

The blain is a watery vesicle in the second joint of the wing. It should be lanced, and the hawk kept quiet until the wing is strong again.

For a " snurt," or cold in the head, Bert recommends the root of wild primrose dried in an oven and powdered. The powder is to be blown into the nares of the hawk. Or the leaves of the wild primrose may be distilled, and the nares bathed with the juice.

Craye is a stoppage in the " tewel," or lower bowel. It is said that the meat should be washed in distilled haws, or a decoction of primprivet, or drawn through milk warm from the cow.

Rye is a swelling in the head, which is said to be produced

by keeping the hawk without hot meat, and is cured in the way which may be conjectured.

Prynne is a malady of the eyes, for which it is recommended to bathe them with the juice of daisy leaves, or a decoction of powdered egg-shell, yolk of hard-boiled egg, and a quarter as much rock alum.

For a bruise Bert advises clarified honey, boiled with half as much stone pitch.

Some old writers declare that a hawk's appetite may be improved by steeping her meat in claret and the yolk of an egg ; that when she is slow at casting, or in digesting her food, she should have a mustard-seed made up with honey into a pill.   In such cases she should certainly have plenty of tirings ; and fresh water should be kept within her reach, so that she may sip it at any time if so inclined.   Sweet things are good for a goshawk, which is something of a sweet-tooth.   A good scouring for a sparrow-hawk is pounded sugar-candy and butter mixed with beef. Sugar-candy and olive oil are both good purgatives for getting rid of the internal fat or grease.   For giving a tone to the stomach, cloves, nutmeg, and ginger are beneficial.   And the most celebrated of all ingredients for compounding hawk medicines is " mummy."   One very distinguished modern falconer, having read in the ancient books endless references to this medicament, wrote to another equally distinguished authority to ask, " What is mummy ? "   The answer, which is too good not to be repeated here, was, " Mummy is mummy."   That is perhaps as much as the greatest Egyptologist can say !

CHAPTER XVII

MOULTING

A MOST important period in the life of any hawk arrives when she begins to undergo the ordeal of moulting. The annual or biennial change of plumage which occurs naturally in almost all birds affects more or less powerfully their health and condition, robbing them for the time of a certain amount of their strength and vigour, as well as depriving them of a part of the actual mechanical apparatus which serves as their means of locomotion. Thus we have seen that skylarks, when putting on a new set of feathers in August, are very much less able to escape from a hawk than when that process has been completed. To the hawk, whose very subsistence depends mainly upon his flying powers, it is obvious that the loss of any big feathers in the wing must be at least a very serious inconvenience, especially if it is combined with a weakening of the whole bodily organism. Nature has not, therefore, allowed the young hawk to mate or breed until after the first moult. At the time when he or she would naturally be busied with family cares—that is, when she is nearly a year old—the minor but still formidable effort of moulting is deemed a sufficient trial. Only when, after assuming the adult plumage, she has kept herself through the whole of a second winter is she called upon to undertake the arduous task of feeding not only herself, but also two or three ravenous and helpless youngsters. The first moult of the young hawk is also arranged to take place at that time of year when it is least difficult for her to find her own living. While the big feathers of her nestling plumage are falling out and being slowly replaced by new ones, the bird world is full of newly-fledged quarry, or at least of quarry which are not yet very strong upon the wing. In other words, the moulting of hawks naturally takes place in summer, just when they are most able to dispense with a part of their flying apparatus and of their energy.

Wild hawks vary a good deal in the date at which they drop their first feather, but trained hawks can be made to vary still more. Experience soon showed that a certain diet and regimen would hurry on the moult and expedite its progress, whereas another would defer and protract it. The young falconer will reflect betimes which of these treatments will best suit his plans, and act accordingly, remembering that, having once decided, he cannot without great inconvenience and even some risk adopt a different system. In any event he will, except in the case of rook-hawks, find himself in some difficulty, for the moulting process is in any case a long one. It is reckoned by months rather than by weeks. In peregrines, which are notoriously slow and bad moulters, it may last a half-year. If ever it is completed in three months the falconer may think himself lucky ; and the worst of it is, that the moulting months generally include August and September. The earliest day on which a feather can be dropped is usually well on in March or often early in April, and this is in the case of eyesses, for the passage hawks can hardly be induced to begin till a good deal later. Unless, therefore, the falconer can hurry the feathers down, he will hardly get his hawk even through the moult, and far less ready for active work, by September 1. We shall see, moreover, that the faster the moulting process is pushed on the less fit will the hawk be at the end of it to immediately take the field.

It is thus, in at least nine cases out of ten, practically impossible to fly a hawk in full plumage at rooks in the spring, and afterwards to fly the same hawk also in full plumage at game in August or September. And whether she has been flown in the early part of the year or not, it is still almost equally difficult to so arrange that she shall fly in full feather in the early part of the game season. Hence it is that an eyess of the year, when flown as soon as she is fully trained, comes usually into the field better equipped in the way of feathers than what may be called her elders and betters. Occasionally the moult of a passage hawk, or even adult eyess, can be deferred until August or even September, but this result is not to be reckoned upon with any certainty. The youthful grouse or partridges and their rather hard-worked parents, the adolescent or moulting lark, and inexperienced blackbird, ought all to be a little grateful to Dame Nature for having ordained that they should be pitted against hawks which are either young themselves or else have to take the air with shortened sail.

Many modern falconers, abandoning all attempts to fully moult their hawks in time for the game season, fly them irrespectively of the condition in which their feathers may be. That is to say, instead of shutting up their hawk, as the old falconers commonly did, when she drops the first feather, and keeping her inactive in the mews until the last new one has come down, they simply go on giving her her daily exercise just as if nothing had happened, and almost, if not quite, ignore the moult. It is wonderful how well some hawks acquit themselves under such disadvantageous conditions, and how little difference to a really fast and clever flyer is made by the loss of even two of the biggest feathers in each wing. On the other hand, a slow hawk, especially if she is not over-gifted with brains, so as to be able to make her head save her wings, is apt to cut rather a poor figure when flown in the middle of the moult at grouse. One of the chief drawbacks incident to this plan—especially with peregrines—is that when flying hard they often moult so badly. Full feeding—or rather overfeeding—is necessary to many trained hawks if they are to moult fast and well; and, of course, when expected to fly in the field they cannot exactly be overfed. Well fed, even to the verge of excessive generosity, they must be, or the new feathers will come down narrow and weak, or even the moult may cease. But to overfeed a passage hawk before putting her up to wait on, is to court the loss of her. Consequently the falconer who flies grouse with a falcon in the moult is confronted with an awkward dilemma. If he keeps his hawk sharp-set he is quite likely to see her leave off moulting, at least for a time, beginning again perhaps later on, and thus protracting the moulting season to an unconscionable length. If, on the other hand, he attempts to keep her fat, he may be pretty sure that she will be disobedient and slow at coming to the lure, and he will be tormented by a constant fear that she will despise it altogether and choose her own place in which to moult at liberty.

Suppose, however, that the falconer, having flown his eyess through the game season or his passage hawk through the rook-hawking season, desires to get her into moult as quickly as possible and through it without delay. While still flying her to the lure for exercise he will take care that she is bountifully dealt with in the matter of rations. He will reserve for her one of the most cosy places in the hawk-house; and when she sits out at her block he will be specially careful that she is never exposed to uncomfortable draughts or damp or chilly winds. He will encourage her to bathe, in the open air if it is fine and warm, or indoors if the weather is bad, and will, if necessary, take the chill off the bath water. He will carry her often and give her tirings, and, in short, make rather a pet of her; and one morning, as he comes up to her place on the screen-perch, he will espy beneath it a big broad feather shaped rather like the blade of a butter-knife. This will be the seventh feather of one of the moulter's wings. Sticking it into his hat, presently to be transferred to a rack on the wall, which will hold the remaining big feathers as they drop, he will then carry off my lady to her quarters in the moulting-room.

This apartment, in the words of a high authority, should be so "cleane, handsome, and well kept, that your hawke may rejoyce and delight greatly in it." We may perhaps have our doubts whether any hawk would delight as much in the most palatial prison-house as in the fresh air of the least picturesque mountain or forest; but, at anyrate, a clean, cheerful, and well-lighted room pleases her better than a dismal garret. A well-ordered moulting-room is a somewhat luxurious apartment, and cannot be provided without some trouble and expense. It should not be cramped in size, but big enough to allow the hawk at least to stretch her wings in a short flight from one end of it to the other. The walls should have no projecting corners, and if they are hung with some soft protecting stuff it will be all the better. The windows—except in those very commendable cases where the room is lighted by a skylight—will be guarded on the inside by perpendicular bars of smooth wood or cane; and the floor will be laid at least more than an inch deep with sawdust or dry sand. Fixed upright into the floor will be a block or two, with padded top; and the room, near its two ends, nearest and farthest from the window, will be crossed by perches, one of which at least should also be well padded. If it is intended that the hawk, or hawks, for which the room is designed shall be left mostly alone in solitary occupation, a bath may be left on the floor; but, as in any case the bath must be emptied and refilled pretty often by some person entering the room, it may be as well to let the bath, when unused, remain outside, where it can be kept clean instead of dirty. The door of the moulting-room should open outwards; and it is a good plan to make it close of its own accord by a weight or spring, to minimise the chance of its being inadvertently left open.

Goshawks should never be moulted in company, and the bigger falcons only when known to be good-tempered, and that with a companion of the same sex. Tiercels, unless especially cantankerous, may moult in the same room, and the same thing may be said of female sparrow-hawks. All the other small hawks may moult in company with others of the same sex. In fact, in the case of merlins and kestrels there is no harm in associating the two sexes, provided all occupants of the club-room are kept, as they should be, constantly provided with plenty of food. I am, however, disposed to think that when merlins are loose together a good deal of chevying about takes place, which is apt to be dangerous to the growing feathers when the moult is nearly over.

The moulting-room should never be cold, and still less damp. In very wet and chilly weather artificial heat may be used in moderation. For instance, there may be a small fire in the room underneath, or the flue of a lighted fire may pass up one of the sides of the room itself. The window also should by all means face the south rather than the north. The moult is quicker and better when a hawk is kept warm, whereas anything like a chill may check, or at least retard, it seriously. Yet there is, of course, a difference between warmth and stuffiness. Of the two evils, however, I am inclined to believe, with the ancients, that over-ventilation is worse than over-closeness—if, at least, you are anxious to get quickly through with the moult.

The food for a moulting hawk should be nutritious without being too heavy. It should be good and very plentiful. In fact, the bird should be able to eat whenever she has a fancy to, and to eat as much as she will. Accordingly, each time that rations are served out they should be ample to last until the next supply will be forthcoming. In quality the viands may be rich and high-flavoured, if the hawk can stomach them. John Barr moulted a falcon in an exceedingly short space of time by supplying her constantly with the heads, necks, and pinions of fat ducks, keeping her mostly under a small tented shelter, upon the outside of which a summer sun beat down with almost ferocious force. He declared that the feathers, nourished by the fat contained in these succulent meals, came down broader and stronger, as well as faster, than he had ever known in other instances. Thus a "grene goose" was anciently recommended for moulting hawks' diet, and on the same principle an ideal food for moulting merlins or sparrow-hawks would be fat quails. These little hawks are, however, often nauseated by eating birds which are very fat. The heads, necks, and pinions of fowls should always be given freely to moulting hawks, not only because the meat on them is of a good kind, but because they make capital tirings, and so provide exercise at a time when exercise is very difficult to find. Mice for the small hawks, rats for goshawks, and rabbits for the other big hawks, should also be often supplied ; and plenty of castings should be given, or the internal fat which accumulates in a moulting hawk will either rob her of her appetite or cause some obstinate and perhaps dangerous disorder.

It is not to be supposed that the ancient falconers, who were so fond of physicking their hawks, could omit to discover artificial methods of expediting the moult. A couple of specimens of fashionable prescriptions may be worth quoting for just what they are worth : "When ye meane to further the mewing of your hawke, take of the snayles that have shelles, stampe them shelles and all, strayning them through a cloth, and with the oyle that comes thereof wash hir meate two or three tymes. Also take of the snayles that lie in running streames, give your hawke of them in the morning ; for that will both scowre hir and nourish hir greatly, and setteth hir up and maketh hir to mew apace. Master Michelin, in his *Book of the King of Cyprus*, sayeth thus : 'Cut an adder in two parts and seeth him in water, and with that water and wheate togither fede your pullets, pigeons, turtles, and other birds which you intend to allow your hawkes that are slack to mewe, and soone after they shall mewe their feathers apace.' "

The personal attention paid to a moulting hawk varies very widely. Some falconers make frequent visits to the room, and habituate the captive to come to the fist, and be carried and handled and maintained in a very tame state. The ancient falconers—and some of our own time—gave themselves very little trouble, and left the moulting hawks pretty much to their own devices. Probably the one course has nearly as much to commend it as the other. It seems more amiable and business-like to keep up, even during the off-season, that friendly intercourse with your hawk which is natural among friends, and even some of those habits of obedience which you have so laboriously taught. On the other hand, while you are giving your hawk a holiday, you may almost as well give her a real one as do it by halves. She will very possibly moult a little quicker, perhaps a little better, if she has no worry at all, and can concentrate her whole energies upon the mere growing of feathers, just as she did when in the nest, instead of having to bother herself about jumping to the fist—a mere perfunctory act of meaningless duty, devoid of practical use or result.

The falconer will, at least once a day, visit the moulting-room, if it is only for the purpose of changing the bath water, clearing away the castings and the stray feathers of birds that have been plucked and eaten, and gathering up any feathers which may have been dropped by the hawk herself. The order in which these feathers fall is admirably arranged, so that each new feather as it successively appears in the place of one that has dropped out finds itself between two completely grown feathers, either old or new, one on each side, between which it can grow down with a protector right and left of it. The deck feathers, *i.e.* the central feathers of the tail, are the first to drop, and in the wings the " beam " or longest feathers are about the latest to fall. By this time the smaller feathers of the body and other parts will have mostly been changed. By rights, of course, the change should be universal and complete, but in peregrines and lanners it is often not so. Very commonly one of the former may be seen with several brown feathers interspersed among the light grey plumage of the first moult. A falconer must be rather over-fastidious if he is put out at this ; but there is more reason for complaint when rusty-looking primaries, well worn in the nestling stage of existence, persist in keeping their places amongst the brand-new shafts and webs of flight feathers just come down. A blue hawk thus parti-coloured, looks as if there was something wrong with her ; and the owner is apt to fancy, whether rightly or wrongly I cannot say, that the old feathers abnormally left in are not as serviceable as new ones would have been. At anyrate, most falconers consider it rather a feather in their cap to have their hawks "clean moulted," that is to say, with a complete suit of new feathers on their bodies.

Occasionally it happens that without any apparent reason an eyess drops out some of her nestling feathers almost as soon as they have come fully down, or, as the old falconers termed it, as soon as she is "summed." I have known a jack-merlin, well hacked and fully trained, and in first-rate condition, drop his two deck feathers while sitting quietly on the pole-cadge on the way to be flown in the field, and have seen him just after-

wards fly as well as ever, and give a good account of a ringing
lark. When any such little mishap occurs the hawk must of
course be kept as high fed and fat as he can be consistently
with proper obedience. The jack I speak of found himself, in
consequence of his misfortune, promoted to a position of special
favour among his fellows. An extra allowance of the best sort
of food was daily permitted to him. When he flew well—which,
by the way, he always did—he had nearly as much as he liked
to eat. And when by reason of this very high feeding he
refused to come to the dead lure, a lark was generally walked
up by beaters driving towards him as he sat on a rick, so that
he might be indulged with the flight for which his vain little
soul was longing. Or, if this could not be done, he was left on
his self-chosen perch until one of the other hawks went up after
a ringing lark, when he would come up like a meteor across the
sky, and join in, sometimes to the great chagrin of the other
hawk, which had started under the impression that she was to
have the field to herself. In due course the new feathers grew
down, having the pretty blue-grey hue of the adult plumage,
and thus contrasting conspicuously with the five brown feathers
on either side of them. Before the lark season was over they
were fully down ; and my lord was quite a curiosity, looking
rather as if some waggish under-falconer had imped the two
middle feathers of his tail with a couple of wood-pigeon's feathers
instead of the proper ones.

A hawk which has once been moulted in captivity is said
to be "intermewed." When the moulting hawk, which has been
mewed in the old-fashioned way to get through the process, is
"summed" with her new suit, the falconer must not suppose
that the troubles of the ordeal are over. Before the newly be-
dizened beauty can be flown again with any success she must
be got into condition, and, if suffered to get wild during her long
incarceration, she must undergo a fresh ordeal of reclamation.
The old falconers give elaborate directions for conditioning a
hawk when "drawn" from the mews. It would be more tedious
than profitable to reproduce their prescriptions, most of which
recommend nostrums too fanciful for this matter-of-fact age.
Almost as well might a modern trainer be advised to get his
man fit by means of the terrific potions and purges upon which
Caunt and Belcher were brought into condition. In these days
we are partly too timid, and partly, I suspect, also too lazy, to
compound together some score of ingredients, more or less
poisonous or distasteful, and administer the product to an

unwilling patient in the rather sanguine expectation that it will cure and not kill. A simpler treatment is preferred for producing a result which is, after all, simple enough. The problem is to get rid of that accumulation of fat which, in a time of almost complete inactivity and overfeeding, has encumbered the heart and liver and other internal organs of the hawk, and until it is removed will make her dull, sluggish, and unmanageable. This should certainly be done by medicine of some kind; and the sooner it is done, after the flight feathers are fully down, the better. Any attempt to reduce the superfluous fat, or to produce an appetite by means of mere hunger, would be a great mistake. The hawk would lose in strength and weight much more than she gained in condition; and it would be a long time before, by dieting alone, you could get rid of the mischief which a couple of doses would almost put an end to immediately. A simple purge and a simple emetic should be administered in any case; and if the hawk is of a vivacious disposition, and has not grown dull in the mews, this may be found a sufficient physicking. For the former nothing seems to be better than rhubarb. A convenient mode of dosing a peregrine is in the form of a Cockle's pill, which may either be wrapped up in tissue paper and pushed down the throat with a small stick, or concealed in a tough morsel of meat which the hawk swallows bodily. A merlin or female sparrow-hawk should not have more than half one of these pills for a dose; and a jack or musket even less than this. Goshawks may have more than the small hawks, but not so much as a peregrine. For those who want a more orthodox and time-honoured prescription, the following may serve:—" Take Aloes Cicotrine and graines of Filander, otherwise called Stavesaker, and Cassia Fistula, as much of the one as of the other, to the mountenance of a beane, togither, and when ye have beaten it into powder put it into a henne's gut of an inch long, tied fast at both ends: then convey it into hir in the morning, so as she may put it over, and that must be after shee hath cast, if she had any casting at al. Then set your hawke by the fire or in the sunne, and feede hir with a quicke chicken, or some other live warme meate two houres after." Even in those days, however, it is plain that there were some misguided heretics who rebelled against the long-winded precepts of the esoteric school of hawk-doctors. "Neverthelesse, in stead of the sayd aloes, ye may at youre discretion use common pilles, such as Potecaries give men to make them loose-bodied. And many are of opinion that they be much better than that other

of aloes: for the pilles drive downward and scowre more strongly
and with greater effect."

It was an almost invariable rule with the old falconers to give
washed meat to a hawk after the moult. Many of them, indeed,
began to do so for about ten or fifteen days before the end of
the moult; and in the case of hawks which are now intended
to be flown as soon as possible, some preliminary steps of the
kind should be taken while the last feathers are growing fully
down. Washed meat is better than short rations in such a
case as this, where if you reduce the hawk's strength a little it
is no great matter as long as she does not get thin withal. But
the grand desideratum for a newly-moulted hawk is plenty of
carrying. The effect of this discipline upon a wild-caught hawk
has been already described; it is quite as magical, and still
more speedy in its results in the case of one which has become
wild in the mews. This is one of the good things of which one
cannot have too much. It is more than one man's work to
carry a single hawk as much as she ought to be carried when
fresh from the moult. If, therefore, there is not a man available for each, let the one which is not being carried be pegged
down at her block if it is fine, or confined to the perch if it is
not, and provided with a tiring until there is someone who
can take her again on his fist. Tirings must be kept going
assiduously for the sake of the exercise, and for the first few
days all food that is not tirings should be given on the fist. In
short, the trainer must go through, with a moulted hawk, most
of the same processes, more or less modified according to the
character of the hawk, as he went through when first reclaiming
and making her to the lure.

Long-winged hawks are, of course, less troublesome to
reduce to orderly habits after the moult than sparrow-hawks
or goshawks. But then they require longer to get into wind.
For this purpose they must be called off to longer and longer
distances, and made to stoop hard at the lure. At first their
flight will be very heavy, and their desire to mount non-
existent. After a minute's stooping at the lure they will have
their mouths open. It will perhaps be quite difficult to keep
them on the wing. But they must not be excused; and the
much-enduring trainer must have the patience to wait, swinging
the lure until it pleases my lady to come to it, and be keen in
the cause. It is altogether impossible to say how long it will
be from the time when she is taken out of the moulting-room
to the day when she can take the field once more. A haggard,

dosed successfully, and dieted with lucky precision, may surprise you by getting fit quite quickly, whereas an eyess which you expected to bring into fettle in a few days may prove more restive than she did when taken up from hack. There is luck as well as skill in the treatment of each hawk. But carrying is the *sine quâ non*; and the more a man carries his hawk the better chance he has of observing how his treatment works, and whether it should be modified in one way or another. The best hawks, when well moulted, will often become even better the next year; and there is no reason why a moderate or even a poor hawk should not improve. Newly-moulted hawks should not be brailed, nor allowed to be bareheaded in any place where they are likely to bate. And of course great care will be taken for some little time that they are not left in a damp or draughty place or in the rain.

CHAPTER XVIII

Virtue and Vice

CONSIDERING the great variety which exists in the character, shape, size, colour, and appearance of hawks, it may be easily supposed that they differ also in strength, speed, and general capability. Perhaps the most notable of all points in which they are distinguished is in the matter of temper. Not only will the young birds from different eyries be unlike in this respect, but the very same nest may produce one good-tempered hawk, and another sulky; one bold and confiding, another timid and suspicious; one vivacious and greedy after her food, and another dull, sluggish, and indifferent about her meals. Nor are these discrepancies the result, apparently, of any different dieting or treatment. They exhibit themselves in eyesses in the very earliest days of hack, or even before, and usually continue for a long time, if not for life. No doubt a good-tempered hawk may, by falling into bad hands, be changed into a bad-tempered one; and some of those which seemed worst tempered when first caught, or when first taken up from hack, have by skilful management become quite amiable and well-behaved. But the amount of care and art required for the one sort is very different from that needed for the other; and very few beginners will be likely to achieve much success with a pupil which is thoroughly unmanageable by nature. Sparrow-hawks, especially eyesses, are, as has already been said, the most naturally untamable of the hawks usually trained, with golden eagles a pretty good second; and the most amenable are hobbies and merlins, which often seem as if they rather liked being trained. Nothing more need be said here about tempers than that with a troublesome pupil the trainer must be extra patient and extra cautious, and be continually on his guard against making a mistake. Hawks are from their earliest days very good judges of character; and the more distrustful and apt to take offence any one of them may be, the more determined must the falconer show himself to keep his temper and exhibit a philosophic calm in his demeanour. The petulance and restiveness which some hawks display vanish to an extraordinary extent if such ebullitions of temper are quietly ignored, and the offender, apparently wishing to make herself designedly disagreeable, finds herself treated as if she had played quite an amiable part. But the least sign of impatience or anger on the part of the falconer is noted by an ill-conditioned hawk, which thereupon seems to take a real delight in further aggravating her imprudent or hasty master.

There is a whole world of difference between the breaking of dogs and the breaking of hawks. The former know when they deserve punishment, and actually expect it. They respect a man for chastising them when they have done wrong, and rather despise him if he ignores the fault. A hawk, on the other hand, must never be punished, at least openly. To strike a hawk, or rate her, is to forfeit at once her respect, and what may be called her affection. A dog is a slave by immemorial habit. He knows intuitively that he is dependent upon man as a master. But the hawk, if she is worth her salt, knows nothing of the kind. Turn her loose, and instead of starving or begging, like the lost dog, she will well shift for herself. She looks upon man as an ally rather than a master. She likes to be treated as a friend and equal, rather than as a dependant and a servant. Falcons, especially,—that is, the females of the long-winged hawks,—are excessively proud, and even haughty ; and are mortally offended if any indignity is offered them. But no matter what the hawk may be, the true policy is constant kindliness, or at least the outward semblance of it—a policy of rewards and not of punishments. Endeavour always to impress upon her the idea that you are her very best friend ; that her chief enjoyments in life are due to your foresight and assistance ; that her food, her bath, the block on which she stands at ease, the well-padded, sheltered perch, and, last but not least, the opportunities for good and successful flights, are provided by you. Then will she, in the language of the mediæval falconers, rejoice at the sight of you, and like no place so well as the fist. Then will she fly the better when your voice cheers her on, and begin her meal more comfortably when you are standing or sitting by. It is well to treat the ill-tempered hawk somewhat as Mrs. Gummidge was treated, by making allowances. Possibly she may some day surprise you by the display of unsuspected virtues.

Passing from the mental to the bodily characteristics of hawks, we find that occasionally two hawks are so alike that it is almost impossible to distinguish them except by their jesses, while others of the same kind and sex are so dissimilar that a stranger may find it difficult to believe that they do not belong to different species.   There are, naturally enough, good and bad hawks of every shape, size, and colour; and it would be very rash to pronounce off-hand at the first sight of one that she is worth more than any other.   Nevertheless there are certain peculiarities which are found in the average of instances, taking many together, to belong more commonly to the best hawks, and others which in the great majority of cases betray the bad performer.   These have always been remarked.   They are mentioned in many ancient books, written in many languages; and there can be no doubt that after taking a good look at several individuals, an experienced judge will pick out those which he would prefer to possess if he had the choice.   John Barr told me upon this subject a rather pleasant story.   He was travelling southwards with a large number of hawks by train, when at an intermediate station he met with the late Prince Dhuleep Singh, who during a great part of his life was a most enthusiastic and successful falconer, by whom Barr was at one time employed.   The Prince immediately inspected the hawks, which, I believe, were the same that were afterwards flown at Epsom, and in the course of conversation pointed out in their order the hawks which were likely to do best.   The falconer mentally noted the selection thus made, and afterwards found that it was accurately justified by the result.

It is somewhat curious that the same characteristics which in one species of hawks mark out an individual for admiration or the reverse, are mostly found to serve a like purpose in the other species.   The following short remarks, therefore, unless when otherwise specified, may be taken as applying to hawks in general.

One of the very first points of which a critic will take note is the foot of a hawk.   Long toes are a great merit; and if they are slender and well separated at the bases, it will be all the better.   Nor is there anything mysterious or unnatural in this, for, the wider the area which the hawk's foot can cover, the better chance she obviously has of catching hold with one talon or the other of the quarry at which she strikes.   Another notable characteristic of the best feet is that they fasten themselves naturally with a clinging grip to the object of which they take hold, adhering so closely to a glove or any soft surface that they seem almost to be glued or stuck to it, and can only with difficulty be removed. In fact, the feet of some hawks, when they have taken a firm hold, can only be got off by picking the talons or claws out one after another with the hand. The hawks which thus clutch are almost always good killers in the field. Many falconers attach some importance to the colour of a hawk's feet. Major Fisher declares that a nestling peregrine with yellow feet is of little worth, and that the best colour is lead-grey or greenish grey. Merlins in their early days often have very pale feet, but some of the best of them, when in high condition and fed daily on freshly-killed larks, will put on a bright yellow and even a somewhat orange hue. Bright colours are undoubtedly a sign of health, though they may not be of strength, speed, or courage. The power which a hawk has in her feet seems usually to be a sure indication of corresponding vigour in the rest of her body.

The head of a specially good hawk is seldom big or round, but wedge-shaped, narrowing from the back rapidly towards the base of the beak, and rather flat on the top than dome-shaped ; and there is a prominent eyebrow, with a keen eye, very full and bright. The shoulders come very high up, and are square, as they would be called in a man. There is a great deal of breadth in the upper back and in the breast, where the pectoral muscles are situated, and these muscles may be felt by the hand extending in a firm and ample bulk under the upper points of the wings. The wings themselves have also an appearance of size and strength, and each feather, if separated from the next, is seen to have a broad web and stout shaft. The same may be said of the tail feathers ; but in these no extra length is desirable. A short tail with plenty of strength and solidity is better both for useful and ornamental purposes ; and a hawk with a long flexible train like a kestrel is not to be preferred. A strong and fast hawk often folds her wings close together, so that the points cross one another quite high up over the tail. The nostrils of a hawk should be large, and the beak short. No indication can be derived from the general colour of the feathers, whether dark or light. As regards size, there is a prejudice against big falcons and small tiercels ; but this does not hold good with regard to the short-winged hawks, in which strength is often the chief desideratum. In the case of peregrines a very large falcon is often clumsy ; and the majority of brilliant performers whose names have come down with honour in the annals of falconry, were rather under than over the average size. One of the most famous peregrines of this century (Aurora by name) was of such an intermediate size that her owner for some considerable time mistook the sex. As for merlins, I do not remember any exceptionally big one that was not particularly stupid and remarkably slow. A specially small jack, however, is by no means invariably a duffer.

So much for the appearance of hawks when standing at ease on the block or perch. As soon as they are put on the wing the task of distinguishing between them in point of merit becomes very much more easy. The good hawk, when in good condition, has a buoyancy in the air which is wanting in the other. She flies with less effort, and as if she liked the exercise. It seems as natural to her to fly in a slanting line upwards as on a level. When she spreads her wings and sails along they are held out to the very farthest possible extent, and kept "flat": that is to say, the tips are on a level with the back of the head, or even a little above it. The fast flier does not usually go along steadily through the air, moving, as a boating man would say, on an even keel. On a windy day one wing is often higher than the other, and her course swerves more or less from time to time as she utilises or counteracts with a marvellous art, not understood of men, the wayward pressure of the disturbed air. If you have to choose between a hack hawk, which makes her way along with regular beats of beautifully even wings, like a heron or a dove, and one which hurls herself forward in unexpected lines like a lapwing, by all means choose the latter. Do not suppose that either lapwings or haggard peregrines go crooked by accident, or because they know no better. They can go straight enough if they choose, and will do so if it happens to be their game to play. But just as a skater, having only one skate on the ice, can go along if he moves in divergent lines but not if he attempts to keep a straight line, so it seems that by a sort of zigzaggy course more pace can be got up than by mere plodding straightforward work. It is only after watching many hundreds of flights that a man can hope even to begin to understand how birds, both pursuer and pursued, manœuvere in the air, trimming their sails, so to speak, so as to increase to the utmost, the one the momentum of her stoop, and the other the speed and suddenness of its shift.

Haggards, and the cleverest younger falcons, fly more with the outer part of the wing than with the part nearest the body. They work, in fact, rather with the joint which in the human body is the wrist than by the movement of the whole arm from the shoulder. The saving of labour so effected is obvious enough. Only, in order to fly thus, the shoulders must be thrown very far back, and the chest far more widely opened than it is by most eyesses. When a hawk in stretching her wings while standing on the block raises them far above her head, or when, having bated off, she hangs down from the fist, and, flopping with her wings, brings them so near together behind her that they seem almost about to touch, be sure that that hawk will fly better than one which carries her wings back to about a level with her back only. It is in stooping at the lure that you can judge best as to the merits of rook-hawks or lark-hawks, while, of course, those of game-hawks and duck-hawks are best tested by merely waiting on. In the latter and more simple case that hawk will be preferred which goes up quickest and to the highest pitch without raking away too far. But note, in stooping to the lure, which comes at it with the most headlong dash, and, having missed it, throws up soonest and highest. In a hard flight that hawk is most successful which after each stoop shoots up farthest, rebounding, as it were, from the unsuccessful stoop, and so keeping the command of the air, so that the quarry, even after the cleverest shift, still finds his adversary on a higher level than himself. The best hawks take great delight in stooping at the lure, and may be cheered when they make a brilliant cut at it, which will increase their excitement and zest. Sometimes, getting to a distance from the falconer, they will rush in at their very best speed, and, on the lure being twitched aside, will shoot up almost in a perpendicular line; then, turning a sort of half-somersault, they will come down in almost the same perpendicular line with the way of the original impetus apparently still on them. A good "footer" at the lure is usually a good footer at her quarry; and good footing is one of the most deadly qualities any hawk can possess.

Another remarkable thing about hawks is that those which are the best-tempered are generally the boldest, strongest, and best fliers. The reason is doubtless that bad temper proceeds to a large extent from timidity; and timidity of mind is, in nine cases out of ten, either due to bodily weakness, or at least connected with it. By bad temper I do not, of course, understand mere anger. Some of the hawks which are the fiercest and most furious when first taken out of the bow-net, prove the easiest to reclaim, and the most obedient when trained. Sulkiness is the worst of the natural vices, and it is unfortunately common enough, not only in goshawks, which are notorious for it, but in all kinds of hawks. Out of one nest I have had one merlin which was almost the best-tempered and one which was almost the worst-tempered that ever I saw. Eyesses are more commonly sulky than passage hawks, and very often display signs of this defect in the days of hack. Later on this develops into some more specific vice, which will perhaps need great care and patience to cure or modify. A short notice of the vices most prevalent amongst hawks will not be out of place, for the treatment of these disorders is almost as well worth understanding as that of their bodily ailments.

Carrying is a fault with which the falconer will generally first become acquainted. The word is ill-chosen, or rather ill-adapted from the Norman "charrier." It would have been better if our ancestors had used such a term as "bolting" or "lifting," so that no confusion need have arisen between the word carrying, as applied to holding a hawk on the fist, and as applied to the hawk's action in taking up and flying away with her food. However, be the name what it may, the practice is one to which all hawks are more or less naturally addicted, although some in a very much greater degree than others. Merlins and hobbies are the most notorious offenders, and wild-caught hawks of the long-winged kinds, though not always troublesome in this way, must be prevented for a long time from developing this habit, or they will infallibly become spoilt and lost. In the chapter on Training, some directions are given for guarding against this predisposition, and curing the mischief when it has already arisen. But of all safeguards and remedies, by far the best is the habit already referred to of constantly instilling into the hawk the idea that your near presence is a thing to be desired, and not disliked. If a merlin or any other hawk shows the least inclination to carry when flying to the lure, or when being taken up from it, I would, for a time at least, never go near her on any occasion without taking a piece of food in the hand and giving it to her. By this means in a few days she will look out for your coming, and even listen for your step with all the pleasurable expectation that other tame animals await the coming of their feeder. And in taking her up have always on your hand a piece of food which is either more tempting or at least more easily

devoured than that which she has in her foot.   Let the tit-bit
be a "mess of pottage"—but not necessarily a big one—for the
immediate fruition of which the silly bird (as Turbervile calls
her) will barter away all the prospective advantages of a freshly-
killed partridge or a dainty pigeon.   These latter have to be
plucked, mark you, before they can be eaten, whereas the bright
red morsel in your hand can be begun at once, without any such
trouble and delay.

In bad cases the vice of carrying may be corrected by a
rather strong remedy, which, like all other hawking devices, has
long been practised.   Before resorting to it, see that the lure
which you are going to use, whether live or dead, is quite a light
one, but very firmly fixed up, so that no part of it, or no part
of the food with which it is garnished, can come away.   Then
exercise your ill-behaved hawk in whatever way you prefer, and
let her ultimately get the lure and have it on the ground in her
foot.   This lure will have a fairly long creance to it ; and you
will keep hold all the time of the end of the line.   Now, as your
hawk is on the ground with her food, begin to make in as if you
were approaching her after a real flight.   You may, however, do
so much less cautiously.   If she bolts with her meal, let her go four
or five yards, and then, with a sharp, sudden pull on the string,
twitch the whole apparatus out of her foot, and let it come flying
back towards you.   What with the "way" that the hawk has
on her, and the suddenness of your pull on the string, the lure,
if properly fixed up, is bound to be jerked away ; and my lady
will have to trouble herself to turn round and come back towards
you.   But, of course, if you so arrange your lure that it will
part, and the edible portion of it remain with the hawk, while
the inedible comes back to you with the creance, you will have
done ten times more harm than you expected to do good.   A
few lessons of this kind will often cure even a determined carrier.   But I have known merlins which were cunning enough
never to carry a light lure, knowing from experience that it would
be a mere waste of time, and yet, when they had taken a wild
lark, never doubted that they could make off with it if they
liked.

There is a special sort of carrying to which many long-winged
hawks are prone, and it is still more difficult to cure than the
practice commonly so called.   A hawk which is much fed on
the fist, and little on the ground—especially on damp or uncomfortable ground—will, after taking her quarry and killing it,
stand still on the ground, looking round with a restless air.   And

after a while, thinking, apparently, that the spot where she is is not exactly the most convenient that could be found for a meal, will get up, pelt in hand, and fly off in search of one more desirable. This is done out of no feeling of mistrust or deliberate conviction that her prize is likely to be taken from her. Thus the fact that the hawk is quite tame, and even likes your company at her dinner, is no safeguard against this vexatious habit. I have known a jack-merlin which was frequently easy to take up, bolt with a full-sized lark, and carry it, as if it weighed no more than a feather, for nearly half a mile, searching for a place which was good enough for my lord to picnic on, and disdaining several flat mounds which lay in his way, and which would have formed luxurious tables. The same hawk once carried a lark about six hundred yards in one direction, and then, seeing no specially attractive ground on that side, came back the whole way, and, flying past at about fifty yards distance, settled on a rough, dirty heap two or three hundred yards in a different direction. Had he gone straight on for the same length of time in the original direction, he would either have been lost and left out, or only found by accident after a search of long duration. Sometimes a hawk, too dainty to feed on the ground amongst prickly stubble or tall, wet turnip-leaves, will go off with her quarry into a tree, which is not a particularly comfortable dining-place, but which she chooses to prefer. Mr. St. Quintin had a fine falcon which persisted in this vice, until he actually got rid of her.

Other hawks, especially merlins, delight in going off to ricks to plume and eat their quarry. There are not many trees in places where the best merlins are flown, but there are always plenty of ricks. Sometimes it is possible to climb these structures ; and many a time has the falconer, if a small man, been hoisted up on the shoulders of some stalwart friend, or, if he is stalwart himself, has given a back to some smaller man, or even a man and a boy, ladderwise. Often, however, the rick is unclimbable. Then what is to be done? for you cannot drag a ladder for miles over the downs. The surest way is to carry a long coil of string, with a bullet at one end. Stand at one side of the rick on which your hawk is quietly and contentedly plucking her victim ; sling the bullet over the top of the rick, and as nearly over the head of the hawk herself as your skill and the wind will allow. Then, if you have an attendant, let him take hold of the end of the string which has no bullet attached, and which has not gone flying over the rick. If you have no companion, peg down this last-mentioned end at a good distance from the rick. Then walk to the other side and pick up the bullet. Pulling the string taut, drag it sideways, so that the line scrapes along the top of the rick, and, coming to the hawk's self-chosen dining-place, sweeps the whole affair, dinner, hawk, and all, away. If the line should get entangled in the quarry, so much the better; you can pull it down to the ground. If not, the hawk may, of course, carry to another rick, and recommence the same trick. But after repeated scrapings-off she generally gets sick of the worry, and condescends to go down to the ground.

A simpler and more unceremonious way of interfering with the offender is to pelt her with clods of earth, or even flints, until one of them either hits her or goes so near that she thinks it advisable to decamp. I have known a hawk sit so stolidly on a rick that though flints went within two inches on either side of her, she took no notice, and went on eating. Others, old offenders, know as well as their master what happens when they go to rick. They would be rather surprised if they did not see him bending down as he makes his way towards them, collecting suitable missiles, and if he did not begin at once the familiar sport of hawk-stoning. Such hawks may be called rick-hawks ; and they are about as trying to the temper as anything which the falconer has to contend with. They are, however, not quite so bad as tree-hawks. A falconer who is possessed of one of these last-named treasures must add to his other accomplishments that of being a good shot with a small stone.

What remedy there is for the hawk which carries out of pure caprice it is not easy to say. In the first place, she must be habituated to take some of her food on the ground—tirings anyhow, which hitherto have perhaps been taken on the block or the perch. Let them be fastened down by a peg or a weight, sometimes on damp ground, sometimes even in prickly stubbles, so that the over-dainty hawk may learn that eating on the ground is not so bad after all. Then she ought to be flown sharp-set, so that, being in a hurry for her food, she should be glad enough to pluck it quickly and on the first place where she alights. Give this sort of hawk as large a quantity of flying as ever you can. Fly her, if you have the choice, at the most difficult quarry, and in the most difficult places. Never mind so much if she succeeds or not. It is better to lose a few rooks or partridges than to lose your hawk. Fly her, therefore, as often and as hard as you can. Never mind whether her score or her average is bad. It is better to make a poor score than to think your hawk is a good one when she isn't. A good deal of the restlessness which makes a hawk flit about with her quarry is due to her being short of exercise. If, therefore, you can make your hawk fly more, either at the lure or in the field, than she has a mind to, she is much less likely to go fooling about before attending to the business of feeding herself. Of course it is very difficult to do this, as twenty or thirty miles more or less is a mere exercise canter for a peregrine. But many trained hawks get a great deal less than this in a whole day.

There is a device which I should like to see tried with a carrying hawk, but it requires some patience and good temper. Get some stuffed birds of the proper kind, at which you mean to fly your hawk ; use them, unweighted, as lures, and when the hawk has taken them and come down, let go the string and approach her cautiously with food in hand as if you were making in to her after killing a real bird. If she bolts, let her go and make what she can of the stuffed bird. About twenty minutes after you will have her back, furious, but perhaps less ready to bolt away from the food in your hand—a sadder, but possibly a wiser, hawk.

When a hawk, being carried on the fist bareheaded, ready to be thrown off at quarry, keeps jumping off in a tiresome way at nothing, ten to one she is not quite ready to fly. Better put on her hood and let her wait for an hour or so, and go on with another hawk, if you have one to fly, and, if not, light a pipe. Hurry no man's hawks, not even your own.

It would be rather a misnomer to call soaring a vice. This, which is one of the most beautiful accomplishments of the wild falcon, is the natural mode of taking daily exercise. To see it in perfection, look at a wild peregrine or a wild hobby—you have there what enthusiasts describe as the poetry of motion. All hawks, eagles and vultures soar by nature. It is their way of stretching their wings, and of taking the air where it is cool and fresh. Kestrels do a sort of humble soaring in search of their food, and hobbies actually feed themselves, like swifts, on the wing. To say, therefore, that a trained hawk which adopts this orthodox method of keeping herself fit is thereby committing a fault, is rather hard upon her. Nevertheless it is a very vexatious habit, when over-indulged in, and, speaking from a practical point of view, is not to be too much encouraged Hobbies, when flown in the middle of the day, even sharp-set, will stay up constantly for a quarter of an hour and even more, taking little apparent notice of the swung lure, or at the most striking at it without catching hold, or at least coming down with it to the ground. To do them justice, they seldom go far away, but often look as if they meant to do so, which, indeed, they occasionally do, especially at migrating times. But a peregrine which has taken to the soar often seems so engrossed in the pleasant occupation as to forget all about mundane affairs, and, sailing along in ever-widening circles, drifts farther and farther down-wind, until the falconer, if unmounted, can keep her in view no longer. Then, when she is beginning to tire of her amusement, and to remember that she has, after all, a crop to fill, she will very likely wing her way back to where she last saw the falconer wistfully swinging her despised lure. But what if an unlucky pigeon then heaves in sight? or if some unsuspecting yokel puts up a partridge or a rook? There is nothing to prevent her from having a shot at it : and, if she kills, good-bye to my lady for that day. If you find her, it will be more by good luck than anything else.

Hawks will go soaring because they are short of exercise, because they feel hot from insufficient bathing, or because, not being particularly hungry, they prefer a few minutes' free roaming about to immediately dining. Consequently a hawk which has shown herself fond of the practice and slow at coming to the dead lure, should be offered a bath whenever she is at all likely to take it—once a day, in very hot weather. She should have lots of flying and stooping to the lure, for, as she is fond of the upper air, there is the less chance of her hanging about round the falconer and spoiling her pitch. Finally, she should be a bit keen after her food before she is put on the wing. Soaring and waiting on are analogous things, or rather they are the same with a difference. The best game-hawks, which wait on mountains high, are soaring as they do so ; that is, the movement of the wings is the same, but the difference is that the waiter-on is, as it were, anchored to a fixed point below— the man or the dog, whereas the soarer is merely floating about like a yacht which has no particular destination.

The vice of raking away differs only from that of soaring away by the fact that it may be done at any height. Half-trained hawks, before they have done any real work in the field, are very apt to wait on in the wrong place. They know as much as that they are expected to keep within sight of the falconer, but not that they ought to be directly overhead ; and, through laziness, or because they prefer stooping at the lure up-wind, they allow themselves to drift away to lee. Hardly

have they come up level with the man than they at once fall
back on the wind, lowering their pitch, if pitch it can be called,
so that for all useful purposes their attendance is a mere sham,
and they might as well be on the falconer's glove. Repeating
this idiotic performance in the field, they are some hundreds of
yards to leeward, and at a low elevation, when the grouse or
partridge get up, and a stern-chase ensues, in which the quarry,
going up-wind, gets the best of it. For this annoying vice there
is no direct remedy. Experience may be expected to teach
the young hawk better. One plan is to let loose pigeons,
while the hawk is so waiting on, so that, after missing some,
by reason of raking and low flying, and perhaps catching others
when flying properly, she may understand at last how success
is to be had.

Checking is a crime to which we are not now so much
exposed as were the old falconers. Bird life is not so abundant
now, at least in England, that a hawk is confronted often with
an *embarras de richesses*, and leaves her legitimate quarry for a
stray bird of a different species. Eyesses, indeed, if kept to
one quarry, will often hardly be induced to pursue any other.
Passage hawks are more ready to check at birds which cross
their path. It would be rather too much to expect a haggard
falcon, which in her time has struck down birds of fifty different
kinds, to discriminate very nicely between a plump partridge
and a fat wood-pigeon when Providence threw either within
reach of an easy stoop. It is when a passage hawk has been
flown at rooks in the spring, and afterwards at game in the
game season, that there is the chief danger of checking. As
long as the sable quarry is alone attempted the risk is not
great. The hawk is flown out of the hood at quarry actually
in sight. It is only when that quarry has saved itself that the
temptation to check occurs, and at that moment there are, or
ought to be, lures waving near at hand. But encourage the
rook-hawk to become a game-hawk, and the case is altogether
changed. She has to go up alone, with nothing particular in
view, and wait aloft till the falconer springs her quarry. Moreover, she knows now that rooks are not the only lawful game.
She is at full liberty to go at grouse; and, if grouse, why not
wood-pigeons and house-pigeons, gulls, or curlew? Why not
anything which is desirable, and which "tempts her roving
eyes"?

The besetting sin of the checking peregrine is the chase of
pigeons, wild and tame. Often, it must be admitted, this sin is

the outcome of the falconer's own action. Has he not himself used a pigeon as a live lure? Has he not, when teaching his pupil to wait on, let loose a pigeon with the express intention that she should fly it? If he has never had occasion to do so in training his passage hawk he has been exceptionally lucky. As regards pigeons, it is generally pretty easy to break peregrines of checking at them as soon as they have once begun to fly at game. To achieve this feat get a good number of very good pigeons—say a dozen, the faster the better ; make the hawk wait on at a short distance—say 600 yards—from some covert in which the pigeon, if he can get as far, will be safe from pursuit ; then, while the hawk is waiting on on that side of you which is farthest from the covert, let go one of the pigeons. The hawk will start, but the pigeon, if a good one, will manage to make the covert ; the hawk will throw up, and, if all is well, come down to your dead lure. Repeat this performance, always making as sure as you can that the pigeon will save himself, until your pupil has got sick of the whole business, and at last refuses to go for such disappointing quarry. If you can put in, between whiles, an easy flight at a grouse or partridge, and reward the hawk well upon it, the contrast will be all the more striking, and she will begin to have a settled conviction that game-hawking is capital fun, whereas pigeon-hawking is a fraud. It is obvious that a somewhat similar trick may be used with regard to other birds besides pigeons— flying the hawk in impossible places at those which you don't want her to pursue, and in easy places at those which you do.

Some hawks, which ought to know better, from laziness or want of condition, will not remain on the wing, but go off, after a few turns in the air, to a tree or to the ground, and there sit waiting for the lure, or till the spirit moves them to stir. This is disheartening conduct, quite unworthy of a ladylike or gentlemanly hawk, and disgraceful in a falcon-gentle. Yet so it is that many of these high-born dames, and not a few tiercels also of noble birth, are so lost to a sense of their own dignity that they give way to this degrading weakness, and demean themselves to the level of a base-born short-wing. What is to be done with them? Various devices have been tried with varying success. In the first place, as the hawk behaves in an ignoble manner, she cannot complain if you treat her in ignoble wise. You may therefore ride at her as she sits on the ground, and force her to get up, or you may throw clods at her, and drive her out of her tree ; but the surest plan—only it requires time and patience—is to let her cure herself. Light a pipe and sit down in a comfortable place, if such there be, and leave the sinner alone until the spirit does move her to stir. At some time or other, varying from five minutes to five hours, she will want the lure badly enough. Then let her come for it. Keep her waiting on or stooping at the lure till she has had a good dose of it, and if she goes off to perch again, wait again till she will work for her living. Show her, in fact, that in coming to the lure she is conferring no great favour on you, as she seemed to imagine, but rather that the boot is on the other leg. Next time it is more than probable that she will work a little rather than go fasting, when she might have a good meal at once. If you have time and patience to read her a few such lessons she may gradually be brought to exhibit some activity. But give her a dose as well. For liver has probably something to do with the matter, as well as mere laziness.

A hawk which is hood-shy is a plague to you and to herself. Very few hawks exhibit this vice except through the trainer's fault. But trainers are not all good hooders; and a few bungling and unsuccessful attempts at hooding will make even the best-natured hawk hate the very sight of the hood. If, therefore, the beginner is not clever at the art, let him practise on a kestrel. Or, if he will have one of the better hawks, let him get a skilful hand to break her to the hood. To hood a hawk which is already broken is a comparatively easy matter; but it is the nature of a hawk, as of any other creature, to dislike being blindfolded, and the wonder is that hawks can be made to submit to it as readily as they do. Occasionally a hawk has such a rooted objection to the proceeding that the cleverest man never succeeds in quite overcoming it. Vesta, already mentioned, was hood-shy, though in good hands; but even then the objection felt by the sufferer can only by a perversion of terms be rightly called a vice. Hood-shyness, even in a pronounced form, has often been cured, and, as has already been said, a hood-shy hawk cannot be considered fully trained. Whenever the hawk is difficult to hood, she should be handled constantly, and the trainer should almost always have a hood in his right hand. The actual condition of being hooded is not disagreeable to many hawks—it is the indignity and discomfort involved in the process of putting on the apparatus that give rise to the trouble. The smaller the hawk, the more difficult she is to hood; and the mischief is not only that the hawk's feathers are in danger whenever she is hooded against her will, but also that her temper is ruffled, and the relations between her and her trainer become strained.

One of the most annoying errors into which a hawk can fall, is a belief in her own vocal powers. No hawk ever has at all a musical voice, and the exercise of it, even in moderation, can quite well be dispensed with. Unfortunately, most eyesses which have been taken very young from the nest develop quite early in life a tendency to cry out. When there are several of them together they often catch the habit from one another, and becoming worse as their feathers come down, are by the time they are ready to fly confirmed "screamers." No cure has, I believe, been discovered for this vice, except that of turning them out to hack, which in nine cases out of ten proves successful. I have several times known a family of hawks when first turned out, to keep up for the first day or two an almost incessant screeching, and yet I have taken up the same birds at the end of hack completely cured. Generally, as soon as a young hawk finds that she can expend all her superfluous energy in flying about, and that no sort of attention is ever paid to her eloquence, she gets tired of indulging in the weakness. I know, however, of a case where hobbies too early taken were actually lost at hack, and never came at all either to lure or hack board, and yet continued to scream when quite wild for at least more than a week afterwards.

Passage hawks, I believe, never scream. It is often supposed that no wild hawks scream, and this, I think, is as a rule true. But I have heard young wild kestrels scream for a few days after they could fly, and one lot of wild merlins, though they were fully summed, and had probably been already driven away by the parents to shift for themselves, were what may be called bad screamers. They would scream while soaring, ten minutes at a time, and at such a height that the sound could only just be heard. It is true that there were trained merlins about at the time, and possibly they may have been calling to them. It is quite a common thing for hawks which are entirely free from the vice to call out when they see another hawk unexpectedly. They will do it even when they see their own likenesses in a looking-glass.

If the hawk, after being well hacked, still retains vestiges of the bad habit, there is yet another chance. The flying and killing wild quarry has often a magical effect in curing this vice, which would seem, like some other malpractices, to be largely the result of idleness. Still there are instances where, in spite of all the advantages which an eyess enjoys, she will persist in screaming. Some of them will go so far as to scream with the hood on, though this is rare. As a rule a screaming hawk is not a good performer. And she ought to be a very good one, in order to make it worth the falconer's while to be plagued with her. If you turn her adrift you may possibly, after a few days, catch her again and find her cured; and if not, you will not have suffered a very severe loss.

A still more disheartening fault is that of "refusing." People who know nothing at all about falconry are apt to suppose that when once you have "tamed" your hawk, and can call her back to you when you like, the only thing which remains to be done is to walk with her into a field, show her a bird, and let her go. That she should fail to pursue it is a contingency which does not present itself to their minds. It is, however, unfortunately one that constantly occurs, not only with eyesses, but also with the boldest of wild-caught hawks. The novice gets his hawk into a fine state of obedience. She will come a long distance to the lure as soon as it is produced. But when the long-expected day arrives for the first flight at a wild quarry, and perhaps an expectant field of friends turns out to see the sport, the wild bird is put up, the hawk is thrown off with a lusty shout, and, without taking the smallest notice of her intended victim, goes quietly on her way either to wait on for the lure or to take perch in a pleasant spot. Even when hawks have been entered, and have begun to fly in earnest, you cannot be absolutely sure when you cast them off whether they will be in the humour to do their best. They may begin the flight in apparently faultless style, and go up bravely in the most orthodox of rings after the ringing quarry. And then as they seem to be getting on terms with their rook or lark, you may see the fatal spreading of their wings, and have the painful conviction forced upon you that they have shown the white feather and thrown up the game. This vice—of "flying tail to tail," as the old falconers term it—is a most disheartening one for a beginner to meet with; so much so, that some old writers regard such a hawk as hopeless, and advise giving her away to a friend! I have found it strongly developed in the only two hobbies I ever tried to train; and a like result has, to my knowledge, followed in several other instances. These hawks have made rings and followed a wild lark up. But they have never taken even so much as a bad one! I had a merlin which out of 41 flights killed 40 larks. But the one occasion when she missed she refused—or at least left the lark in the air. Possibly this was because she was flown too soon after the last flight. But the disgrace remains recorded against her name in the quarry-book.

To guard against this sad catastrophe you must encourage your hawk ; that is, you must keep up her courage, which is the thing most severely tested in a ringing flight. You must feed her well ; yet keep her digestion in perfect order. And you must strengthen her muscles by constant hard exercise. It is not enough for her to go out and kill a couple of indifferent rooks in two or three short easy flights. If there is not enough good quarry—difficult quarry—to be found for her, you can give her a good spell of stooping at the lure, or in the case of a game-hawk, a long waiting on when the wind is highest, pro-bably about midday. She must have tirings galore. And if she has refused once, fly her sharp-set the next time. Hawks will refuse through being too fat as well as through being too lean. Avoid, if possible, giving your best hawks bad quarry, or your worst hawks any that are too good. The former may refuse a specially good one because they are accustomed to take duffers, and the latter may refuse because they have not yet gained con-fidence in their own powers. Goshawks are capricious creatures ; they will refuse a leveret, and half an hour later fly well at a full-grown hare Other hawks may refuse if flown too early in the day, and yet do a fine performance if tried again later on. With a hawk that persistently refuses you should try every remedy that your ingenuity will suggest as likely to inspire her with a proper sense of her duty. Try feeding up ; try flying her very hungry. Physic her for liver, with one prescription after another. And if all fail, give the hawk away, or, better still, cast her loose in an open country where the keepers don't shoot hawks. She then will have the choice between working and starv-ing ; and she will very soon know how to decide the question.

The last, and in one way the most serious, vice which has to be referred to, is that of "running cunning." I do not think it is common, if even it prevails at all among passage hawks ; and what there is to be said about it in the case of eyesses, has been said in the chapter on Lost Hawks, *à propos* of Ruy Lopez.

We have thus a list of seven deadly sins, or so-called sins, to which trained hawks are prone—carrying (better called lift-ing), refusing, checking, perching, hood-shyness, screaming, and running cunning. There are a few minor faults which hardly amount to more than peccadilloes, and deserve only a passing notice. Sometimes a hawk will keep bating off in a tiresome way. This is when she is strong and well, but short of exercise, and perhaps a bit feverish. The remedy is simply to hood her up. It is far less annoyance to her to stand hooded than to fatigue or worry herself by constant tugging and straining at her jesses. But, as a matter of fact, for hawks to stand hooded for any reasonable time is no annoyance to them at all, after they have worn the hood a few times. If it were, we should find that they suffered from it in health, strength, temper, or somehow, which is not known to be the case. Merlins, however, and male sparrow-hawks should be left unhooded more than other hawks. And they must not be expected to fly, like peregrines, immediately the hood is removed. The same cause will induce hawks sometimes to pick and pull at their jesses or at the covering of the perch, or even at the glove. The remedy is to smear the jesses or perch or glove with aloes or some bitter preparation, which is distasteful to them, but will do no harm if they like to go on picking, but rather good.

It has been said (p. 32) that goshawks and sparrow-hawks cannot be flown in casts (*i.e.* two of them together). This is on account of the great probability that they will fight or "crab." There is also, in the case of long-winged hawks, some danger that the like trouble may arise, especially if one or both of the individuals thrown off has a bad temper of her own. Accordingly, it is often well that each hawk intended to be used for double flights should be first flown single a few times, until she has become keen after her quarry, so that she may be too intent upon the pursuit of it to quarrel with her colleague, when flown double. But eyesses which have been well hacked and well reclaimed are seldom addicted to this vice, which is still more rare in passagers. As to the difficulties attending double flights with merlins, see the remarks made at page 141 ; and as to entering a young hawk with the assistance of an older one as "make-hawk," see pages 113, 142.

Some hawks, especially the wild-caught, will not bathe, but after tasting the water in the bath, and perhaps making as if they would go in, hesitate for a long time, and at last jump back to their block. Some will not even "bowse," or sip the water. This is vexatious, for bathing undoubtedly improves the feathers besides merely cleaning them, and keeps the hawks free from parasites and from small attacks of feverishness. It also cleans their feet, and makes them more hardy and robust. The best plan in such cases is to see that the bath-water is never too cold, to let a hawk which bathes well bathe in the sight of the recusant, and to keep the bath on fine days within reach of the latter. Such a hawk should also have her feet bathed now and then while on the perch ; and her beak should be kept clear of any scraps or stains which may remain on it after feeding. This wiping of the beak should, however, be done in any case, if the hawk is not careful herself about feaking, or rubbing the refuse off her mandibles.

Such is the rather long list of faults and vices. Let us not end up the chapter with these, but hark back to the virtues, and remind the reader that these are also great. Speed, courage, mounting, and footing: these may be called the cardinal virtues. Some hawks are born with some or all of them : some achieve them ; while upon others—well, they must be thrust. The mode of treatment suggested in the preceding pages has been found by long experience to be the best for developing the good qualities in a hawk as well as for eliminating the bad. Exercise and practice are the essential requisites. Nature is then working on the trainer's side. Every hawk should be made as often as possible to earn her food by hard work. And every hawk should be encouraged to take a pleasure in her work and a pride in herself. Exercise means speed ; and speed means success. With success will naturally come courage ; and excellence in mounting and footing is no more than the inevitable result of proper practice in the right sort of flights. All hawks in the wild state can kill many sorts of quarry. All trained hawks, therefore, should be able to take at least one. But if any man expects to become a falconer off-hand, he will be disappointed. If he will begin moderately, with one hawk,—a kestrel for choice,—and train her single-handed and completely, he will soon be able to attempt much greater things.

CHAPTER XIX

Anecdotes and Adventures

IF history is rightly called the practical illustration of philo-
sophy, then the quarry-book may be considered with
justice the tangible test of the falconer's theories. In many
cases a handful of experience is worth a cart-load of advice;
and a trainer who has lost a valuable hawk by treating her in a
bad way is not likely to forget in a hurry how bad that system
proved. Some entertaining and very instructive anecdotes may
be found scattered about in the old books, and more especially
in that of Charles d'Arcussia, Lord of Esparron and Revest,
the Italian who was falconer to Louis XIII., and was honoured
by him with special favour. This treatise, which is difficult to
procure, is well worth perusal, not only for the descriptions contained in it of remarkable flights, but for the sound sense of
many of the precepts given. Between the French and Italian
schools of falconry, as of fencing, a sort of friendly rivalry
existed; and the Italian, who had become a Frenchman, may
be said, in a way, to have represented both.

Coming to more modern times, a great many interesting
details of a historical and anecdotal kind are given in the works
already mentioned, published during the last fifty or sixty years,
beginning with the fine illustrated volume of Schlegel and
Wulverhorst, and including the new edition of Mr. J. E. Harting's
Hints. Without going over any of the ground covered by these
writers, I propose to add a few notes of actual experiences
within the memory of man. For most of these I am indebted
to the kindness of brother-falconers, who have supplied them at
some trouble to themselves, and whom I desire to thank heartily
for their friendly aid.

The powers of a trained peregrine are severely tested by a
first-rate house-pigeon, which is one of the fastest of flying
things, shifts well, and lives usually in fine condition, taking

plenty of exercise.   Adrian Möllen told me that a fellow-country-man of his, vilipending his passage hawks which he was then train-ing for the campaign at herons at the Loo, offered to bet that three of his own pigeons would beat any hawk Möllen could produce. As the hawks were not Möllen's, and it is always quite on the cards that a flight at a fast pigeon may result in the loss of the hawk, the falconer had to ask leave before accepting the bet.   The king's brother, who then represented the Loo Club in Holland, readily gave permission, and, I think, also offered to pay if the hawk lost.   Anyhow, a day was fixed, and a small party assembled on the most open part of the Loo.   The fal-coner had stipulated that he should give the signal for the release of the pigeons by the owner.   His fastest falcon was then put on the wing, and as she waited on Möllen gave the word.   The pigeon started ; the hawk stooped, and, after a good flight, killed. She was allowed to eat the brain, and the rest of the pelt was thrown to the disconcerted fancier.   A second pigeon was then prepared.   The hawk again waited on, and the signal was again given.   This time, however, the pigeon was taken at the first stoop.   " Out with your third pigeon," cried Möllen, elated with the double victory.   But the countryman elected to pay, and not to play.   "My third gold piece is lost anyhow," he sadly remarked.   " Better pay my money, and save my remaining pigeon, than find I have to lose both."

The statement that a peregrine cutting down a grouse or partridge without binding kills it "stone-dead" in the air, is doubtless occasionally true.   But to suppose that this is a com-mon occurrence would be a great mistake.   Much more often the partridge is stunned or dazed, the wing broken, or the back or neck dislocated.   But the force with which a game-bird comes down when hit in the air is often very great, and enough in itself to almost fatally bruise it.   I have mentioned that a falcon of Major Fisher's knocked down a grouse on fairly level ground which, so great was the impact, rebounded from the earth, and came down again fifteen yards from the place where it first fell. Larks and other birds often dash themselves hard against the ground in shifting downwards from the stoop, and bound up again like balls.

Peregrines, when on their day and intent on killing, will sometimes do more execution than would readily be believed. Not very long ago a tiercel stooped at a covey, cut down a bird, and threw up with the intention of descending to seize the victim. But at the height to which his impetus had carried him up he was right above the remainder of the covey, which was speeding away at a short distance above the ground. Changing his mind, therefore, the tiercel stooped again at one of the fugitives. He cut this down also, and shot up again, likewise over the retreating birds. For a second time the temptation proved too great, and with a third stoop he took a third partridge.

John Barr was flying a ger-tiercel at a pigeon on Epsom Downs, not far from Tattenham Corner. But the hawk was no match for the pigeon, which evaded all his stoops. Instead, however, of making off and thanking his lucky stars, this over-vain bird stayed fooling around. Confident that the ger would not or could not catch him, he sailed about, as if "chaffing" the big hawk and challenging him to do his worst. At this moment an amateur falconer came on the Downs by the Grand Stand, carrying a falcon (peregrine) of by no means first-rate powers, but keen to fly, and a good waiter on. Getting on to the open ground, this gentleman threw off his falcon. But neither he nor his falcon at first saw the pigeon, nor did the latter, intent on his game with the ger, espy the distant foe. Thus the hawk had time to get up some way before there was any suspicion on either side that there was sport to be had. As soon as the falcon did cast eyes on the inadvertent pigeon, she fortunately went up higher, instead of starting in pursuit, as some eyesses would have done. As she got to a pretty good pitch the pigeon at last became aware that there was a second enemy in the field, or rather in the air, and began to gird up his loins for flight in bitter earnest. It was, however, now too late. The falcon towered far above, and on the other side was the "allied power," the ger. Another ten seconds and the falcon came down with a will, threw up, and at the second shot did for the too imprudent joker. The amateur had the laugh at John Barr for some days afterwards, having "wiped his ger's eye" with a peregrine.

Mr. Riley, who has had so much success with the short-winged hawks, had thrown off a goshawk at a rabbit, which ran past some old hollow pollard ashes. As he passed, out jumped a fox and joined in the chase. This, however, boded no great good for the hawk; and her owner raised so unearthly a noise that reynard turned aside into the fence just as the goshawk took the rabbit only two or three yards away. On another occasion a rabbit was ferreted out by the side of a mill-pool. The ferret was close on his traces, and he jumped deliberately into the pool and swam across. Mr. Riley, who, like a good austringer, loves fair play above all things, thought it a shame to fly a wet rabbit, and would not throw off his goshawk. However, when the rabbit was on dry land he went so well that Mr. Riley let the hawk go. The rabbit was caught ; and when he was taken from the hawk he was found to be quite dry ! But whether his wet skin had been dried up by terror or by the violence of his exertions, or how else, is a mystery still unsolved. One day, having had bad luck with partridges, Sir Tristram, owned and trained by the same gentleman, was indulged with a pigeon. The big pointer included in the party, and which was a great ally of the goshawk, was at the time roaming about. As the hawk was pluming the pigeon on the ground, the dog came romping along. But when he had accidentally got within eight yards of Sir Tristram, the latter left his meal, and, flying straight for the pointer, gave him a good sound box on the ear, which sent him flying, the hawk then returning, well satisfied, to his food.

Hawks have been known to kill quarry with a leash and swivel still attached to their jesses. I have known a merlin with a long leash on follow a lark up in rings several hundred feet high, but she could not get on terms with him. What is, however, perhaps still more astonishing, I have seen a merlin with a whole dead lark in her foot pursue and strike down one that was uninjured. I was with a friend in a very open place. Each of us had a merlin to fly ; and we walked different ways. My chance came first ; and the lark, after a flight of moderate length, was taken under some open railings surrounding a dry pond. Hardly was this flight over, and the hawk beginning to plume her lark, when my friend's hawk started after a lark from the opposite side of the pond. This lark happened also to make for the same place—not that the railings were at all likely to save him, but because he thought he could dodge round and round the posts and under the bars, and so put off the fatal moment. Larks seem often to think that any shelter is better than none at all. Accordingly, round and round the rails this second lark twisted and turned, passing sometimes within a yard or two of the place where my hawk stood on her dead lark watching the fun. The other hawk meanwhile made shot after shot, but could not foot her quarry. "She"—that was the name of my merlin—looked on more and more excitedly. At last she could stand it no longer, but getting up, dead lark and all, she mounted a bit and stooped. As the lark was diving underneath a rail she hit it, first shot, with a resounding whack— not with her feet, for they were both encumbered by the dead quarry, but with the dead quarry itself ! The lark was, of course, not held, but projected forwards and downwards about three feet to the ground ; and before he could get up again the other hawk was on him.

I was flying the same hawk in a very big stubble-field. A lark got up—a ground lark, but a fast one—and away they went, zigzagging along the surface of the field. They had gone a long way, but not far enough to be out of sight, when they both suddenly vanished. Running up, I found a deep depression in the ground, where years ago a big pit had been dug. This accounted for the disappearance. But what had happened after that? If the lark had been taken, where was he? And where was his captor? A small heap of dry sticks at the bottom of the hollow was searched in vain. There seemed to be no other hiding-place. At length a tiny hole was seen—the mouth of a rabbit-burrow. And out of this, in another half-minute, emerged the little hawk. The lark had gone in, and she after it, but after some groping about in the dark had failed to find the wily fugitive.

Only a few days afterwards the sister of this hawk started after a first-rate ringing lark. Both of them went out of sight, drifting at a great height towards a village a mile off. We ran towards it at our best pace, fearing some disaster ; but when half-way to it saw the hawk coming back to the lure. Well, we were glad enough that she had not killed in any cottage garden, and, taking her back up-wind, went on with the day's programme. As it was getting dark we had to walk through the same village on the way home. " Did you find your 'awk ? " asked a cottager. " What hawk ? " " Why, one of your 'awks chased a lark into the passage o' th' public there, and would a' caught 'im too, only there was a cat in the passage up and grabbed the lark before the 'awk was on 'im ; and the 'awk looked as savage as thunder, and 'ooked it out, and went over there where you come from."

Bee Cottage stands desolate in a very big valley, with hills sloping gradually down to it on almost all sides. A ringing lark, with a merlin close at his heels, got within reach of this shelter from above the hillside to windward, and shot down to it like a bullet, with the hawk a few yards behind. It was too far to see from the hillside where, but he put in somewhere on the premises. A diligent search, however, in hedge, bush, coal-shed, and everywhere, led to no result. The door was shut and locked : so were the windows. No one seemed to have lived in the place for months. More searching, without any sign of lark or hawk. Yet they undoubtedly came down here, and never came out again. Outside, they could have been seen anywhere for half a mile. At last I saw that there was a small pane of glass gone in one of the downstair windows. Through that opening I looked ; and there sat my lady, with a fluffy heap round her feet. So far, so good. But the room was full of bees, some dead, and some alive ! What was to be done?

Colonel Sanford owned, hacked, and trained a very first-rate merlin called Orkney, which killed no less than ten larks in a single day in single flights, thus surpassing Queen, which took nine in single flights and one in double. This Orkney, after a very long flight, put a lark into a flock of sheep. But she marked the exact spot, underneath a sheep, where the fugitive stopped, and, taking perch on a neighbouring wether, kept her eye on the place. The sheep moved on, leaving the ground clear ; and Orkney jumped as nearly as she could guess on the right spot. She failed, however, to grab the lark, which got up again and promptly took refuge under another sheep. Again the little hawk took stand on the next bleater, marking still more carefully the hiding-place of the quarry. Again the animals walked on, and this time perseverance was rewarded, and the lark was carried in triumph from the woolly protectors which had so nearly saved him. The same hawk once drove a lark into a small hole where she could see nothing of him but the tail. After some reflection she put in her beak and grasped steadily the feathers of the tail. Then with an unhurried pull she drew him far enough out of the hole to be able to get at him with her foot.

The best hawk I ever had was the merlin Eva. She was never beaten in fair flight by any lark during the whole of the moulting season ; and she killed one (fully moulted, of course) as late as 7th November. One day she mounted an immense height after a ringing lark, bested him, and had had three shots, when a wild merlin joined in. After this the two hawks flew in concert just as if they had been trained in the same stable. Stoop for stoop, in regular alternations, they worked this plucky lark down by a few yards at each shift, neither I nor James Retford, who was running with me, being able to distinguish which was which. At last, when the lark had been driven down to within about 300 feet of the ground, there were two fine stoops in quick succession, the second of which was fatal. " Which is it ? " I gasped, inquiring of the experienced falconer. " The wild one," I think, he answered, sinking down breathless on the down. It was not, though. The wild hawk, furious, turned away, and, to vent her rage, made a savage shot at the ears of a hare which happened at the moment to be running along the valley ; while Eva, descending slowly on the side of the down, had just recovered her breath by the time I got up.

On a second occasion Eva was almost equally high, and still ringing to get above her lark, when she suddenly spread her wings and swerved in her course. At the same moment Major Fisher, who was out on horseback, shouted, " The wild merlin ! " But this time Eva was not going to join in any duet. The wild hawk had come up on a much lower level than the trained one had attained, possibly thinking that when Eva had done the hard work of the early stoops she might cut in and reap the benefit. At anyrate, Eva was not to be so dealt with. Poising herself like a falcon when the grouse get up, she turned over and came down with every ounce of force she could muster right at the interloper. Of course she did not hit her. The two went off, stooping at one another, and were soon out of sight. Major Fisher rode after them, field-glass in hand, predicting that the wild hawk would chase Eva away. But in less than two minutes he espied a merlin coming back ; and the trained hawk, in one long slanting fall from out of sight, descended daintily upon the lure held in her owner's fist.

Queen was a first-rate merlin—sister of Jubilee, and also, though younger by a year, of Tagrag. She started at a ringing lark in a very open place, and it was a case of hard running, for there were no markers out. Before half a mile was covered they were over a sloping brow. By a desperate spurt I reached the ridge, when the hawk was in sight again. The ground sloped downwards for half a mile more ; and in the valley, far away, was a sheepfold, with sheep, shepherd, and a dog. For this fold the quarry was of course making. Anyhow, there would be the shepherd to mark ; and a shout might reach even his rather inattentive ear. It was too far to see the hawk as she stooped ; but when she threw up, and when she turned over, the sunlight caught the under-surface of her wing or tail, and showed where she was ; and the last gleam came from painfully near the sheep. The running was easier downhill ; and soon the shepherd was within hail. " Where is the hawk ? " Reply inaudible up-wind. Thirty yards farther on the words could be heard, " Gone back where you come from." Then, of course, she had lost the lark—rather luckily, having regard to the dog —and had passed me unnoticed, flying low. Well, the hill must be mounted again and the lure kept going.   There, too, is surely a glimpse of Queen herself, just vanishing over the sky-line.   She will be gone back to the place where her sister is pegged down.   Ten minutes' walking and running, and this place is in sight.   But no sign of Queen.   Five minutes' more luring, and at last a hawk comes in sight,—not making directly for the lure, however, but hanging about and keeping well away.   Strange conduct in this merlin, which rather liked the lure!   And now she begins waiting on, and soaring,—a rare amusement with this very practical-minded hawk.   Round and round, farther and farther down-wind, away we go, Queen hardly now even looking at the lure.   Soon the hawk is too far to keep in sight without very fast running.   Had I been fresh, probably I should have run hard.   But I was far from fresh.   And the behaviour of Queen was very queer.

Suddenly a new idea evolved itself.   What if it was not Queen at all, but a wild merlin?   It might be well to search a bit, anyhow, where Queen was last seen in her own undoubted personality.   Searching, therefore, became the word—rather late in the day.   And on a patch of new-ploughed fallow, barely distinguishable from the clods of brown earth, there stood my lady, with a litter of feathers round her, calmly eating the remains of a lark, and wondering what on earth I was about. She had taken the lark with that very last stoop for which I had seen her turn over, at the very edge of the sheepfold, and, not liking the proximity of the dog, had carried her booty well away, taking the direction from which she had come, as the dog was on the other side.   The wild hawk had been too late to join in the flight, but had seen the kill, and had come down perhaps with a vague idea of robbing Queen.   Thinking better of any such attempt—which would not have ended pleasantly— she had been inquisitive as to the lure, and thinking the whole affair rather singular, had soared about, waiting to see what would happen next.

Ruy Lopez was a jack which rather fancied himself, and had something in his style of flying of the tactics of a haggard peregrine.   That is, he would start in a different direction from the quarry, so that strangers would suppose he had no designs upon it, and afterwards turn and make an immensely long stoop at it all across the air.   But on one occasion he had a very close personal experience of the stooping of peregrines.   He was lost ; and no one knew anything of his whereabouts.   It so happened that James and William Retford, Major Fisher's falconers, were out with a pointer and a falcon named Black Lady. The dog stood, but in a queer and rather doubtful way; and Black Lady was thrown off. When she had got to her pitch the men ran in. But instead of partridges, there got up out of the swedes the unexpected shape of Ruy Lopez, he having been quietly discussing there a lark which he had just killed. Down came the falcon, better pleased, as hawks are, at such a chase than one at a mere partridge. And the falconers describe the flight as beyond measure exciting. They thought each stoop would be the last, and declared that the small hawk saved himself several times by a hair's-breadth. At length, however, he got in under a stook of wheat. No doubt the falconers thought it was a near thing. And possibly it was; but as far as my own experience goes, trained peregrines cannot get within a yard of a good trained merlin. I have seen them try; and the merlin has shifted with contemptuous ease. Major Fisher, however, as already mentioned, had a tiercel which made it very hot for a wild merlin, and, as he thinks, very nearly caught it. I have seen one of his eyess tiercels take a kestrel with apparent ease at the first stoop. But that is certainly quite a different matter.

The already long list which has been given of mischances and maladies which beset trained hawks is even yet not complete. In India the wild eagles are a serious nuisance, coming down from the high altitudes at which they soar, and obliging the hawks to shift for their own safety just when they are expected and expecting to give a good account of their own quarry. In England, hawks which are pegged out in any but a quiet private place are exposed to the attack of any chance dog. I do not know that cats will deliberately attack even the smallest jack, either by day or by night. But a tame cat which had gone mad once made an onslaught on the trained peregrines belonging to the O. H. C., and with such ferocity that quite a large number of them died of their wounds. Mr. A. W. Reed, an experienced and enthusiastic amateur falconer, had some very valuable hawks, including a ger and some Eastern varieties, pegged out on a lawn in Essex. A neighbouring householder, being troubled by sparrows, laid down poisoned grain. The sparrows took the grain, and, dying as they flew over the place where the hawks were, fell down on the ground near the blocks. Of course the hawks ate them ; and, equally of course, the hawks were poisoned. And, advice being taken, it was considered useless to take proceedings against the offender.

Cases of deliberate hawk-murder are now punishable by

law.   All falconers are highly indebted to Mr. E. C. Pinckney for having demonstrated this fact conclusively in a local tribunal. He extracted £10 in damages from a neighbour who had shot at and killed his game-hawk, although the latter set up the usual defence, pretending that he was unaware that the hawk was a tame one.   The judge held that, as he was aware that his neighbour kept trained hawks, if he shot at one, he did so at his own peril, just as a man would who shot at a house-pigeon or escaped parrot.   More lately still, Mr. A. W. Reed has been awarded £5 at the Kingston County Court as damages from a neighbour who had wilfully shot his trained peregrine.   The precedents, as far as they go, are most valuable.   Unfortunately they do not, of course, go very far.   But a falconer will be well advised, having regard to them, to send notices in registered letters, when going into any district, to all such people as are likely to prove mischievous.

INDEX